Democracy's Body
Judson Dance Theater
1962-1964

Democracy's Body

Judson Dance Theater, 1962–1964

Sally Banes

Duke University Press   Durham and London 1993

Third printing, 2002
© 1993 Sally Rachel Banes
All rights reserved
Printed in the United States of America on acid-free paper ∞
This book was previously published by UMI Research Press
(Michigan) in 1980 and 1983.

Library of Congress Cataloging-in-Publication Data
Banes, Sally. Democracy's body: Judson Dance Therater,
1962–1964 / Sally Banes.
Reprint. Previously published: Ann Arbor, Mich. : UMI
Research Press, c1983. Includes bibliographical references (p.)
and index. ISBN 0-8223-1399-5
1. Judson Dance Theater--History. I. Title.
GV1786.J82B36 1993
792.8′09747′1--dc20   93-21760 CIP

Contents

List of Illustrations

Acknowledgments

I am grateful to Michael Kirby for his counsel and his patient, painstaking reading of the text and to Selma Jeanne Cohen, Ted Hoffman, Michael Miller, and Robert Sklar for their advice and criticism. For help in the research, editing, and preparation of the manuscript, I would like to thank Jack Anderson, the Bennington College Judson Project, Adam Brightman, Dan Cameron, Tony Carruthers, the staff of the Dance Research Collection of the Library and Museum of the Performing Arts (New York Public Library at Lincoln Center), Kyle de Camp, Gautam Dasgupta, George Dorris, Jon Hendricks, Wendy Japhet, Jill Johnston, the staff of Judson Memorial Church, M Mark, Bonnie Marranca, Katy Matheson, Barbara and Peter Moore, Wendy Perron, Carole and Tony Pipolo, and Burt Supree. The many participants in Judson Dance Theater listed in the bibliography generously gave me time and information, letting me look through personal files and documents and suffering hours of questioning. Finally, as always, Noël Carroll was a generous and incisive colleague, as well as an encouraging friend.

Introduction

In the summer of 1962, a group of young choreographers decided to present a concert of works they had made for Robert Dunn's choreography class, taught from 1960 through 1962 at Merce Cunningham's studio in the Living Theater building. These choreographers were not all dancers by training; their numbers included visual artists and musicians. Dunn himself had studied music theory with John Cage, the avant-garde composer and Cunningham's collaborator, at the New School for Social Research.

In looking for a place to show their experimental work in a professional concert format, the group found a welcome at Judson Memorial Church, a liberal Protestant congregation that was housed on the south end of Washington Square in Greenwich Village. There the ministry and parishioners had long been active in reform politics, civil rights, and arts activities. Already the site of Happenings, the Judson Poets' Theater, film screenings, and the Judson Gallery, where exhibitions of Pop Art and political art were held, the Judson Church soon also became the center for avant-garde dance in the city.

A Concert of Dance #1 was open to the public free of charge. It lasted for several hours, with twenty-three dances on the program by fourteen choreographers. This concert, given on 6 July 1962, proved to be the beginning of a historic process that changed the shape of dance history. It was the seedbed for post-modern dance, the first avant-garde movement in dance theater since the modern dance of the 1930s and 1940s. The choreographers of the Judson Dance Theater radically questioned dance aesthetics, both in their dances and in their weekly discussions. They rejected the codification of both ballet and modern dance. They questioned the traditional dance concert format and explored the nature of dance performance. They also discovered a cooperative method for producing dance concerts. For young artists who did not want to be judged by older authorities in the field, or who wanted the freedom to experiment in a familiar space that was easily accessible, this was an alternative to uptown juried concerts. Attracting a grassroots audience of Greenwich Village artists and intellectuals, the Judson Dance Theater affected the entire community and flourished as a popular center of experimentation.

The group that put on A Concert of Dance #1 was invited to continue meeting and performing at the church. Over the course of the next two years, nearly two hundred dances were given by the Judson Dance Theater (as the group began to call itself by April 1963), either at Judson Memorial Church, or under the group's auspices in other locations. When in the autumn of 1962 Robert Dunn did not continue his choreography class, the group began to meet independently on a weekly basis, first at Yvonne Rainer's studio and then at the church.

This book provides an account of the Judson Dance Theater and documents the dances the group produced and the dynamics of the workshop itself. So much important work and theory in dance grew out of Judson Dance Theater that numerous myths and misconceptions about the group and the work have arisen. Although several books on post-modern dance have recently been published, there is still no comprehensive study of the origins of this entire movement in the fertile experimentation that took place at Judson. Don McDonagh's *The Rise & Fall & Rise of Modern Dance* includes an interview with Robert Dunn and some material on the Judson choreographers, but the book does not provide extensive documentation. It is, rather, a survey of modern dance in the 1960s and 1970s. It does not differentiate between Judson Dance Theater as a collective entity and work by members of the workshop after the collective disbanded. McDonagh's work also does not draw sharp distinctions between avant-garde dance and the modern dance that is contemporary while following the older traditions of composition, technique, and performance. Anne Livet's *Contemporary Dance* is an anthology of useful interviews with some of the Judson choreographers, as well as historical and critical essays by Michael Kirby, Deborah Jowitt, Clive Barnes, and Don McDonagh. These essays are transcripts of lectures given at the Fort Worth Art Museum. However, Livet's book also does not attempt to document all the dances choreographed by these people during the Judson years: choreographers who were not part of the Judson Dance Theater are included in this book. My own *Terpsichore in Sneakers: Post-Modern Dance* examines the work of ten choreographers and one group, taking into account some of the Judson dances, in the context of the careers of the choreographers concerned, and discussing the new aesthetics and activities in dance beginning with Judson Dance Theater. But *Terpsichore in Sneakers* is selective, covering the work of only some of the members of the Judson workshop, and the book includes chapters on three choreographers who were not part of the workshop, as well as a chapter on Grand Union, an improvisational collective formed in 1970, long after the Judson days. Jill Johnston's *Marmalade Me* and her reviews of dance concerts in the *Village Voice* give a lively account of the Judson Dance Theater performances and polemics, but they present only a partial view of the events, and *Marmalade Me* also covers events in the mid-1960s and later years.

One problem faced in writing this book was the definition of Judson Dance Theater in terms of both chronology and personnel. James Waring, for instance, was a choreographer who choreographed one dance in Concert #12, gave evenings of his own choreography at Judson Church (which were sometimes publicized as presented by Judson Dance Theater), and used members of the workshop in his dance company. However, Waring was never a member of the Judson workshop. He was an influence on many of the younger dancers who were members of the cooperative; he was one of the avant-garde choreographers of the 1950s whose teaching and choreography helped to set the stage for the emergence of the Judson Dance Theater. But he did not consider himself, nor did the group consider him, part of Judson Dance Theater. Therefore, his work is excluded from this book, except for *Imperceptible Elongation*, in Concert #12. The same is true for other mentors of the Judson group, like Aileen Passloff, Beverly Schmidt, and Katherine Litz. Also, concerts of dance given at Judson Church after the group dispersed are still advertised as Judson Dance Theater events. However, it is commonly agreed that the original Judson Dance Theater — that is, the cooperative group that originally took on this name and produced concerts that grew out of weekly workshops at the church — no longer was an entity after the last numbered concert, Concert of Dance #16, on 29 April 1964. In fact, the name Judson Dance Theater nowhere appears on the posters or programs for *The Palace of the Dragon Prince*, a ballet by Fred Herko, one of the original workshop members. The term Judson Dance Theater, then, will be used in the narrowest possible sense, to mean the choreographers associated with the cooperative group and workshop, and the body of their choreography in Concerts #1 through #16, plus four evening-long concerts featuring the choreography of four individuals in that group: *Terrain* by Yvonne Rainer; *Afternoon* by Steve Paxton; "Motorcycle" by Judith Dunn; and *Fantastic Gardens* by Elaine Summers.

The above list illustrates the system of punctuation I have used throughout the book: names of dance works are underlined; evenings comprising various dances are enclosed in quotation marks, except for non-titled evenings, like A Concert of Dance #1; parts of dances are also enclosed in quotation marks. Thus, *Motorcycle* is one of the dances in "Motorcycle," as is *Astronomy Hill*; but "Play" is one of the sections of *Terrain*.

Another problem faced in this book is that confronting any attempt to recapture a performance that has very little written text. Any history of performance is fragmentary; the historian tries to assemble as many fragments as possible. The account of Judson Dance Theater is a collection of images, narratives, partial recollections, imperfect reminiscences, and a few scores. I have used oral history as much as possible, interviewing all the members of Judson Dance Theater I could locate, as well as other people peripherally involved with the project. Facts were checked against written sources but, as the reader will discover, sometimes sources conflicted and the "true" version was impossible to discover. During the interviews, questions were posed about Judson Dance Theater as an artistic and social milieu. Questions were also asked about the specific details of the dances and concerts, such as: What was the structure of the dance? What was its intention in terms of form? Content? How did it use time? Space? Movement? How long was it? Was there music? What kind? What was the relationship between the dancing and the music? Were there special costumes or lighting effects? Were props or scenery used in the dance? How was the dance taught to the dancers? Were scores used, either in choreographing or teaching the dance? How long was the rehearsal period? How many people were in the dance? Where did they come from? What was the audience response? How did the dance fit into the concert as a whole? What was the concert like as an event? How did this dance relate to other works (dance or nondance) by the same person? By other choreographers? How did it relate to contemporary artworks? Interview subjects were also asked about the works of choreographers other than themselves.

Besides these live interviews, information was also collected from videotaped interviews, some of which I conducted, carried out by the Bennington College Judson Project, as well as from printed programs, scores (in the form of written or drawn notations), notes, letters, journals, diaries, films, reconstructions of the dances (live or on videotape), and photographs. I have made extensive use of the archive at Judson Memorial Church, the Dance Research Collection of the Library and Museum of the Performing Arts (New York Public Library at Lincoln Center), and the private files of several choreographers, as well as the photographic files of Peter Moore.

The book unfolds chronologically. The first chapter documents the seminal dance composition course given by Robert Dunn at the Cunningham studio from 1960 through 1962. Here most of the works performed publicly at the first Judson concert were first shown and discussed. Dunn's teaching methods, the choreographic structures and the methods used in class, and the artistic milieu within which the class functioned are examined. The second chapter is devoted to the first Judson concert, A Concert of Dance #1. Chapter 3 covers the second concert, given later that summer in Woodstock, New York; the convening of the workshop in the fall of 1962; the dynamics of the workshop; and Concerts #3 and #4, the first series of concerts to be produced from the workshop. In Chapter 4 two watershed events in the dynamics of the group are considered: *Terrain* by Yvonne Rainer, the first solo choreography produced by the workshop as a separate evening of dance, and Concert #5 in Washington, D.C., an event that signaled the consolidation of a nucleus within the larger group, and that nucleus's ties with the visual art community. Chapter 5 documents Concerts #6, #7, and #8 at the Judson Church and Concerts #9 through #12 at the Gramercy Arts Theater during the summer of 1963. And Chapter 6 documents the final season of the Judson Dance Theater as a workshop and cooperative producing agent, considering Concerts #13 through #16 and three solo choreography concerts: *Afternoon* by Steve Paxton, "Motorcycle," by Judith Dunn, and *Fantastic Gardens* by Elaine Summers.

In many ways the blossoming of the Judson Dance Theater as a center for avant-garde activity in dance was a fortuitous occurrence. Robert Dunn offered his class; a number of young dancers who were ready and willing to experiment at a professional level came to the class, where they formed a rich medium for some of Dunn's ideas, as well as their own. There were models among older choreographers in two senses: the older avant-garde of the 1950s, like Merce Cunningham, James Waring, Paul Taylor, Aileen Passloff, Beverly Schmidt, and Merle Marsicano, provided a precedent for breaking with the modern dance "academy,"[1] and the academy itself provided the methods, techniques, and definitions that were once avant-garde but now served as the givens of the art—there to be sampled, borrowed, criticized, subverted. Finally, the church was there for the asking: a large space to dance in, with performance and rehearsal facilities free of charge.

The time was ripe for such a movement in dance in Greenwich Village, for both theoretical and practical reasons. The country's postwar mood of pragmatism was reflected in the various arts, from the Happenings that made use of environments at hand, to the New Realism, or Pop Art depiction of figures and objects and making reference to industrial subjects and styles. The economy was expanding, and the new Kennedy administration stressed youth, art, and culture. There were few grants for individual dancers, but there was a spirit of willing participation and an interest in using inexpensive materials; one could live cheaply and make art cheaply. In Greenwich Village, beatnik culture had catalyzed a renaissance of the "bohemia" that had long been the reputation of the neighborhood. The area was an intensive center of theatrical, literary, and artistic activities, and ideas spread freely and flowed from one art form to another. The philosophical fascinations with Zen Buddhism, existentialism, and phenomenology fit well with certain aspects of American art in the late 1950s and early 1960s. The concreteness of existence, the interest in the everyday actions people practice, the questions of identity, both individual and collective, that were the topics of these philosophical systems — at least in their popular versions — were appropriate questions for modernist artists after the middle of the twentieth century. The phenomenological exhortation "Zu den Sachen!" ("To the Things!") was echoed in the manifestoes of artists in every field. Poetry, music, theater, and dance stressed performance more than the literary aspect of their forms, aspiring to more immediacy, more "presentness," more concrete experience. The descriptive, methodological thrust of phenomenology found an analogy in the reflexive formalism of the various arts and the movement toward descriptive criticism. If the Village was a place where artists and intellectuals gathered to partake of the diversity and community spirit that gathering created, and to pursue a new identity that could only be formed in such a community, it was also the place where they examined the identities of those arts, working at the edges of artistic conventions and analyzing the process of making that art.

American modern dance, since its beginnings at the turn of this century, has been a series of avant-gardes. Each generation called for a new set of subjects, a new dance technique, a new relationship to musical, literary, visual, and theatrical arts. By the late 1950s, a number of choreographers were considered more radical than the dominant modern dance choreographers and teachers, such as Martha Graham, José Limón, Tamiris, and Hanya Holm. Merce Cunningham, who had been a soloist in Martha Graham's company, combined the flexible spine used in modern dance with the crisp footwork of classical ballet in a technique that was precise and articulate. His experimentation with chance in choreography affected the look of his work in a number of ways: It decentralized space, created unexpected and often witty combinations of body parts in movement, and decentralized time in the dance in the sense that there were no logical climaxes or developments. A working relationship with John Cage allied Cunningham to the most advanced movements in music; the method of collaboration was that the music and the dancing simply occupied the same space at the same time. Although juxtaposition sometimes lent dramatic expressiveness to either music or dance, such correspondences were not planned. The Cunningham-Cage collaboration was an important influence on the Judson Dance Theater. Some of the members of Cunningham's company participated in Judson, and the Judson dancers respected Cunningham's accomplishments as a choreographer — rebelling against what was sometimes felt as a hierarchy of authority in modern dance and cleansing the dance of its often psychological overtones. The dancers learned from Cage's teachings — his interest in Zen Buddhism, in moving from music toward theater, in the writings of Antonin Artaud, in chance methods, in the value of the everyday. Through Cage, a younger generation of artists found a heritage in the history of European avant-garde art and performance.

James Waring, a choreographer and artist who was born in San Francisco and trained in ballet technique on the west coast and at School of American Ballet in New York, was another crucial influence on the Judson group. Like Cunningham, Waring taught technique; he also taught composition classes to his students beginning in the late 1950s. Waring's influence on the Judson group was both practical — several Judson dancers gained performing experience in dancing in Waring's works — and aesthetic — Waring taught his protégés a great deal about collage techniques, music, theater, and art. Waring, Paul Taylor, David Vaughan, Aileen Passloff, and several others were involved in Dance Associates, a choreographers' cooperative organized in 1951. And socially, Waring was a link between the dance world and a group of poets — including Diane di Prima, Alan Marlowe, and others — who were also connected to the Living Theater.

Several of the Judson group studied with Ann Halprin in San Francisco. From Halprin came another kind of freedom in dance: freedom to follow intuition and impulse in improvisation. Related to this freedom was a desire to be closer to nature; students worked out-of-doors on an open platform in the mountains of Marin County. Halprin also encouraged an analytic approach to anatomy and kinesiology; students were asked to understand and analyze the physical changes they experienced during the course of their improvisations.

Besides these three teachers, other choreographers influenced the Judson dancers. Aileen Passloff was trained in ballet but, lacking the typical ballet dancer's body, was determined to choreograph her own style of dances. She became noted not only for her wit and theatricality, her collaborations with visual artists and avant-garde composers, but also for her independence, as were Beverly Schmidt, who had danced with Alwin Nikolais, and Merle Marsicano.

The Judson aesthetic, as this books shows, was never monolithic. Rather, the Judson situation was deliberately undefined, unrestricted. Styles of choreography grew out of the groundwork done at Judson, but the wealth of dances created by Judson Dance Theater show, above all, a remarkable diversity. Still, within the group a few specific themes and interests arose, just as eventually several choreographers emerged as the most productive and influential. Within the Judson workshop, a commitment to democratic or collective process led on the one hand to methods that metaphorically seemed to stand for freedom (like improvisation, spontaneous determination, chance), and on the other hand to a refined consciousness of the process of choreographic choice. In general, questions of technique and its perfection were considered less important than formal compositional problems. This was true in part because the performers available to the choreographers were a mixture of experienced and inexperienced, trained and untrained dancers. But also, it was an aesthetic and even political choice, allowing for full participation by all the workshop members and giving the works an unpolished, spontaneous, "natural" appearance. Questions of the relationship of music to dance were explored anew. Perhaps even more important than the individual dances given at Judson concerts was the attitude that anything might be called a dance and looked at as a dance; the work of a visual artist, a filmmaker, a musician might be considered a dance, just as activities done by a dancer, although not recognizable as theatrical dance, might be reexamined and "made strange" because they were framed as art.

In retrospect, several important individual choreographic styles grew out of the rich culture at Judson: Yvonne Rainer's dialectical work, mixing ordinary or grotesque movement with traditional dance techniques, pushing the body's operations and coordination to the limits, and testing extremes of freedom and control in the choreographic process; Steve Paxton's fusions of nature and culture, his framing of mundane actions like eating and walking as noteworthy for attention and perception, his flattening of time; Robert Morris's task dances, using objects to focus the attention of both performer and audience and his references within the works to other artworks, creating an historical context for the work in the work; Lucinda Childs's cool performance style, rooted first in handling of objects and later in pure movement structures; Trisha Brown's improvisations and flyaway movements. This analytic, reductive wing of the post-modern dance movement was one aspect of Judson. A second aspect was the theatrical, often humorous, baroque style — in the work, for example, of David Gordon, Fred Herko, and Arlene Rothlein. A third aspect was the multimedia work exemplified in Elaine Summers's *Fantastic Gardens* and, later, Judith Dunn's *Last Point*. Work developed along all three of these lines in the later 1960s and 1970s, but it was the analytic, reductive side of the Judson work that proposed and tested theories of dance as art.

1

Robert Dunn's Workshop

John Cage asked Robert Dunn to teach a class in choreography at the Merce Cunningham studio in the fall of 1960.[1] Dunn had taken Cage's class in "Composition of Experimental Music," taught at the New School for Social Research from 1956 to 1960,[2] as had the writers Jackson Mac-Low and Dick Higgins, the composer Toshi Ichiyanagi, and Al Hansen, George Brecht, and Allan Kaprow, all of whom were later associated with Happenings and Events. The classes Cage gave were small and participatory. Cage later wrote of his teaching method:

> I began each series of classes by meeting the students, attempting to find out what they had done in the field of music, and letting them know what I myself was doing at the time. The catalogue had promised a survey of contemporary music, but this was given only incidentally and in reference to the work of the students themselves or to my own work. For, after the first two classes, generally, the sessions were given over to the performance and discussion of student works.[3]

Dick Higgins remembers that Cage spoke about notation, prepared a piano, gave the class problems to solve, and when the students demonstrated their solutions, discussed the philosophy of each piece. "The technique of the piece was seldom mentioned, except that inconsistencies and incongruities would be noted." Higgins, who credited the class with contributing to the development of Happenings, writes that "the best thing that happened to us in Cage's class was the sense he gave us that 'anything goes,' at least potentially."[4] Al Hansen came to Cage's class interested chiefly in film; he had read in writings by Sergei Eisenstein that "all the art forms meet in the film frame." Hansen also traces Happenings back to Cage's course and his own realization, by the end of it, that "all art forms...meet...in the eyeball. In the head of the observer."[5] He remembers that the class members often brought their friends to class, and it was there that Hansen met artists such as George Segal, Jim Dine, Larry Poons, filmmaker Harvey Gross, and regular class members Florence

Tarlow and Scott Hyde. "To a great extent, and probably to John Cage's disgust, the class became a little version of Black Mountain College."[6]

According to Remy Charlip, then a member of Merce Cunningham's company, the dancers in the company asked John Cage to give a modern dance composition class — as an antidote to Louis Horst's class — in 1957 or 1958. Cage consented, and in the class, which lasted for about six months, taught in a way that was "very free." "Everyone did a piece and then we talked about it, I think in a similar way to how Bob [Dunn] later did it," explains Charlip. Charlip made a dance, called *Crosswords for the Cunningham Company*, in which he took a crossword puzzle and colored in the squares in an arbitrary order with four different colored pencils. "Each dancer had a square, and each person had a color, and when you came to a color, you went to that other person to get a movement." Jo Anne Melsher did a dance to music with a line of people. Charlip says that on the first day of Robert Dunn's class, Dunn showed the *Crosswords* score to his students.[7] James Waring had also taught an "experimental" composition class, at the Living Theater, in 1959 and 1960.[8]

Dunn was not a dancer or choreographer. He was the accompanist at the Cunningham and other modern dance studios at the time. Dunn thinks that Cage asked him to teach choreography because Dunn had a knowledge of contemporary dance and other art forms, and because Cunningham was not inclined to teach composition.[9] Dunn, married then to Cunningham dancer Judith Dunn, was born in Oklahoma in 1928. He studied music composition and theory at New England Conservatory, where he earned a bachelor's degree. He worked in opera as a vocal repertoire coach and accompanist. From 1955 to 1958 he studied dance at Boston Conservatory of Music, chiefly with Jan Veen, a student of Mary Wigman and Harold Kreutzberg; Dunn also taught percussion for dancers at the Boston Conservatory. In 1958, when Cunningham performed in Boston, Dunn accompanied him and was asked to work at the American Dance Festival at Connecticut College that summer. In the fall of that year, Dunn moved to New York, where he worked for Martha Graham and Merce Cunningham as a pianist for rehearsals, classes, and performances. During his years as an accompanist he also worked for José Limón, Helen Tamiris, Pearl Lang, Jane Dudley, Paul Taylor, and James Waring. He no longer danced, but he studied Tai Chi Chuan and Yoga.[10]

Cunningham donated the use of his studio at 14th Street and Sixth Avenue free of charge for Dunn's classes, which ran about two and a half hours, for ten to twelve sessions per course. Dunn charged a fee of twelve to fifteen dollars for the entire course "for each solvent student," except returning students, who were allowed to take subsequent courses without further payment.[11] During some of the classes, Cunningham sat in his dressing room behind the studio where, Dunn claims, he was listening to the discussion.[12]

Robert Dunn had seen the composition classes given by Louis Horst, Martha Graham's music director, who demanded rigid adherence to musical forms; he had seen those given by Doris Humphrey, who assessed dances according to their theatrical tensions and resolutions.[13] Dunn found the atmosphere in those classes, in which young dancers studied every summer at the American Dance Festival sessions, "so oppressive that it was incredible. If indeed I helped liberate people from Louis [Horst] and Doris [Humphrey] (who was a great woman, but still) — . . . that was well worth doing."[14]

Unlike Horst, who used preclassic forms, and modern music by composers such as Béla Bartók, Zoltan Kodaly, Alexander Scriabin, Arnold Schönberg, and Aaron Copland, Dunn taught his students the musical structures of later composers, like Cage and the European avant-gardists Karlheinz Stockhausen and Pierre Boulez.[15] These chance and indeterminate structures were given to the students not as musical forms, but as time-structures "derived from and applicable to all the arts or future arts which might take place in time."[16] John Cage's use of noise and silence in music and his move toward theatrics in musical performance were two influences on Dunn's thinking in this regard.[17]

Dunn's classes, both in their heritage from Cage and in their eclectic assimilation of various cultural preoccupations of the 1960s — including Zen Buddhism, Taoism, existentialism, and scientism — were a microcosm of New York's avant-garde art world. It was an art world small enough for poets, painters, dancers, actors, and musicians to know each other and each other's work. So, many of the ideas circulating in the various artistic and social networks around Greenwich Village found their way into the dances and discussions in Dunn's courses. To Dunn, the classes were a generalized "clearinghouse for structures derived from various sources of contemporary action: dance, music, painting, sculpture, Happenings, literature."[18]

But literature was the area least plumbed because, according to Dunn, "we were feeling that dance had been so super-literary in a very destructive way. Burroughs had just come on the scene, making a break in texture with the New American Poetry. Even before he did the cut-ups, his work was collage, hard-edged, perceptually obsessive. A lot of people had read *Naked Lunch*. And all of us had some attachment to the Dadaists."[19]

The concrete approach Dunn used in the class was modeled after Cage's class. But Dunn had felt an unsatisfying lag in productivity as

Cage's classes progressed, and so he added assignments for the choreography students, "materials and ideas put forth for their possible suggestiveness to further work. This was a bit of stategic 'irrigation' of the garden plot, it being very clear to me at the time that the all-necessary seeds were provided by each member of the class."[20] These materials included Cage's graphic production of the chance score for *Fontana Mix* and the number structure of Erik Satie's *Trois Gymnopédies*.[21] Other assignments dealt with an abstract time constraint, e.g., "Make a five-minute dance in half an hour."[22] Others involved collaborations in which autonomous personal control had to be relinquished within a "semi-independent" working situation.[23] Still others had to do with the subject matter, though this was rarer: "Make a dance about nothing special."[24]

Louis Horst had also used Satie's music in teaching modern forms of musical structures for dance composition. But Horst's approach to teaching was more prescriptive and rigid than Dunn's. For example, Horst used one of the *Gnossiennes* as a study in "archaism," in which two-dimensional design of the body is achieved by distortion, tension, formality. The archaic composition was to emphasize "planal design," arresting life "in attitudes that breathe at the same time a potential of movement." Horst prescribed performing the *Gnossienne* study so slowly that the dance would imitate slow-motion cinematography.[25] He also suggested Satie's *Danse de la Brouette* as an accompaniment to an exercise in asymmetrical rhythm. He wrote that the "uneven, oblique, unstable" movement done to a 5/4 rhythm was especially appropriate to express the scattered, frantic feeling of a Madison Avenue executive or a housewife. But, he warned, the "feeling of unbalance [should] not [be] destroyed by gestures which create a too symmetrical design in space."[26] In other words, the quality of expression in the movements in a Horst composition assignment was to resemble the emotion suggested by the musical accompaniment.

In his book *Modern Dance Forms*, Horst gave young choreographers a checklist for evaluating their compositions:

1. Is the work sufficiently beautiful and is its movement delineation striking and ingenious?
2. Is the *formal design* rational and clear?
3. Is its *rhythmic structure* distinct and effective?
4. Does it contain sufficient fullness?
5. Is the demand of *contrast* adequately respected, and the bane of *monotony* avoided?[27]

In a world where concepts of beauty had long since been challenged, where art works that embraced monotony and eschewed rational design had been made at least since Duchamp and the Dadaists, Horst's rules seemed old-fashioned, even though he was still applying them through the early 1960s. (The book, a record of his teaching methods, was published in 1961.) Comments Horst made in his classes, also recorded in *Modern Dance Forms,* strikingly reveal the difference between his method and Dunn's:

> You always have to know where you're going—how things look to the audience. You must do the impossible. A dancer is an aesthetic acrobat—*must* be—so you can do anything you want to do....A quarter of an inch makes a difference—that sort of exactitude that makes it professional. Nothing casual should happen on stage anyway....
> I know it hurts. You didn't think it was going to be fun, did you? Dance and be happy?[28]

When Dunn used Satie, his approach was entirely different: "I played the piece and gave them a number structure and they composed a dance, separate from the music but structured with the music in a sort of dovetailing way without any mickey-mousing."[29] The separateness of the dancing from the musical structure was typical of Cunningham's collaborations with Cage and other composers.

In fulfilling their assignments in Dunn's class, students were allowed wide latitude in terms of methods, materials, and structures; as in the Cage class, the discussion focused on how these choices were arrived at and how well the choreographer had succeeded in carrying out his or her intention. The analytic method used in the discussions was also inspired by Cage's ideas about musical form:

> Structure in music is its divisibility into successive parts from phrases to long sections. Form is content, the continuity. Method is the means of controlling the continuity from note to note. The material of music is sound and silence. Integrating these is composing.[30]

Cage was a rich font of principles and methods, but, as noted above, he was not Dunn's only influence. At the time Dunn did not want to be only a musician, preferring the "model of a sort of errant philosopher-poet adventuring in various media, including that of the social occasions surrounding the work." He later wrote of his ideas about teaching as originating in quite disparate sources:

> I was impressed by what I had come to know about Bauhaus education in the arts, particularly from the writings of Moholy-Nagy, in its emphasis on the nature of materials and on basic structural elements. Association with John Cage had led to the project of constantly extending perceptive boundaries and contexts. From Heidegger, Sartre, Far Eastern Buddhism, and Taoism, in some personal amalgam, I had the notion in teaching of making a "clearing," a sort of "space of nothing," in which things could appear and grow in their own nature. Before each class I made the attempt to attain this state of mind, of course with varying success.[31]

Heidegger's writings about the human "world" in which we exist and act but which is not of our making, and about "things-in-the-world" which constitute our everyday existence, together with Sartre's stress on consciousness, find analogues in the interest, among the artists of the late 1950s and early 1960s, in using ordinary objects and amplifying perception of their thingness in relation to the beingness of humanity. For Heidegger, the social world consists of a set of relations between humans, tools, and natural things. This "world," where people manipulate things and use up materials, is in constant strife with the "earth," or natural realm, which remains impenetrable and secluded. The artwork functions as the bridge between these two realms, paradoxically bringing the earth into the world without violating it. The truth that is present in nature takes on a social—i.e., historical—existence. In the artwork, a framework that sets off the thingly nature of an object fashioned by humans is created.

> The rock comes to bear and rest and so first becomes rock; metals come to glitter and shimmer, colors to glow, tones to sing, the word to speak. All this comes forth as the work sets itself back into the massiveness and heaviness of stone, into the firmness and pliancy of wood, into the hardness and luster of metal, into the lighting and darkening of color, into the clang of tone, and into the naming power of the word.[32]

The artwork shows us that, "at bottom, the ordinary is not ordinary; it is extraordinary, uncanny."[33]

Heidegger's thoughts on art and its mystical relation to the natural realm, as well as the Western interpretation of Zen Buddhism as an anti-intellectual discipline, valuing spontaneity and meditation on the simplicity of everyday things, must have been attractive to a generation that had lived through the politically and socially anxious 1950s. After the "conspicuous consumption" of postwar American life, to live simply and naturally seemed an antidote; after an age of conformism and social pressure, especially for women, people thirsted for the "liberation" and sense of personal autonomy spontaneous behavior connotes, which often seems everywhere present in the natural world.

The use of chance methods and indeterminacy by composers such as Cage, Stockhausen, Earle Brown, Morton Feldman, Christian Wolff, and other avant-garde composers in the United States and Europe in the 1950s had brought about a new form of musical notation, both as a means of generating a fixed score (but able to express different qualities than those conveyed by traditional notation) and as a way of indicating parameters for a performer who might take an actively creative role in interpreting from the score. Labanotation and other, more personal, movement notation systems were available but not widely known to dancers and choreographers at the time of Dunn's classes. The *writing* of dances—the "-graphy" in choreography—was crucial to the composition process Dunn outlined for his students, not necessarily in the sense of permanently recording what the dance was, but in order to objectify the composition process, both by creating nonintuitive choices and by viewing the total range of possibilities for the dance.

> Whether we use any other writing material in between, we certainly do inscribe dances on the bodies of the dancers, as a group. We inscribe dances on the body of the theater. When I say choreography, I am always talking about choreography/improvisation....By planning the dance in a written or drawn manner, you have a very clear view of the dance and its possibilities. Laban's idea was very secondarily to make a *Tanzschrift*, a dance-writing, a way to record. Laban's idea was to make a *Schrifttanz,* to use graphic—written—inscriptions and then to generate activities. Graphic notation is a way of inventing the dance. It is part of the conception of the dance. What the choreographer has to do is to choose a world of movement...to invent or choose the graphic side and invent or choose the correlations.[34]

Dunn alludes to Cocteau's statement "We build traps for poetry" in speaking of the release of physical activity and meaning from graphic scores.

> The human body and its doings are so full of meaning that most of what you have to do is release and channel this meaning. A great deal of cleverness and thought is a wonderful thing to get towards making those traps and releasing that meaning, but they do not guarantee it. When you know your movement vocabulary, you can make a metamorphic transfer of many models of other artworks, the structures and relations within them, out of movement material. The fact that you've used a scientific or philosophical or natural model is absolutely no guarantee of the validity of your work.[35]

For all the diversity of models, the unifying and paradigmatic form of choreography in Dunn's class was the aleatory process, which Merce Cunningham had used since 1951.[36] Says Dunn:

> I came to realize very well that chance is a form of choreography, of dance notation. You set up a table of possibilities. Those dice, as you throw them, are writing. They tell you what to do next.[37]

In the fall of 1960, Dunn's first course began with five students: Paulus Berenson, Marni Mahaffay, Simone (Forti) Morris, Steve Paxton, and Yvonne Rainer.[38] Mahaffay was a young dancer from Portland, Oregon, who had been trained in ballet and then joined Charles Weidman's company when it toured to Portland, partly as a way of getting to New York. Attracted to the Zen idea that the conjunction of disparate elements has meaning and validity, she soon became devoted to Merce Cunningham "and everything surrounding him." She zealously attended every class given at Cunningham's studio, and Dunn's course was no exception. There she first began to understand Cage's precept that any sound is valid as part of music, that any movement is valid as part of a dance—"whether it's a cough, a sniffle, or natural movement." And that continuum of sound and of movement extended, critically, to silence and its correlate, stillness. Mahaffay remembers using charts that outline space, movement, and rhythm options in order to make dances by chance. "The possibilities came out limitless."[39]

> I used the rotation of the moon to make one structure, but it could have been any-thing—for instance, the routine of getting up in the morning and cooking an egg. The path of the moon indicated where things could happen in space, in the dance.[40]

For Mahaffay the ever-present option of stillness—of nothing—was crucial. "When you roll the dice and get stillness, suddenly you are given an image of what preceded that moment—and that creates a kind of medita-tion on the movement." Giving up cherished control over the dance was an experience as compelling as the use of stillness.

> To give up your own clichés, to give up your own movement that you were so attached to, was very exciting. You might only be given enough time to do the beginning of your favorite movement, or to do it much less than you would have preferred to. You ended up putting movements together in ways that weren't at all obvious or expected.[41]

Mahaffay, a very small woman, was interested in the kind of detailed, meticulous movement she had learned in ballet and in Cunningham's tech-nique classes. She remembers one phrase she made within a larger form that involved the folding and unfolding of the body in various careful ways, "like a box opening and closing, very complex and fast." Other stu-dents generally did activity that was less "dancey." Mahaffay recalls Steve Paxton creating a dance that consisted of repeatedly running into the school office to carry out one piece of furniture at a time. Simone Forti did a duet with someone else from the class running together in a large circle for a long time, then breaking that constancy and tension with a series of quiet, abrupt side steps. "The effect of those very simple elements was thrilling. I was so moved by the simplicity and strength of it: the comfort-able, clean, expansive run, the quietness of the stepping. Simone [Forti] brought certain ideas from Ann Halprin into a situation of extreme disci-pline."[42] Mahaffay also remembers Yvonne Rainer doing a meditative study making shapes with her entire body while sitting on the floor.

> It was visual, it was nondance. Those exercises in meditation that several people were involved in came out of Zen and seemed to relate to Merce [Cunningham]'s philosophy.
> You could go to a concert and listen to La Monte Young playing sandpaper for half an hour or forty-five minutes. Sandpaper wears down, and then the sound changes. Or

he would adjust the sandpaper in his hand, changing the rhythm and texture of the sound. There is an impact when one simple element works against another.

At another concert, someone threw a cord of logs down a staircase, and we listened to the sound it made. Or a musician would sit at a grand piano and never touch the keyboard, making sounds with sponges and window-cleaning squeegees, tapping the piano in various ways.

The students in the class were remarkably resourceful, Mahaffay recalls, bringing in ideas from various places and disciplines. Yet Dunn clearly directed the flow of events in the class.

> Everyone was free to be wherever it was they were coming from; somehow it all fit into what Bob [Dunn] was doing. The way he talked about movement was so all-encompassing, you could do anything! There was something very centering and supportive about him, a deep level of understanding that went beyond what he was teaching. I remember him sitting at the piano with a stopwatch, and with a calmness and centeredness that related to Tai Chi.[43]

Steve Paxton grew up in Tucson, Arizona, where he did gymnastics and started dancing in high school to improve his tumbling. He was trained in Graham technique and toured with a performing group directed by his dance teachers, an Episcopal nun and a woman who taught at the local Jewish Community Center. In 1958 Paxton went to Connecticut College for the summer courses in modern dance. That summer Merce Cunningham was teaching at Connecticut College for the first time, and Paxton studied with him as well as with Graham, Doris Humphrey, and José Limón. Paxton came to New York, where he danced with Limón's company and studied at the Cunningham studio.[44] He got a work-study scholarship with Cunningham; his work was to clean up the studio. "I was very much in love with the company at that time because they all seemed very sprightly, sprightly and droll."[45]

From the beginning of Dunn's class, Paxton was interested in challenging all of the assumptions of modern dance, including the methods and habits of people, like Cunningham, whom he respected. He tried to find sources for movement outside of the by-then refined technical vocabulary of the first generation of modern dancers and Cunningham's ballet-derived technique. Rainer remembers Paxton doing a dance that consisted of his sitting on a bench, eating a sandwich. Paxton says of his work in Dunn's class:

> The work that I did there was first of all to flush out all my "why-nots," to go through my "why not" circles as far as I could until getting bored with the question. "Why not?" was a catch-word at that time. It was a very permissive time.

The Living Theater was in the same building as Cunningham, and there were concerts there by the Paper Bag Players, who were zany, and by Jimmy Waring, who was eclectic and droll, by the Living Theater itself, which was my first contact with the rise of political consciousness—where I first saw the peace symbol, where I first saw dope smoked, where they were doing plays like *The Connection* and talking about prison reform. Jackson MacLow did readings there. As an environment it was very permissive and form-oriented. [I.e., the approach to making art was formalist.] A MacLow play was described as a chance operation. James Waring was interested in chance and eclecticism. His dances had all different styles. It didn't seem to matter; nothing that had been done before seemed to matter.

Diane di Prima and other poets were there [at the Living Theater], and I remember lectures that they gave, in which the hostile audience would say, "What are you doing? What has happened to art? And they would say, "We're just making art, and why not?"

They [di Prima and her circle] had a title pool. Everyone would contribute titles, and if you needed a title for something, you just pulled one out. Why not?

Paxton remembers Dunn's style as a teacher as Zen-like.

Dunn himself managed to do something that I've admired ever since. He taught us ideas almost by neglecting us, by mentioning things but tending to disappear at the same time, leaving with a smile. It was rather Zen-like, because how can you teach something that is in a constant state of mutation? What do you teach? He taught forms—Cage forms, Satie forms, basically musical ideas, in rebound, I think initially for him, against Louis Horst's teaching of earlier musical forms, with the idea that music is a key to time, or one of the keys to time. When you listen to a piece of music, you listen to intervals, sections, and structures. You aren't involved with personality and states of presence. So Dunn got us into that.[46]

Paxton never choreographed a dance in response to the Satie assignment. He was less interested in using musical forms—perhaps because Cunningham had already used Satie's music as accompaniment to some of his dances— than in the very process of movement selection itself. For Paxton the history of modern dance had been tainted by cults of personality, and he searched for ways of stripping any trace of the artist's hand from his own work.[47]

Simone Forti was born in Florence, Italy, in 1935. Her family was Jewish, and in 1939 they escaped to Switzerland and then to the United States. Forti grew up in Los Angeles, then studied psychology and sociology at Reed College, where she met Robert Morris. They married and left school in 1956, moving to San Francisco where Morris painted and Forti studied dance with Ann Halprin. Halprin had only recently broken with conventional modern dance. For four years, Forti danced with Halprin in Halprin's outdoor studio near Mount Tamalpais in Kentfield, California, working on free improvisations, kinesiological analysis, and vocal work.[48]

Halprin's studio was a gathering place for other artists who collaborated with the dancers and sometimes taught them. They included the composer La Monte Young, actor John Graham, dancer A. A. Leath, painter Jo Landor, and architect Lawrence Halprin, Ann Halprin's husband. Forti was fascinated by Surrealist films, which she had seen since high school; she read Kurt Schwitters with interest. At Halprin's workshop Forti continued her involvement with fantastic juxtapositions. She, Halprin, and Graham worked together on movement and language improvisations based on intuitive imagery and contrasts. "I felt we were working out of a Zen state. But it wasn't Zen, so we took the word Nez," calling these works the Nez plays. Halprin also taught Forti techniques for inducing a "dance state" in which the body is focused and receptive to impulses that set off movement flow.[49]

In 1959, the Morrises moved to New York. Forti, who was beginning to find the chaos of total improvisation disturbing, looked for other ways of working in dance and theater. Robert Morris gave up painting in the Abstract Expressionist style. Forti took some classes at the Martha Graham studio, where the idea of holding her stomach in repelled her, and then at the Cunningham school, where she found the characteristic speed and fragmentation of Cunningham's style bewildering. Cunningham was brilliant at articulating adult sensations of alienation, she writes, but she felt that "the thing I had to offer was still very close to the holistic and generalized response of infants."[50] She taught at a nursery school, where she noticed the meaningful and satisfying repetitive movements of the children. She listened to La Monte Young's reductive, repetitive music. She saw and then worked in the Happenings of Robert Whitman, and she read about the activities of the Gutai group in Japan, who used artist's materials and actions to create simple, sensuous experiences for audiences.[51]

Forti enjoyed Dunn's workshop sessions, where chance methods became meaningful to her not so much as a repudiation of personal control — she did not mind having control over the work — but as a technique of invoking a past experience — the moment of composition — in present performance. She was impressed with the speed with which Dunn himself worked, and she found his clarification of principles useful.[52] "Bob Dunn asked us to be very specific about our parameters and to invent new ones." One of the first assignments Dunn gave, according to Forti, was to make a dance by combining sets of choices for body parts, durations, parts of the rooms, and left or right directions in space.

> You could end up, for example, with eye, hand, neck; left, right; here, there. And then you would make up slips of paper for each option. So if you picked three combinations arbitrarily, you might get [she demonstrates]: hand, right, there; eye, right, there; eye right, there. And you'd use those results as instructions, as a score to make a dance.[53]

Remy Charlip remembers Forti's dance in response to Dunn's Satie assignment. Forti put different parts of her body against the floor, depending on whether the musical phrase was a five-count, four-count, or three-count measure. "If it was a five she put her head down. If it was three, she just put her two feet down. It was an exquisite dance."[54]

In December of 1960, Forti created two Happenings, *See-Saw* and *Rollers*, for a program at the Reuben Gallery, on which were also Jim Dine's *A Shining Bed* and Claes Oldenburg's *Blackouts*. In both works, Forti used children's playthings to generate movement. In *See-Saw* the movement structure was dictated by a seesaw, to which was attached a toy that made a mooing sound, and in *Rollers* two performers sat in shallow wagons pulled by three ropes.[55]

Robert Dunn remembers Paulus Berenson, who later became a potter, showing the class a long solo and then asking them where they thought the climax of the dance was.

> "Climax" was aesthetically perhaps not a very "in" word at the time, but we felt we had experienced something rather mysteriously impressive in that line, and left him to tell us what. His dance was punctuated by a number of stillnesses of varying lengths, and on his informing us that it occurred during the longest pause, everyone shook their head in happy agreement with this solution.[56]

Yvonne Rainer, born in San Francisco in 1934, had moved to New York in 1956 to study acting. She took classes from Lee Grant, at Herbert Berghof's school, and from Paul Mann, but, dissatisfied with the Method approach, she took some dance classes on the recommendation of a friend. Rainer began dancing in 1957 with Edith Stephen, and in 1959 heightened her commitment to dance, taking two classes a day at the Graham school. Rainer studied ballet, with Lynn Golding and Lisan Kay at Ballet Arts, in addition to modern dance.[57] At that time, Rainer says, she already planned to become a choreographer, partly because she had begun training as a dancer, at age twenty-four, too late to achieve "mastery as a performer of other artists' work."[58] She started taking classes from Cunningham at the end of 1959, and soon after that, she met Simone Forti through Nancy Meehan (a dancer studying at the Graham school). Rainer, Meehan, and Forti met once a week in the spring of 1960 to improvise and share ideas. Rainer's interest in repetition, social contact, unusual positions, and fragmented movement was stimulated in these sessions.[59] (See Chapter 4.)

In the summer of 1960, after taking Cunningham's intensive June course, Rainer went back to California to take Halprin's workshop, on Forti's recommendation. Forti herself attended the class, as did Robert Morris, Ruth Emerson, Trisha Brown, June Ekman, Willis Ward, La Monte Young, A.A. Leath, and John Graham.[60] That fall, Rainer resumed classes at Cunningham's studio, including Dunn's choreography course.[61]

At some point in Dunn's two years of teaching, but probably during the first year, Rainer made a chart that listed body parts (head, hands, voice, spine, foot) and also five possibilities of action for each part. The head could shake, roll, nod slowly, look at the feet, or nod quickly; the hands could touch the knee, shake the fingers, brush the hip, clap, or rub together; the voice could say "eeiioo," "if you insist," "sure," "aaaaa" in a breath, or "First of all, it is a contribution to history"; the spine could round, arch, curve to the side, curve the lower spine, or curve from side to side; the foot could rotate, step out three times, stamp, pat the other foot, or rub the floor.[62] Although the possibilities for the spine are Cunning-hamesque, the use of voice—and the options for the voice—and several of the actions of the head are strikingly original in modern dance. Rainer's use of speech, related to the Dada use of formal and art statements and pure sound, would continue as a salient feature of her work throughout her career. (See Chapter 4.) Rainer composed a dance by grouping points on the chart together, some actions to be performed one at a time and some simultaneously; she inserted four six-count pauses into this phrase. For instance, the dance begins with the hands clapping and the second action is a rotation of the foot. The dance ends with five simultaneous actions: the foot rubs the floor, the hands clap and fingers shake, and the voice says "eeiioo" and "sure."[63]

Another untitled score by Rainer from this period is a spatial plan made by connecting dots on a piece of paper. Also on the paper are scattered words that could indicate movements and body parts in a dance, such as hand, hip, ribs, knee, leg, foot, and recline, walk, creep, squat, hop, leap; numbers from one to ten; and indications for fast and slow.[64]

Rainer thinks she may have been the only person in the class to use all the materials Dunn provided in the beginning of the term.[65] Her *Three Satie Spoons* used the method of Cage's *Fontana Mix* and also the number structure of Satie's *Gymnopédies*. In *Fontana Mix*, Cage marked the imperfections on a piece of paper, drew lines on the paper, and then put a transparent staff or grid across the markings, which were then subject to interpretation by the performers. When Rainer used this graphic method, she made a separate score for each of the three Satie *Gymnopédies*. She decided on the smallest interval, a four-count measure, then counted the total number of measures in a piece and made a staff to correspond to that number. She made a drawing with crayons, using a different color for every phrase in the first section of the music (which then repeated itself), then put the staff on top of the drawing. She laid a straight line at an angle across the staff, and wherever the "guideline" crossed a color, or colors, she performed the corresponding movements, which she had invented, at that point in the duration of the music. Rainer then made a decision about how to fill the unit of time with movement: whether to do a particular movement phrase several times, once slowly, or once and then hold for the rest of the musical phrase.[66] The chance method of *Fontana Mix* resulted in a repetitive structure that was appropriate to Satie's music, because the staff usually crossed the same color for several lines in a row.

Although Rainer was interested in the impersonal quality inherent in the chance method, which created unpredictable juxtapositions, what emerged in her dances was a distinctive movement style, full of eccentricities and fragmentation, arrived at by choice as well as chance. In 1962 Rainer wrote about her movement choices, in a short essay on three dances made for Dunn's class.

> I dance about things that affect me in a very immediate way. These things can be as diverse as the mannerisms of a friend, the facial expression of a woman hallucinating on the subway, the pleasure of an aging ballerina as she demonstrates a classical movement, a pose from an Etruscan mural, a hunchbacked man with cancer, images suggested by fairy tales, children's play, and of course my own body impulses generated in different situations — a classroom, my own studio, being drunk at a party. I am also deliberately involved in a search for the incongruous and in using a wide range of individual human and animal actions — speak, shriek, grunt, slump, bark, look, jump, dance. One or many of these things may appear in a single dance — depending on what I read, see, and hear during the period I am working on that dance. It follows, therefore, that no single dance is about any one idea or story, but rather about a variety of things that in performance fuse together and decide the nature of the whole experience.[67]

The movements themselves could be seen as highly expressive, but the ways in which they were put together resisted the interpretation of a unified plot or characterization.

The movements in *Three Satie Spoons* include stretching the mouth with the index fingers, tracing lines down the body with the index finger, squatting, grasping the foot to the thigh while turning, making semaphoric arm movements, lying down on the side and falling over on the back, extending a trembling bent leg, and a shoulder stand.[68] Among these movements are themes that thread through Rainer's choreography for the rest of her career: one part of the body leading or indicating another part; awkward positions; a subversion of the "pulled-up" dancerly line in limp or trembling limbs; quotations of games and gymnastics. The third section of the dance, performed to the third *Gymnopédie*, also includes sounds: a squeak; "the grass is greener when the sun is yellower"; "ah-ooo-wah-ooo."[69] Rainer threw dice to determine where these sounds should fall in relation to the movement.[70] The use of language and the disjunctiveness between the verbal and visual "tracks" of the work have also threaded through Rainer's *oeuvre*, not only in her choreography, but also in her filmmaking in the 1970s.

In composing *Three Satie Spoons*, Rainer shared Dunn's interest in associating other art forms with dance in her use of Cage's scores and Satie's time structures, as well as in considering the spatial and temporal qualities of sculpture:

> [The] spirit of the piece derives from the simplicity and monotony of Satie's music. I became involved with repetition thru a concern that each movement might be seen as more than a fleeting form, much as one can observe a piece of sculpture for one minute or many minutes.[71]

As Rollo Myers has pointed out, sculptural presentation was Satie's explicit intention, not only in the *Gymnopédies,* but also in the *Gnossiennes* and *Sarabandes.* However, Myers describes the listening experience in slightly different terms than Rainer uses; he calls the three *Gymnopédies* three different views of the same thing, all three of which share an underlying unity.[72] For Rainer, the sculptural aspect dealt not so much with point of view as with permanence.

According to Rainer, Dunn's early classes were informal, with everyone bringing in disparate ideas and Dunn leading the discussions with a mixture of tact and enthusiasm.

> It was a very strange assortment of people. Paul [Berenson] was Graham-trained. He did a very long, complicated solo, with traditional Graham-Cunningham movement. I can't remember how it was discussed. Marni [Mahaffay] did a dance in a little black skirt, tights, and leotard. She did some hip movements and played around with her skirt, as if she were doing a strip tease. Maybe there was some jazz music. I was dumbfounded. I wouldn't have known what to say. And I recall I was impressed by the delicacy and sensitivity that Bob [Dunn] used in dealing with her. That was the great thing about Bob. He got interested in everything. Anything that happened there, he was interested in, and the more unusual it was, and the more unsophisticated, the more things he would find to focus it in some way that would bring out its specialness.[73]

When Dunn offered the course a second time, in the early part of 1961, Ruth Allphon and Judith Dunn joined the others as students.[74] Although some of the students (and the program notes for Concert of Dance #2) refer to both Robert Dunn and Judith Dunn as the teachers of the class, Robert Dunn says that he only asked his wife to assist him while he taught.[75] Judith Dunn confirms this view, writing:

> As a teacher Bob Dunn was outrageous. He allowed interminable rambling discussion, which often strayed wildly from the opening point. He permitted class members to deal with whatever hit their fancy. To examine, consider and present any object, dance collection of words, sounds and what have you in answer to problems he had given for study. He posed questions arising out of the most basic elements—structure, method, material. He was in one respect persistent, as if he had taken as his gospel the words of

the Chinese philosopher Laou T'su [sic], who said, "Favor and disgrace are the things which drive men mad." In other words, evaluation, in terms of "good or bad," "acceptable-rejected," were eliminated from discussion and analysis replaced them. (What did you see, what did you do, what took place, how did you go about constructing and ordering. What are the materials, where did you find or how did you form them, etc.) There was no formula to be filled. Initially this caused some anxiety. What he asked was that invention take place and that work continue to be produced economically and practically in terms of the place we were in, at that time, the Merce Cunningham Studio.[76]

Judith Dunn grew up in Brooklyn. Her mother, a physical therapist, had studied with Martha Graham. Dunn had no childhood ambitions to be a dancer, but she did want to be a professional basketball player when she was in junior high school. She majored in anthropology at Brooklyn College, where she was a member of the modern dance club. She planned to go to graduate school in anthropology, but in 1955 changed her mind and began the master's degree program in dance at Sarah Lawrence. After graduation she got a job teaching dance at Brandeis University, where she discovered how to teach as she went along.[77]

There were no obstacles and few traditions to prevent me from teaching or doing what I wished. Frankly, I had very little idea what was expected of me or how to proceed. I knew I was to meet classes and I had decided in the time allotted I would do both technique and composition. I would just have to invent things from week to week.[78]

When Merce Cunningham visited Boston as a guest teacher, he was encouraging to Judith Dunn, and she moved to New York to study with him. By 1958 she was a member of his company.[79] But until the Robert Dunn choreography class, Judith Dunn had not attempted her own choreography in New York.[80]

At the end of the first year, the choreography class gave a private recital of works made in class, at the Cunningham studio. Rainer showed a dance built on interlocking instructions for five dancers. Each dancer had a path to travel that was one part of a spiderweb-shaped floorplan. Marni Mahaffay's instructions were to "comb your hair, rest, sleep, practice pirouettes or chaîné turns or piqué turns in whatever sequence you wish" along the prescribed route. She could stop at a marked point to bark like a dog. She also had an option to eat the food of the other performers. When everyone else left the stage, Mahaffay was left alone to do two pirouettes, one *en dehors* and one *en dedans*, then to walk off. Ruth Allphon outlined her route with string. She had the option either to practice handstands or cartwheels, or to eat walnuts at prescribed spots. She could also make involuntary sounds, "such as grunts, squeaks, 'whoops!', etc." She could not leave until Paxton escorted her off. Paxton was instructed to creep along his path and between certain points to practice walking on his hands. At one place there was a preset stethoscope, which Paxton could sit down to use, but not necessarily every time he encountered it. If he met Ruth All-phon, he was to help her do handstands. Berenson's directions told him to eat raisins along his route. Whenever another person arrived at the exact center of the space, his instructions were to set down his raisins and do his "standing-in-one-spot bird movement dance." He could stand still to watch at any point, but at certain places he had to sit down "for 10 'bananas'." Rainer's score for her own part has been lost, but she did make two exits, on the second of which Berenson could exit at the same place.[81] The unnamed dance exemplified a number of principles Dunn and the partici-pants had brought to the class: the value of ordinary, even mundane actions, such as combing one's hair or eating; the freedom to exercise a range of options; the value of stillness as an element in the dance; the use of repetition and juxtaposition as structuring devices; and above all, the use of scores to generate and teach the dance.

Also in the end-of-the-year concert was a collaboration between Rainer, Forti, and Allphon. Its title was *Stove Pack Opus,* the result, according to Rainer, of a three-way free association between the choreog-raphers; Forti contributed "stove," Allphon "pack," and Rainer "opus."[82] The score for the dance gives a coded structure for each dancer, indicating intervals of unison movement, stillness, and two instances when the stage was empty. During one of the interludes with an empty stage, barking, whistling, and humming emanated from offstage.[83]

Another dance in the recital was a solo Forti made for a telephone booth. Designed for the booths then in use, which had panes of glass through which the upper part of the user's body was visible, the dance took place in one spot, using only Forti's torso, head, and arms. Forti also read a "dance report," in which she described how the growth of shoots in an onion she was observing caused its weight to shift and ultimately, caused the onion to fall off the bottle on which it rested.[84]

The end-of-the-year recital by Dunn's class was given in May or June 1961. That spring La Monte Young organized a series of concerts at Yoko Ono's loft at 112 Chambers Street. On 26 and 27 May Simone Forti gave a concert of "5 dance constructions + some other things," as part of the series. Other artists who gave concerts or events were Robert Morris, who created an environment that lasted four days; Philip Corner, Jackson MacLow, Toshi Ichiyanagi, Terry Jennings, Henry Flynt, Joseph Byrd, Richard Maxfield, and D. Lindberg.[85] At Forti's concert, the loft was arranged more like an art gallery than like a stage. Different dances took place in various parts of the loft. There were pieces that were based on children's playthings, and *See-Saw* was performed again. *Slant Board*, a ten-minute climbing activity for three or four people, was clearly based on sports. *Huddle*, a cluster of people who took turns climbing each other, was a kind of human jungle gym, meant to be viewed in the round. But here the audience walked around the dance. Several activities were simple, unitary actions lasting or repeating for a long time, much as La Monte Young's music often consisted of single, sustained tones. One of the dances was an accompaniment to a piece of taped music by Young.[86] Forti's game structures were presented simply, without special scene changes or costumes, without special backstage or secret transformations. They were dances without drama or illusion. Each dance consisted of a set of rules that generated an ongoing activity, without artistically arranged phrases, climaxes, or theatricality. These "constructions" simply allowed both dancer and viewer to enjoy the kinesthetic moment and to watch the subtle changes in shape and energy that occurred when the moment extended into longer durations.

During the spring and summer of 1961, more connections were forged between the students at the Cunningham studio and the dancers working with James Waring. The Dunns were friendly with Waring already. Rainer had been impressed by Aileen Passloff's dance *Tea at the Palaz of Hoon,* which she saw in 1960. She knew that Passloff worked closely with James Waring, and in spring 1961 Rainer found herself at Waring's studio. That summer, Waring asked her to perform two solos in a program he was organizing for 31 July at the Living Theater.[87] The program also included Waring's own choreography and dances by Passloff and by Fred Herko, a young dancer who performed with Waring.[88] Rainer danced *Three Satie Spoons* and another dance she had choreographed in the Dunn course, *The Bells*. In that dance, among other actions, Rainer crumpled her right hand into her nose; performed a "backwards traveling turn on one foot as fingers flit around head like insects"; turned her legs in and out while doing jetés; improvised in a staccato, rhythmic movement style while saying "the lewd fat bells of Manhattan"; rubbed her fists in her eyes while walking on tiptoe, saying, "I told you everything was going to be alright, Harry." She did the movement phrases while facing squarely in the various directions of the compass, which had been predetermined by chance.[89]

Michael Smith, the drama critic, reviewed the concert in the *Village Voice*, characterizing the dramatic effects of each dance rather than describing or analyzing its movement. We learn from his review that Waring's *Little Kootch Piece No. 2* was humorously despairing, its "eccentricities all but destroy[ing] communication"; that Passloff's *Rosefish* was about "a hopeless desire to escape," and that it was "danced with fine authority." This concert marked the public debut of both Rainer and Herko as choreographers, although Smith does not make any reference to this fact in his review. He notes that Rainer's solos emphasize form, and he praises her concern with structure as "effective in holding attention." But he sees her dances as studies, wondering where the communication with an audience enters into the performance. "*The Bells* is funny, but maybe for the wrong reasons: the *Satie Spoons* is bleak, introspective, fascinating, private." Herko's *Possibilities for a Pleasant Outing* provided Smith with a change from the otherwise uniformly "bleak landscape." "Mr. Herko seems, more than the others, to derive direct delight from moving, which I'd think would be the basis of all dances." Still, Smith must dramatically interpret Herko's dance: he is, Smith writes, dancing about infantile pleasure in a world dominated by inhibiting adult rationality.[90]

That fall, Robert Dunn again offered a course in choreography at the Cunningham studio. Several more students began to attend. Rainer continued for the third and fourth terms, as did Paxton. The new participants over the course of the year were: Trisha Brown, Ruth Emerson, Alex Hay, Deborah Hay, Fred Herko, Al Kurchin, Dick Levine, Gretchen MacLane, John Herbert McDowell, Joseph Schlichter, Carol Scothorn, and Elaine Summers. Valda Setterfield and David Gordon attended occasionally, with an "ineffable air of being 'in it but *not* of it'." As in Cage's experimental music class, friends of the students often dropped in to observe, and sometimes participate. Dunn remembers Robert Rauschenberg, Jill Johnston, and a young filmmaker, Gene Friedman, as regular visitors, and Remy Charlip, David Vaughan, Robert Morris, Ray Johnson, and Peter Schumann as occasional guests.[91]

Once again Dunn gave a Satie assignment. Rainer again combined *Fontana Mix* with Satie, this time with *Trois Gnossiennes*, to make a duet for herself and Trisha Brown. Punning as she did with the earlier dance, she called it *Satie for Two*.[92] The movement phrases included a "Gauguin sit," a "sloppy skip," a standing position in which the head was turned in profile and the arm wrapped around the head to grasp the forehead while the opposite hip jutted out, a section in which Brown and Rainer touched parts of each other's and their own bodies, an "atom bomb," and various traveling steps. An interlude between the second and third *Gnossiennes* involved both speaking in "children's dialect" and barking and quacking.[93]

Trisha Brown had grown up in Aberdeen, Washington, where as a child she played football, climbed trees, and studied tap, ballet, and acrobatics. She got a bachelor's degree in modern dance at Mills College, where she learned "traditional" modern dance composition according to the rules of Louis Horst and Doris Humphrey. During the summers she studied at Connecticut College, where she took classes from José Limón, Louis Horst, and Merce Cunningham. In 1958, Brown was hired to set up a dance department at Reed College. After a few months, she "exhausted conventional teaching methods," and for the rest of her two years at Reed she taught improvisationally, while also developing her own dance vocabulary.[94]

In the summer of 1960, Brown also went to Halprin's workshop. Simone Forti vividly recalls a study Brown did in Halprin's studio:

> She was holding a broom in her hand. She thrust it out straight ahead, without letting go of the handle. And she thrust it out with such force that the momentum carried her whole body through the air. I still have the image of that broom and Trisha right out in space, traveling in a straight line three feet off the ground.[95]

That fall, Brown came to New York, where she worked on structured improvisations with Forti and Dick Levine. In 1961 she performed in Forti's evening at Yoko Ono's loft.[96] The process of improvisation has been an essential aspect of Brown's work. As she later wrote:

> If you stand back and think about what you are going to do before you do it, there is likely to be a strenuous editing process that stymies the action. On the other hand, if you set yourself loose in an improvisational form, you have to make solutions very quickly and you learn how to. That is the excitement of improvisation. If, however, you just turn the lights out and go gah-gah in circles, that would be therapy or catharsis or your happy hour, but if in the beginning you set a structure and decide to deal with X, Y, and Z materials in a certain way, nail it down even further and say you can only walk forward, you cannot use your voice or you have to do 195 gestures before you hit the wall at the other end of the room, that is an improvisation within set boundaries. That is the principle, for example, behind jazz. The musicians may improvise, but they have a limitation in the structure just as improvisation in dance does. This is what I would call structured improvisation because it locates you in time and place with content.[97]

Young dancers at the beginning of the 1960s, like their peers in every field, and like each new avant-garde generation, were trying to free themselves from the restrictions and rules of what they perceived as an older, more rigid generation. Improvisation in jazz and "classical" music or in dance stood as a metaphor for freedom, but also as a strategy for learning to act spontaneously, for setting one's own rules within a form.

For Brown one of the most valuable features of Dunn's class was the way he approached analysis, not looking for the correct answers to the problems he set, but interested in whatever individual solutions his students discovered for themselves, and in helping them to understand what it was they had created.

> After presenting a dance, each choreographer was asked, "How did you make that dance?" The students were inventing forms rather than using the traditional theme and development or narrative, and the discussion that followed applied nonevaluative criticism to the movement itself and the choreographic structure as well as investigating the

disparity between the two simultaneous experiences, what the artist was making and what the audience saw. This procedure illuminated the interworkings of the dances and minimized value judgements of the choreographer, which for me meant permission, permission to go ahead and do what I wanted to do or had to do—to try out an idea of borderline acceptability.

One of the assignments Brown recalls distinctly was the simple instruction: Make a three-minute dance.

This assignment was totally nonspecific except for duration, and the ambiguity provoked days of sorting through possibilities trying to figure out what time meant, was 60 seconds the only difference between three minutes and four minutes, how do you stop something, why, what relation does time have to movement, and on and on. Dick Levine taught himself to cry and did so for the full time period while I held a stopwatch instructed by him to shout just before the time elapsed, "Stop it! Stop it! Cut it out!" both of us ending at exactly three minutes. That dance is a good example of the practice of substituting one medium, in this case acting/crying, to solve a dance problem.[98]

The interest in time and its perception is related to the 1960s fascination with Zen meditation, with altered sensations of time under the influence of drugs, with phenomenology. It is also related to the extension of nontime arts, like painting and sculpture, into forms that used time—like Happenings and Events—to promote an experience of immediacy, of impermanence, and of duration itself. The perception of time, of space, and of the workings of the body were three major preoccupations of the new, post-modern dance that grew out of Dunn's workshop and the Judson Dance Theater. Of course, not all the students in Dunn's class may have known about Zen Buddhism, the effects of drugs, or phenomenology and existentialism. But there were shared areas of investigation between those who did and those who approached issues of perception and control by other means. And the involvement of Cage, who was the mentor of many young dancers and other artists, in Zen did provide a certain framework for these issues. Paxton recalls:

When I heard Cage talking, it was a more articulate version of what I had mutely been feeling, and I was very drawn to it. It was the first time I had heard anybody talk that way besides myself and my friends. . . [about] attitudes to life in general, with art being just one facet of how to deal with attitudes, how to see them.[99]

Brown and Rauschenberg, discussing Dunn's class, say that Paxton was especially adept at creating dances about duration.

Brown: I can remember Steve [Paxton] presenting pieces that so extended time I couldn't believe it.
Rauschenberg: It was unbearable.

Brown: I thought he had become unconscious. He was extremely interesting. He did not supply any kind of gratification to my expectations or anyone else's. He just did it in his own time, which was not like anything I had ever witnessed.
Rauschenberg: It was in no way compelling. It was just existing. In the same space you were, without any gratifications.[100]

Although Brown and Rauschenberg seem to disagree in the above exchange, my impression was that they both admired the cool, casual and meditative work that Paxton presented. It was exactly because the dance was "in no way compelling," without gratifying expectations, and simply seeming to exist without rushing toward a climax, that the sense of duration was heightened.

Elaine Summers was born in Perth, Australia. When she was five, her family moved to Wellesley Hills, Massachusetts, where at first she went to convent school, but then soon began studying tap and toe dancing. At thirteen she began taking ballet lessons in Boston. She wanted to become a dancer, but, partly because her parents were opposed to her pursuing that career, she trained as an art teacher at Massachusetts College of Art. She continued to dance while at college, and came to New York one summer with her sister to take an intensive workshop at the Graham school, where Cunningham still taught, as did Louis Horst and Erick Hawkins. Summers also studied for a short time at the Juilliard School after graduation. But she had to work nights to afford it, and she began to develop an arthritic hip, so she left Juilliard. She continued to study dance at various studios, including Mary Anthony's, Jean Erdman's, and Merce Cunningham's, and she also began to teach dance. In teaching nondancers, Summers noted the way differently shaped bodies permitted different dynamics and discovered that many of the movements she preferred were not considered dance movements.[101]

During the summers, she and her husband, the artist Carol Summers, went to Woodstock, where Elaine Summers choreographed for the Turnau Opera Company. In the mid-1950s she saw works by James Waring and Aileen Passloff that excited her in much the same way as Cunningham's dances had.

Ballet didn't really excite or interest me, and Martha Graham didn't. But there was a very lively dance scene [that included Cunningham, Waring, and Passloff] and I was more and more thinking about different sized bodies and ordinary movement.

By the time she entered Dunn's class, Summers had taken several composition classes from Louis Horst, which she had enjoyed, partly because she appreciated Horst's keen kinesthetic memory.

Horst's classes were also about structure, but they were more historical. They weren't concept-oriented. One of his courses was based on pre-classic dance forms. You made up a dance of your own, using a pre-classic structure. He was extraordinary. You'd do your dance, and then he'd say, "Fourth measure, second beat, third beat — what did you mean there?"

Summers's impression was that both Dunns taught the class. Judith Dunn may have taken a more active role in assisting Dunn during the third and fourth terms of the class, for many of the students who began taking the class in fall 1961 or spring 1962 refer to it as the Dunns' class. According to Summers:

My feeling is that Judith was teaching alongside of Robert. I remember Robert sitting at the piano and Judith beside the piano, Robert giving out the assignment and Judith participating in it. The extraordinary thing about the class was the clarity of the presentation of Cage's principles, and the clarity of the teaching structure, which both Robert and Judith participated in.

I remember Deborah Hay's dance with a mirror, and I remember a dance that Trisha [Brown] did, where what the dancer did depended on what the audience was doing, like crossing their legs or coughing. That was a chance mechanism.

Summers says that one of the few rules in the class was that the solution to the assignment had to be presented as a complete, finished dance.

You couldn't come in and say, "This is the idea," and then when the critical time came say, "Well, you'll like it better when I do it better or when I get Margot Fonteyn to come in and dance it for me."

Not all the criticisms in class were supportive. One of Summers's earliest dances made in class was based on Debussy's *Ondine*, and she remembers that the class "rejected" it.

I was still afraid to step out from Debussy's structure and I did a dance that was quite romantic. And Steve [Paxton] said, "Well, I don't like the dance and I don't like the structure, and you didn't dance it well." First time out!

So I went home and thought about that a lot and then I thought, "Well, I don't care, I like the structure."

I went back the next week and I did it again, and Steve said, "I still don't like the dance, I don't like the structure, but you danced the hell out of it." And I felt good because I felt that my own feelings about my work were more important to me than what somebody, even someone I respected a great deal, felt. Unconsciously, though I think I was being safe, doing a structure that wasn't chance at all.

But even though I had been rejected tremendously, there was an impersonal aspect in it. The class was very dry. You went, you did your work, and you were totally involved with ideas and concepts, so that if you were rejected, you didn't feel personally destroyed. There was a kind of objectivity in the situation that was caused by Bob and Judy [Dunn], to begin with, plus the intensity of the participants.[102]

Elaine Summers's son Kyle was two years old when Dunn's class began, and at one point Summers brought in a score for Ruth Emerson that used a drawing by the child to dictate movement choices. The drawing was a long vertical scrawl, and Summers divided its length into thirds to determine the timing. In the first third and last third of the dance, the shape of the line dictated the pattern of movements in terms of space, and in the second section of the dance, the shape of the drawing determined the floor pattern. The initial instructions read: "Any length of time in total, but the proportions the same in time as the division in space." Instructions for movements in the first section of the dance read: "Toes, head, 2 hands."; for the middle: "jump, gallop, squiggle"; for the end: "Squiggle, jump, walk."[103] Several chance mechanisms remove the personal involvement of the choreographer from the dance in this instance: the drawing, which shaped the movements in space and along a path, was a "found" drawing, and a drawing by a child who did not have adult, aestheticized design sense; the list of movements corresponding to each section was probably established through another chance procedure; finally, the dance was performed not by the choreographer, but by another dancer, who could install certain of her own choices in the interpretation of the score. Emerson chose to make the dance last a total of eight minutes, with one minute of stillness inserted arbitrarily into each section.[104]

For Dunn's assignment to use a chance mechanism to choose body parts, Summers remembers using a spinning ball to solve the problem.[105] Later, Paxton developed the use of the ball by writing movement choices on it and stopping the diagrammed ball with his index finger or flattening it with a piece of glass to determine the order of the options.[106] Summers remembers that the discussion following the body parts assignment centered on "how difficult it is to break away from body patterns that go together, your own particular clichés or dance clichés in general."[107]

Ruth Emerson had grown up in Urbana, Illinois, where she studied dance in high school with the graduate students of Margaret Erlanger, who had created the dance department at University of Illinois in Champaign-Urbana. Emerson learned Graham technique there, and she remembers that when she saw Cunningham perform in his own work in 1954, she hated him. Twice during college at Radcliffe she went to Connecticut College for the summer sessions with the modern dance establishment. In 1958, she graduated with a degree in mathematics. She had danced during college, where she was president of the Radcliffe Dance Group, and before moving to New York in 1961, Emerson danced with Dancemakers, a small company in Boston, for two years. She returned to Connecticut College for another summer session in 1959.[108]

In 1960, Emerson went to Ann Halprin's workshop for the summer session where she met Rainer, Brown, Forti, and the other students and collaborators who were also in Kentfield that summer. Emerson was still committed to the Graham aesthetic at the time.

> It was very disturbing to see all these things in which people weren't looking for the right answer and they weren't trying to be pretty and famous and do hard steps and all the things I was tremendously anxious to do, and to do better than anyone else. Occasionally I could move without being terribly self-conscious and thinking how it would look. Usually I wanted things to look nice and cheerful. [109]

When she moved to New York, Emerson took classes at the Graham school, but soon she changed to the Cunningham studio. She was coming to appreciate Cunningham's work, and like many of her fellow students, she hoped eventually to be in his dance company. And, like most of the other students in Robert Dunn's class, she took the course in choreography because it was there.

> He accompanied. I can't remember why I decided to take his class. Maybe it was just a social thing that everyone was doing then. I didn't have any deep conviction of what it was going to bring at all. We all wanted to dance more. [110]

During this time, Emerson was also dancing in the company of Pearl Lang, a choreographer who had danced with Martha Graham. In addition she was coauthor of a textbook in mathematics and working at the Center for Programmed Instruction. [111] A Quaker, Emerson was active in The American Friends Service Committee and The General Strike for Peace. [112]

Emerson enjoyed Dunn's commitment to the students as well as his neutral, nonauthoritarian way of teaching.

> For me it was a total change from controlling the process of how you made movement, which was first of all that you were supposed to suffer and improvise and struggle with your interior, which I couldn't bear. I hated it. I remember years of sitting rebelliously in the window sills at Connecticut College while teachers would come and look at me and know that I wasn't doing things right. It was such a relief to take a piece of paper and work on it without someone telling me I was making things the wrong way.
>
> Then when [Dunn] would look at things, he was interested in what happened and how you had done it. He was not at all judgemental about whether you got it right or whether it was art. It was a tremendous relief.

Emerson thinks that one reason Dunn stressed the use of written scores was a purely practical one:

> There was no rehearsal space, and Bob [Dunn] understood that. It was well understood by everybody that most people didn't have a studio of their own. But in another week,

you were expected to come in with something. It was the only practical way of convey-
ing information. You might not see people in the meantime for rehearsal. That was
totally beyond everybody's capacity. So it was expedient in some ways. I enjoyed using
scores very much, for their formality and the graphic aspect.

But also, [Dunn] was interested in having people deal with randomness. Some people
were reluctant to cope with random numbers. There was something good about the telephone book. It was the only way they could do it. Dice or chance seemed too intellectual.[113]

Emerson's studies for the class reflect an appetite for mathematical
conceptualization, a sensitivity to time structures and to the particular
space in the Cunningham studio, and also a thorough commitment to the
chance methodology. One of the scores she created began with a chart
using the following elements: dancer, time, space, speed, and absolute
time. The gamut for each factor included dancers numbered one through
five; ten-second time spans; six different areas of space in the studio, one
of which was offstage; various speeds ranging from stillness to very fast;
and factors of six, rounded off to multiples of five. Apparently Emerson
used a complicated system of throwing dice to determine which choice out
of each gamut fell into the blanks on the chart. One of her notes says,
"Doubles is 2 dancers," and in some spaces in the "dancer" column, there
are, in fact, two numbers listed instead of the customary one. A score for
each dancer, consisting of a time graph in absolute time and the corresponding activity for each part of that time (space, duration, and speed)
was made from the master score.[114]

Another of Emerson's scores uses the streetlight at the corner of 14th
Street and Sixth Avenue, visible through the studio windows, as a cuing
device. The score assigns numbers arbitrarily to the dancers, based on the
color of their hair ("lightest hair lowest number, etc."). The dance could be
performed by three to eight people. The space in the studio was divided
into eight contiguous blocks, six of which were labeled with numbers, and
each of the six windows in the studio was also assigned a number. The
instructions to the dancers read as follows:

Use only enough windows so that 2 people have no window at the beginning. Use
windows and spaces according to number of people.

Beginning: All except 2 "extra" people go to windows as numbered and wait for one
of the 14th St. & 6th Ave. lights to start flashing *"don't walk."* Count the flashes for
one intake of breath, then proceed to your space & perform your dance ½ that number
of times.

Extra people wait for a vacant window & then proceed the same way.

Each person should go through the process twice, first using the "a" part of his space,
& then the "b" part.[115]

One Emerson score from this period contains explicit political content. It is an improvisation with chance cues involving predetermined sounds and actions. Again there is an emphasis on space: six numbered spaces border the walls of the studio, and a seventh (space #1) is a small area that borders space #2. Four of the areas were reserved for the performance of actions: in the other three areas, sounds were to be made. The activity was shaped by a number of factors: first, three to five people each took two slips of paper from one pile of ten "sound" possibilities and one pile of ten "actions." The sounds were: "when she said that I"; "don't go there now with all that in"; "there is a lovely road that goes"; "in the beginning"; "yesterday"; "WORD"; make high sounds; make low sounds; "ban the bomb"; free. The actions were: jumps from two feet to one foot either big or fast; carry someone with you; fast leaps in place; cross arms behind you as far as possible; collapse on floor; arch backwards; sit on the floor and turn; use hands to make sounds; move head and stamp feet; free. Each dancer also chose two numbers from one to seven, from another pile of slips of paper, and each dancer chose two "guide people." A transformation of the numbers on the slips made 1 correspond to 2, 2 to 7, 3 to 1, 4 to 1, 5 to 4, 6 to 6, and 7 to 4. The instructions for using all these factors were:

> Walk or stand at will.
> When your guide goes to your number, go immediately to the appropriate space and do the prescribed sound or action for as long as you want, then resume.
> In case of horn or siren—all cluster together low.[116]

Apparently there was also a dance phrase which the performers did in between sounds and actions.

The movement and verbal content of this dance are strikingly full of reference to nonviolent resistance, and perhaps, in the case of the cluster, to bomb shelters. In conjunction with these highly expressive elements, the cuing from the "leaders" and the arbitrariness of the changes in activity take on a political meaning, suggesting both the need for political organization and the frustration of following a political leader into unknown territory without explanation.

Emerson frequently scribbled scores and notes on the backs of used pieces of paper. Appropriately, on the back of one of the sheets of this score is a crossed-out draft for a notice, which reads:

> Dear Friend,
> Are you interested in reading about non-violent direct action, and talking it over with other people? I would like to know who is interested in meeting one evening a week. In

order not to degenerate into a group of opinions with no material to build on, it seems we should do new reading, with the object of finding out things that we don't already know or think.... [117]

John Herbert McDowell was a composer who had grown up in Scarsdale, New York, and earned a degree in music from Columbia University, studying with Darius Milhaud, among others. McDowell had composed for Paul Taylor, James Waring, and Aileen Passloff, and he worked with Alec Rubin on dramatic improvisation and movement therapy at the Master Institute. [118] His impression, like Summers's, was that both Dunns taught the class.

> The kind of dance teaching that Jimmy[Waring] did in his composition courses, and that Bob and Judy [Dunn] subsequently did in their composition course, which went directly into the Judson group, is historically important. I think the important thing about the Judson group was that it was a focus for a number of things that already had been happening over...five, ten years....Dance had become stultified into old dance, Graham-Humphrey had by then become codified....Merce [Cunningham] and Jimmy [Waring] and a few other people were breaking away, individually. But there was in the air a spirit of change, there were now two codified things, and a whole fresh outlook was needed. [119]

But, McDowell notes, not everyone in the class enjoyed Dunn's approach. "Some people who were not turned on by the sort of thinking that went on in the class simply went and made pieces which they showed in the class."[120] David Gordon and Valda Setterfield were two students who were less enthusiastic about the class than most. Gordon grew up in Manhattan and went to Brooklyn College, where he earned a degree in fine arts and also performed with the school dance club. He began dancing with James Waring in 1956, while still in college. Gordon took technique and composition classes from Waring, and in 1960 presented his first choreography on a program of works by Waring's students, given at the Living Theater.[121]

The dance, *Mama Goes Where Papa Goes*, was a chance-composed duet for Gordon and Setterfield. It opened with Gordon standing on stage, his arms full of rubber balls. He dropped all the balls, waited until they had stopped rolling and bouncing, and walked offstage. Setterfield had a solo composed of jumps strung together without pauses or preparations. At one point in the dance, Setterfield played a cripple who limped in on crutches to be miraculously cured; when Gordon pulled away her crutches, she could walk again. From Waring, Gordon had learned to put together disparate activities and images and to value wit in dancing. He also, from the beginning, was drawn to the panoply of Hollywood myths.[122]

In the summer of 1960, Gordon studied with Cunningham at Connecticut College on scholarship. There he took technique classes from Martha Graham and composition from Louis Horst. After Graham turned her class over to another teacher, Gordon lost interest. And when Gordon refused to conform to Horst's prescribed assignments, Horst lost interest in him.

> [Horst] said ABA: this many beats in the A, this many beats in the B, this many beats in the A. That seemed very sensible, and that seemed to be all the information I needed. And if I were to stand and pick my nose for eighteen beats and then go back to it at the end, that seemed to be perfectly fine, and you couldn't object to that, because I was following the form.[123]

Setterfield, who grew up in London, studied ballet there with Marie Rambert and Audrey de Vos. She worked for an Italian revue to save money to come to the United States where, she had heard from David Vaughan, her height would not be a handicap as it was in the English ballet aesthetic. When she arrived in New York 1958, Vaughan immediately introduced her to James Waring, who asked her something about Zen ("I didn't know what he was talking about") and shortly asked her to dance in his next concert.[124]

Setterfield remembers Horst as "the kind of person who was jolted by anything humorous. He would think it irreverent." Yet when Setterfield, who had learned preclassic forms at the Royal Academy of Ballet, performed her version of a pavanne in Horst's class in 1960, "really an honest-to-god pavanne," Horst thought it was humorous and liked it. "He decided that I was just like Virginia Woolf and he snorted and giggled the whole way through." The rest of the students in the class that summer, as in previous summers, were following Horst's teachings and filling their pavannes with emotional content, "full of lamenting and weeping and waiting."[125]

Gordon and Setterfield married in 1960 and went to Europe for a year. When they came back, Setterfield began to dance with Cunningham, and both went to Dunn's class. According to Setterfield, they had already learned certain very useful lessons about choreography from Waring:

> Why shouldn't something be put in a dance, and what was art, why was it special and particular. One got to be able to do all sorts of things one might have earlier thought were just not suitable, not proper, not appropriate. One learned not to evaluate things as they came to mind.[126]

Gordon thinks he wanted to go to the Dunn classes "to be with a group of my peers and see what everybody else was doing and see what I was doing."[127]

Gordon found the class "amazing," but he was more excited by the other students in the class than by the teaching.

> Judy and Bob [Dunn] were really very rigid about this chance procedure stuff they were teaching. And I had already been through a lot of this chance stuff with Jimmy [Waring]. I wasn't very religious about it. And I couldn't deal with all of the rehashing. Every time somebody got up to do something it was part of the class to take it apart.
> "How did you decide to move your left arm after your right arm?"
> I was trying to find the holes in the teaching, and I did manage to make them feel uncomfortable which was very useful to me at that time.[128]

Setterfield remembers the discussion as less analytic than vague and congratulatory. "'I would really like to say I thought that was a wonderful piece.' 'I thought your piece last week was more wonderful.' That sort of thing."[129]

Rainer recalls that Robert Dunn came under attack during the second year of the course. To begin with, Gordon and Setterfield made it clear that they "thought it was just garbage—the way people performed, their style of performing. They thought there was no critical perspective being brought to bear on the situation." And Rainer herself had choreographic ambitions that were no longer wholly satisfied by the class.

> I began to get fed up with all the chance stuff. That seemed to be the end-all. If you made it by chance, then anything was okay. But I don't remember being particularly vocal about it.
> Something different was obviously needed, and Bob [Dunn] didn't know how to go on. So it was the participants who took it over. Judy and Bob [Dunn], and Valda [Setterfield] and David [Gordon] always had things to say, and they were always at odds.[130]

Robert Dunn thinks that the tension that began to arise stemmed from an anxiety about authority on the part of the students, who were products of a rebellious generation but were not always prepared to face their own free situation.

> My refusal to provide a "recipe" toward which to work for approval or disapproval periodically got me in hot water emotionally with members of the class, so much had this approach been typical of the attitude taken by teachers in this area. I think also I provided rather the wrong kind of surface for the "parental transference" usually and rather troublesomely present in any advanced study still in a teacher-class situation. (I moved from 31-35 during [the Judson years, 1960-64], most of the rest were in their 20s.)

But Dunn was not troubled by this manifestation of anxiety, which he considered part of the learning process.

The "interminable rambling discussion" spoken of by Judith Dunn did indeed take place and was part of a deliberate *askesis*, preventing premature closure before the practically unheard-of had some chance to poke its way into our presence, which it often did. Particularly, the matter of anxiety, whether personal or aesthetic, on the part of teacher or other members of the class, was rather sternly bypassed, in so far as it could be, though this took place by example and contagion rather than as stated doctrine. Allowing this anxiety to take place for dancer and choreographer, and later for the audience, without automatic and unconscious retreat to safer formulae, was of utmost importance in *getting to* the explorations, the dances, and the audience experiences which we felt at that time as somehow crying to be born.[131]

In the fall of 1961, Diane di Prima and Alan Marlowe had founded the American Theater for Poets with the intention of producing plays by poets, and dance and music concerts. From October 1961 through February 1962, they had presented a program of plays at the Off Bowery Gallery at 84 E. 10th Street, with works by Michael McClure, LeRoi Jones, di Prima, John Wieners, Robert Duncan, and James Waring. At the same time they exhibited in the gallery collages by Ray Johnson and photographs by the filmmaker Jack Smith.[132]

In March 1962, the group organized a Poets Festival at the Maidman Playhouse on 42nd Street. The prospectus announces new music by Richard Maxfield, La Monte Young, Philip Corner, and Joseph Byrd; Happenings by Allan Kaprow, Robert Whitman, George Brecht, and Ray Johnson; films by Stan Vanderbeek and Nicola Cernovich; and several dance concerts.[133]

The first of the dance concerts, on 5 March, featured the works of Yvonne Rainer and Fred Herko. Rainer danced *The Bells*, *Three Satie Spoons*, and *Three Seascapes* (made that year in Dunn's class and described in Chapter 3). She and Trisha Brown danced in Rainer's *Satie for Two*. Rainer also did a collaborative duet with Dariusz Hochman, called *Grass* and dedicated to the Great Wallendas. Herko presented *Edge*, a long group work for actors and dancers.[134]

The concert was widely reviewed, with reactions ranging from the horrified to the delighted. Lillian Moore, whose review appeared the next day in the *New York Herald Tribune*, describes the scene in the theater lobby as a chaotic gathering of seedy "beatnik types." She discusses *The Bells*, *Satie for Two*, and *Three Seascapes*, and concludes her review by explaining that she was "obliged to forgo" the rest of the concert. Herko is mentioned in the headline, but nowhere in the body of the review.[135] Marcia Marks, writing in *Dance Magazine*, calls the concert an example of meaningless nonconformism. She thinks Rainer's work suffers from repetitiveness, and considers *Edge* "a heavy-handed attempt at nonsensicality."[136]

Lelia K. Telberg wrote about the concert for Louis Horst's *Dance Observer*. Telberg opens her review with a sympathetic contextual framework:

> Yvonne Rainer and Fred Herko are part of the trend in which young experimental choreographers are searching for new—. New what? Form? Content? Technique? Significance? There is no standard Form for modern dance; "anti-form" or "chance" form is in itself a form. . . . Emotional involvement is frowned upon; it must be abstract, unrelated—a crystallized, pure style. Pure Dance—each decade had its own interpretation.

Telberg, though not unqualifiedly enthusiastic, finds much to like in the dances. She considers both choreographers gifted, thinks *Satie Spoons* "charming" and *Satie for Two* Rainer's best work. She is impressed by Rainer's strong "inner image," which captivated the audience.[137]

Jill Johnston, writing about the event in the *Village Voice,* was prophetically moved. Johnston, who had taken classes at Limón's studio while going to graduate school at Columbia University, met Louis Horst when she got a job in the dance research department of the New York Public Library around 1958. Horst asked Johnston to write for *Dance Observer* and, after she wrote a favorable review of James Waring, Johnston remembers, Remy Charlip befriended her at the library and encouraged her to look at Cunningham's and other avant-garde dances. It was Charlip and Waring, she claims, who soon arranged for Johnston to review dance in the *Village Voice.*[138] She pronounces the concert the wave of the future, noting the connection to Robert Dunn's course, which, she predicts, will have a strong bearing on coming developments in choreography. She compares Herko's dance-play to a Rauschenberg combine. In *Edge*, she states, the various dance events and dramatic occurrences "seemed to move forward and backward, or skip all around in time, and to have no origin, no destination, and no Simple Simon meanings." Johnston explains the conceptual groundwork for Rainer's *The Bells* and *Satie for Two*, associating this choreographic strategy with Gertrude Stein's circular, repetitive writing style.[139]

Another concert, on 13 March, presented work by Waring, Passloff, Emerson, Rainer, Brown, and Herko. For Maxine Munt, Brown's *Trillium* (see Chapter 4) was "with its taut construction and nice performance. . . the high point of the evening." Munt had a mixed response to this group of avant-garde dances.

> The concert field has long needed new directions, fresh talent, and performing opportunities, so we welcome any efforts in presenting them. You may like some of the works, or none; you may find them confusing, or even absurd; you may miss quality and beauty of movement, but no matter—here are dancers at work and some of them are very promising. . . . Are the offerings of this group really studio studies? Is this man-

ner of working just a means of complaining or a form of catharsis? Will they develop into something meaningful or remain where they are? Will they prove that form, content, beauty, and affirmation are not necessary to the art of dance? We shall watch with interest and continue to hope.[140]

Jill Johnston much preferred this program to Allan Kaprow's *A Service for the Dead*, given on 22 May at the Maidman. She invokes Antonin Artaud:

Isn't this [Kaprow's happening] still what Artaud meant when he said: "There is still one hellish, truly accursed thing in our time, it is our artistic dallying with forms, instead of being like victims burnt at the stake, signaling through the flame"?... If there is going to be any "artistic dallying with forms" I much prefer this sort of dallying [the dancers'] to that clatterbang burlesque of a fertility rite that didn't dally enough to be interesting Art and wasn't real enough to be a moving experience.[141]

In regard to Rainer's *Dance for 3 People and 6 Arms* (See Chapter 2), Johnston pronounced Rainer "not 'promising' but 'arrived.'"[142]

Johnston accurately perceived that the work of these choreographers was new and significant both in terms of the historical development of choreography as an art and in terms of its relationship to the other arts. Beginning with "Fresh Winds,"[143] as she titled her review of the March 5 concert, Johnston enthusiastically followed and championed the burgeoning of a new, pluralistic generation of choreographers—one which, as the body of her criticism shows, she saw as actively installing in dance new values of democracy, humanism, decentralization, and freedom.

2

"A Concert of Dance" at Judson Church

By the end of Dunn's spring choreography course in 1962, the students wanted to put on a public concert of works they had been showing to each other in class and to their friends in the end-of-the-year recitals. "There was a body of work which it was called a shame to waste without at least a public showing, and Judson was asked and they were agreeable. But it was intended as a one-shot concert," as John Herbert McDowell succinctly put it.[1] "And [we decided to put on the concert for] just the adventure of it," Steve Paxton adds. "Going out and doing something elsewhere. The Living Theater was too small."[2]

Yvonne Rainer, who had just seen the first Judson Poets' Theater production in the choir loft of Judson Memorial Church, suggested that the class look into holding the concert there. Also, the students knew that the church had been the site of several Happenings. Paxton met with Al Carmines, the minister in charge of the church arts program, and set up a date for an audition.[3] On the appointed date, Paxton, Rainer, Ruth Emerson, and perhaps Robert and Judith Dunn went to the church, where Paxton, Rainer, and Emerson danced.[4] Rainer danced *Three Satie Spoons,* Emerson her *Timepiece,* and Paxton may have performed *Transit.*[5] Paxton's memory of the audition is that "It was a pretty weak showing. But they said, 'Fine.'"[6] Emerson, who thinks that much of the impetus in planning the concert came from Rainer, who was ready to show her accumulated work, recalls:

> Steve [Paxton] and Yvonne [Rainer] and I went down one very hot evening, and I think I was asked just because I was around. I remember having the feeling that Al wondered if we'd take all our clothes off or do something terrible. We did a couple of pieces. We came prepared to be really serious and to show him how we worked. I don't even know if he saw all our pieces. After ten minutes he said, "Oh this is wonderful, this is great. No problem," and we all started laughing.[7]

Judson Memorial Church, a Greco-Roman building at 55 Washington Square South, at the corner of Thompson Street, was designed by Stanford

White in 1892. Its stained glass windows were designed by John La Farge, and its baptistry was built by Herbert Adams from plans by Augustus St. Gaudens. The church was built by Edward Judson in memory of his father, Adoniram Judson, who went to Burma in 1811 as one of the first American missionaries. The younger Judson, who thought a ministry in Greenwich Village could be as difficult a challenge as the conversion of Burmese Buddhists, placed a copy of his father's Burmese translation of the Bible in the cornerstone of the church.[8] The church, dually affiliated with the American Baptist Church and the United Church of Christ, had since its founding two goals: community service and refraining from proselytizing in a community that was primarily Italian Catholic.[9] The church set up a water fountain at the corner of Thompson Street and Washington Square, to provide fresh, clean water for poor city dwellers, sponsored a summer fresh-air camp, and later opened health clinics and a gymnasium. The church was a base for labor union organizing in the 1930s and for the civil rights movement, school integration activities, and drug addiction rehabilitation programs in the 1960s. In 1961, the parish had played an active role in overturning a ban on folksinging in Washington Square, after a year of protests and sit-ins, and in the same year the chief minister, Howard Moody, had been elected head of the Village Independent Democrats.[10]

After World War II, when many of the church's members had moved out of the city, Robert Spike, minister from 1948 to 1955, started an arts program, partly out of personal inclination and partly to stimulate the life of the church. Concerts and plays were given and paintings exhibited. Then Howard Moody, who came to the church in 1956, organized the Judson Gallery, which showed works by Pop artists Jim Dine, Tom Wesselman, Daniel Spoerri, Red Grooms, and Claes Oldenburg as early as 1959.[11] The "Judson Group" put on a program of Happenings, *Ray Gun Spex*, in early 1960, and later that year Dine presented his *Apple Shrine*, an environment. A group called the Judson Studio Players performed *Faust* in the sanctuary of the church in 1959; Carl Dreyer's film *Joan of Arc* was shown there in 1958 and his *The Day of Wrath* in 1959.[12] In 1960, when Moody decided to start a resident theater group in the church, he hired Al Carmines, who had just graduated from Union Theological Seminary, to coordinate the arts program and organize the Judson Poets' Theater.[13]

Carmines had grown up in Virginia, where he studied piano. He wanted at first to go to Juilliard for musical training, but instead he went to college at Swarthmore, where he majored in English and philosophy. After Paul Tillich came to lecture at Swarthmore and spoke personally to Carmines about religious faith, Carmines decided to enter the ministry. While a student at Union Theological Seminary, Carmines went to parties for divinity students at Judson Church, but also, in 1958 he claims to have attended an early Kaprow Happening there. When he heard there was an opening for someone to run the arts program at the church, he applied for the position. And when Carmines became associate minister, for the first two years on a part-time basis while he earned a master's degree, he continued the church policy of aiding as many artists as possible, and of supporting the avant-garde without censorship.[14]

The first production at the Poets' Theater, on 18 November 1961, was a double bill of one-act plays: Guillaume Apollinaire's *The Breasts of Tiresias*, and Joel Oppenheimer's *The Great American Desert*.[15] About two weeks later, on 3 December 1961, Carmines organized a "Hall of Issues" at the Judson Gallery. The public was invited to make statements "about any social, political or esthetic concern. . . in the form of paintings or poems or posters or essays or a sentence or a sculpture or a newspaper clipping or photos or an assemblage and pin-it-tack-it or tape-it-hang-it or set-it-up."[16] For four weeks in a row, the Hall of Issues was open each Sunday from two until five in the afternoon for contributions and then, for public viewing, from six to ten Sunday through Wednesday evenings. On Wednesday evenings a meeting was held to discuss the issues and plan actions.[17] During the season of 1961–1962, Judson Poets' Theater presented three more programs of one-acts (opening in January, March, and May) and in May Peter Schumann, with the Alchemy Players, gave a masked dance/play, *Totentanz*. In the summer of 1962, Carmines began writing music based on popular forms for Judson Poets' Theater, beginning with George Dennison's *Vaudeville Skit*. Carmines's attitude toward making theater in the church, as he told an interviewer in 1966, was unconventional for a minister.

> When I started the theater in 1961, with the help of Robert Nichols, who's an architect and playwright, we had two principles. One, not to do religious drama. Two, no censoring after acceptance. . . . [The fact that our plays are performed in] a church liberates me more than any other place would. I've discovered for myself that God doesn't disappear when you don't talk about Him.
> Like a lot of ministers, the real world was not part of my life. Ministers are often preoccupied with themselves. The theater broke it all open for me. A source of revelation.[18]

Carmines remembers that when the dancers approached him to ask whether they could put on a concert in the church,

> I was scared of the kind of dance they did. I was used to ballet, maybe Martha Graham. I hadn't seen Merce Cunningham. I said they'd have to give their first three concerts in the gymnasium, and the board of church would have to decide whether it was proper to do in the sanctuary.[19]

Robert Dunn was as interested as his students in presenting their dances as professional work.

> I had seen these people who had studied with Louis [Horst] and Doris [Humphrey] and they were in their thirties and forties. They'd done a lot of choreography. They were presented at the Y [M-YWHA on 92nd Street and Lexington Avenue] in group concerts, always as if they were still students. They were little Marthas and little this and little that. It was awful.
>
> The circumstance was that more people got interested in seeing our workshops, and I said, "I'm sick of that, let's present our workshops as a professional concert of dance."

Dunn suggested calling the evening A Concert of Dance to invoke a historical tradition of nonnarrative dance and to suggest an intimate, chamber presentation.

> Concert of Dance meant non-narrative. It meant coming away from a literal, narrative presentation, with hard-core theatrical dance—like [Graham's] *Clytemnestra*, or [Anna Sokolow's] *Rooms*. Coming away from characterization. There was a musical sense in the title. One was going to see qualities and atmospheres.
>
> And there was a historical tradition I was wanting to refer back to. It had to do with Sybil Shearer. It had to do with Isadora Duncan. It also suggested the closeness between audience and performer of Yeats's plays, not quite thoroughly theatrical. It was admitted that the performers were in the same room as the spectators.[20]

Robert Dunn selected the order of the dances on the program.[21] Paxton remembers that "it was largely reasons of necessity that determined what had to follow what; who had time to be where when, who needed to be free at a certain time, so they could make their changes. Certain things weren't possible."[22] Also, "Dunn made the order of the dances, including some that were shown with each other, which was a popular idea at that time: 'Let's have chocolate and strawberry at the same time.'"[23] According to Rainer, "The selection of the program had been hammered out at numerous gab sessions, with Bob Dunn as the cool-headed prow of a sometimes over-heated ship. He was responsible for the organization of the program."[24] Elaine Summers's recollection is that:

> Steve [Paxton] and Yvonne [Rainer] and Bob [Dunn] and Judy [Dunn] said, "Let's do a concert and everyone can pick one work of their own, or two, and it can be anything you want. Make your own decision about what you're going to present, and let's do a concert in July. It'll be hot, and there won't be anyone there, and we'll just have a wonderful time." And then we all did whatever it was we had to do.
>
> Everyone in the group was extremely responsible. Everybody had their chores to do, and everybody did them. And lo and behold, we had this concert. And we had so much material it started at eight and went until midnight. It was hot in there, ninety degrees, and we were totally amazed because so many people came. It was absolutely crushed![25]

Steve Paxton and Fred Herko formed the publicity committee. Paxton designed the flyer, which is plain, clear, but also witty in its hint of repetition and reversal. Herko wrote the press release, dated for release 22 June, which explains that the "young professional dancers" involved in A Concert of Dance use a variety of choreographic techniques. The participants are named: Bill Davis, Judith Dunn, Robert Dunn, Ruth Emerson, Deborah Hay, Fred Herko, Richard Goldberg, David Gordon, Gretchen Maclane [sic], John Herbert McDowell, Steve Paxton, Rudy Perez, Yvonne Rainer, Carol Scothorn, Elaine Summers, Jennifer Tipton. This notice lists choreographers and performers together as participants, without setting up a hierarchy of status. "Indeterminacy, rules specifying situations, improvisations, spontaneous determination, and various other means" are named as choreographic strategies, and a concluding paragraph states that the event will show a diversity of work, and that the concert will "be of interest as it signalizes a new concern on the part of the younger dancers to explore dance with the concerns and responsibilities of the choreographer as well as those of the performer."[26] An abbreviated version of this notice, consisting of the first paragraph and including the names of all the participants, appeared in the *Village Voice* on 28 June.[27] The flyer was sent to the names on the church mailing list, which had been augmented with the names of the dancers' friends and acquaintances.[28]

The program for the concert lists the following other discharges of responsibilities: lighting design, Carol Scothorn; lighting operation, Alex Hay; musical direction, Robert Dunn and John Herbert McDowell; costume consultant, Ruth Emerson; stage manager, Judith Dunn; film projector operation, Eugene Freeman [sic]; advisory, Judith Dunn, Robert Dunn.[29]

The concert was given in the sanctuary of the church, one flight up from the street-level entrance on Washington Square. A curtain hung down from the edge of the choir loft, at the opposite end of the room from the altar, serving as a divider between the lobby-entrance and the performing space in the sanctuary proper. It also served as a backdrop for the "stage," which simply was the space in front of the curtain, and an architectural rhythm for this setting was provided by four columns supporting the loft. The audience walked in through the lobby, across the bare space, and to their seats.[30] At that time, the church still held traditional "high Baptist" services. There was a pulpit and a large cross at the altar, at the south end of the sanctuary, and the congregation sat in moveable pews facing the altar. The Poets' Theater performed in the choir loft, not on the sanctuary floor. The dancers disturbed the arrangement of the sanctuary by moving the pews around and putting them against the altar, facing north, and along the sides of the room, clearing the rest of the space for the dancing.[31]

A Concert of Dance [#1] was arranged in a slightly asymmetrical balance of solo and group dances, solos by men and by women, dances with and without music, and live and recorded music, talking and singing, slow and fast and variable tempi, simple and complex choreographic structures, plain and fancy costumes. The twenty-three items on the program were divided into fifteen units. Dance number one was actually a film, and it was billed under a musical term: *Overture*.[32] So from the moment the concert started, the irreverent trespassing of artistic boundaries was present. A group work followed, then a solo by a woman, then three solos by men, then another group work. In mirror sequence, the next six dances were: group, male solo, three female solos, another group. The only duet was performed during intermission. Following intermission, there were nine more dances: group, two male solos, group, two female solos, male solo, female solo, group. Two pieces of music by Erik Satie (probably the same piece) were heard on the first half of the program, but in between them were two dances in silence which themselves sandwiched a dance to music by Marc-Antoine Charpentier. Yet *Cartridge Music* by John Cage, also used for two different dances, was played once as the dances were done either simultaneously or overlapping one another.

A number of other aspects of this concert would later become essential features of the Judson Dance Theater: the democratic spirit of the enterprise; a joyous defiance of rules — both choreographic and social; a refusal to capitulate to the requirements of "communication" and "meaning" that were generally regarded as the purpose of even avant-garde theater; a radical questioning, at times through serious analysis, at times through satire, of what constitutes the basic materials and traditions of dance.

As the audience entered the sanctuary at 8:15, a film was being projected. This was Robert Dunn's idea.[33] McDowell recalls:

> [The film] was Bob Dunn's doing and was beautiful. The dance concert was announced to start at 8:30. The audience was admitted at 8:15 and they went upstairs into the sanctuary to find that in order to get to their seats they had to walk across a movie that was going on. It was embarrassing, and Bob's whole point was to discombobulate them, to quash their expectations. This movie consisted of some chance-edited footage by Elaine [Summers] and test footage that I made, all of which was blue-y. . . . And W.C. Fields in *The Bank Dick*. And we went on exactly precisely for fifteen minutes. The last sequence in the film was the final chase scene from *The Bank Dick*. And then there was a marvelous segue between the unexpected film and the dance. The first dance, which was by Ruth Emerson, started on the dot of 8:30. As the movie was just about to go off, the six or so people involved came out, the movie sort of dissolved into the dance, and as the stage lights came up the dancers were already on stage and the dance had already started.[34]

The authors of *Overture* are listed as W.C. Fields, Eugene Freeman [sic],

John Herbert McDowell, Mark Sagers, and Elaine Summers. Summers was learning filmmaking from Gene Friedman, an assistant cameraman in commercial television and cinema. Friedman was also a friend of John Herbert McDowell's. Summers remembers being so stimulated by the chance methods Dunn taught that she suggested making a chance movie. Friedman had been giving Summers assignments that, though they were traditional problems for beginning filmmakers, bear a striking similarity to some of Dunn's assignments.

> He would say, "Take a three-minute reel of film and do a complete story nonverbally with it. And no cutting, you have to do it in the camera." And then he would want one that had zooms.
>
> So I had a lot of scrap movies, and Gene [Friedman] was contributing not only his guruship but also films—tail ends of movies, called short ends, from the tv stations where he was working. And John [Herbert McDowell] had some W.C. Fields movies.
>
> John, Gene and I got together and used a chance system from the telephone book. We took all the film strips, and we rolled them up, and we put them in a big paper bag. They had numbers on them, like one foot, two feet, three feet. We'd get a number from the telephone book, like 234-5654, and we'd have to put the film strips together in that sequence.
>
> I remember saying "This certainly brings out the stubborn in one, because I don't want to put a two-foot strip here, I want to use a six foot one." And of course that was one of the exciting things about the chance method. You suddenly realize that you have a lot of opinions.[35]

According to McDowell, some of the segments were upsidedown and backwards.[36]

Allen Hughes, the dance critic for the *New York Times*, called *Overture* "a moving picture 'assemblage'" and wrote, in his review of the concert:

> The overture was, perhaps, the key to the success of the evening, for through its random juxtaposition of unrelated subjects—children playing, trucks parked under the West Side Highway, Mr. Fields, and so on—the audience was quickly transported out of the everyday world where events are supposed to be governed by logic, even if they are not.[37]

Judith Dunn, John Herbert McDowell, Steve Paxton, Yvonne Rainer, and Elaine Summers danced in Ruth Emerson's *Narrative*, a three-section dance. Each dancer was given a score that indicated walking patterns, focus, and tempo, and also cues for action based on the other dancers' actions. The instructions are not dramatic or psychologically descriptive; they refer to abstract movements and individual focus, rather than interaction. For instance, directions to dancer B (Paxton) include the directive, "Take great care never to focus on G [Rainer] or direct your movement at her." Three of the dancers walked along geometrical paths during part one: Paxton along diagonals, Dunn along a rectangle, and Summers along a circle; McDowell walked at random backwards, and Rainer walked at random sideways. The focus for each dancer was quite specific, and each one had to cue his or her tempo to the rates of the other dancers. In the second section, Dunn sat with focus down, Paxton did a movement pattern (two quick diagonal extensions of the foot and arm, and a turning arm gesture in plié, with focus up) seven times, and Rainer did another movement pattern (fouetté with arms, break at elbow and relax), four times. (The scores for the second section for the other two dancers have been lost.) Part three orchestrated patterned exits, chiefly along diagonal lines.[38]

Narrative was not taught or written with expressive overtones in psychological terms, but Emerson says that she was trying to make it a dramatic dance.

> Dramatic in the sense that by placing people in the space and by turning them in different directions, I could show something about relationships. There was little that happened, except people changed their [spatial and temporal] relationships to one another. It had very little tension, which is what I obviously would have liked to achieve. I didn't feel it was a brilliant success. I think I did not know very much about groups of people and was finding out more about *my* body and how to construct material for me. That was more productive.[39]

The first live dance on the program, then, was a new twist on an old modern dance theme. The title suggests a literal meaning, of the sort the older generation of modern dancers always offered an audience. And modern dance choreographers used diagonal lines to connote dramatic tensions. But Emerson's *Narrative* was a drama without specific or coherent symbolic meaning.

The next dance on the program, also listed under item number two, was Emerson's own solo *Timepiece*. It was another dance structured by chance, based on a chart that extended the categories she had worked with on earlier dances. It had columns for quality (percussive or sustained); timing (on a scale of one to six, ranging from very slow to very fast); time (units of fifteen seconds, multiplied by factors ranging from one to six); movement (five possibilities: "red bag, untying; turn, jump, jump; hands, head, plié; walking forward side back side side; heron leg to floor"); space time (ten, twenty, thirty, forty, fifty, or stillness); space (five areas of the stage plus offstage); front (direction for the facing of the body, with four square directions, four diagonals, and one wild choice, marked "?"); and high, low, or medium levels in space.[40] The qualities having to do with movement and timing were put together, along the graph of absolute time, separately from the qualities dealing with space. Thus changes in area, facing, and level in space might occur during a single movement phrase. *Time-piece* started out with stillness, "to my utter horror," Emerson recalls. "I had to get over the fact that I could start a piece with forty seconds of stillness. One of the reasons I liked the piece was that I learned I could do that."[41]

Paxton remembers Emerson's dancing in *Timepiece* as "boundy." "Very long limbed. Not particularly articulate. A lot of large shapes, big sweeps."

> We talked a lot about her performance, because she looked very glazed when she performed. I remember trying to encourage her to be less glazed. And I remember Judith Dunn looking disapproving, because that's how she looked when she performed. But somehow that was appropriate to her.[42]

The question of the dancer's performing presence was one of the issues about dance this group was trying to understand and resolve in a way appropriate to their emerging styles.

"We didn't want to emote," Paxton explains. "On the other hand, the glazed look was obviously becoming or already had become a cliché."[43]

Timepiece, with its components tightly governed by various independent temporal controls, punningly refers to a stopwatch or clock, the legendary accoutrement of both John Cage and Robert Dunn. It also seems an appropriate step, in terms of the increasingly upset expectations of the audience, in instructing the spectator. After the first dance made clear what this new work would *not* be, the second dance presented a paradigmatic chance dance, an example of what much of the new work *would* be.

Unit number three on the program comprised three solos by men, which may have indicated that they were performed simultaneously, or else that they were performed in close sequence, without a break. These were Herko's *Once or Twice a Week I Put on Sneakers to Go Uptown* (music: Erik Satie; pianist: Robert Dunn; costume: Remy Charlip); Paxton's *Transit*; and McDowell's *February Fun at Bucharest*.

Jill Johnston describes *Once or Twice a Week . . .*:

> Herko did a barefoot Suzie-Q in a tassel-veil head-dress, moving around the big open performing area. . .in a semi-circle, doing only the barefoot Suzie-Q with sometimes a lazy arm snaking up and collapsing down. [And] with no alteration of pace or accent.[44]

The Suzie-Q is structurally quite similar to the Twist. Allen Hughes devoted one-fifth of his review to this dance.

> Fred Herko came out dressed in multicolored bath or beach robe with a veil of lightweight metal chains covering his head and face. . . .One's attention was riveted to his

dance, which was no more than a kind of unvaried shuffling movement around the floor to the accompaniment of a piano piece by Erik Satie. (Satie, incidentally, would have loved it.)

This was the *Sneakers* dance, but Mr. Herko was barefoot all the while.[45]

Remy Charlip remembers that he made a cap based on an African design for Herko, with strings of beads ending with small shells that hung down over his forehead, expressly to emphasize the swaying movement that was the dance's motif. Charlip also thinks the title was a kind of ironic reverse snobbishness: if the bohemians and avant-gardists downtown danced proudly in bare feet, then to put on sneakers was to dress up, to go to haute uptown.[46]

Herko died in 1964, so it is impossible to find out about his intentions or methods of any of his dances. Paxton was not impressed by Herko's work in general.

It seemed very campy and self-conscious, which wasn't at all my interest. As I remember he was a collagist with an arch performance manner. You would get ballet movement, none of it very high energy. Maybe a few jetés every now and then. As a dancer his real forte was some very, very elegant lines. But in terms of actual movement, transitions from one well-defined place to another, he did it rather nervously. Holding a position was more what he did than moving from place to place.[47]

Hughes describes Herko's style more enthusiastically.

His dances were architecturally organized. He didn't just go willy-nilly from here to there. He always had a sense of theatrical structure. Herko was a performer with charisma. He had a performer's instinct. He may not have been a great choreographer; I'm not suggesting that. I'm only saying that he vitalized that movement. He gave it a vividness that many of the others did not. Herko was the brightest performing star of all. He was a happy exhibitionist, which makes theater. Therefore he really wouldn't allow himself to go too far off into inner-somethings, because he never wanted to lose his public.[48]

Al Carmines, with whom Herko worked in the Judson Poets' Theater, recalls that Herko's work "always included humor and pathos and high-class camp. He was an unusual actor, and audiences adored him. He learned to be totally accessible to an audience."[49]

Andy Warhol, who met Herko at the San Remo Coffee Shop at Bleecker and MacDougal Streets in Greenwich Village, remembers him as "a very intense, handsome guy in his twenties...who conceived of everything in terms of dance."[50]

Herko was born in Ossining, New York, where he had grown up, according to one account, studying piano and ballet, possibly at School of

American Ballet, the school attached to the New York City Ballet.[51] But Warhol writes that Herko's dance training began much later:

> He was one of those sweet guys that everybody loved to do things for simply because he never remembered to do anything for himself.
>
> He could do so many things well, but he couldn't support himself on his dancing or any of his other talents. He was brilliant but not disciplined—the exact type of person I would become involved with over and over and over again during the sixties. You had to love these people more because they loved themselves less. Freddy eventually just burned himself out with amphetamine; his talent was too much for his temperament. At the end of '64 he choreographed his own death and danced out a window on Cornelia Street....
>
> He didn't start taking dancing lessons till he was nineteen. After he graduated from high school in a small town just north of New York City, he enrolled in NYU night school—during the day he gave piano lessons. Eventually, he transferred to Juilliard School of Music, but he didn't do well there; he kept missing classes and exams. But when he saw the American Ballet Theater's performance of *Giselle*—which was the first dancing he'd ever seen aside from on television—he suddenly felt he had to become a dancer. He applied for a scholarship to the American Ballet Theater School, got one, and within a year was choreographing himself in one of their programs. He was involved in some off-Broadway productions, too—going on tour in New England and up to Canada. Pretty soon he was on one of those Sunday morning dance shows on television.
>
> Then he went on "The Ed Sullivan Show" and got stage fright.
>
> The scary thing is how you could dance in front of so many small audiences so often and never even have it occur to you that dancing in front of national television cameras might completely freak you. When Freddy got out onto Ed Sullivan's stage, all of a sudden, he confided to me, he felt as if the blood in his wrists had stopped flowing, and he had to ask someone from the back row to trade places with him in the front line. Afterward he ran out of the theater and back down to the Village, to the security he felt there.[52]

Steve Paxton's *Transit*, following *Once or Twice a Week...*, was a solo that presented a spectrum of movement styles, from classical dance (ballet) to "marked dance" (technical movement performed without the high energy usually expended in performance) to pedestrian movement. It also presented a spectrum of speeds, from running to slow motion.[53] Paxton would perform a classical ballet phrase, then repeat it in a marked version, run at different speeds, and stand in tense or relaxed positions. "It was just taking items and playing their scales."[54] It was an analysis by dissection, in a sense, of ballet movement, which is recognizable on stage by one of its essential components: a taut charged body. In much the same way, Eadweard Muybridge's photographs had broken down the movements of animals and humans, including dancers, around the turn of the century when modern dance began.

Transit, which Paxton refers to as a collage, was made specifically for the first concert at Judson Church, not for Robert Dunn's class. It was eight minutes long, and Paxton performed it in black tights and leotard and bare feet, in silence. He rehearsed it for a month; most of that time was spent perfecting the ballet phrase, which was "a pet phrase of Margaret Craske's. That's why I wanted it, because it was coming from her." Paxton had learned the phrase from Carolyn Brown, who went regularly to Craske's studio in the Metropolitan Opera studios for ballet classes, as did other members of the Cunningham company. Paxton went to Craske only occasionally.[55]

John Herbert McDowell had grown up in Scarsdale, attending the Putney School in Vermont, where he had worked on shows in the Putney Summer Repertory Theater, and went to college at Colgate University. He remembers seeing Kurt Jooss's company perform *The Green Table* in Yonkers when he was a child, and he also saw Martha Graham's company. In 1949, on graduation from college, he got a job as a television director and producer in Cleveland, Ohio, and then was drafted and stationed in Long Island City where he worked on films for the army. When McDowell got out of the army, in 1952, he was twenty-five years old. He decided to study music at Columbia University. Within a year, through teachers at Columbia, McDowell was working with dancers. His first composition for dance was written for Richard Englund. Through Dance Associates, an organization for cooperative work among choreographers that had been formed by James Waring and David Vaughan, McDowell met and worked with Waring, Paul Taylor, and Aileen Passloff. In 1961, working on Taylor's *Insects and Heroes*, McDowell had needed a pianist and found Robert Dunn. Interested in movement, partly through movement courses he had taken with Alec Rubin at the Master Institute, in the same building with Dance Associates, McDowell joined Dunn's choreography course.[56]

McDowell was among the performers and choreographers on the Judson concert with the least formal dance training. Jill Johnston wrote approvingly about both his performance and his choreography in *February Fun at Bucharest*:

> John Herbert McDowell is a composer. He has no dance training.... Having no ties or tensions arising from a training and having an inordinate sense of fun, McDowell distinguishes himself as a "natural"—not a natural dancer (although you could think of it that way if you're not too set in your idea of what dancing is): I mean a natural person going about the business at hand, which in this case consisted of a few zany actions performed in a red sock and a yellow sweater.[57]

Diane di Prima describes the dance as "John McDowell in a red sock, leaping about like a demented pixie."[58] McDowell remembers that he stood on his head in front of a mirror and pulled his hair out. But set against these "zany actions" was the baroque weight of music by Charpentier. McDowell says the music had nothing to do with the dancing; he simply had to use other people's music to his own dances.[59] Perhaps McDowell's choice was also governed by an ironic tribute to a special alliance between theatrical dance and religion that preceded Judson Church: Charpentier was, after all, one of the most memorable composers of Louis XIV's court, a court renowned for its opera-ballets. And Charpentier had two specialties, theatrical and religious music.[60]

The dance listed as item number four on the program was Elaine Summers's *Instant Chance*. Summers used huge numbered styrofoam blocks, which had been carved into different shapes and painted different colors on different surfaces, to cue movement for dancers. The dancers would throw the blocks up in the air. Each dancer had a separate movement choice in response to the three different factors that fell top up. The shape dictated the place or type of movement; the color, the rate of speed; the number, the rhythm. For instance, Ruth Emerson's score indicates that for the cone, her movement should be in the air; for the cube, in relevé; for the column, standing; for the sphere, sitting or kneeling; for the oblong, on the floor. If she saw yellow, she should move very fast; blue, fast; purple, medium; red, slow; pink, very slow. The instruction for the numbers read: "Repeat movement, every movement 5 times but the number equals a rhythm. $1 = 1$ (an insistent pulse), $2 = 2/4$, $3 = 3/4$, $5 = 5/4$."[61] Each performer was also assigned a color and an identifying mechanism; Ruth Emerson, called Pink, wore a pink leotard.[62]

A later score with different sets of instructions indicates that the same components for shapes were reshuffled and redistributed for each performance (i.e., in the later score, Pink's instructions for shapes are: tensing and walking; rippling; stretching and collapsing; swinging; and breathing in and out. But Pink's former instructions are also present in directions to other dancers, e.g., Yellow has the direction relevé for the column; Blue has high in the air for the triangle, and so on.) Also, in the later score the numbers and colors govern different aspects of the dance.[63]

Watching a reconstruction of *Instant Chance*, I was struck by the childlike nature of the dance.[64] The dancers throw their "dice" as though they were beach balls or giant block toys. They rush to perform their actions as soon as the shapes land. The performers' concentration on doing the task at hand—over and over—and their apparently short attention spans, as they abandon one movement for no obvious reason to throw their "dice" for the next instruction, gives the whole dance the look of a satisfying game. Though each performer is highly self-absorbed, there is some interaction. The instructions for this performance (which may not have been included in the original) often had one dancer lifting his colleagues one at a time, or interrupting, or in other ways intervening in their movements. The others nonchalantly carried on with their activities. The effect was that of a bratty child bothering his playmates. This score also set dancers climbing up the altar and scampering along it, with seemingly innocent irreverence.

Summers says that she called the dance *Instant Chance* because she felt that most chance dances used hidden operations. The moves were determined by chance beforehand, but then the dance was set; the audience had no way of knowing, from watching the dance, what method the choreographer had used. In *Instant Chance* the display of the method was central to the viewing of the dance. Summers set up rules for her dancers (Ruth Emerson, Deborah Hay, Fred Herko, Gretchen MacLane, Steve Paxton, John Herbert McDowell, and Summers herself), but how these rules would come to be expressed depended on both the rolling of the "dice" and the immediate decisions those circumstances prompted in the dancers. Even the choreographer could not predict what the dance would look like from performance to performance. Summers gave very broad parameters for movement choices, so her control was quite loose. The use of arbitrary rules, similar to the spirit of children's rule games, was one method for achieving the coveted performing value of spontaneity.

> You knew what the operation was but you didn't know what the realization of the movement would be. If red and one meant cover space and leap, I didn't know how that person was going to leap, or how they were going to cover space.

With this score, Summers was trying to confront the glazed or overly expressive faces that plagued so much of modern dance, and to produce instead a look of engagement and intelligent concentration.

> I love the way that people look when they're dancing and at the same time they're having to realize a score. I think they look totally different, much more interesting. A part of them is creatively involved. It's not that interpreting choreography as a dancer isn't creative, but it's not as totally engaging. That engagement takes the dancer automatically away from the presentation of face and body. In the Judson group, people were interested in getting out of that, they didn't want it.
> It was hard to find people who were willing to do a dance without that [artificial presentation of facial expression]. We had trained for years to come out and have a certain presentation that made everybody feel secure. So that the audience could say to themselves about a dancer, "She knows what she's doing." But to wash all that away and simply do the movement as straightforwardly as you could was wonderful.[65]

Again, the values that were put forth by this dance, as in many of the dances on this first program, were values of spontaneity, matter-of-factness, pluralism, and freedom of choice and of action.

Hughes explained the mechanism of the dance to his readers in the *New York Times*, but he could not explain his reaction to it:

> Six performers appeared to be playing on a beach. They had various objects, including a ball, that they tossed around like dice, and the objects were numbered. The numbers that came up on the objects probably gave the dancers clues as to what they would do next. In any event, there was movement of all kinds going on steadily, and for some reason or other, it was interesting much of the time.[66]

According to David Gordon, whose *Helen's Dance* was item number five on the concert, that dance was one of the weapons he used to make Dunn's class uncomfortable.

> The primary concern of the Dunns was to teach chance procedures, and they rigidly persevered against any chance occurrence that might alter the course of an evening's schedule. A flick of the long yellow pad and "let's get on with what we have to do" generally put an end to spontaneous discussion. The dogmatic approach of the class often irritated me, and I sought ways to beat the system. *Helen's Dance* was made to a piece by Satie as a class assignment. We were given the options of using the music in various ways. None of these options included the possibility of ignoring the music, which is what I chose to do. The apartment that I lived in then was a three-room railroad flat, and I had no studio space available to me so I made a long narrow piece that moved through the three rooms. I performed it in about twelve feet of space at the Judson. *Helen's Dance* was a series of twenty-odd activities performed in a straight line, one after another, including some gestural dance material. Miming planting a flower was one of the things.
>
> The costume, I remember, had black-and-white striped tights and a black-and-white geometrically patterned top trimmed with jet fringe.... The piece was named for a friend who died of cancer at that time, and it became inexorably confused with her death in my mind until I realized that I was performing it in a terribly sentimental fashion, and I never did it again.[67]

Like Herko, like Forti, like La Monte Young, and perhaps even like Satie in a way that he never intended, Gordon amplified concentration on a single phenomenon — to get closer to the facts of things. To list things is an elemental form.

Number six on the program comprised three solos: Deborah Hay in her *5 Things*, Gretchen MacLane in her *Qubic*, and Hay again, this time in *Rain Fur*. All three dances were done in silence, and it may be that they overlapped in some way.[68]

Hay, born in Brooklyn in 1941, was one of the youngest dancers in the group. She had been dancing nearly all her life, beginning lessons with her mother, who taught ballet, tap, acrobatics, and toe dancing. Hay's mother, who had danced professionally in various ballet corps in New York City, and who had tapped with Adele and Fred Astaire, taught dance classes in Brooklyn in the basement of the local synagogue for the neighborhood children. After several years, her mother started looking for other teachers for Hay. "She was very balanced, very centered, very earth-motivated. I got that from her—just being here and getting my feet planted. I also got from her the sense of daily discipline, working every day." Hay went on to study and perform with Bill Frank, who taught at Henry Street Playhouse. "He gave me an abandonment to movement that I hadn't had. He was a wonderful teacher and friend." In 1961, Hay went to the Connecticut College summer session and became interested in Merce Cunningham's work. "I used to sneak into the auditorium at night and watch the rehearsals lying on my stomach in the balcony. I had never before experienced the magic that he still has. What I learned from watching him was something about performance: When he's dancing he looks like he's listening with his entire body." When Hay returned to New York that summer, she married Alex Hay, whom she had met when she was teaching dance at the Police Athletic League, where he was teaching art. That fall she took Robert Dunn's composition class, and she remembers that "the Judson thing was something Alex and I decided to do together." She remembers the Dunn class as extraordinarily supportive; she felt like "the baby of the group" and appreciated that support. She had studied composition with Bill Frank and with Ruth Currier, and had choreographed the dances for the musicals her high school had produced. But in Dunn's class, she felt a sense of relief that there were no value judgments, and that "I was free of the notion that I was the center of the universe, and that gave me space to play."[69]

Hay destroyed her scores when she moved away from New York in 1971, and she remembers very little about her early dances at the Judson. She thinks that in *Rain Fur* she lay down on the floor in front of the audience, with her back to them, "in a very familiar, painterly lying posture." She then rolled over to the other side and faced the audience.[70] Perhaps this is the dance that Rainer recalls from the first concert, in which Hay wore a skirt made of small hoops that hobbled her, restricting her movement possibilities severely.[71]

Gretchen MacLane grew up in Chicago, where she studied ballet, tap, and character dancing. "My teacher, Edna McRae, trained you to make money as a dancer, which actually I never did," she says. In college at Mount Holyoke, MacLane belonged to the dance club, along with Barbara Dilley who later, under her married name, Barbara Lloyd, would dance in Cunningham's company and in some of the Judson dances. MacLane choreographed a dance for the annual college dance concert which "no one'd seen anything like" and won a scholarship to Connecticut College for the summer of 1960. It was her first encounter with modern dance. She loved watching ballet and show dancing, was left cold by Graham and Limón, but after she saw Cunningham's *Night Wandering* — a duet for himself and Carolyn Brown — she "was moved, for the first time, by modern dance." In New York, MacLane danced with Charles Weidman, took composition classes with Lucas Hoving ("I never had the nerve to take Louis Horst's class," she says), and then took Robert Dunn's class as a palliative for the rigidity of other composition classes she had known. About her *Qubic* she recalls only that it was made for Dunn's class, and that it must have been in response to an assignment about space, because she named it after the three-dimensional tic-tac-toe game then popular (pronounced "cubic").[72]

Paxton remembers that in Dunn's class MacLane was "somebody who had a gift for being really droll and constantly fought it."[73] MacLane remembers watching Paxton's work and being "bored out of my mind. But it wasn't bad being bored in those days."[74]

The twelfth dance in the concert (but number seven on the printed program) was Yvonne Rainer's indeterminate *Dance for 3 People and 6 Arms*.[75] It had been performed on the 24 March program at the Maidman Playhouse, in the New York Poets' Theater festival. Rainer describes the dance as "a trio consisting of an improvised sequence of predetermined activities."[76] It was danced first by Rainer, William Davis, and Trisha Brown, and at the Judson concert Judith Dunn replaced Brown, who was in California for the summer.[77]

The movement options, as might be predicted from the title, emphasized the dominance of the arms, though the whole body was set in motion. The arms often led, worked independently of, or were set against the rest of the body's motion. In a sense the dance was a probing analysis of the function of the ballet port de bras. The choices that the dancers could exercise comprised ten "movements," three "actions," and two "positions." At the beginning of the dance, the three performers stood upstage for a moment, then all three did one of the "movements," number three: a turned-in attitude with "spread-eagle arms" that pulled the body around to turn, the whole thing traveling downstage. For the next fifteen minutes, the performers freely made their own choices from the gamut supplied by Rainer, except for one restriction: When anyone started one of the "actions" — which Rainer describes as "'Blam-blam. Blam. Blam-blam,' accompanied by flat-footed jumping about" — the other two had to stop what they were doing and join in.

Rainer's examination of arm movements included a ballet port de bras, nicknamed "Flapper," done with limp arms while the dancer traveled forward in a relaxed, alternating fourth position. In another "movement" the body engaged in "foot-play with one hand 'consciously' moving the other hand about the body. Hands alternate being 'animate' and 'inanimate.'" Another "movement" was a series of activities including a relevé with the right palm gliding up the nose, scratching the arm while walking in a circle, then throwing the head back while bending the knees in parallel plié. The arms "swim" or droop, the hands place themselves on the body while the dancer walks in plié and squeaks, or the hands clasp the ankles during bourrée steps, or the hand and head vibrate while the rest of the body collapses into a squat. The other two "actions," besides the flat-footed "blam-blam," were: moving the arms as quickly as possible and simultaneously descending to a prone position, as slowly as possible: and rocking from side to side while the hands play a sort of game with the head—trying to clasp each other without the head noticing. The two "positions" were: "ghoul"; and "twist with eyeballs up—perched on one leg. Placed either d[own]s[tage] right or d.s. left."[78]

After the first performance of *Dance for 3 People and 6 Arms*, at the Maidman, Jill Johnston called it "dazzling" and announced that Rainer was no longer a "promising" choreographer, but one who had "arrived." Johnston lauds the creative role the dancers were given in putting the choreography into action.

> No two performances will ever be alike, and the situation puts the dancers as well as the choreographer in the role of creators. The given material is so lively and various that a rich, natural complexity is inevitable.[79]

Maxine Munt, writing in *Show Business* about the same concert, thought the dance "redundant and disaffectingly gauche."[80]

William Davis recalls that dance as one of his most memorable, happiest performing moments.

> I remember waiting for the curtain to go up at the Maidman Theater. I think it was the first time dancers were waiting for a curtain to go up without having any idea whatsoever of the shape the dance was going to take.
> That kind of thing was being done musically [in the work of Cage and his colleagues]. What it really resembled was jazz musicianship, more than chance operations, because we were all working for a time when we might, for example, do this, or seeing what someone else is doing, think "Oh yes, I can connect this to that," or "They're doing fine, I'll just let them go at it." It's a sense of shape taking place in three people's minds as the dance is going on. It was wonderful to perform.[81]

The demands of the movements themselves so taxed the dancers' coordination that to be as aware of each other's moves as Davis describes required a finely tuned sensitivity to the other performers. Extending logically John Cage's use of indeterminate music scores—something Cunningham had not attempted—Rainer created a dance that both gave control generously to the dancers and also demanded their utmost concentration, attention, and intelligence.

Intermission, numbered eight on the program, followed *Dance for 3 People and 6 Arms*. The program noted that coffee would be served in the lobby. But also, Rainer presented a *Divertissement*, in the tradition of ballet entr'actes in European operas. Spoofing dance partnering, Rainer and Davis entered the sanctuary from behind the curtain, grasping each other clumsily. Their legs interlocked so that they could barely walk, and only sideways. They stumbled across the floor, lurching through three or four different steps, then exited through the lobby.[82]

In a way, *Divertissement* was a comment on Rainer's own work and the work of her colleagues as well as on traditional theatrical dance. Coming directly after *Dance for 3 People and 6 Arms*, probably the most radical dance on the program in terms of its structure and materials, *Divertissement* acknowledged that *Dance for 3*...and the other unconventional dances on the program were not devoid of roots in a historical dance tradition.

After intermission came Elaine Summers's *The Daily Wake*, number nine on the program and the fourteenth dance. This was a group piece based on reading newspapers as scores. The credits say that the "structure [was] realized by the following performers: Ruth Emerson, Sally Gross, John Herbert McDowell, Rudy Perez, Carol Scothorn." The music was by Robert Dunn, John Herbert McDowell, Elaine Summers, and Arthur Williams, a downtown playwright.[83] Summers herself made up a movement sequence inspired by the scores, then gave the dancers written instructions specifying movement qualities for the three sections of the dance. She personally taught them a series of poses taken from photographs in the newspaper. The dance began in stillness. Then all five dancers performed individual dances at individual tempi during the first section of the piece. When finished, each assumed the first pose assigned them for section two, until all five had assumed poses, and the series, including group poses, began. The positions included the twist, swimming, an umpire, soldiers, a handshake, Rockefeller, a bride, graduation, and a Pantino advertisement. In the third section, each dancer was assigned certain numbered movement phrases, certain actions and qualities to apply to these phrases, a floor pattern that corresponded graphically to a newspaper layout design, and a time pattern.[84]

Summers explains her use of the newspaper as a score:

The Daily Wake was based on the front page of a daily newspaper, the *Daily News*. What they have reported is already dead and finished, so it has a wake-like quality. I took the front page and laid it out on the floor and used the words in it to structure the dance, and used the photographs in it so that they progressed on the surface of the page as if it were a map. If you start analyzing that way, you get deeper and deeper. You get more clues for structure, like how many paragraphs are there? Beginning with *The*

> *Daily Wake*, I became very interested in using photos as resource material, and other structures as maps.[85]

The interest in photographic freeze-frames of movement, which also informed Paxton's *Proxy*, signals an analytic concern with the moment-to-moment process of human movement, almost as if the choreographers wished to appropriate the filmmaker's ability to slow down a film and watch it frame by frame. It is also another strategy for making movement without submitting to personal taste.

Number ten on the evening's format was David Gordon's *Mannequin Dance* and Fred Herko's collaboration with Cecil Taylor, *Like Most People — for Soren*.[86]

According to Gordon,

> *Mannequin Dance* was made, in response to another class assignment, while standing in a bathtub waiting for A-200 to take effect on a bad case of crabs. In the piece, I turn very slowly from facing stage right to diagonally upstage left and slowly make my way down to lie on the floor. That about covers the territory that a bathtub had to offer. The piece took about nine minutes to perform, during which I sang "Second Hand Rose" (after Fanny Brice and *before* Barbra Streisand) and "Get Married Shirley," two songs to which I had become addicted. It was slow, tedious, concentrated, theatrical, virtuosic, and long. I wore a bloody biology lab coat given me by a biology-teaching artist friend [Barbara Kastle].[87]

After he began to lower himself to the floor, Gordon raised his hands gradually until they extended out in front of him and wiggled his fingers slowly and regularly. The effect was both soothing and macabre.[88] Besides the singing, more music was provided by James Waring, who passed out balloons to the audience, asked them to blow up the balloons and to let the air out slowly.[89]

> The reason the piece was called *Mannequin Dance*...was that I had had the idea to rent department-store mannequins and place them dressed or nude at various points in the performing area and to perform the piece ten times in one evening with two or three-minute intermissions between performances. During the intermissions, the mannequins would be moved to different positions, or have their costumes changed. I never performed it more than once in an evening, and I never rented the mannequins, but the name stuck.[90]

Diane di Prima, who was fascinated by Gordon's singing during *Mannequin Dance*, wrote about the intangibly touching qualities of his performance. "David Gordon stands still a lot. The flow of the energy, like a good crystal set. The receiving and giving out one operation, no dichotomy there. One incredible dance, *Mannequin*, where he moved slowly from one off balance plié to one other, *singing* all the while, [was] somehow terribly moving."[91]

Jill Johnston wrote of Gordon's two dances on that concert:

> For my free time David Gordon did two extraordinary dances on that program. He did some movement nobody ever saw before. Like the body bent off center, the head awkwardly strained back, the elbows squeezed into the ribs as the flattened hands and forearms made the painful beauty of spastic helplessness. As though the body were straining, yelling, against an involuntary violence. Molloy and Malone should be so lucky.[92]

Rainer and Gordon were not the first modern choreographers to use awkward movements. The modern dancers of the 1930s were criticized for using distortion and dissonance in their choreography, and they responded by arguing that these were the qualities necessary to represent modern times.[93] The awkwardnesses of Rainer and Gordon, however, were not symbolically expressive. They did not mean pain, as the Graham contractions in *Lamentation* signified. In the matter-of-fact attitude toward life and art, and movement as one component of both, awkwardness is one part of a gamut of movement and bodily possibilities—and perhaps a more intriguing one, because less familiar in art but more familiar in life, to young artists who had never seen the modern dance of the 1930s, but only its mutated descendants (like Cunningham's dances) and its more diluted forms (later Graham and her epigones).

Perhaps Fred Herko met Cecil Taylor, the jazz musician, through LeRoi Jones and Diane di Prima, the coeditors of *The Floating Bear*, a literary newsletter. In the winter of 1961–1962, James Waring, Herko, and Cecil Taylor had helped put the *"Bear"* out at di Prima's, a social locus for the community of artists and poets in the East Village. Di Prima remembers that,

> In the winter of 1961–1962 we held gatherings at my East 4th Street pad every other Sunday. There was a regular marathon ball thing going on there for a few issues. Whole bunches of people would come over to help: painters, musicians, a whole lot of outside help. The typing on those particular issues was done by James Waring who's a choreographer and painter. Cecil Taylor ran the mimeograph machine, and Fred Herko and I collated, and we all addressed envelopes. I would have the issues more or less edited ahead of time, and the whole thing would be typed, run off, collated, and addressed in about a day and a half. Sometimes we would stay up together all Sunday night and have it in the mail by Monday morning. That petered out when it got to be spring and people had other things to do.[94]

Herko lived upstairs from di Prima, whom he had been close to since the mid-1950s.[05] Herko had already written theater reviews for the *"Bear,"*[96] and in January 1962 he had published a scathing attack on Paul Taylor in the *"Bear,"* accusing Taylor of lacking love and therefore making alienated dances.

Paul Taylor — A History

What has happened?
Once there was Dance Associates, they performed at the Master Institute. Paul Taylor was a Dance Associate, so was James Waring.

Mr. Taylor danced *The Least Flycatcher* and *Three Epitaphs* and others. Then Dance Associates disintegrated. Mr. Taylor gave a concert with two beautiful dances, one to a tape of "at the tone, the time will be—" and another of rain. Then other concerts in which nothing happened. And now this latest one.

Mr. Taylor made dances because he loved making them — he loved to dance them.

Love is ultimately beautiful.
Love is interesting.
Love is exciting.
It was lovely to watch Paul Taylor.
Paul Taylor is not lovely to watch.
Paul Taylor is not exciting.
Paul Taylor is not interesting.
Paul Taylor is not ultimately beautiful.
It is hard to watch Paul Taylor working at his job.
A job is not interesting or beautiful or exciting.[97]

On the same page in that issue of *The Floating Bear* are notices for performances by Aileen Passloff and Company at The Fashion Institute of Technology, with music by Richard Maxfield, and performances by James Waring and Dance Company, with music and designs by George Brecht, Remy Charlip, Richard Maxfield, Erik Satie, and Robert Watts.[98] Clearly certain lines were being drawn between different wings of the avant-garde in dance. Herko was aligning himself with the romantics, like Waring and Passloff — the expressionists in the perennial debate in dance history on expression versus technique. As di Prima later explained it, there was "a continuing argument at the time between people who wanted art to have no obvious emotional content and people who found that a bit boring. The younger generation of dancers, of whom Freddie [Herko] was one, had learned a lot from John Cage and his people, and they began incorporating stories into their dance, old Chinese myths, for instance, or they used a lot of color or some other kind of emotional content."[99] The argument continued directly in the pages of the *"Bear."* In March, Edwin Denby's response to Herko was published. Denby was a dance critic well-known for his appreciation of the technically refined dance idioms of George Balanchine and Merce Cunningham, and a poet. He wrote, after quoting from Herko's review, against the romantic ideals of art. "Herko is judging Taylor by an idea. The idea—the idea of love and art and The Unsoiled Life—is shit. If Taylor fails by that, he's doing fine. Herko had better watch his language."[100]

The Floating Bear primarily published new poetry, but it also carried reviews of music, art, theater, and dance, especially reviews written by poets. The connection between the poets and jazz musicians is clear by early 1961, when Jones (in a notice signed Koenig) recommends in the *"Bear"* that John Coltrane's new album "must be heard."[101] The script of Michael McClure's *!The Feast!*, published in October 1961, was dedicated to Ornette Coleman.[102] In the December 1961 issue, Alan Marlowe's review of the first Judson Poets' Theater production appears on the same page with a review by Gilbert Sorrentino of a performance by Sonny Rollins.[103] Cecil Taylor, Ornette Coleman, and other young jazz musicians considered in the avant-garde of black music were playing in coffee houses and lofts in East Village and on the lower East Side when more conventional bop musicians were booked in jazz clubs.[104] The innovations Taylor, Coleman, and others were bringing to jazz in the early 1960s were analogous to those the Judson dancers brought to modern dance, in terms of form; the avant-garde in jazz, however, wanted to restore seriousness to a form that had been tarnished by the requirements of entertainment and easy listening, while the dancers wanted to bring the snobbish high art of modern dance down to a human scale. LeRoi Jones writes of Taylor's and Coleman's achievement:

> What these musicians have done, basically, is to restore to jazz its valid separation from, and anarchic disregard of, Western popular forms. They have used the music of the forties with its jagged, exciting rhythms as an initial reference and have restored the hegemony of blues as the most important basic form in Afro-American music. They have also restored improvisation to its traditional role of invaluable significance, again removing jazz from the hands of the less than gifted arranger and the fashionable diluter (though no doubt these will show up in time)....What Coleman and Taylor have done is to approach a kind of jazz that is practically nonchordal and in many cases atonal....Their music does not depend on constantly stated chords for its direction and shape. Nor does it pretend to accept the formal considerations of the bar, or measure, line....It considers the *total area* of its existence as a means to evolve, to move, as an intelligently shaped musical concept, from its beginning to its end.[105]

It seems likely that Herko and Taylor met through di Prima and the *Floating Bear* circle, because their collaboration is dedicated to Soren Agenoux, another member of that circle, whose pseudonym was taken from Kierkegaard and the French translation of "on one's knees,"[106] and who later published satires on the *"Bear,"* called *The Sinking Bear*, which he mimeographed at Judson Church and circulated in the gay artists' community.[107]

The only extant description of *Like Most People* is di Prima's review of it in *The Floating Bear*. Di Prima was frank about her friend's shortcomings.

> Fred Herko's work still less clearly defined than those two [Gordon and Rainer]. [It] seems to come from more varied places. His dances happen inside his costumes a lot. [In] *Once or Twice a Week I Put on Sneakers to Go Uptown*, a dance to Satie where he traveled around the stage his feet carried him, his arm made an occasional very simple gesture, he wore a kind of lampshade on his head. And *Like Most People* he performed inside one of those Mexican hammocks (bright colored stripes) and Cecil Taylor played the piano. It was some of Cecil's very exciting playing, and after a while the dance started to work with it, and the whole thing turned into something marvelous and unexpected. [108]

Paxton remembers that Taylor fell asleep backstage and Herko woke him up just before the dance began. Taylor "stumbled right out and started to play." [109]

Steve Paxton had made *Proxy* while on tour with the Cunningham company in 1961. A trio, it was a "slowpaced dance in four sections, with two photo movement scores for [sections] two and three; instructions for [sections] one and four." The dance involved a great deal of walking; standing in a basin full of ball bearings; getting into poses taken from photographs; drinking a glass of water; and eating a pear. Paxton speaks of the dance as a response to work in Dunn's class with John Cage's scores.

> My feeling about making movement and subjecting it to chance processes was that one further step was needed, which was to arrive at movement by chance. That final choice, of making movement, always bothered my logic somehow. If you had the chance process, why couldn't it be chance all the way? [110]

The methods Paxton used to select the movement itself at the most basic level were another attempt to get away from the cult of personal imitation that surrounded modern dance, a cult that began with the direct transmission of movements from teacher to pupil and ended with a hierarchically structured dance company. In *Proxy*, that learning process was mediated by the use of a photo score.

> That was a selection process but one removed from actually deciding what to do with the pictures, because I made the score and then handed it over to the performers, and they could take a linear or circular path through the score. You could start any place you wanted to, but then you went all the way through it. You did as many repeats as were indicated, and you went back and forth as indicated. But how long it took and what you did in between postures was not set at all. It was one big area of choice not at all influenced by the choreographer. The only thing I did in rehearsing the work was to go over it with them and talk about the details of the postures.

We looked at the dance and discussed whether they'd accurately done the picture scores or not and worked on getting it more accurate. We talked about the possibilities of how to interpret the scores, because there's a confusion: When you're looking at a picture score you can interpret the picture right or the audience right, in the same way in which when you're in class and the teacher sticks out the left foot, you're supposed to automatically stick out your right foot. That convention was questioned. We went through the various points in the process to see what would make people feel secure. And then they gave a secure performance. It was relaxed and it had its own authority.

I thought I was solving a complex problem with the scores, and the walking initially didn't seem like much of a problem. But I realized that I spent two or four hours a day in class and then there were rehearsals. But the rest of the day, my body was still doing something that I was not in control of and didn't understand. And the walking was the first example of trying to get to that material—what the pedestrian technique is. What walking is.[111]

The score had been made by gluing cut-out photographs of people walking and engaged in sports, and cartoon images (Mutt and Jeff, and one from a travel advertisement) on a large piece of brown paper. A moveable red dot marked the beginning the dancer had chosen. Paxton made the score large enough for the dancers to be able to look at it on the wall without stopping their dance.[112]

Robert Dunn has remarked that Paxton's method of making the score for *Proxy* was close to Marcel Duchamp's work, rather than Cage's.

He cut the images out, dropped them on various places, let them float down, then glued them in place. One of them was a photo of a baseball player sliding for the base. Those stop photos are very beautiful.

I'm not sure how he got the lines between the images. If he had been John Cage, he would have found a big piece of plastic and he would have drawn some paths on the plastic and dropped the plastic freely on the figures of the players and that would give him the sequence of the dance. Then, when he got through with that, he'd make another version of the same dance, picking the plastic up, turning it over, and dropping it again.[113]

Paxton rehearsed the dance only enough times to find out how long it was. He remembers rehearsing three or four times, and discovering that the dance lasted for twenty-three minutes. "[The timing] hardly ever varied, even though there were a lot of choices."[114]

The first section was eating and drinking. A small square had been marked off with yellow tape on the floor, and one dancer came into the square, sat down, and ate a pear. The next person came out, stood in the square, and drank a glass of water. Then the walking section started. The dancers walked around the backdrop seven times in large circles. On one of the circuits, the basin with ballbearings was deposited on the floor, and one of the dancers stood in it while another dancer pulled her around. In the center two sections, the picture scores were performed, and in the final section the dancers walked again and picked up the basin.[115]

> [The amount and repetitiveness of walking were intended] to reduce pacing so that every quality was introduced and developed in a very placid way.
>
> Walking is something you can't tamper with. If you say "ordinary walking," you get a wide range of materials. And the more you tamper with it, the less it has the quality of being just the thing. It starts to look like somebody with a problem on their mind or somebody with an infirmity instead of just someone walking. I tried not to tamper with it too much, so that it wasn't too special and it just occurred.

The title was a deliberate play on words, on several levels of meaning.

> The word as a proxy for the dance, the title being the encapsulation of the thing. And the fact that the dancers made decisions about what the movement was. Also, a proxy marriage is one in which a picture is used instead of the person's actually being there.[116]

The implication is that, as in Zen, the participant can also be the detached observer who—through emotional neutrality, repetition of simple actions, and concentration on ordinary things—can transcend personal attachment.

One of the assignments Robert Dunn had given the class was to take something, cut it up, and reassemble it. Both Carol Scothorn and Ruth Emerson had done their dances for this assignment to Cage's *Cartridge Music*. *Proxy* was number eleven on the first concert program, and the Scothorn and Emerson cut-ups, *Isolations* and *Shoulder r*, together with *Cartridge Music*, are listed as number twelve. Scothorn had chosen to cut up some Labanotation scores, and, while making the piece, according to Emerson, she "had a horrible time. The first thing she had to do was shorten her neck. She almost gave up the whole project, but she's a very stubborn person and she worked it out." Scothorn, who was a dance teacher at University of California at Los Angeles, was in New York City for the year to study Labanotation.[117]

Emerson doesn't remember what kind of material she herself cut up, but her score indicates that she also used elements from Labanotation. Her score for *Shoulder r* lists space-covering movements: walk, run, triplet, crawl, skip, hop. It lists spaces: five spaces plus offstage. It lists geometric patterns: yin-yang circle (◐), circle, vertical rectangle ([]), horizontal rectangle (▢), triangle, wavy line (∿). It also gives elements of timing and of absolute time. Then there was a second set of elements—body parts: right leg, arm, hand, ribs, head, foot, and left leg, arm, hand, shoulder, hips, spine. Also in the second group was movement quality: percussive, swinging, violent, sustained, rotary, heavy. Further instructions included low and high levels, stillness, in the air, sit down; contact floor, focus right, forward, left, down, up, back, stillness, front facing, and smile. The first set of elements was reshuffled and set in one order; the second group was also recombined and laid next to the first series along the same time grid, sometimes overlapping. For example, during the first five seconds, the elements were: triplet 4 very slow ↗↳ low; ribs spine slow rotary floor; for the next fifteen seconds, the first part of the chart reads: 4- △ high; while for the first five of those seconds it also reads: ribs hips–rotary floor; and the next ten seconds reads: head spine very fast rotary smile.[118]

Although Emerson does not remember what the dance looked like, in trying to reconstruct it from the score it seems evident to me that Emerson's response to Dunn's cut-up assignment must have been as demanding to perform as Scothorn's had been. She had to keep track of both locomotion and the changing movement of separate body parts. Despite the fact that the score sometimes calls for very slow movement, the dance (as I interpret it) has a quality of wild abandon, as if the body were going off in countless directions all at once. There is an awkwardness that comes from the juxtaposition of actions and levels that was present in the work of early Taylor and Cunningham.

Emerson's title was also a joke, because "shoulder r" was one element that never entered into the list at all.

Emerson thinks that Scothorn's and her solos may have been performed together in different parts of the space, or that one started while the other was going on, so that they overlapped in time.[119]

Perhaps it is not a coincidence that the Dadaists, who celebrated the use of chance techniques as well as musical analogues in composing their works, collaborated with the dance students at Laban's school in Ascona, including Sophie Taeuber, Mary Wigman, Susanne Perrottet, Maja Kruscek, and Käthe Wulff.[120] The cut-up was known to be a chance method favored by Hans Arp and Tristan Tzara. Tzara's "Manifesto on feeble love and bitter love," which had been published in English in Robert Motherwell's *The Dada Painters and Poets* in 1951, gave instructions on how to make a dadaist poem:

To make a dadaist poem
Take a newspaper.
Take a pair of scissors.
Choose an article as long as you are planning to make your poem.
Cut out the article.
Then cut out each of the words that make up this article and put
    them in a bag.
Shake it gently.
Then take out the scraps one after the other in the order in
    which they left the bag.
Copy conscientiously.
The poem will be like you.

And here you are a writer, infinitely original and endowed with a sensibility that is charming though beyond the understanding of the vulgar.[121]

According to Hans Richter, the Dadaists used chance methods to understand more clearly the totality of experience.

This experience taught us that we were not so firmly rooted in the knowable world as people would have us believe. We felt that we were coming into contact with something different, something that surrounded and interpenetrated *us* just as we overflowed into *it*. . . . Beneath it all lay a genuine mental and emotional experience that gave us wings to fly—and to look down upon the absurdities of the "real" and earnest world. . . . Chance appeared to us as a magical procedure by which one could transcend the barriers of causality and of conscious volition, and by which the inner eye and ear became more acute, so that new sequences of thoughts and experiences made their appearance. For us, chance was the "unconscious mind" that Freud had discovered in 1900.

Richter attributes to the antirational use of chance methods the breakdown of boundaries between the separate art forms that also characterized Greenwich Village in the early 1960s.

In the years that followed, our freedom from preconceived ideas about processes and techniques frequently led us beyond the frontiers of individual artistic categories. From painting to sculpture, from pictorial art to typography, collage, photography, photomontage, from abstract art to pictures painted on long paper scrolls, from scroll-pictures to the cinema, to the relief, to the *objet trouvé*, to the ready-made. As the boundaries between the arts became indistinct, painters turned to poetry and poets to painting.

And Richter attributes the source of these methods to a situation of world crisis that the generation of artists born just before World War II and living through an adolescence during the Korean War and a young adulthood in the shadow of the testing of nuclear weapons also lived through.

Compared with all previous "isms," Dada must have seemed hopelessly anarchic.

But for us, who lived through it, this was not so. On the contrary, it was something meaningful, necessary and life-giving. The official belief in the infallibility of reason, logic and causality seemed to us senseless—as senseless as the destruction of the world and the systematic elimination of every particle of human feeling. This was the reason why we were forced to look for something which would re-establish our humanity. What we needed to find was a "balance between heaven and hell," a new unity combining chance and design.

We had adopted chance, the voice of the unconscious—the soul, if you like—as a protest against the rigidity of straight-line thinking.

Another link between the Dadaists and the ideas of Cage and his followers was an interest in Eastern mysticism. According to Richter, another purpose of using chance techniques was:

to restore to the work of art its primeval magic power, and to find the way back to the immediacy it had lost through contact with the classicism of people like Lessing, Winckelmann, and Goethe. By appealing directly to the unconscious, which is part and parcel of chance, we sought to restore to the work of art something of the numinous quality of which art has been the vehicle since time immemorial, the incantatory power that we seek, in this age of general unbelief, more than ever.[122]

Raoul Hausmann and other Dadaists were familiar with the *Tao Te Ching* and other Taoist writings, and Hausmann wrote in 1921:

The partial inexplicability of Dada is refreshing for us like the actual inexplicability of the world—whether one calls the spiritual trump Tao, Brahm, Om, God, Energy, Spirit, Indifference, or anything else, the same cheeks still get puffed out while one does so.[123]

The confluence of chance techniques and mystical philosophy in both Dada and New York avant-garde art world of the 1950s and 1960s is intriguing, especially because one could espouse the identical techniques in the service of diametrically opposed world views. For those in the Judson group, like Robert Dunn or Steve Paxton, who embraced some of the ideas of Zen or other mystical systems, chance, collage, automatism, and other methods were ways to free oneself from the tyranny of the self; to put oneself freely in the larger stream of the cosmos, or the unconsciousness, or God. For others, like Yvonne Rainer, these very techniques were a way to bring art out of the realm of "incantatory power," to remove from art its mythic, "numinous power."

William Davis had been interested in dancing since he was a child, in southern California. His mother, a junior high school teacher, ran an after-school dance group and later taught ballroom dancing. Davis remembers that his first dance hero was Ray Bolger's Scarecrow in the *Wizard of Oz*; for a variety show in grammar school he worked out a routine in which he was a scarecrow dancing with a chorus of other children dressed as radishes and cabbages. He joined a ballroom dancing club and a square dancing group, performed in school shows and plays through junior high and high school, and began studying tap dancing in Los Angeles. He also began studying modern dance, at the Lester Horton School, where he continued to attend classes during vacations when in college at Stanford. At Stanford he acted and danced in dramatic productions, as well as directing, choreographing, and designing sets and costumes. There he met Jenny Hunter, a choreographer who worked with Ann Halprin, who had been hired to choreograph Menotti's *The Unicorn, the Gorgon, and the Manticore*. Hunter told Davis about Merce Cunningham, and in 1959, after graduating from Stanford, he went to New York to study with him. During his first year at Cunningham's studio, he also took classes daily at the

Graham studio but then, on Cunningham's advice, changed to ballet classes at the Joffrey studio. He joined Cunningham's company in 1961. Davis had not taken Dunn's choreography class, but he was close to many of the students who had, because they were all in the dance classes together both at Cunningham's studio and at the Joffrey school, and because he danced in Cunningham's company with Steve Paxton and Judith Dunn. He was dancing with Rainer in Waring's work. Also, he was performing in Rainer's *Dance for 3 People and 6 Arms* on the first Judson program. He was invited to contribute a dance.[124]

Davis' *Crayon* was number thirteen in the evening. It was a solo accompanied by three rock-and-roll songs: "I Love You," by the Volumes; "Hey Little Girl," by Dee Clark; and "Baby, Oh Baby," by the Shells. In the tradition of Merce Cunningham and John Cage, the dancing was not done to the music, but coexisted with it, in time and space, an effect that was jarring when the music had the propulsive beat of rock-and-roll. The dance began in silence, and after about twenty seconds the three songs followed in sequence. Davis explains:

> I was hoping to set up an exhilarating surprise, and I felt if I didn't establish a kinetic line first, it might not be possible to keep any separation. The movement was to ride along on top of the sound like riding a wave, and I wanted a paddling head start, so to speak, to get ahead of the crest and avoid being swamped in the rhythm or the sentiment of the music.
>
> The first record was the Volumes' "I Love You," which takes off with insistent rhythm and a loud rush of harmonic sweetness of sound and lyrics. This was pre-Beatles, and pop music was still just for its own audience. It went straight for sentimental force.[125]

There were no popular dance steps in *Crayon*, nor were there characterizations or movement jokes. "It wasn't overtly funny, though I remember that people reacted with laughter. I hoped there was a certain wit in the movement phrasing, but mainly it was amusing, or at least that's what I hoped, in the way something exhilarating can be amusing."[126]

The costume was a rust-colored leotard and tights with a red heart painted on the chest, referring to the lyrics of the songs in a brash, pop style. Davis recalls that he was inspired by the rose and skull tattoo images Robert Rauschenberg had used on two costumes for Cunningham's *Antic Meet*. The dance lasted eight or nine minutes. Davis writes about the movements:

> At the time I was most involved in the movement itself: that is just inventing steps; working up movement phrases that had some sort of vitality and resonance (at least for me); fitting things together; figuring out how to get from one point to the next. I suppose the movement must have seemed Cunninghamesque, with overtones of ballet,

though I don't think there were any actual "Cunningham steps" in it. What I was interested in was not so much the repertory of steps in the Cunningham technique, as the wonderful dynamics of Merce's own dancing, mainly the orchestration of energy — the development of energy around the space, and from parts of the body to other parts. At that time, I didn't think of what Merce did as a "style." It was just dancing — at its most splendid.

Of the actual movements, among the few things I can remember are a large, vertical-circling one-arm port de bras, rather like the "lyre strumming" in Balanchine's *Apollo*; a horizontal circling of one hand around the head (as though wiping a giant halo) while the other hand shimmered palm down out to the side at the end of a straight, extended arm; and some skittering, rabbit-hopping, two-step jumps in relevé plié on a downstage diagonal.

The title set the tone for the meaning and the mood of the dance.

I suppose I was thinking of a writing instrument, something that describes a linear design, scrawls a message; of a dance solo as something like the choreographic parallel to a line drawing, being made by one thing moving in space — the only relationships being of the dancer to the space (and the parts of the dancer's body to one another). Also the word has a simple, kinetic, bright sound, which seemed right.

"The moving finger writes. . . ."

There were several uses of a pointing finger in the dance, to indicate a direction of energy, or just as little emblems — like Paul Klee arrows.[127]

Walter Sorell, reviewing *Crayon* at a later concert, tries to guess whether Davis's method was chance or improvisation (it was neither), but concludes that Davis showed "how far one can go and still get away with it because. . .it was one piece and held my attention."[128] Sorell implies in his review of the entire concert (which also presented works by Phyllis Lamhut and Yvonne Rainer) that it was emblematic of a hip, angry younger generation of rebels. Perhaps, despite Davis's repudiation of characterization, the dance did exude the sense of joyous defiance that popular songs in the early 1960s extolled.

Paxton remembers being thrilled by *Crayon*.

It seemed like a logical thing to do in a way; it was a collagist mentality. But no one was collaging what was really current. Everybody [in dance] seemed to be into esoterica or surreal qualities in their work. Bill [Davis] seemed to be pretty up front about including the whole realm of pop music in the dance scene, suggesting a kind of earthiness and raunchiness that was totally lacking otherwise. Everybody else was either in an intellectual sphere or involved in artistic choice-making that included fairly decadent, decorative art. [*Crayon*] was very refreshing in this slightly rarified atmosphere.[129]

Following *Crayon*, Rainer performed item number fourteen, her solo *Ordinary Dance*. Choreographed during the time of Dunn's class, *Ordinary Dance* was not a solution to an assignment, nor did it spring from a score or chance technique. "By then I was simply stringing movement together," Rainer says. "Unrelated, unthematic phrases, with some repetition."[130] While she danced, Rainer spoke, reciting a poetic autobiography that listed her addresses in San Francisco, Berkeley, and Chicago, up to her first New York address; her grade school teachers; and atmospheric sounds.

> It began in 1934. I think it was November 1934. Or was it November 24, 1934? College Avenue was before my time. Geary Street. That's the impression I got. Yes. Geary Street with too much sun and windows open to the sea. No birth certificate. Then came the dark alley of 1914 and the empty elevated lot of Golden Gate Avenue. A fire started in a drawer. No more fires, no no. Los Gatos and Daly City belong in here somewhere: singing among the deaf-mutes. And of course, Sunnyside, but I won't go into that — no point. Seventh Avenue with Parnassus looming above Hugo Street. It always glittered over there. Oh yes, I forgot to mention Gilroy: the two-wheeled cart which moved the earth.

> 1941–42. The story gets denser around here. 1-2-3-4-5. MacDonald, Barrett, Myers, King, Myers, McCarthy, Kermoian, Pepina. 5-6-7-8-9. I'm not going to be able to talk for a while.

> Uh. Let's see. Panhandle, early morning. Uh, let's see. Panhandle, early morning. White, white, white. Uh, let's see. Panhandle, early morning. White, white, white. White, whaat, whaat, whaat. Whack whack whack, whack whack whack, whack whack WHACK! Oh yes, I forgot to mention Detner.

> It's going to get cosmic any minute now, Yes. Here it comes: Roosevelt. Gravel and industry. But not for long. September, 1952. Pierce St. Then came the long haul to the riverside bloodstream looped through with portwinesap.

> Oak St. Scott St. Over the bathroomed tunnel. But I'm really not telling you much lately, am I. Nevertheless, it does go forward. 1956: After the moon-milked water shock: Bank treatment. 21-25-63-57-14. So, that's the story. Oh yes, I forgot to mention North Pinegrove. Also 88th Street. But I'll have to demonstrate that.[131]

The dance began as Rainer entered and squatted. She immediately began speaking. From the squat she did an elbow stand, fell over, and got up. She stamped her foot heavily and repetitively, each time she said "Whack." For the most part, however, the words, which were written after the movement was made, did not correspond to the rhythms or the connotations of movement. At one point Rainer imitated with her face an eccentric woman — "my loony-bin subway impersonation." Two extant photographs show frozen instants of other movements. In one, Rainer went up on relevé with right knee up to the side and the arms outstretched, holding the pose momentarily, and then bringing the leg and arm in sharply, dipping the torso over and standing up straight again, very quickly. In the other, her torso curved to the left with her head held upright while she walked forward, saying "Yes yes yes yes yes."[132]

Rainer began making the dance from fairy-tale imagery. One of the movements (the subway impersonation) was taken from a chance lecture she had given in Dunn's class (see Chapter 3). Other movements are recognizable as hallmarks of her style, which savored incongruities and awkwardness: the squatting and falling, the bent torso with the head craning upright. Rainer was involved at this point not only in wrenching the body into unexpected, clumsy configurations, but also in heightening the difficulty of the dancer's action by engaging the memory in simultaneously recalling the text and the complicated movement phrases.

In 1962, Rainer wrote:

> When working on *Ordinary Dance* I set out to make a dramatic dance about Grimm's *Fairy Tales*. Finally abandoned this idea while keeping some movement images that had been inspired by several of the fairy tales.
> Nevertheless, the dance retained its dramatic flavor, mainly thru dealing with fragments of observed behavior in different kinds of people—a ballerina demonstrating classical movements, a woman hallucinating on the subway. This is juxtaposed with pure dance movement and a simultaneous narrative.[133]

William Davis remembers his viewing of *Ordinary Dance* as a numbing, dazzling experience.[134] According to Lucinda Childs, "What knocked me out was the fact that it had such a valid performance quality. Even though if you think about it — and I had never seen this before—if you had said this girl is going to walk around and do this thing and talk, I would think you were kidding, or crazy. And instead, it was completely spellbinding. She could have been talking about anything. She had a manner of delivery that was very matter-of-fact."[135]

Sorell, reviewing a later performance (on the program with *Crayon*), wrote:

> *Ordinary Dance* is extraordinary as an autobiographical outcry, in its dramatic fusion of word and movement, telling story told breathlessly by Yvonne who, however, did not lose her breath nor the dynamic pulsebeat of the dance nor her audience. *Ordinary Dance* roused me from the stupor into which you fall when you protest against madness with another kind of madness for more than an hour and a half.[136]

According to Maxine Munt, writing in *Show Business*,

> [Rainer] is completely at home in this approach to dance, and her absoption and projection in this particular work were complete, even though she employed more talking and grunting than usual.[137]

Reviewing the Judson concert, Johnston wrote about *Ordinary Dance*:

> It is an ordinary dance because it is autobiographical and Miss Rainer does a lot of talking while she moves, ordinary-type talking, telling you the facts. . . . Poetry of facts. The title has its ironic aspect. The dance is out of the ordinary. Like Gordon, she did

some movement nobody ever saw before. I can't say any more now except to note the audience responded tumultuously, and we had good reason.[138]

Di Prima predicted that *Ordinary Dance* would become a classic. "Naming streets out of her past, moving in her inimitable manner, pausing and twitching, lyric and wooden, a system of Dante's hell in dance, personal as any hell, but terrifyingly clear to the observer."[139]

Though the dance was a series of fragments, the pieces added up, for the viewer, to an expression of the shattered experience of alienation. It was a dramatic dance. But its power derived from the meanings that flowed from the rubbing together of disparate elements, rather than from explicit content.

The first concert ended, around midnight, with a collaboration between Alex Hay, Deborah Hay, and Charles Rotmil, called *Rafladan*. Rotmil played a Japanese flute, Deborah Hay danced, and Alex Hay moved a flashlight around. "I don't think we consulted each other," Alex Hay recalls. "We just did it." His part of the collaboration was to make a frame—invoking his profession as a painter—and stand behind it, so that his own activity could be seen metaphorically as a painting. "I stood in back of the square in the dark and just did things with little pinlights, flew them around."[140]

Paxton recalls that in *Rafladan*,

Alex [Hay] and Charles Rotmil were background and Deborah [Hay] danced sporadically, in a very strong performance. At that time, as she described it a few years later, she had absolutely nothing on her mind. She was a strong and serious performer, not as technically clear as she became a few years later, but obviously a very interesting young, quiet woman, with a lot of passion in her movement, of a kind that was refreshing, especially in my context because I was working with such passionless ideas. One of the movements she did was to pull her arms up and drum her ribs with her fingers. And Alex and Charles at the end, when the lights faded, wrote things in the air with flashlights, leaving afterimages.[141]

The concert had begun in darkness with a film projection fading up into a lighted dance. It ended by fading back into darkness while the dancing continued. From start to finish the question of what constituted a dance was raised. In *Rafladan*, the dancing happened in the dark, suggesting that the movements of a person not directly visible might still fall within the realm of dance. One could see Alex Hay's movements indirectly by watching the lights as he manipulated them. But Deborah Hay's movements were present to the spectators only by implication.

All the critics who attended the concert realized immediately that it was a signal event in the history of modern dance. Allen Hughes, who began his review pointing out that "there was hardly anything conventional about it," concluded that "the same group may appear together on another occasion, and have a total flop. The chances are, however, that their experiments will influence dance development in this country somehow, and because this seems likely, the are worth watching."[142] Hughes, who had seen earlier concerts by Rainer and Herko, had only recently replaced John Martin, the *New York Times'* first dance critic, the venerable champion of historic modern dance during his tenure at the *Times* from 1927 to 1962. According to Hughes, Martin too went to see the new dance but refused to write about any performances that happened below 14th Street. "I had a year before John Martin left in which I didn't write, but immersed myself in dance performances," says Hughes, who had just joined the newspaper as a music critic.

> I went to everything that happened in New York; I also went to Europe and saw things there. Mr. Martin had been very conservative. He went to most things at least once, but he only wrote about what he liked or liked the idea of. When I became dance critic, the paper asked me to broaden the coverage. I had seen bits of experimental dance and as far as I was concerned, it was going to happen and therefore my place was to be there.

Hughes, trained primarily as a music critic, was not considered knowledgeable as a dance critic by many members of the dance community. After Hughes reviewed the Judson concert, he noticed that his colleagues snubbed him.

> The dance establishment wasn't very big then; it was *Dance Magazine, Dance News,* the *Times* and the [*New York Herald*] *Trib[une]*. And that was it. Jill Johnston did all sorts of things downtown, but she was not part of it. After I wrote this piece, when I saw my colleagues they turned up their noses. The implication was that since I was new I didn't know anything.[143]

Diane di Prima wrote, after concluding that Gordon, Rainer, and Herko stood out as new choreographers "of definite promise":

> At this distance, the evening retains its excitement, the high one feels being in on a beginning: these people working out of a tradition (all three are, or have been, members of James Waring's Dance Company, all three have studied with Merce Cunningham and have been highly influenced by both of these masters) yet in each case doing something that was distinctly *theirs*, unborrowed, defined. Yvonne Rainer to a large extent summing up existing techniques, Fred Herko and David Gordon in their unsimilar ways marching uncautiously forward into what may be new romanticisms. Interesting, too, that for all the dance is once more pushing at its so-called boundaries: David's talking and singing in *Mannequin*, Yvonne's street names in *Ordinary Dance*, and Freddie's costumes and that jazz, right there w/him. ok.[144]

Jill Johnston's prophecy in the *Village Voice* was the most extreme:

> This was an important program in bringing together a number of young talents who stand apart from the past and who could make the present of modern dance more exciting than it's been for twenty years (except for an individual here and there who always makes it regardless of the general inertia). Almost all these dancers and choreographers were in Robert Dunn's composition class at the Living Theater. [145]

The dancers, too, were delighted with the results of the Judson concert. Rainer writes of that evening:

> We were all wildly enthusiastic afterwards, and with good reason. Aside from the enthusiasm of the audience [of about 300], the church seemed a positive alternative to the once-a-year hire-a-hall mode of operating that had plagued the struggling modern dancer before. Here we could present things more frequently, more informally, and more cheaply, and—most important of all—more cooperatively. [146]

The first Judson concert had incorporated choreographic techniques and human values that reflected and commented on both the smaller dance and art world and the larger social world the dancers inhabited. Through chance, collage, free association, cooperative choice-making, slow meditation, repetition, lists, handling objects, playing games, and solving tasks, the dancers and the dances described a world: a world very much like an innocent American dream pocked with intimations of anxiety; a world of physicality, bold action, free choice, plurality, democracy, spontaneity, imagination, love, fun, and adventure. A world where traditions existed to be freely sampled or ridiculed. But also, a world where that very freedom was interwoven with the experience of a shattered, fragmented universe.

3

The Judson Workshop

In June 1962, the Supreme Court ruled official prayers in public schools unconstitutional. On 1 July Algeria won its independence from France. The United States resumed atmospheric nuclear testing for the first time since 1958 on 7 July, the day after the Judson concert. On 10 July, Martin Luther King, Jr. was jailed in Georgia for leading a demonstration the previous December, and on the same day Telstar was sent into space. In late August, the U.S. announced that the U.S.S.R. was pouring arms and military personnel into Cuba. All summer long, demonstrators protested in sit-ins against segregation. The world was changing very quickly, and dance was a highly visible part of the flux. The Twist had become a widespread fad; the Peppermint Lounge was an internationally known social spot. Two ballet companies — Jerome Robbins's Ballets: U.S.A. and the American Ballet Theater — performed at the White House in the spring. The Kennedy administration made clear its commitment to art over entertainment. And the *New York Times* called the young ballet dancers who performed *Billy the Kid* for an audience of distinguished government officials "as American as the twist."[1] The New York State Council on the Arts subsidized state tours by New York City Ballet and American Ballet Theater. Over the summer, City Ballet prepared for its fall tour to the Soviet Union, while New Yorkers anticipated the upcoming visit of the Bolshoi Ballet.[2] America's young ballet tradition was becoming an important part of the national cultural life, and if modern dance still had its special audience, Americans in general were becoming more and more aware of the various kinds of dance, both theatrical and social, that artists, entertainers, socialites and young people were dancing.

For four weeks, beginning 10 July, Merce Cunningham taught a composition class from 8:00 to 10:00 PM on Tuesdays and Thursdays.[3] The class had been announced in a Cunningham studio circular as "Class in Experimental Dance Composition," with Cunningham, Judith Dunn, and Robert Dunn listed as teachers. But the Dunns did not, in fact, coteach.[4] It was the first time Cunningham had taught such a course, and he based it on his *Suite by Chance*, a dance choreographed in 1953 using a gamut of movement choices and pennies, which he tossed to determine the order of the movements.[5] Members of Dunn's class and of the Cunningham company, as well as other students at the studio — including Lucinda Childs and Meredith Monk, two students of Judith Dunn's at Sarah Lawrence College — participated in the class. After learning Cunningham's methods for *Suite by Chance*, the students made their own movements, then paired up and taught their own versions of the dance to their partners.[6]

After the success of the Judson concert in July, Elaine Summers organized another Concert of Dance, this time in Woodstock, New York, an artists' community with a lively summer program. The concert took place at the Turnau Opera House, where Summers worked as a choreographer. On the day of the concert, either 31 August or 1 September, Summers's husband, Carol Summers, built the stage out ten feet.[7] Nine dancers came up from New York City to perform in the program, presenting nine dances and the film *Overture*. Of the nine dances, one was a collaboration by Laura de Freitas, June Ekman, and Sally Gross; two were choreographed by Ruth Emerson; three were by Elaine Summers; and three were by Elizabeth Keen. Six of the dances had already been seen in the July concert at Judson church. The Woodstock concert was produced by M. Edgar Rosenblum and the Turnau Opera Association, stage-managed by Carol Summers, and lighted by David Thuesen. The program note explained the genesis of the concert:

> We would like to acknowledge our debt to Robert and Judith Dunn, who provided a framework in which dancers could freely explore their art and themselves. This program represents a number of approaches to dance and choreography which were investigated with the Dunns. Some of the works utilize indeterminate or chance techniques, spontaneous determination, improvisation.[8]

The concert was organized into a more regular, symmetrical format than the first concert had been. After the film *Overture*, there were five dances, alternating between group and solo works, before the intermission. The second half of the program began with a group dance followed by two solos, and ended with Summers's three-part *Suite*, a finale that concluded by engaging the audience in the Twist. All of the solos on the program were by women. Most of the dances were accompanied by music.[9] Elaine Summers's *Instant Chance*, danced by Ekman, Emerson, Rudy Perez, and Summers, followed *Overture*. Third on the concert program was *Dawning*, a solo to jazz music by Elizabeth Keen. Next came Emerson's *Narrative*, danced by Emerson, Sally Gross, John Herbert McDowell, Perez, and Summers, with music by McDowell; the fifth item was another jazz solo by

Keen, called *Sea Tangle*. The sixth number was *32.16 Feet per Second Squared*, structured and improvised by de Freitas, Ekman, and Gross. After intermission were Summers's *Newspaper Dance* (a new title for *The Daily Wake*), danced by Emerson, Gross, McDowell, and Perez; *This Perhapsy*, another solo by Keen—this time to spoken poetry by e.e. cummings; Emerson's solo *Timepiece*; and finally, Summers's *Suite*.

Elizabeth Keen was a dancer with Paul Taylor's company who was beginning to work independently on her own choreography. Keen had grown up in Huntington, Long Island, where as a child she studied dance at summer camp and both ballet and modern dance at Adelphi College Children's Theater. She then studied Dalcroze eurhythmics with Mita Rom, ballet at the School of American Ballet, and Graham technique at the Juilliard Preparatory Division, during high school. Keen began college at Radcliffe, but, committed to the dance activity in New York City, transferred to Barnard College, where she majored in the history of religion and continued to study dance. After graduation, Keen danced with the Tamiris-Nagrin Company, Pearl Lang, and Paul Taylor. She joined the Taylor company in November 1961 and soon after danced in *Insects and Heroes*. She studied composition with Louis Horst and Helen Tamiris, and besides dance, she studied mime with Etienne Decroux.[10] A reviewer wrote of a later performance of *Dawning*:

> Danced to perfection to a hurrying jazz score by Don Friedman, Miss Keen seemed to be forever asking where is the most satisfying movement? Here? No, there. No, let us go on to the next. Each phrase flowed inexorably to the next and carried the dancer on, one is sure, long after the curtain fell.[11]

According to Don McDonagh, Keen's early dances were choreographed in the mode she had learned at the Tamiris-Nagrin studio: "Movement was supposed to be dramatically motivated and to be about something." The restlessness of the movement corresponded to the agitation of the jazz, and *Dawning* presented an impression of anxiety and fragmentary dissociation. Keen's *Sea Tangle*, which she had danced at the Tamiris-Nagrin studio under the title *Magnetic X*, was about shifting directions and weightlessness in space and underwater travel. McDonagh gives the following account of Keen's choreographic process in *Sea Tangle*:

> Keen initially approached the dance by imagining herself into the part in much the same way that an actor might prepare himself for a role, and tried to conceive of her body magnetized and pulled in different directions. As she developed the dance, the sea parallel exerted more influence on her imagination, with its images of strands of seaweed floating and entwining. It was an interpretive rendering of reality and at the same time offered the abstract-movement interest of parts of the body working independently of one another.[12]

This Perhapsy was unusual for Keen in its nonjazz accompaniment. Here, according to McDonagh, Keen attempted to use movement in an abstract way, not necessarily illustrating the meaning of the words, and occasionally she let the dance phrases "go 'across' the words." It was Keen's first use of language in dance, a technique that would become a hallmark of her style.[13]

Laura de Freitas, June Ekman, and Sally Gross danced together in Merle Marsicano's company. Sally Gross, who had met Elaine Summers at an improvisation concert at Jean Erdman's studio earlier in 1962, had danced in *The Daily Wake* in the July concert at Judson church. She remembers that she, de Freitas, and Ekman frequently improvised together and, since Summers had asked all three of them to perform in her dances at Woodstock, Summers invited them to contribute a piece on the program.

> The three of us got together beforehand, we set up a structure, and then we left up to chance what it would look like in space and how long the time would be. What we did, basically, was fall. It was just fall and recovery. We started together and for timing we just took as long as we could fall. It must have lasted five or six minutes. There was no sound. We fell from standing to the floor by spinning, twisting, whatever it was that brought you to the floor, and that was it.[14]

The improvisational quality of the dance originated, in part, due to practical reasons. The dancers had to rehearse in New York City, then adapt their pieces quickly to the stage in Woodstock, because all of the performers on the program were staying at Summers's house and they arrived only a day or two before the concert. Summers had done the publicity by herself, in advance. "She'd been to Woodstock many summers and people knew about her. She put out an announcement, and a flyer was distributed. There was a summer art colony with interested people. It was a nice audience and a comfortable space," Gross remembers.[15]

Sally Gross had grown up on the lower East Side in New York City. Her first experience in dance was performing in *The Mikado* in summer camp at age fourteen. She studied for a short time at Henry Street Settlement House, with Rose Lichner, who was teaching for Nikolais. When she went to Brooklyn College, Gross joined the college dance club, where she met Judith Dunn (then Judith Goldsmith), and she resumed dance classes at Henry Street. After college, Gross married, had two children, and continued to study full-time with Nikolais, taking classes in theory, composition, percussion, improvisation, and pedagogy, as well as technique in the Wigman-Holm style. In 1956, Gross met Laura de Freitas, who introduced her to Drid Williams, a ballet teacher who taught alignment and placement based on the kinesiological studies of Mabel Todd. Gross did typing for

Williams in exchange for classes. In 1957, Gross went to San Francisco to work with Ann Halprin. There she met Simone Forti. Returning to New York later in 1957, Gross continued to work with both Williams and Nikolais, then after 1959 with Erick Hawkins and Merce Cunningham. From 1959 to 1962 she studied and performed with Marsicano.[16]

For Gross, who had broken up with her husband and was trying to support two children and dance at the same time, working with Elaine Summers in 1962 was a relief, partly because Summers demanded so little time from her.

> When she asked me if I wanted to dance in *The Daily Wake*, I said, "Well, I have two children, I don't really have much time." I had just danced with Merle [Marsicano], and the kids had gotten chicken pox, and even though I hadn't missed one rehearsal, she thought I was not a serious person, having problems like this to attend to. She didn't want you to bring your personal life to work. Elaine [Summers] said, "Oh, that's all right, there's no problem with rehearsals. I'll just send you this thing in the mail. You read it over. If you have any questions you can call me. But don't worry, we'll just get together a couple of times before the performance." That was a real shock to me.
>
> And also, she said, "You can wear anything you want." And I remember that in the first concert I wore a red sleeveless leotard, no tights, no bra, and I didn't shave my legs. I knew I was the first person who ever came out on a dance stage looking like that.[17]

Jill Johnston had met Sally Gross through Marilyn Wood, a dancer with Cunningham's company, and Gross claims that it was because of their friendship that Johnston came to the first Judson concert.[18] For Johnston, Gross and her husband symbolized an entire way of life, the world of jazz musicians, poets, and artists, the world of lower East Broadway.

> I was enchanted by her lifestyle. Or I should say, I was amazed. It was so different from my proper, Protestant life. There were kids' drawing all over the walls, the ceilings and walls were peeling, the floors sloped, and everybody seemed to be having a good time. There were drums around, and they did strange things. They seemed to be living a vital existence. They knew exciting people – black jazz artists and stuff. I was suddenly caught up in a swirling social life. We'd go to the Dom, a discotheque of the early 60s, and the Cedar Bar. We'd make the rounds of the bars, and go to big parties and do the Twist and all the other latest dances and any other thing, finally, that you felt like doing, and go to hear the jazz musicians. She was my introduction to that entire world. Those people that she knew all connected up with the Judson somehow. The Grosses had kids, and they were living high, and they were trying to figure out how to survive.[19]

Johnston also went up to Woodstock for the second concert, and she wrote a short review of the evening in the *Village Voice*. She says of the collaborative dance:

> [De Freitas, Ekman, and Gross] did an exciting falling dance titled "31.16 [sic] feet per second squared" (the acceleration at which a body falls through space), which was per-

haps too long—although the first sixty seconds or so were a kinesthetic shot in the arm for anybody who has any doubts about the raw power of a body to give in to itself *after* the initial impulse of falling: pure joy![20]

Walter Gutman, a wealthy stockbroker, aspiring avant-garde poet, patron of the arts, and an admirer of "muscle molls," as he put it, also went to the Woodstock concert. His account of the evening gives the impression that the dancers were "Elaine Summers' group." Most memorable for Gutman were *32.16 Feet*...and a party following the concert, where Johnston went swimming fully clothed. He writes, in a 1970 tribute to Johnston:

> I should mention the behind of Laura de Freitas. Laura danced with June Ekman and Sally Gross at the Woodstock performance of Elaine Summers' group, after which Jill [Johnston] fell off the diving board. Laura attempted to introduce a variation into the general dance [con]cept, which is that the dance should be based on some dynamic force coming from some fragment of the feet—like a toe—or both feet, by falling on her behind. As I watched her deliberately fall backward on her behind—not once but several times, I could not help but feel that here was my dream woman—who Jill had said I should write about. You have to have a powerful behind in order to make falling on it a deliberately important part of a highly intellectual dance concept, and Laura—a beautiful and powerful—but feminine and seductive as well as intellectual woman—had it. Her effort to bring behinds into the dance did not succeed beyond this concert. That is why I am commemorating it here. If falling on their behinds had become as common—- anywhere near, that is—as standing, walking, or toeing in their feet, Laura would long ago have been recognized as one of the powerfully original minds of the dance world. But the dance world—even the most avant garde—still has certain set ideas. There are parts of the body which convey the soul and others which upset the soul, and the behind—a very great behind, that is—is still considered to belong to these. My soul was upset by Laura, and it tingles now as I write about it.
>
> Well, I am sort of imitating Jill by digressing to Laura, but then Jill claims that she got some stylistic ideas from the way I wrote when she was doing some editing for me.[21]

Elaine Summers's *Suite* could be interpreted as an up-to-date tribute to Louis Horst, or a new twist on Horst's method. The three sections of the dance were named for musical forms: "Galliard," "Saraband," [sic] and "Twist." Summers, who had originally met McDowell when she was studying with Waring, asked the composer to help her structure the music for her *Suite* "correctly."[22] The choreographer and composer went to the Peppermint Lounge to do research for the final section.[23] McDowell wrote a "Gigue," perhaps as accompaniment for the "Twist" movement in this suite. McDowell says of his method in "Gigue":

> I got every Bach gigue I had in the house, which turned out to be 18, and I made out an arbitrary list or order for them by shuffling cards and then I looked at the first note of every one of them and I made an 18-note row out of whatever those first notes happened to be. Then I made the rhythm in the same way. And it was astonishing. It was very peculiar and something I never would have done in my life.[24]

None of the sections in *Suite* was called "Gigue"; a gigue usually ends a dance suite.

The dances were structured by chance from a gamut of movements appropriate to the dance form but not necessarily in the historical style of the dance. According to Summers:

> A 16th-century galliard has a particular style; we didn't do it in that style. But it also has, say, so many jumps per measure, so many beats in the measure, and the emphasis is on such-and-such a beat. John [McDowell] wrote a new galliard, with that structure in mind, and I took the dance movement, with that structure in mind. You still have to hop on the second beat, for instance.
>
> I kept the formal elements and did not use the style of presentation of the historical dance form. And then at the end, I tacked on a Twist. Using it in the same way. And we invited the audience to come up and do the dance with us at the end.[25]

Sally Gross explains, "You didn't really get out there and do the twist, as you would to Chubby Checkers. Watching it, you might not know that it was the Twist, because the movements were broken up and rearranged. And I remember that mine was done in slow time."[26]

In *Suite*, Ekman, Gross, and Perez danced the "Galliard"; Emerson danced a solo "Saraband" all the dancers in the evening's program, except de Freitas—i.e., Ekman, Emerson, Gross, Keen, McDowell, Perez, and Carol and Elaine Summers—danced the "Twist."[27]

In the fall of 1962 Robert Dunn did not continue his choreography class. Judith Dunn later wrote, "Forever is no time and a long time. I believe it was expected that Bob Dunn's class would continue indefinitely. After two years he stopped teaching, but the activity went on."[28] Rainer felt that "although it had been quite a while since I had relied on Bob [Dunn] for direction, I missed the contact and the discussions."[29] One day at the Cunningham studio, Rainer suggested to Paxton that they call a meeting of people who might want to work together on their own, and Paxton immediately posted a sign on the studio bulletin board. A week later, a group of dancers, musicians, and artists met at Smith's bar, across the street from the Cunningham–Living Theater building, to discuss where and when to hold a new workshop. Rainer offered the studio she had shared, since the fall of 1961, with Waring and Passloff, above the St. Mark's Playhouse at the corner of Second Avenue and St. Mark's Place. The group began to meet there on Monday nights, after Waring's technique class.[30] Meanwhile, Waring and di Prima had organized a Monday night lecture series, meeting on alternate Mondays beginning October 1, also at the studio. *The Floating Bear* had announced in August that the series would feature Valda Setterfield, David Gordon, George Brecht, Jill Johnston, and others.[31] The choreography workshop changed its meeting night to Tuesday.[32] The lecture series was complementary to, rather than competitive with, the choreography workshop; it involved many of the same people, but in a different capacity.

Rainer, for instance, gave a lecture in the Waring–di Prima series. It was a chance-structured lecture, based on character observations and short speeches written on sheets of colored construction paper, that she had originally made for Robert Dunn's class. The lecture allowed Rainer to demonstrate and talk about her method simultaneously. One of the movement possibilities was "jump rope." Another was "stark hand action while trying to speak—'you,' 'I,' 'I know what's wrong,' etc."; still another was the "subway lady attending tea party" that Rainer had also used in *Ordinary Dance*. Sometimes the monologue involved didacticism, personal revelation, and absurd utterances, as in the "subway lady" section:

> The chance operation is useful when one is in a quandary, is in a stalemate with one's body, is immobilized by habits no longer useful, is in need of clues to new images, or—as in my case—when not knowing what one knows or doesn't know about beginning the long climb into oneself that leads out and away into the bright world and giddyap-giddyap.

The monologue that corresponds to the action "ah ha ha" sets forth a serious philosophical argument for the use of the chance method in a world where the presence and disconnectedness of things is a more powerful experience than the perception of causation:

> I am beginning to think that there is not really such a thing as cause and effect. The fact that one thing apparently follows from another out of necessity, destiny, history, naturally, perversity, precocity, inhumanity, or hip-hip-hooray—is a comforting belief. In the absence of belief, the possibilities of the world become inexhaustible. I am I and I do what I have to do—not by virtue of the unhappy childhood, the psychotic mama, the fanatical daddy, the tortured adolescence, the open-mouthed early twenties, the closed-mouth late twenties. I am I in that there exists the possibility of wanting to be watchful, and the possibility of wanting to be autonomous. I am I because I go into the street and the sun shakes my hand. I am I because the bum takes a polite pee in the gutter, shielding his activity with his overcoat. I am I because once in a great while I can be awed. I was born in a cage, I grew up in a cage, I continue to live in a cage—but goddamn it—it doesn't matter—because all things are possible, and it can be spring again.

Rainer also argued that the use of chance does not eradicate the image in a work of art.

> The chance operation versus the image. By image I mean personal vision, fantasy, or dream and attendant atmosphere.

> There is no innate contradiction between the chance operation and the image.

> Aside from the image possibilities in the use of chance—and by this I mean the assimilation of the results of a chance operation into one's own personal language and

imagery—all this aside—it is possible for the chance result and the image result to co-exist.

It is also possible for the image to influence one's interpretation of the chance operation.

It is also possible for the image to be so strong and insistent that it makes other kinds of investigation unnecessary.

It is also possible—and very gratifying when it happens to me—for the chance operation to control certain aspects of a larger image. But here again is a situation where the image—also the experience and life of the artist—has been affected by the use of chance.[33]

At the end of October, the artist Robert Morris wrote a statement about the lecture series, noting the problems of communication in an impermanent, often undocumented art form; praising the dancers for their intellectual clarity; and expressing the hope that dance might, partly through these efforts, become an autonomous art form, no longer relying on ideas and methods of the other arts. The essay includes barbs aimed at those choreographers whose "limit of exploration is the imposition of chance procedures to alter the continuity of Grahamesque expressionism." Morris names a few examples of "recent and wonderful rumblings of subversion":

Peter Schumann's new archaicism—the attempt to find out just what it is to swing an arm and stamp a foot, searching out what a purely kinesthetic rhythm might be; Yvonne Rainer's elaboration of an "associational" approach brought in part from the West Coast where, in the work of Ann Halprin, the materials of the dance are extended to include responses to the stream of consciousness within the head of the dancer—interplays between words and movements; and the transfixing imagery of David Gordon's expressionism which lies beyond official dance technique.[34]

Morris submits that at the biweekly sessions "one is struck not so much by what actually gets said but by the fact that such a situation exists." He predicts that this situation "may prove that Virgil Thomson's comment about dancers being completely auto-erotic and therefore without conversation is, at last, no longer a contemporary observation." Recommending that dancers attend the sessions, Morris closes his remarks by staking out one of the critical positions in the Judson Dance Theater aesthetic: "Perhaps dance is moving toward dance, toward its own free identity and does not have any historical obligation to submit to a metamorphosis into theater."[35] Among the sets of contrasting categories in the body of work presented by Judson Dance Theater, the theatrical versus the nontheatrical dance would represent one obvious distinction.

After about a month in the Rainer-Waring-Passloff studio, the choreography workshop moved, perhaps because of scheduling problems, to the

Judson Church, where they met on Tuesday nights in the basement gymnasium.[36] McDowell remembers the sequence of events after the first concert slightly differently:

> The church was pleased by the results of the first concert and asked if it could become a steadier thing, and we decided that a once-a-week meeting would be a good idea and started operating as a workshop and subsequently all the concerts were drawn from works and things that happened in that workshop.[37]

The workshop sessions were open to all who wished to attend and, as in Robert Dunn's class, the choreographer showed the dance and then the group discussed it. "We agreed in the early days that one wouldn't say 'I don't like it,' or things like that," explains Trisha Brown. "The choreographer would say 'This is my intention; was it there?' That is the direction the discussion followed. Whoever had something to show or do did it and got other people to do it with them."[38] According to Alex Hay, "The energy was incredible. All I would think about each week, for about a year, was the Judson Workshop."[39]

Not every member of the workshop attended regularly. Lucinda Childs recalls that she only attended if she had a dance she wanted to show.[40] For the core members of the group, however, the commitment was intense. According to Elaine Summers:

> We met every single week for over two years. During the second year Christmas and New Year's fell on the workshop night; the one social thing we ever did was that we had a New Year's party after the class was over.
>
> The meetings usually started at eight o'clock and would end between eleven and midnight. Once we got to Judson and it was no longer a class, we set up a rotating chairmanship. The chairman got to say what kind of criticism we were to indulge in that evening.
>
> Steve [Paxton] once said, "You may say anything you like, but it must be one sentence long, and it must be something that you actually saw." And everybody did as they were told.
>
> Another night, when [Paxton] set things up, he said, "You must bring a dance that does not have the qualities you always use in your dances. Elaine," he told me, "you are not to be wistful."
>
> The rule continued from the classes that there were to be no excuses. You did this dance, you put it out front, and then whatever was said was the criticism and you listened to that. It was wonderfully objective. That made you free to be honest about what you saw. For me it meant taking criticism without feeling destroyed. "Where do you go from there?" became apparent. The criticism was extremely precise.
>
> One night Steve [Paxton] and Judith [Dunn] did a dance in which she sat on one of those trays you find in cafeterias. Someone said, when they'd finished, "Judith, did you mean to point your toe?" And she said, "Oh no, did I point my toe? Well, could I do it again?" And they went through the whole dance all over again, while Judith concentrated on doing it without pointing her toes.

One point of that is that we were an audience for each other that was willing to look at a dance a second time, just for a single movement. Another point is that we weren't saying to her, "You shouldn't point your toes." We wanted to know whether she really did want to, or whether she shared the struggle many of us were having about training and mannerisms. I personally had a lot to shed to get down to what I wanted in movement.[41]

From the first meeting, decisions were reached about the way the evenings would be run.[42] Ruth Emerson proposed that the group follow the Quaker method of arriving at group decisions by consensus rather than by taking a majority vote, which would still leave some participants dissatisfied. According to Emerson:

I remember feeling that it was important to make decisions by consensus rather than majority vote. That was partly a political feeling, because we all felt that establishment dance and choreography had discriminated against us in an authoritarian way. I was working as a volunteer at the American Friends Service Committee, and that made me want to work in my daily life and work situations in the way that people were trained to struggle with problems at AFSC. I guess I did try to articulate those ideas at Judson. I had a conviction that a consensus was better than a democratic vote. The majority would always end up with some minority.

There were other forces at work, too: people wanting very much to do their own work, finding out how to do that, and having confidence in themselves, which goes with making your own work. For me it was a very happy time, in which I thought all these things were working well.[43]

The consensus procedure required that sometimes as many as twenty people come to a unanimous decision. And, as Summers explains, "that meant there was no politicking. There was no point in getting three or four more people on your side. Everyone had to agree that this was the way it was going to be done. And that really made things go much faster."[44]

Judith Dunn writes of the workshop's method:

At the beginning there was no central authority or hierarchical structure operating. The group concerts and the workshop were cooperative and voluntary with a nondiscriminatory policy regarding works performed and workshop members. (James Waring once said in a fit of pique, "Judson Dance Theater is the world!") No important [decisions] were made until everyone concerned and present agreed. On occasion this method was time-consuming but in my opinion not at all wasteful. Later, in the second year, as the workshop grew in popularity, organization became a problem and changes began to take place. Voluntary chairmen were called for workshop meetings, and a committee was chosen (by election) to administrate group concerts.[45]

Another internal rule of the group was that the weekly sessions were not for rehearsal purposes. "You might get to the church early, but once the meeting started, you couldn't be somewhere else rehearsing and then come in late with your piece. You had to be there for the whole thing, see everybody's work, and of course you were dying to see everybody's work."[46]

By January the group was ready to present another concert. Although Robert Dunn did not attend the workshop, either as a teacher or as a participant, his former students asked him to help them organize the program. Robert Rauschenberg, who had come to several sessions and offered comments and advice,[47] is listed with Dunn under the title "advisory" on the program.[48] The workshop had generated so much material that two concerts were held, on 29 and 30 January 1963.

Lucinda Childs and William Davis are listed as the publicity committee.[49] William Davis designed the flyer, a collage using photographs and *New York Times* typeface.[50] Rainer helped them with the mailing and press release.[51] Like the publicity for the first concert, the press release for A Concert of Dance #3 and A Concert of Dance #4 stresses the use of various compositional methods and the pluralism of styles within the group. But, unlike the first notice, this statement emphasizes the participation of non-dancers. It also implies the presence of a permanent, ongoing group.

> These two concerts are in the series initiated at the church 6 July 1962, and continued at Woodstock, N.Y., in August, with the aim of periodically presenting the work of dancers, composers, and various non-dancers working with ideas related to dance. The methods of composition of the works in this series range from the traditional ones which predetermine all elements of a piece to those which establish a situation, environment, or basic set of instructions governing one or more aspects of a work—thus allowing details and continuity to become manifest in a spontaneous or indeterminate manner.
>
> It is hoped that the contents of this series will not so much reflect a single point of view as convey a spirit of inquiry into the nature of new possibilities.[52]

The lighting design for the concert was done by William Linich, the musical direction by Philip Corner, costume consulting by Ruth Emerson, and stage managing by Linda Sidon.[53] Sidon danced with Waring.[54] Linich had been introduced to the group by Herko;[55] they lived together, but later that year Linich changed his name to Billy Name and moved into Andy Warhol's Factory.[56] According to Warhol, Linich had been a waiter at Serendipity, dabbled in art, loved opera, regularly took amphetamines, and entertained the Greenwich Village "A-men" at the Factory. Linich furnished the Factory with discarded items he found on the street and turned its interior silver.

> [Linich and his friend Ondine] loved Maria Callas best of all. . . . They always said how great they thought it was that she was killing her voice and not holding anything back, not saving anything for tomorrow. They could really identify with that. When they'd go

on and on about her, I'd think of Freddy Herko, the way he would just dance and dance until he dropped. The amphetamine people believed in throwing themselves into every extreme — sing until you choke, dance until you drop, brush your hair till you sprain your arm. . . .

It was the perfect time to think silver. Silver was the future, it was spacy — the astronauts wore silver suits — Shepard, Grissom, and Glenn had already been up in them, and their equipment was silver, too. And silver was also the past — the Silver Screen — Hollywood actresses photographed in silver sets.

And maybe more than anything, silver was narcissism — mirrors were backed with silver.[57]

Concerts #3 and #4 were performed in the church gym, where the workshop met. The audience was seated with their backs to the long south wall facing the door; above their heads was a cage enclosing a balcony storage area, and to their right was a basketball hoop and a radiator built into the east, short side wall.[58] Linich set up a simple lighting system for the room which, according to Paxton, "wasn't very successful because the lights were low-powered and the ceilings were high and the throw was quite far. But nobody was into heavy-duty tech anyway, in those days. It was enough light to see."[59]

With Philip Corner's participation a new artistic and social network joined the Judson group. Corner, a composer who had grown up in New York, had gone to City College and then studied with Oliver Messaien in France. Although Messaien, like Cage, was interested in rhythm as the basis of music and, also like Cage, often was inspired by non-Western music, Corner felt ill at ease in the European intellectual music community.

The state of mind I was working in did not resound with the mental life there. I felt my work was more improvisatory or visionary. I wrote pieces, but I worked out of a sense of vision, and that vision was very clear. The idea of systematizing it by twelve-tone or some other rational principle that automatically generates all the results seemed hostile to my way of working. When I came back [to the United States], it was a question of desperate importance to connect with people like John Cage. My sense of intuition also permitted me to have an interest in jazz. Certainly the American composers were a step away from the overriding European intellectual oppression, where everything had to be justified, rationalized, proven, theoretized, polemicized, and everything else.

Corner got to know Cage, Morton Feldman — whose more intuitive approach he preferred to Cage's pervasive systems — Earle Brown, and Christian Wolff, as well as other music performers, like Dick Higgins, Al Hansen, Alison Knowles, and Yoko Ono, whom Corner did not think of as composers. "I still thought of Dick Higgins as theater, Alison Knowles as a visual artist, and Yoko Ono as a poet." Corner spent two years in the army, stationed in Korea, where he learned calligraphy and borrowed certain aspects of Korean music, such as gliding tones, sharp juxtapositions, and heterophonic structure, in which a group of musicians plays the same melody in different meters. When he returned to New York, in 1961, he found that "the whole scene had opened up. Abstract Expressionism is dead; there's Pop Art. La Monte [Young] was here from California, Joe Jones was making his musical, automatic, self-playing instruments, George Maciunas was around, George Brecht was doing very minimal kinds of things." Corner was involved with these people, who were soon to form the Fluxus neo-Dada music group, but also with more "traditional" avant-garde musicians, like Malcolm Goldstein, whom he met while in graduate school at Columbia University, and James Tenney, an experimental composer in residence at Bell Telephone Laboratories. "All of these people kept on being professional musicians and composers in the strictest sense." Corner, Goldstein, and Tenney organized Tone Roads concerts at the New School, where they played compositions by Charles Ives, Carl Ruggles, Edward Varèse, Cage, and Feldman, as well as their own works. They included Fluxus performances and events on their new music program. "None of these worlds was incompatible. All of these people were around, and if you were at all interested in painting, poetry, or dance, you met them. People would use each other in their works. The barriers were breaking down; everyone brought in special qualities."[60]

In May 1962, Corner and Higgins had organized an evening of performance at the Living Theater. The program included Higgins's *Two Generous Women*, three renditions of La Monte Young's *Poem for Chairs, Tables, Benches*, Philip Krumm's *Lecture on Where to Go From Here*, with sound by Corner, and Carolee Schneemann's *An Environment for Sounds and Motions*, made with Corner and performed by Judy Ratner, Yvonne Rainer, Malcolm Goldstein, Arlene Rothlein, and Andre Cadet, with lighting by William Linich. Schneemann, a painter at that time, lived with Tenney; Arlene Rothlein was a dancer who was married to Malcolm Goldstein.[61]

Through Corner—who was friendly with Rainer—Schneemann, Tenney, Goldstein, and Rothlein began attending the Judson workshops.

Concerts #3 and #4 were distinctive not only because they represented a consolidation of the group and its identification with the Judson Church, but also because the composers played a large role in the performances themselves. The dancers and nondancers who choreographed works for these concerts had moved beyond their models of Cage and Cunningham. In terms of the relationships of dance to music as well as in terms of the kinds of structures and movements in the dances themselves, those choreographers who danced with Cunningham, either in his company or in his studio, showed a marked departure from the essential features of his work.

Rainer twice used romantic music: Berlioz in *We Shall Run* and Rachmaninoff in *Three Seascapes*. Paxton made a piece of music for his collaboration with Rainer, *Word Words*; the "music" was a separate physical activity, performed on a different night. If Cunningham's dance need not be related to Cage's music, except that they existed in the same time, Paxton posited an even more distant relationship between the elements. Philip Corner's dance, *Certain Distilling Processes*, was primarily a musical experience, in which the movement of the dancers served as conducting cues to the musicians. Some of the dances had no music; others used music in a more "traditional" way: choreographers used preexisting accompaniment or asked one of the available composers to create a piece specifically tailored to their piece. In terms of the choreographic structures, repetition and improvisation emerged as two modes neither Cunningham nor the other influences on the group (except Ann Halprin) were accustomed to use. The movements themselves ranged from those generated by tasks or instructions, as in Carolee Schneemann's *Newspaper Event*, to the even, quotidian jog of *We Shall Run,* to the violent, single-minded whacking with instruments of *War* (by Robert Huot and Robert Morris), to the pantomime of Paxton's *English,* to the lyricism of Arlene Rothlein's *It Seemed to Me There Was Dust in the Garden and Grass in My Room.*

Again the concerts were structured in slightly asymmetrical, unexpected ways. Concert #3 consisted of nine dances, each one this time considered a single unit. It began with *We Shall Run*, a grand dance that others might have turned into a finale. It continued with *Giraffe*, a solo of almost violent energy by Emerson, then Paxton and Rainer's low-key, repetitive nude duet *Word Words*, then Summers's *Suite*, which again seems like a natural finale. But instead of breaking for intermission after *Suite*, the evening continued with Scothorn's *The Lazarite*, a solo. Then came intermission, followed by Rainer's three-part, repetitive solo *Three Seascapes*, Herko's tough solo *Little Gym Dance Before the Wall for Dorothy*, Davis's crystalline pas de deux to radio music, *Field*, and finally, Schneemann's physical collage of materials, movements, and bodies, *Newspaper Event*.[62]

On the next night, there were also nine dances, but Paxton's *Music for Word Words* was treated like a prelude to the concert itself, so the numbering of the dances began with his *English,* again a large-scale group piece. Lucinda Childs's *Pastime*, a solo, followed, and then two contrasting duets: Brown's *Lightfall* and the Huot-Morris *War*. Intermission followed, then another large group dance, Deborah Hay's *City Dance*; Rothlein's solo; Judith Dunn's duet *Index*; and the final piece, a huge-scale finale with twenty-two performers, Corner's *Certain Distilling Processes*.[63]

Jill Johnston announced the blossoming of the Judson group as a new entity in her review in the *Village Voice*, nearly a month after the double concert. She celebrated Judson's anarchic variety.

> In the Judson concerts there is a big, pliable, inchoate matrix of independent, original activity which knows itself even while looking for itself. The core of dancer-choreographers engaging in these concerts, as well as those who drop in and out, constitute a kind of loose, free-wheeling phalanx which is more than enough to fill that uncomfortable vacuum left by the decline, around 1945, of the first modern dance.
>
> One of the good things about the Judson concerts is the indiscriminate attitude of including just about as many dancers or nondancers (in as many kinds of actions and movement) as seem willing to participate. The programs may tighten up later on, but for the moment a certain amount of indiscrimination makes the most encouraging situation for everybody concerned. If that sounds provisional, I would add that I think it's great to be as inclusive as possible, because it's more like life that way. On a large, unwieldy program many experiences are available, and you can love it or hate it or fall asleep and not be too concerned about getting your trouble's worth every foot of the time.
>
> Be that as it may, there have been enough dancers on these programs to make the boat rock with dangerous excitement. The possibilities of form and movement have become unlimited. There is no way to make a dance; there is no kind of movement that can't be included in these dances; there is no kind of sound that is not proper for accompaniment. Only the integrity of the performer is at stake, the integrity to do the business at hand, to be inside that business, so that the action and the performer become one. The sluggish run of a non-dancer can be as moving and important as the beautifully extended leap of a dancer.[64]

Johnston saw in the Judson work correspondences with her rhetorical notions of modernity, freedom, and democracy—a generous, all-embracing celebration of the variety and vitality of American life. But even Maxine Munt, a more traditional, judgmental critic, wrote in *Show Business,* "Over the past year or so [the choreographers involved in the Judson workshop's] programs have ranged from benumbing boredom to intense concentration for the watchers, and if the boredom averages one half of the evenings the remaining half is worth a walk from any point of the city."[65]

For Johnston, Rainer's *We Shall Run* was a particularly resonant dance, celebrating the heroism of ordinary people.[66] Accompanied by the "Tuba Mirum" section of Hector Berlioz's *Requiem*, the dance consisted of seven minutes of jogging by twelve dancers and nondancers, in various floor patterns. The dancers lined up at the side of the room and waited for a moment, then began their inexorable movement, arms held waist-level as they jogged regularly in clumps. Occasionally one or two people broke out of their groups to run alone. Finally, the groups swept together to form a central, slowly whirling vortex that pulled each person firmly into it.[67] The dancers in the first performance were Trisha Brown, Lucinda Childs, Philip Corner, June Ekman, Ruth Emerson, Malcolm Goldstein, Sally

Gross, Alex Hay, Deborah Hay, Tony Holder, Carol Scothorn, and John Worden.[68]

Rainer later wrote of her use of repetition in *We Shall Run*:

> I have rarely used the kind of repetition that causes "one thing" to go on for a very long time, as La Monte Young has done in music and David Gordon and Simone [Forti] Whitman have done in dancing. *We Shall Run* bordered on it. It was a 7-minute piece for 12 people with a very bombastic portion of Berlioz' *Requiem*. The only movement was a steady trot, but the constantly shifting patterns and re-grouping of runners were as essential to the effect as the sameness of the movement. The object here was not repetition as a formal device but to produce an ironic interplay with the virtuosity and flamboyance of the music.[69]

Despite its apparent simplicity, *We Shall Run* was not an easy dance to perform. Childs recalls:

> It was the very first piece on the evening, and it was my debut in the whole Judson thing. We all came out, and I remember worrying that I was going to forget it. I had my own solo the next night; I was a total nervous wreck. The piece was very complex. You had to go over here and make a little circle, and come back here and make a big circle. It was hard to keep it in my head. But we did it. You broke off from the group here and there, but you always had to remember where you splintered out to. You couldn't just drift, and if you got in the wrong group you wouldn't know what they were doing.[70]

Tony Holder made his own score of flip cards in order to remember the sequences of groupings. Although Rainer had made a written score in the form of floor plans, she did not use her own score to teach the group.

> She wanted everybody to learn it. She'd walk around and talk you through it and play the music. Then we'd literally run through it. And then she would say, "Yes," or "Start that part sooner." We would run, then clump together, then run. We'd do diagonals or short straight lines or circles or spirals. I thought it was very complicated, though the movement wasn't complicated. And I thought everybody else was so much smarter than I was, because they could remember it and I couldn't.[71]

Explaining the work to those of his readers who perhaps were accustomed to seeing or reading about story ballets and dramatic modern dance, Allen Hughes wrote:

> In Miss Rainer's *We Shall Run*, 12 dancers ran to a movement from Berlioz' *Requiem*. Sometimes they ran as a pack, sometimes they divided into groups, sometimes they huddled for an instant, but only as a respite from the gentle, rhythmic running that almost became hypnotic before it ended. And all the while, the singing of Berlioz went on. Crazy you think? Non-dance? Who's to say? If it isn't dance, what is it?[72]

To Johnston, the dance was expressive in a way that the more abstract works of Cunningham perhaps were not, but subtly so:

> Standing in a line, before they began to run, with impassive attention, [the performers] looked like what they were: people. No "attitudes," just waiting to execute the play. Then they ran, an even jog (not always in step, or course), running and running, back and forth across the gymnasium, moving in compact groups—a pervasive collective feeling, as the rhythm accumulated insistence, that finally bloomed absolutely heroic. The heroism of the ordinary. No plots or pretensions. People running. Hooray for people.[73]

Giraffe was a dance that Emerson characterizes as full of "violent, casting-the-body-around movement, which was very liberating to me."[74] She did not use a chart or chance score in choreographing the solo, but instead used movement that "was invented without thinking about it beforehand. It had a lot of energy, crashing up and down out of the floor. It was quite a rough dance to do; my feet would always be calloused and scabbed afterwards. At the time it was nice to be able to put out all that energy and to feel very strong." The dance had nothing to do with giraffes or their movements. The title, Emerson explains, was just "a kind of handle" for the dance. "I always wanted to have titles that were just one word, as a matter of personal taste." Reviewers, however, were determined to find a connection between the wildness of the movement, the musical score by McDowell, and the title. "Of course," Emerson notes ironically, "what we were really trying to do was to get away from those kinds of connections."[75]

Natalie Jaffe, who reviewed a later performance of *Giraffe* in the *New York Times*, writes, "Ruth Emerson, with the aid of some chilling, undisciplined jungle sounds, evoked the regal separateness of a giraffe in a piece as strong and watchful as the beast itself."[76]

Emerson's second performance of *Giraffe*, reviewed by Jaffe, was on a program of work by young choreographers, produced by Contemporary Dance, Inc. at the 92nd Street YMHA in April 1963. The auditions for the jury for that program had already been held before the Judson concerts #3 and #4 were organized, and several of the Judson group had brought dances to the auditions. Paxton's and Rainer's dance *Word Words*, third on Concert #3, was a stinging response to the snobbish attitude of the jury toward downtown work. Paxton explains:

> We had introduced some pieces for a small group of people who held sway at the YMHA, hoping for a wider audience and a chance to do work. It later got back to us that one of them had said, those people at Judson all look alike to me. So we made this dance that was done as a solo, a solo, and then as a duet; the same movements each

time. I don't know exactly what we did, but at least there was room for comparison. The title was mine; it was one of a series of self-reflexive titles.[77]

The dance was a ten-minute sequence of movements, performed first as a solo by Rainer, then by Paxton, then as a duet by both, in exact unison.[78] The movements contributed by Paxton were complex, Cunninghamesque actions, as Rainer recalls, "quite challenging for me to do; I hadn't performed any of that in public although by that time I was pretty proficient at it." Rainer's contribution included twisting poses and very tiny, repetitive gestures.[79]

According to McDowell,

> She did a long, seven-minute, like, solo, while he leaned against the wall, and then he came out and did a long solo. And then after a while you realized that it was exactly the same dance — while she leaned against the wall. And then she came out and they did the same together. So the whole dance lasted, like, 20-plus minutes. And in rehearsal it was pretty boring, and they decided, like, the day before, that they were going to take off their clothes, and that made it very interesting, and the audience was like this, you could have heard a pin drop.[80]

Rainer does not accept this apocryphal account.

> *We* didn't think the dance was boring. We had tried it out in Rauschenberg's loft for an audience of Bob and Judy Dunn and Rauschenberg. It felt all right to us, and they liked it. So we did it.
>
> Steve [Paxton] wanted us to look as much alike as possible. He thought of gorilla suits, Santa Claus suits, playing around with our faces to re-draw them so they'd look alike. That didn't work. And then we decided on a chaste version of nudity. We were afraid that in the church it would upset some people. We asked Al Carmines; he said he didn't mind. At that time it was illegal to dance totally nude. We obeyed the law: I wore pasties and we both wore g-strings.[81]

Because the program ambiguously credits the choreography of *Word Words* to "Steve Paxton (with Yvonne Rainer),"[82] several of the critics attributed it solely to Paxton. Hughes expresses his appreciation for the repetitive structure of the dance in emphasizing the movement for its own sake:

> Perhaps you would have preferred one of the more sedate offerings of the evening, Steve Paxton's *Words Words* [sic], which he and Miss Rainer did wearing only what the French call "caches-sexes." This was, in effect, a dance in the nude, and its purpose was evidently to show that after the first surprise, nudity makes no difference at all. The dance was dignified, and by showing the same choreography three times (as a solo by each of the performers plus a repetition as a unison duet), Mr. Paxton made sure that

the dancing impressed itself upon the spectator as the significant aspect of the whole thing.

At the end, the performers might as well have been wearing fur coats for all the difference their lack of apparel made.[83]

Johnston saw the costumes as a comment on the standard modern dance costume, the leotard and tights which are suggestive of nudity. She found the dance ultimately rather puritanical. And like Hughes, she did not appreciate the title's indication of the dance's structure.

Mr. Paxton and Miss Rainer danced the former's *Words Words* [sic] naked — that is, naked except for one or two items required by law. The exposure was a natural extension (removal) of the revealing tights and leotards most dancers wear. And if the shock at first distracted from the dance, the novelty wore off soon enough and you were left with two bodies (you could watch the bodies, too) in a dance that was classically pure and not terribly interesting. . . . If the length of the dance and the absence of contact (neuter, sexually) were meant to offset the nudity, I didn't mind. But I wouldn't have minded some relationship either. Since they both performed with total clarity and self-possession, anything would seem possible, in retrospect at least.[84]

The fourth dance on the program was Elaine Summers's *Suite*, which Johnston simply described as "funny and well-timed, much better than the Woodstock version."[85] Munt thought it "trite, but fortunately short."[86] This time the "Galliard" was danced by Rudy Perez, Summers, and John Worden; "Sarabande" [sic] again by Emerson; and "Twist" by Trisha Brown, Philip Corner, Ruth Emerson, Malcolm Goldstein, John Herbert McDowell, Gretchen MacLane, Perez, Arlene Rothlein, Carolee Schneemann, Carol Summers, Elaine Summers, Jennifer Tipton, and Worden.[87]

The fifth dance, Carol Scothorn's *The Lazarite*, was an homage to Doris Humphrey, who had died in 1958.[88] Scothorn had been awarded the second Doris Humphrey Fellowship at the Connecticut College American Dance Festival, in 1962. Part of the fellowship included the performance fee for a new work, and Scothorn first performed *The Lazarite* at the Festival on 11 August 1962. The musical accompaniment was by Daniel Jahn.[89] Munt thought the dance "sentimental and oddly 'old,' but [Scothorn] is a good performer." According to Rainer, "it had a lot of early modern dance movements, Humphrey-like swings." Johnston thought the dance "communicated the idea that 'there is no death.'"[90]

After intermission came the sixth dance, Rainer's *Three Seascapes*, which she had already performed on the March 5, 1962 program at the Maidman Playhouse. Rainer describes the dance as:

[A] solo in three parts: 1) Running around the periphery of the space in a black overcoat during the last movement of Rachmaninoff's Second Piano Concerto. 2) Traveling with slow-motion undulations on an upstage-to-downstage diagonal during La Monte Young's *Poem for Tables, Chairs, Benches*. 3) Screaming fit downstage right in a pile of white gauze and black overcoat.[91]

She calls the first section of the dance "an even more ironic use [than in *We Shall Run*]" of the interplay between repetitious movement and flamboyant music, especially because she used a "bad recording" of the Rachmaninoff accompaniment. "The 2nd episode of the same solo is probably the purest example of repetition in my work: traveling on a diagonal with slow-motion undulations of pelvis and vague hand gestures....The movement was simple enough so that it could be observed as 'one thing.'"

Although to some the dance might have simply seemed like three disconnected actions, Marks, reviewing its first performance, found dramatic meaning in every part. She thought the second section suggested that Rainer was at sea, making her way "through imaginary waves to the squalling of chairs pushed across the lobby floor," and that in the third section Rainer "awoke screaming from a nightmare."[93]

Johnston, reviewing *Three Seascapes* in 1962, admired Rainer's Gertrude Stein–like use of repetition in several of her works, and noted the rigorous formal quality in this dance:

> In *Three Seascapes* Miss Rainer makes three incidents employing the same method even more stringently. First she dog-trots all over the stage, and sometimes lies down and gets up, wearing a black coat, to a luscious and amplified movement from the Rachmaninoff Second Piano Concerto. Two, she progresses ONCE across the stage, like a slow-motion spastic, if you can believe it, to the accompaniment of a number of tables and chairs moaning, scraping across the floor in the lobby....And three, she puts her black coat over a long piece of white gauze, lies down under both, and has a beautiful fit of screaming in a flying mess of coat and gauze.[94]

Lelia K. Telberg, writing about the first performance in *Dance Observer*, simply labeled *Three Seascapes* "far out."[95]

One way that *Three Seascapes* functioned didactically was in its use of quite disparate sound accompaniments. Although Rainer did not use any traditional, metrically corresponding choreography with music, she did list three types of sound that, even if set against movements that correspond to them in no way, provided expressive overlays for those movements. The powerfully romantic music, the repetitive, dissonant "new" music, and the violent sounds issuing from the dancer's own body were three of a number of possibilities of the relationship between sound and movement; i.e., the movement could correspond to the sound, counterpose the sound, or exist independently of it—and if independent, the movement could take on the expressive meaning of the juxtaposed sound.

After *Three Seascapes* came Herko's *Little Gym Dance before the Wall for Dorothy*, dedicated to Dorothy Podber, a friend of Herko's.[96] Johnston describes the dance in two contradictory reports:

> Fred Herko's *Little Gym Dance Before the Wall for Dorothy* is a wonderful vignette: coming in straight out down the middle, removing jacket and boots, and sauntering off casually straight out down the middle.[97]

> I recall with wry affection Herko's *Little Dance Before the Gym Wall for Dorothy* [sic], in which he confronted the audience with his typical blend of audacious vanity and cynicism, then danced rings around himself in another characteristic mixture of technical finesse and baroque flourish, and finally swaggered off like the impossible renegade and accomplished dancer that he was.[98]

Whichever version is correct, Maxine Munt only commented, "Fred Herko is indeed the enfant terrible and his *Little Gym Dance*...shouted 'look at me, look at me'; he has yet to prove he belongs with this group."[99]

William Davis's *Field* was the eighth dance in Concert #3. Like Rainer's *Three Seascapes*, *Field* played with the ambiguities of expressive dramatization that emerge from juxtapositions of separate items. But in *Field* the movements were not always accompanied by the same sounds; the dancing was fixed but the sounds were indeterminate. *Field* was a duet for Davis and Barbara [Dilley] Lloyd. The dancers wore transistor radios attached to belts. The program credits the musical accompaniment as follows: "for Mr. Davis, radio station WABC; for Miss Lloyd, radio station WINS."[100] Both stations were popular music stations that interspersed rock music with news reports and commercial announcements.

According to Davis:

> I was interested in different kinds of partnering images in the context of the double sound source, some from social dancing, some from concert dancing, ballet partnering. And I imagine there was inevitably a certain ironic commentary on those "two hearts beating as one" images. But I was also, of course, very involved with the physical problems and possibilities of lifting, counterbalancing weights, supporting; with the evolution of those configurations, and how they can arise out of two related solos, or resolve back into two related solos. I was trying to work out some interesting variations on some classical themes.
>
> While there were quite a few lifts of various kinds in the dance, and some short bits of social ballroom dancing, there were also many sequences where the relationships were just those between two people dancing in the same space, sometimes fairly distant from one another.[101]

The dance lasted for around fifteen minutes, and both dancers wore leotards and tights. Lloyd also wore crystal earrings and a bracelet, "as a slight echo of a 'comedy of manners' quality in parts of the dance," Davis recalls. "Also, I was associating crystal with radios."[102]

The movement was not improvised, but at times the correspondences with the words or music on the radios struck spectators as impossibly apt. Johnston wrote in her review, "I have to mention that just when they came lyrically together Miss Lloyd's radio decided to broadcast 'Moon River.'"[103] Davis wore a knee pad because he had hurt his leg during rehearsal. His radio broadcast a news report on a baseball player who had hurt his knee.[104]

> It may have seemed occasionally that the movement was either improvised or designed flexibly so that we could pick up on things that occurred in the sound, because "meanings" arose frequently and radio broadcasts are obviously not predictable. But, given the character of the movement (although I think this would happen with almost any movement) and the range of material broadcast by both stations, certain expressive coincidences were inevitable. They were part of the nature of the piece. In performance, we were not reacting to anything in the sound.

The physical fact of the radio's closeness to the body, seeming almost a part of the dancer's body, also gave the sound accompaniment a special expressive value.

> There was a moment when I was standing behind Barbara [Lloyd], supporting her in attitude, with my right hand resting at her waist, near her radio, and our left arms together out in 2nd position. She was on relevé, and as she centered the attitude balance, I carefully turned off her radio, and stepped slowly back away from her to the rear of the space. My radio continued to play as I stood at a distance, and Barbara held the balance a very long time in silence. She finally stretched it out into arabesque, and then stepped out into the next sequence of movement and turned on her radio again.
>
> Remy Charlip talked to me at some length about that moment, which he thought appalling. He said it was as though I had stifled her, or strangled her. I was startled at that interpretation, because my conscious intention was to focus on the precarious stillness of the balance, to suspend the sound as the movement was suspended, like a held breath. But, Freudian considerations apart, I suppose it was a perfectly appropriate reaction, since one of the things I wanted with the radios was that sense of separate, personal aura coming from each of us.

About the title, Davis explains that, like *Crayon* in the first concert, the word resonated with various sorts of meaning.

> I was thinking of an electro-magnetic field, or a field of superimposed radio waves. Of an invisibly patterned or loaded atmosphere, an emotional field. And also of field in the sense of a physical space, a field of action.[105]

The ninth dance was *Newspaper Event*, choreographed by Carolee Schneemann. Schneemann had been making collages and paintings since the early 1950s, and, after graduate school in painting at the University of Illinois, she moved to New York in 1961 with the composer James Tenney.

Through Tenney, Schneemann met Corner and Goldstein. Tenney worked as composer-in-residence at Bell Telephone Labs in New Jersey, where he met Billy Klüver, a Swedish engineer who was interested in avant-garde art, occasionally assisting artists with technical aspects of their work and making touring and financial connections between artists and the Swedish government. Through Klüver, Schneemann began to go to environments and Happenings; she appeared in Claes Oldenburg's *Store Days* in February 1962, and in May she created her own "display" in collaboration with Philip Corner, *An Environment for Sounds and Motions.*[106] She began taking dance classes with Arlene Rothlein, whom she met through Goldstein, and Corner suggested that Schneemann join the choreography workshop then meeting at Rainer's studio. There she first worked on *Newspaper Event* and a children's fantasy unrealized until 1969, *Banana Hands.*[107]

Schneemann's sensibility was a sensuous one, luxuriating in colors, textures, moving forms. Influenced by Artaud, whose *The Theater and Its Double* she had read in 1960, as well as by Wilhelm Reich, D'Arcy Thompson, and Henri Focillon, she evolved a personal aesthetic that was nature-embracing and emotionally charged. She rejected chance methods and the Zen serenity that informed other artists' use of everyday things in their natural states. She wanted to use "what moves me," she wrote not "the Frozen, the expanse of slight sensation, the twist to existing conventions: not to be shocked, disturbed, startled, not to exercise the senses thoroughly. . . .to be left as you were found, undisturbed, confirmed in all expectations."[108] In regard to aleatory techniques, she also felt the need to take a position:

> I don't work with "chance methods" because "method" does not assume evidence of the senses; chance is a depth run on intent, and I keep it open, "formless." "Chance method" is a contrary process for my needs and a semantic contradiction which carries seeds of its own exhaustion in its hand clasp of chance-to-method. Method as orderly procedure, way to classification, arrangement—like a bag into which gestalten insight allows chance to pour; what might happen, possibility, unpredictable agent, unknown forces. . .so corralled, netted, become a closing in. Depth run of it—"chance," is way of necessity to surface and tentacled riches are not captured by method.
>
> Process with material/image leads exploratively, spontaneously. Chance, recognition and insistence with discoveries *is* field of action. Visual-kinesthetic sources are not abstract-theoretical conceptions for my process. In bearing. Slug and release—fling it out and pull in the nets; expect to be surprised.[109]

Schneemann's paintings sometimes had moving parts in them. She saw her "concretions"—performances—as extensions of those painting-constructions. "Performers of glass, fabric, wood. . .all are potent as variable gesture units: color, light and sound will contrast or enforce the quality of a particular gesture's area of action and its emotional texture." But at the same time, she acknowledged an interest in the differences between the relatively static object and the performance-in-time. The audience might be more active physically in a performance but, she felt, ironically, it is visually more passive when confronted with fleeting sensations and images.

> The force of a performance is necessarily more aggressive and immediate in its effect — *it* is projective. The steady exploration and repeated viewing which the eye is required to make with my painting-constructions is reversed in the performance situation where the spectator is overwhelmed with changing recognitions, carried emotionally by a flux of evocative actions and led or held by the specific time sequence which marks the duration of a performance.[110]

In making her concretions, Schneemann used space and time as additional components in which to extend the articulation of elements she used in her static constructions; for specific aesthetic reasons, she was not interested in editing the material to meet theatrical expectations.

> I have the sense that in learning, our best developments grow from works which initially strike us as "too much"; those which are intriguing, demanding, that lead us to experiences which we feel we cannot encompass, but which simultaneously provoke and encourage our efforts. Such works have the effect of containing more than we can assimilate; they maintain attraction and stimulation for our continuing attention. We persevere with that strange joy and agitation by which we sense unpredictable rewards from our relationship to them. These "rewards" put to question — as they enlarge and enrich — correspondences we have already discovered between what we deeply feel and how our expressive life finds structure.[111]

Schneemann used the word "concretion" to define her performances because she held that through gesticulation and gestation the "fundamental life of any material I use is concretized." With dancers that gesticulation could occur in any part of the body as well as through the voice.[112]

In *Newspaper Event* each of seven dancers was assigned body parts: spine, Arlene Rothlein; legs/face, Ruth Emerson; shoulders/arms, Deborah Hay; neck/feet, Yvonne Rainer; hands, Carol Summers; head, Elaine Summers; fingers, John Worden. Schneemann herself was "free agent/crawling." The dancers used the assigned body parts as the source and focus of their movements. In a sense their goal was to create objects rather than to dance.

> The source of emphasis, of internal focus and projective insistence was to determine all functions or actions in relation and contrast to the overall movements of the body. Phrasing, duration, repetition, the "scale" of gesture, would all be improvised within the centralized and overlapping movements generated by the instructions. The ruminative, meditative attitude evoked in working concertedly, in making something with the hands seemed a basic sensory value rarely explored publicly.[113]

The performers entered with cartons full of newspapers. Schneemann brought in benches and stools. The dancers "unfold and throw newspaper cascades in the central area, fast as possible. Thickest amount of paper in the center, then outward...in a circular sweep." Each dancer then followed his or her instructions. Rothlein and Emerson were to use horizonality; Hay was to use the refrain "I'll huff and I'll puff" both as energy and in her voice. Rainer's instructions involved making a huge pedestal out of newspapers, becoming tiny and then large, engulfing someone. Both Carol and Elaine Summers were instructed to "make yourself a little something to wear from the newspapers." Carol Summers had a vocal refrain, "That's beautiful," while Elaine Summers's line was "I need breakfast." Worden's actions were meant to be private and self-indulgent, and if anyone came near the "little something amusing" he was making, his response was to call them "you little prick" or "you dumb ass." Schneemann, as the free agent, timed the action, which lasted for ten minutes, and also planted flags on performers, crawling with the flag in her mouth to do so.[114]

Newspaper Event was based on the idea of "an organism interchanging its parts (phagocyte)." Schneemann outlines five principles in her construction of the piece:

> 1) The primary experience is the body as your own environment. 2) The body within the actual, particular environment. 3) The materials of that environment — soft, responsive, tactile, active, maleable (paper...paper). 4) The active environment of one another. 5) The visual structure of the bodies and material defining space.

Schneemann had watched the dancers in the workshop using random movements, chance methods, and nontechnical movement, but was disappointed that they seemed to be working as autonomous entities even in group dances. Her response, in *Newspaper Event,* was to provide a framework within which they could interact physically and spontaneously.

> I wanted touch, contact, tactile materials, shocks — boundaries of self and group to be meshed and mutually evolving. *Newspaper Event* was a first attempt to provide specific instructions through which contact and improvisation could activate neglected thresholds of awareness. Individuals would create their own activity and its momentum, while responding to and incorporating the "intrusions" and unexpected conjunctions with others....There was no underlying basis of abstract structure or rule, no pre-determined movement patterns.[115]

Jill Johnston thought *Newspaper Event* a "mad orgy" that was an "attraction."[116] Allen Hughes was intrigued by the performance, even though he thought its effect was partly accidental.

> Did you ever see a dance accompanied, decorated and — in a sense — dictated by the shredding of newspapers? I am not sure I have either, but in this program Miss Schnee-

mann had a number of dancers involved in what was titled *Newspaper Event*, and I assume she thought what they did was dancing. Perhaps it was.

In any case, it was surprisingly intriguing visually, and it actually — if accidentally — built to a climax despite its improvisational character. Each dancer had been given an action-motif to perform as he or she went through the business of tearing up the papers and romping in them, and these motifs collided in many interesting ways.

One girl, for example, rolled on the floor, another went through the motions of dressmaking with papers, a man knelt on the floor, and from time to time dancers jumped on his back. Other dancers had other characteristic movements. Unfortunately, they had also been given motifs to speak at random, and these weakened the impact of the whole.[117]

Concert #4 began with an unnumbered item, perhaps meant to be a prelude or an overture: Steve Paxton's *Music for Word Words*. It consisted of the inflation and deflation of a twelve-foot square "transparent plastic room with arms and legs. Paxton inside, deflating room into costume which was worn as he left. Rainer with tape recorder catching ambient sounds: audience entry, vacuum cleaner, deflation."[118] The "music" was performed separately from the dance; *Word Words*, on the previous night, had been performed in silence. Paxton was specifically interested in creating a situation that contrasted with Cunningham's method of collaborating with composers. He also cites Aileen Passloff's influence; in some of her concerts, the music came in between the dances. "You had music, dance, music, dance. It was music for the dance, but everything came sequentially, not simultaneously."[119] Munt, commenting that Paxton and Davis had "galvanized the atmosphere and at the same time added to the excessive length and repetition" on the first night's concert, disapproved of *Music for Word Words* and thought Concert #4 "not as good" as the previous night. "Shame on you Steve Paxton," she wrote, "for the monotony of *Music for Word Words*, fortunately I had a good book with me."[120]

The dance that was numbered one on the printed program was Paxton's *English*, performed by Trisha Brown, Lucinda Childs, Ruth Emerson, Deborah Hay, Tony Holder, Shielah Komer, Paxton, Rainer, Rothlein, Linda Sidon, and Jennifer Tipton.[121] Paxton describes the dance:

Group configurations done no faster than a walk. Pedestrian activities mimed in middle section. Properties: 3 plastic screens, 6-½' × 3' hung at thirds of the performing space width, 1 & 3 near audience, 2 upstage. Skin-colored make-up over face and brows.[122]

Tony Holder's recollection is that Paxton again made a score using sports photographs.

There was a chorus that marched across the stage. People would face in different directions and mime some everyday object or event — cooking or washing — and then they'd go back to the chorus. The chorus just marched back and forth. One or two soloists performed the score, which had to do with a catcher jumping up in the air and game positions. You'd go from one position to another, and how you made the transition Steve [Paxton] didn't really care.[123]

Childs thought *English* was less hard-edged, more loosely constructed than *Proxy*.[124] According to Rainer,

> "*English*" was another one of Steve [Paxton]'s intricate, Jesuitical titles. "English" is one of those words that both is itself and stands for something — both symbol and sign. Again he was involved with trying to make everyone look alike. So all of these people soaped out their lips and eyebrows and put on pale, fleshtone pancake makeup. We all came in with these pie-faces, marching in a line, some people facing forward and some people facing backward. Then there were a lot of moving configurations, taken from group photographs, in which each person had one role in the group. It would start in one place, and then one person at a time would walk to another point — say, on a diagonal — so that the whole configuration would gradually be repositioned. One of the poses was a "tango-kiss," in which Steve and I went downstage center, I bent backwards, and he bent over me.[125]

Lucinda Childs was the first person in the Judson workshop who asked Philip Corner to compose music for her dance. The dance was *Pastime*, item number two on Concert #4. *Pastime* was a solo in three parts, a succinct statement involving three different angles of viewing the body and its movements. Childs says that it lasted for eleven or twelve minutes,[126] but a program for a later performance lists its duration as five minutes.[127] In the first section, Childs walked along a predetermined pathway: entering the gym; turning to the right, then walking downstage for a few steps and further downstage right; then along the length of the gym, in front of the audience; then turning left to walk upstage.[128] The movement happened primarily in her right leg, "going in and out, isolated," and involved standing in profile repeatedly.[129] After a blackout, Childs appeared inside a blue jersey bag, sitting on the floor.[130] The same kinds of movements were done by the right leg, but this time coming in and out of the bag, expanding and contracting its shape. Childs had already performed this section as a student at Sarah Lawrence and had made this part of the dance partly as a satire on Alwin Nikolais, who often used stretchy fabrics and various props to distort the shape of his dancers' bodies. This part of *Pastime* might have reminded viewers also of Martha Graham's *Lamentation* (1930), a solo that used such a costume expressively to create a tension and contraction of the body in a highly visible shape. For Childs, the "bag section" in *Pastime* was meant to be humorous. "It was funny to see this foot slowly going out of the bag. I could stretch the bag the entire length of my body. At one point it completely flattened out. And people laughed at that section." In the final section, Childs presented a back view of her body, with her head dropped down so that her face could be seen from the top. "It was like another profile."[131]

Childs wanted the sounds of water to accompany her dance, and she had made a tape herself. But she couldn't isolate the sounds of water from ambient sounds, and she asked Corner to help her.[132] As Corner remembers:

> She had recorded a few drips and drops of water on a cheap tape recorder and then asked for help with it. I listened to the material and said, "Would you mind if I just started from scratch? Let me take the idea of water, but I think I can do better."
>
> She said "Fine," so I did a piece with the spray and gurgling of faucets, and I made three different pieces for that dance. I made more music than I needed, because you couldn't tell exactly how long Lucinda's dance was going to last. That clarified something: that the music, in formal terms, was endless. I wasn't doing something with a built-in climax, movement, or necessity. I was doing something that had endless variety, but was essentially constant. The kind of thing La Monte [Young] was doing at the time is the other end of the same pole. It doesn't matter if you have one event that never changes or a hundred thousand events which are changing all the time.
>
> At that time it seemed not to be enough. Just to stay with that for seven or eight minutes? It took me a long time to do it. But since then I've done a lot of pieces that go on and on, including a piece that was one note lasting for five days.
>
> The music for *Pastime* also turned out to be prophetic. My Korean name means "Contemplating Waterfall," and it was given to me by my calligraphy teacher. I have realized that I have a very passionate feeling for water, and I've since done many water pieces.[133]

Paxton remembers Childs's early work, especially *Pastime*, as "like haikus. Terse. And she was another glazed performer, but on her it looked fantastic, maybe because she has a mannequin's face, and one is used to their impassiveness. Her face simply projected in some way." The "bag section" reminded Paxton strongly of Graham and Nikolais. "It had a slightly ironic quality, but always very cool and very concise. Everything seemed quite considered and quite right and very calmly done."[134]

Childs auditioned *Pastime* for the Young Choreographers Concert at the YMHA, and it was accepted, she thinks, "because it probably had some vaguely traditional look." She remembers that the jury selecting the dances were shocked by the work of the Judson choreographers.

> Lucas Hoving was freaking out. Yvonne [Rainer] did *Ordinary Dance*. Steven [Paxton] came out and ate an apple. [Hoving] said at some point, "For this they studied ballet?" We were all going to Mia Slavenska's class every day. By then I had stopped studying with Cunningham, because I was involved with Jimmy [Waring]. Everybody seemed to be going to Slavenska, so I went too. You had to keep your body together, even though there was a dichotomy between the discipline of that technique and the actual activity you were involved in.[135]

Louis Horst, reviewing *Pastime* at the YMHA, complained that Corner's music "sounded as though all the plumbing at the Y was out of order."[136] Jaffe thought the dance expressed the alienation of people in the modern, mechanized world. "Lucinda Childs...condensed a world of blankets into a dance to the sound of water, rushing maddeningly in and out of enormous automatic washing machines. It...left one with the feeling that laundry is not the only thing that comes out of the machine spotless and without human character."[137] Johnston called it "an intense, cryptic solo of three episodes, including a very difficult part, moving so slowly, seated in a piece of manipulated material."[138]

Childs had grown up in New York City, where she was born in 1940. As a child she had taken dance classes, but she aspired to be an actress. At fifteen, she began taking classes from Hanya Holm, who had come to the United States in the 1930s as an exponent of Mary Wigman's technique. At sixteen, Childs went to Colorado to study in Tamiris's summer session and, after performing with Tamiris, decided to become a dancer. Tamiris encouraged her to go to college at Sarah Lawrence, where Childs studied with Bessie Schönberg, Judith Dunn, and visiting teachers, including Merce Cunningham. On graduation she moved to New York City and immediately began classes at the Cunningham studio, where she had also attended classes during school vacations. While in college, she had studied with Nikolais. "Until Merce [Cunningham] came along, I was very interested in Nikolais' composition process, the way he would get people to build phrases. He was interesting, and I was very interested in Beverly Schmidt [who danced with Nikolais]. I would come into New York just to see her solo concerts."[139]

Trisha Brown's *Lightfall*, a structured improvisation for herself and Steve Paxton, was the third dance on the program. Based on "violent contact" improvisation Brown had been investigating with Simone Forti and Dick Levine, *Lightfall* was a series of stillnesses and perchings, to music by Simone [Forti] Morris.[140] The music was a tape of Forti whistling. Paxton and Brown would jostle up against each other in a high crouching position, then one would leap up on the other's back.[141] Paxton recalls, "I never fully comprehended the structure. We got it together in kind of a rush, and it was a bit of a tease to remember. There were sections of leaping up onto each other's backs, running sections, and turning sections. It had a casual movement quality with quite a lot of really rigorous endeavors."[142] Munt thought *Lightfall* "a total disappointment after [Brown's] *Trillium* [performed at the Maidman Playhouse] last season."[143] Johnston, however, admired Brown's use of improvisation and relaxed spontaneity.

Using the simple action of waiting (football style, hands on knees) as a recurrent "base," the dancers initiated a spontaneous series of interferences — ass-bumping and back-hopping—which were artless, playful excursions in quiet expectancy and unusual surprises. Miss Brown has a genius for improvisation, for being ready when the moment calls, for being "there" when the moment arrives. Such facility is no mere tongue-wagging, but the result of an interior calm and confidence and of highly developed kinesthetic responses. She's really relaxed and beautiful.[144]

The next dance was a collaboration between Robert Morris and Robert Huot, two artists. Called *War*, it consisted of the two men, dressed in "armor" that was a collage of found objects, whacking at each other with sticks and releasing white doves, while La Monte Young played gong music *to Henry Flynt, April 1960*.[145] Rainer recalls *War* as "incredible."

> The whole place was in darkness, and La Monte [Young] was up in the cage. He very slowly made the gong vibrate with soft beats. That went on for a good five minutes. The lights went up, these two guys in these outlandish costumes released two pigeons and ran toward each other, yelling and screaming at the top of their lungs, beat at each other with wooden weapons, which splintered, and the lights went off. And that was the piece.
>
> They had padding and one of them had a shield with a picture of Eisenhower on it. It was somewhere between medieval and pop art.[146]

Henry Flynt, to whom Young had dedicated his composition, was one of the composers who had participated in the series at Yoko Ono's loft in 1961. Rainer went to Flynt's concert there and reports that "the outstanding event of the evening was Henry Flynt holding a taut rubber band up to his own ear and plucking it."[147]

Paxton describes *War*, which he did not like:

> The came on dressed like Tweedledee and Tweedledum, hugely camouflaged and armored, with wooden swords and gauntlets, and they whacked away at each other for a while. They really laid into each other. And then at the end they released doves from the interior of their costumes, which flocked up to the ceiling. It was a very successful piece in terms of the audience reaction. I thought it was a piece of shit. Where was the concept? What was this political cartooning that was going on? I just didn't understand it, I suppose.
>
> Something as light-hearted as that just went right by me. I was very seriously interested in self-reflexive titles and pedestrian movements. There was an anti-war movement then, certainly an anti-nuclear movement, but this didn't seem about that, this was just preposterous.[148]

Listing *War* as one of the "attractions" of the series, Johnston writes that the piece was "Bob Huot and Bob Morris dressed (smothered) in the most incredible, gorgeous panoply and trying to kill each other for real."[149]

After intermission, Deborah Hay's *City Dance*, number five on the program, followed.[150] Jill Johnston called it "an imaginative abstraction of hurried motion in complex, dispersed patterns."[151] According to Emerson,

Hay had made a score for the dance by "collecting data," listening to the sounds outside her basement apartment and timing them over several days.[152] The dancers (Brown, Childs, Emerson, D. Hay, MacLane, Paxton, and Rainer)[153] wore leotards and tights with different everyday items; Brown, for instance wore a scarf, Paxton a headband, Rainer gloves, and Emerson a pointed hat.[154] The music is credited to Richard Andrews.[155] Perhaps *City Dance*, too, was seen by those who looked for dramatic meaning as a piece about the loneliness of modern life.

Dance number six was Arlene Rothlein's *It Seemed to Me There Was Dust in the Garden and Grass in My Room*, dedicated to Mary Rudman, with music by Malcolm Goldstein.[156] Made in honor of Rothlein's aunt, who had recently left a mental institution, the dance was a lyric solo.[157] Paxton and Childs both remember only that it was "romantic."[158] Munt thought Rothlein's solo was "the one outstanding event of this evening. . . . [Rothlein] is a lovely lyrical dancer with a true feel for movement, light as a feather, but again, oh so long."[159] Johnston writes:

> And Arlene Rothlein she was a sweet breath of spiced lilacs in her solo *It Seemed to Me There Was Dust in the Garden and Grass in My Room*. I loved this mixed-up patchwork piece, even though several transitions were awkward because a few gestures were not truly assimilated.[160]

Rothlein, born in New York in 1939, began to dance while a student at Erasmus Hall High School. She studied at the New Dance Group, with Mary Anthony, and at Cunningham's studio.[161] By 1963 she was performing with James Waring.[162] She also auditioned for the YMHA concert and was chosen to perform her solo there. Jaffe thought Rothlein's dance on the Young Choreographer's Concert, like Keen's *Dawning*, contributed to her own feeling that "modern dance is a most perfect medium to communicate the tensions of our world, with a laugh and poignant loveliness in the bargain."

> *It Seemed to Me There Was Dust in the Garden and Grass in My Room* by Arlene Rothlein was also full of meaning and perception. It turned eclecticism into a nightmare and made one wonder if the dilettante is not the unhappiest man on earth. Miss Rothlein managed to convey in one short piece all the exhaustion of trying to keep up with every period of music and dance while achieving real involvement in none.[163]

Judith Dunn's *Index,* a duet for herself and Steve Paxton, was number seven on the program. The music was by Robert Dunn.[164] Although Judith Dunn had participated in Robert Dunn's choreography class as an assistant, she had not made any dances of her own in the class. She had stage-managed Concert #1 at the Judson and danced in several dances on that first program, but *Index* was the first piece she choreographed and showed publicly since joining Cunningham's company. The chance to do her own choreography soon led to her leaving Cunningham to work on her own. Judith Dunn believed strongly in the value of chance as a choreographic method, and she used aleatory techniques to create *Index.* The movement phrases included Dunn giving Paxton five coins while he held his hands behind his back, Dunn leaning against Paxton with her back arched and her hands behind her head, then sliding down to the floor and stepping on her hands. The dance took Dunn several weeks to make, and she considered it quite elaborate. When she finished the dance, she realized that it seemed dramatically expressive. "It was all about conflicts, and I didn't start out to make it that way at all."[165]

According to Paxton, "it had a lot of references to indexes, including index fingers. One of the things I had to do was hop turns, very quickly, in arabesque — an airplane or helicopter propeller image — rolling onstage."[166]

Robert Dunn describes the music he made for *Index*:

> I prepared a score for [a] small chorus of 6 to 8 people, giving each a set of cards with instructions for performing vowel and consonant sounds, and asking them to prepare vocal events from their own combinations and sequencing of these, following certain guidelines. In rehearsal and performance I served as conductor, controlling the density of the sound by signalling the performers as to entries and silences, varying loudnesses, and choice of events. The concert was in the downstairs gymnasium of the church, and the chorus was placed behind the audience seated on bleachers, in a small cage probably for the storage of sports equipment. It was purposefully made to resemble in effect the electronic music of the day, without the sizable expense of electronic gadgetry, and perhaps with a somewhat troubling extra dimension from its live human source.[167]

Jill Johnston does not write about the dance in terms of the accidental expressive value Judith Dunn saw in it, but in purely formal terms:

> This is a long, impressive dance combining many rigorous or lyric phrases and "events." What I liked especially was a phrase near the beginning when Miss Dunn leans against her partner, looks at him long and soft, turns and slides slowly down his torso. Aside from the beauty of contact, I liked it because it was one of few moments when Miss Dunn relaxed from the neck up. As a dancer of fine command and technical accomplishment, she could afford to be more indulgent. Another arresting episode was a jagged succession of tense pretended balances followed by lunges of one at the other around the neck to make both collapse and crash on the floor.[168]

The final event of the evening was Philip Corner's *Certain Distilling Processes,* a musical composition in which four dancers (Davis, Rainer, Rothlein, and Beverly Schmidt) were the conductors of seventeen "performers" who made music on a variety of objects. The performers were: Ansel Baldonado, Joseph Bloom, Joseph Byrd, Michael Corner, Philip Corner, Robert Dunn, Malcolm Goldstein, John Herbert McDowell, Charlotte Moorman, Eric Regener, Joshua Rifkin, Barbara Salthe, Stan Salthe, Carolee Schneemann, Florence Tarlow, Philip Wofford, and Vincent Wright. Norma Marder sang.[169]

Corner had given each dancer a score of calligraphic drawings. The dancer-conductors made gestures according to their interpretations of the drawings, and then the musicians assigned to watch certain dancers reinterpreted those gestures into sounds.[170] Thus the composer's score became music after two sets of translations by several sets of autonomous groups, in much the same way that Paxton hoped his dancers would learn the dance at a remove from the personal mark of the choreographer.

Beverly Schmidt remembers:

> Philip [Corner] came over to the house one day, and he had a big roll of butcher's paper, and he had made a graphic score, that looked like calligraphy. He gave each performer a copy of it, and we just worked on our own. We did not come together until the end. I interpreted it in my own way. I don't know if all the conductors had the same score. I just very conscientiously studied the score. I did something that was very set, very specific, and very detailed. And then there was a group of musicians who followed me. I didn't see them before hand, and they didn't know what I was going to do, I guess. But they had certain cues to pick up from me.
>
> I remember that one of the performers—maybe it was Yvonne [Rainer]—came up with a solution that involved putting a sweater on and taking it off. And I thought, "Gee, that's interesting; I got a totally different interpretation of it." It was based on a purely visual thing, a shape. I somehow related the shape in the space of what I did to the picture that I saw. And since I had a background of abstraction in working with space and shape and time, it was easy enough to connect to that. I also had costumes, and I remember putting things on and taking them off, but it was less pedestrian; it was different. I never really got into the pedestrian style of what the Judson people did. There was a contingent there that made everything very leisurely, the way it would be in real life. I never took that up as a style.[171]

Johnston found *Certain Distilling Processes* "an amazing musical event" and the seventeen performers "intriguing."[172] Munt thought both final events—Schneemann's *Newspaper Event* on Concert #3 and Corner's *Certain Distilling Processes* on Concert #4—were, predictably, "production numbers," and boring ones at that, "nothing more than exercises in improvisation for an acting class, or a group of first graders, or twenty minutes of self-indulgence, sometimes vulgar, sometimes silly, but never evocative."[173]

With her review of Concerts #3 and #4, Maxine Munt concluded that "within this group they are already beginning to quote each other, to achieve the sameness of look and performance, which could become a dead end."[174] Jill Johnston was far more sanguine, even enthusiastic:

> The revolution in dance is upon us. The revolution has been going on for fifteen years. But now the numbers of people are impressive. Just a little over a year ago you could

still despair over the rare occasions when you might see the few isolated choreographers who made anything worthwhile because they were proceeding (and continue) alone to make dance within themselves and of the present moment.

Johnston singled out Rainer as "the greatest thing since Isadora crossed the Atlantic, or St. Denis saw that Egyptian cigarette poster, or any other important moments you can think of in the lives of several astonishing ladies a few decades ago."[175]

Concerts #3 and #4 were a historical step for the Judson workshop group for a number of reasons. First, they represented a consolidation as well as a broadening of the group: They were the first fruits of the cooperative activity that had matured independently of Robert Dunn's class, and they were the product of other networks of artists outside the Waring-Cunningham circles. The musicians and visual artists played a far greater role as collaborators in these concerts, on the whole, than they had in the past. Second, the range of dances on the program showed not only the variety of choreographic and technical styles, but also the consideration of the roots and branches of modern dance, its past and its future. These were dances, like Scothorn's *The Lazarite,* that stood firmly within a particular tradition; dances, like Davis's *Field,* that proudly called on a number of dance techniques while experimenting with the theatrical aspects in an avant-garde manner; dances, like Summers's *Suite* or Childs's *Pastime,* that manipulated or satirized historical or personal styles. There were also dances, like Rainer's *We Shall Run* and Paxton's *English,* Schneemann's *Newspaper Event,* and Corner's *Certain Distilling Processes,* that redefined the physical activity necessary to define an action as a dance. Nondance movement was called into service as material for a dance, raising the aesthetic point that the material that goes into a dance may not be the criterion that distinguishes it as an art work. Third, as discussed above, the relationship of dance to music was investigated and resolved in a variety of ways. Fourth, the relationship of language to dance, both in titling and in the performance itself, was examined. The nature of costumes—from the near nudity of *Word Words* to the shaggy armor of *War* to the leather jacket and boots of *Little Gym Dance Before the Wall for Dorothy*—was similarly scrutinized. Like Pop artists, the Judson choreographers were fascinated by the everyday and put mundane objects and activities in their dances in ways that "made them strange," as the Russian Formalist critics had described in literature. A newspaper used as clothing or as something to shred and play in; a radio blaring banally as the background for a romantic pas de deux; references to football and other athletics, to social dancing, to daily activities—all these elements were a way of making the viewer stop to examine more closely the things one ordinarily takes for granted. And finally, the choreographic structures themselves departed from traditional methods in that they often focused on the movement itself, calling attention to its details in a way very little choreography had before. Rather than an image, a story, an atmosphere, or a phrase, the various choreographic strategies (repetition, improvisation, task instructions, "one thing," frozen moments) foregrounded the movements, the smallest possible segment of a dance work. In many ways, the dances were expressive — they seemed to be "about" alienation, rebellion, human vulnerability. But very often through formal techniques of distancing — as in *Certain Distilling Processes,* the photographic poses of *English,* the chance scores of *Index,* the nudity of *Word Words,* the cartoon violence of *War* — a sense of humanity shone through, a human scale and intimacy that early modern dance once had but eventually lost.

4

The Plot Thickens

On 28 and 29 April 1963, Yvonne Rainer presented an evening-length work in five sections for six dancers. The work was called *Terrain*. The first concert held in the sanctuary of the church since the workshop had begun the previous fall, it was also the first event that used the title Judson Dance Theater in its publicity. The advertisement in the *Village Voice* in the issue before the concert gives the following credits: "Music: Philip Corner, J. S. Bach. Essays: Spencer Holst. Lighting: Robert Rauschenberg. Dancers: Trisha Brown, William Davis, Judith Dunn, Steve Paxton, Albert Reid, [and Rainer]." Rainer had asked the workshop whether it would sponsor a solo evening (solo in the sense of presenting one person's choreography), and the group approved.[1]

Rainer had been working on *Terrain* since the fall of 1962, and her concerns in this dance are clear extensions of her explorations since even before Robert Dunn's class: the use of traditional dance forms threaded through with subversive, out-of-whack elements; repetition; the use of language in dance; the incorporation of natural movement and games; "loony bin" material; the fragmenting of movement and sound in a collage format; the permission for the dancers to make choices and exercise freedom within an overall structure.

On 1 December 1962, Rainer had completed several of the solos from *Terrain*, and these she performed on "A Program for Sounds and Bodies," at Beverly Schmidt's loft, 2 Pitt Street, titled *from the solo section*. The program also included *Animals* by Susan Kaufman with music by Joseph Byrd; *Lovely Music* by Philip Corner; *Three Tape Pieces* of music by James Tenney; *Lamentations of Jeremiah* by Malcolm Goldstein; and *Second Finale* by Philip Corner. Rainer performed four of the five solos from *Terrain*: "Spencer Holst #2 ('On Evil')," "Walking Solo," "Death Solo," and "Spencer Holst #1 ('On the Truth')."[2] The two Spencer Holst solos were identical in terms of their choreography. They began with a somersault and the arms then rising to overhead with a sharp flapping of the palms, then a sudden drop into plié, the arms opening to the side with the palms out. Twenty-three other movement sequences followed, many of them in styles and methods similar to the movement choices in *Dance for 3 People and 6 Arms,* although here there were more phrases and they were more complex. There were movements done as slowly as possible. There were simple, straightforward, athletic movements, like lying on the floor, bringing the legs straight up, bending the knees, rolling to the right. There were ballet steps in which the taut ballet line was collapsed by an undulating or hunched torso, limp wrists, a turned-in knee, or stiff, unyielding knees and elbows. There were movements made seemingly as cumbersome as possible—as in a cross-legged sit, collapse, and roll, after which the entire body was coiled up around the left leg, then hopped and collapsed. There was a quotation from jazz dancing—the arms held straight out to the side, fingers spread wide, while the legs alternated turning in to draw across the body, then hopping out to the side. At times parts of the body "led" other parts. Once the right hand scratched the ear. Toward the end of the Holst solos, there was a "narcissistic" movement involving watching the right hand running up the left arm, looking inside one's leotard, looking over the right shoulder and trying to peer down one's back, watching the left hand move down the right arm and slowly going into a parallel plié, ending on the left knee with the right hand coming up to the chin. The shorter Holst essay ended with this movement, then coming into a first position with the hands on hips, facing the audience. The longer Holst essay continued through three more actions, then ended in the same calm stance. During the course of this complex list of constantly changing, often polyrhythmic movement, Rainer recited prose by Spencer Holst. She had chosen two brief essays Holst had published privately in 1960 and distributed through the auspices of the Living Theater. "On the Truth" is a humorous, matter-of-fact tale about an essay Holst wrote about his great-grandfather, in which some of the "facts" turned out to be false. A philologist friend advises him to let the essay stand; she says, "The philology is not important to the essay. It is irrelevant." The essay concludes: " 'Vera!' I laughed, aghast, astonished, and amazed. What a way to use the word philology! What do you mean? What is philology? The truth?' " The second essay, "On Evil," is a more imagistic—but still quite direct, in terms of style—account of an attempt to "transfix the devil": a down-to-earth narrative about visions and a nightmare. Some of the sounds in "On Evil" bear a striking resemblance to the sound effects Rainer had already been using in her dances. Holst describes a vision, "a burning picture, a sacrifice to Blake. An embarrassment, cogs, clashes, and clangs—flashes in a dozen different brains—of alarm clocks, rattling bells, and buzzered twangs, and splintering glasses-crashes." Later, in a description of a nightmare: "The noise seemed louder...and as I fell forward, running, falling...blind...

the sounds kept pace with me...never behind me...never in front...
always on my right...and coming now obviously closer...not more than
10 feet away from me...tfff...tfff...tfff...."[3]

"Walking Solo" had nine elements, which were ordered and repeated
according to extemporaneous decisions in performance. All nine were variations on walking, including one with turns and an occasionally flung leg;
one completely asymmetrical, with one leg in bent relevé and the other leg
straight and flat-footed, "limp with bent swimming arms"; one that went
from a sudden high, taut, swooping arabesque to a squatting walk with undulating back; one with the arm crooking around the head, a trailing leg,
and a tumble. "Death Solo" was another choreographed sequence of
movement, with sharp, jackknifing actions, distorted facial positions—
including a frozen rictus grin with the hands gripping each other, held high
above the head—and a slow, stiff walk with the head turned, the mouth
open to emit a low, constant, loud, "a-eiou" wail.[4]

The solos, like the Holst essays, are matter-of-fact in their attitude
toward life and the body. The titles alone indicate both their directness and
their elemental status: walking, death, truth, evil. "Sleep" would come
later, in the April performance. The movements constitute a sampling of a
wide range of repertories: dance steps, children's play, sports, extreme or
unusual body states—from refined virtuosity to the grotesque. They challenge the dancer by putting every body part as well as the voice into play
simultaneously; they challenge the viewer by presenting movements with
shocking, frightening, and ugly connotations as well as those valued more
positively as graceful, strong, swift, or elegant.

The Pitt Street loft concerts drew a small audience who knew about
the events by word of mouth. On another program, or perhaps on the same
evening but unannounced on the printed program, Rainer performed
Three Satie Spoons at Pitt Street. The filmmaker Hollis Frampton remembers seeing Rainer for the first time there and feeling that she had challenged the entire tradition of modern dance when she made noises. Modern
dance had established certain cultural expectations, among them the mute-
ness of the dancer. Frampton recalls:

> In the middle of *Three Satie Spoons* she started making *noises*: little mewing sounds,
> squeaks, bleats. I was electrified, because it was totally disjunctive within the situation.
> There she was in a black leotard, doing something that *looked like* a dance. There was
> music. And then she did something that seemed to have nothing to do with dance; and
> there was the momentary question: Is she going crazy? Is this the moment? Are we wit-
> nessing it? Are *we* going crazy? Dance had been mute. The vocal capability of the
> dancer had been put beyond the pale. No mouth, or at most, the fixed mannequin smile
> of the ballerina. That brief performance of Yvonne's was totally memorable for me, not
> so much because of the choreography, or the music, or the skill of that young person.

What was memorable was a violent disruption of, a transgression against, the culturally expected, that had been introduced into the very heart of the thing. What was important was not that she made the specific noises that she did, but that that single gesture broke open the whole decorum of dance.[5]

Frampton compares this achievement in Rainer's work with the "violent ruptures of decorum" that powered so much of Rauschenberg's combines and his own methods of "physically tortur[ing] the surface of film," and other breaches in the traditions of painting and sculpture that raised the question of whether the object could be considered a member of that tradition.[6] In the *Terrain* solos, perhaps even more than in her previous choreography, Rainer's incorporation of the entire range of human movement and posture suddenly raised similar issues, challenging the very notion that dance can be recognized as a particular kind of movement, or even as a way of putting different kinds of movement together.

By February 1963, Rainer had finished "Duet Section," which would be the second part of *Terrain,* and she and Trisha Brown performed it on 15 February in a concert at Judson Hall, on Fifty-Seventh Street, that also included Rainer's *Ordinary Dance* and works by Phyllis Lamhut, Albert Reid, and William Davis. Rainer and Brown wore black tights and black lace push-up brassieres; their feet were bare. The music was a dense collage by Philip Corner, on tape, that included fragments of Massenet's opera *Thaïs,* music by Cecil Taylor and Clementi, and African music. In the first part of "Duet Section," Rainer performed a ballet adagio that she had learned in Nina Stroganova's intermediate ballet class at Ballet Arts studio, while Brown performed a solo that combined balletic movements in the head and upper body with burlesque bumps and grinds in the pelvis and lower back. "Duet Section" concluded with both dancers performing a sequence of nineteen "cheesecake" poses — such as standing into one hip with the head up, mouth open, one hand under the opposite breast and the other hand crooked limply toward the body; or one knee crossing the other leg, the hands crossed over the chest to rest on the shoulders, the back rounded, and the glance coy over one shoulder. This section ended with a movement nicknamed "palsy," which Rainer no longer remembers, and "wrestling," in which she and Brown, on all fours, climbed over and under one another. The poses were accompanied by "Meditation" from *Thaïs,* filtered electronically to sound eerie and attenuated, "lending a goofy overtone to our cheesecake postures," according to Rainer.[7]

Walter Sorell, reviewing the Judson Hall concert in a satirically "hip" tone, in *Dance Observer,* was very taken with both of Rainer's dances, seeing in her work a power that he can only attribute to a "male will."

I dig Yvonne. Her nuttiness has method and Gestalt. There is a male will in her wedded to a fantastic caprice. There is something fresh about her, I mean both connotations:

refreshing and forward, bold and obtrusive. In her "Duet Section" with Trisha Brown, she has taken a model as model, put sense into posing and caught the tragic aspect of clowning.[8]

Maxine Munt, however, thought that in "Duet Section," Rainer "contributed the only moment of vulgarity [in the Judson Hall concert], of tawdriness.... Two girls in black tights and revealing black lace bras are ridiculous, unless there is a reason, which she clearly didn't make clear."[9]

But to Rainer herself, as well as to some of her more sympathetic viewers, the reason to make ridiculous, goofy movements was perfectly clear:

> They so violated the conventions and standards of beauty and grace in a dancer that I felt were dominating me. I felt self-conscious about not coming up to those standards that were still dominating the training. I remember saying, "I will never get into the Cunningham company; yet here I am, a perfectly good, strong personality." Merce needed people who could do things in a certain way and had that balletic leg maneuverability. Unlike Jimmy [Waring], who took on a lot of misfits, Merce always had a classical look to his dancing. But even when Jimmy made dancey movement, it was always balletic.[10]

Rainer's dance seemed to say not only that any movement might be available as a choreographic choice, but also that any body, any person, could be worth watching.

By April, Rainer had completed the other three sections of *Terrain*—"Diagonal," "Play," and "Bach"—and had taught them to the other dancers. She also taught each dancer two of the solos. The group rehearsed in Rainer's Second Avenue studio for several months. According to Paxton, Rainer was precise and confident in choreographing the work on the group.

> The amazing thing about it was that it was Yvonne's first presentation and it displayed her real genius for organization. She has incredible drive and patience with that kind of work. In rehearsal she was calm, direct, right to the point—hard-working without being driven. She showed people the movement material, and then we rehearsed it. There were sections where one had choices.
>
> Working with Yvonne was a fairly intense rehearsal experience. We worked a couple of times a week for several months, but for her it must have been even longer, because the work was always totally prepared by the time she taught it. When we put new material together, she was always very clear about what she wanted or what freedom she wanted us to exercise.
>
> I have very pleasant memories of performing [*Terrain*]. It had some fairly virtuosic dancing that was a great challenge. The Spencer Holst solo was the first time that I performed speaking; I remember trying to get the sense of the story across while moving and going through all kinds of perambulations. And it was also a nice company. The people who were in the piece were quite intent on working on the material.[11]

Apparently the dancers chose which two solos they wanted to perform. Albert Reid recalls that although he admired Rainer's use of the voice while dancing, he preferred not to be vocal when he moved. He chose to do the "Sleep" and "Death" solos, partly for that reason, and partly because the movements in them appealed to him. " 'Death' had a very strange quality, with the tooth business, like a rictus grin. The movements weren't reminiscent of death; you didn't wilt and die. It was very hard to get the leg and arm sequences together and to do them right, because one part of the body was going one way and the other part was doing something else." Reid felt that *Terrain* was a watershed for him. He had been dancing in Alwin Nikolais's company and, tiring of the simplistic humor he felt was at the base of Nikolais's choreography, was studying with Merce Cunningham and at the Joffrey ballet school. He was attracted to the demands of Cunningham's technique; soon after, he was to join Cunningham's company. He had been choreographing his own works, and through his involvement in *Terrain* he became more committed to questioning movement conventions. "*Terrain* was shocking in the sense that it was different and exciting."12

Robert Rauschenberg designed the flyer for the evening. He also designed the lighting, which, like the lighting he did for Cunningham's company, was clear and bright. Paxton explains the genesis of Rauschenberg's style as a lighting designer in terms of both aesthetic preference and self-preservation:

> Bob [Rauschenberg] was doing the costumes for Cunningham and Nicola Cernovich was doing the lighting. Cernovich liked using saturated color. And Bob's costumes were always subjected to Nick's lighting, so I think that's how Bob decided to do the lights, too. His idea of lighting was that it shouldn't interfere. He liked clear colors and lots of white; in general, he tried to create an atmosphere for the piece that didn't get in the way. The atmosphere was almost always calm, bright, and very present. The objects and people always showed in their own way.
> By 1963, when he did the lights for *Terrain,* he'd been lighting for Merce for two years. When he started, he knew absolutely nothing about it; by this time, he was quite proficient. The lighting at Judson was pretty limited, with a six-dimmer board and only a few instruments. But I remember that the "Solo Section" and "Bach" were brightly lit; I remember high diagonals of ungelled light coming down in "Bach."13

According to Rainer, Rauschenberg had set up a single pole coming forward from the choir loft, with all the instruments in the center of the "stage," focused on different parts of the floor. It reminded Rainer of a boxing arena, with the clear, bright, even illumination and the lighting instruments visible, close to the performing area.14

The dancers wore black leotards and tights, except in "Duet," when Rainer and Brown wore black tights and Hollywood Vassarette brassieres.

Rainer slyly undermined the cult of personality in modern dance by adding white t-shirts or blouses to the costumes of some of the dancers during some of the sections. In "Diagonal," Davis, Reid, and Rainer were the "stars" singled out by white tops; in "Play," Dunn, Davis, and Brown wore white; in "Bach," Davis and Paxton wore white; during the "Solo Section," all the dancers wore black.

Terrain began with a kind of overture in which the six performers, staying in a clump, traversed the space along a diagonal, exited to the "out of bounds" space created by the imaginary lines the columns behind the performing area created, then reentered and walked all the way downstage and across the front, then out on a jagged line, pausing for a few seconds before each turn of direction. It was as if Rainer were displaying to the audience her basic materials: the dancers and the space. The first section in the dance proper was "Diagonal," a rule game that involved two categories of movements done traveling along the diagonal. Ten of the movements — which were numbered — could be done by any number of performers, from one to six; four of the choices — designated by letters — could be performed only by one or two. The movements were performed along either of the diagonals bisecting the performing area, always from upstage to downstage. A number of rules governed the actions of the dancers. They grouped and regrouped and performed the actions according to the signals (letters or numbers) that were called out. Special instructions regulated how one could leave or enter a group, or how a splinter group could form. "Sometimes," Rainer writes, "two groups would start simultaneously from two different corners, nearly collide in the center, somehow work through each other, and find that they were comprised of new numbers who had switched groups midway." The group movements included simple options like walking, running, crawling with stiff legs; a typical dance-class triplet run with a turn; and several more eccentric combinations — like walking with legs apart and stiff, the cheeks puffed and the fingers spread on either side of the face, running with the torso completely horizontal and the hands cupped over the ears and the face turned toward the audience, or waddling with arms windmilling, or walking in a squat, or jumping while the legs thrusted, the arms jerked, and the left shoulder and hip met. In one of these options, the group ran and halfway down hoisted the caller of that option high in the air. The four more complex combinations for one or two performers included running as if shot, in imitation of Jean-Paul Belmondo in the last scene of Godard's film *Breathless*. They also included distorted ballet steps, disjunctive movements of the legs and arms, and, in option D, four different leaps. Intermixed with these options and rules was another game, called "Passing and Jostling," in which the performer passed in front of another person, jostled him or her, and stood still until jostled by someone. There were more rules concerning moving back and forth between the two games.[15]

The diagonal line of the stage is one traditional path, according to classical ballet conventions, for the ballerina as she performs her solo variation. In several ballets it is also used to line up the corps de ballet in symmetrical patterns. Doris Humphrey, the most analytic of the modern dance choreographers, noted that the upstage right to downstage left diagonal is the most powerful path on the stage. But the diagonal is as potent in the daily life of the dancer as it is in the stage space: every dance class ends with sequences of movements that travel along the diagonal, which in practical terms is the longest line in any room. This ubiquitousness of the diagonal had occurred to Rainer as early as 1960, when for six months she shared a studio with Simone Forti and Ruth Ravon. The three would experiment together on different basic forms. Rainer recalls:

> In a class, it's leap, run, run, and the whole class does leap, run, run or whatever it is. When we did it, one person would go across with some movement, and the next person would use a movement in response to or influenced by the previous movement. The constant was the diagonal. Then we got into fancy things, like two at a time or going in opposite directions.
> As with a lot of things that Simone introduced—although I don't remember whether she introduced that—I was very impressed with the simplicity of it. Even though I'd taken a lot of classes, and you always ended by going across the diagonal, the fact that we were doing it *there* made me suddenly see it differently.[16]

Near the end of "Diagonal," which lasted about twelve minutes, Rainer and Brown changed into their "Duet" costumes. "Diagonal" continued until they returned. After "Duet" came "Solo Section." As noted above, each dancer had chosen two solos and in performance executed each one twice; he or she could also choose when to perform the solos, subject to certain restrictions. For example, Rainer wanted the Holst essays to be heard clearly, so only one Holst solo could be performed at a time. No more than three solos could occur simultaneously. In addition to "Spencer Holst #1 ('On the Truth')," "Spencer Holst #2 ('On Evil')" "Walking," and "Death," Rainer had added a fifth solo, "Sleep." This was a series of activities done close to the floor, often revolving around a manipulation of objects, which included a white vase, a small sandstone turtle, a glass paperweight, a toy gun, two hats, several dried mango pits, and a carpet bag into which all the other objects were placed at times. A yellow street barricade, brought into the space after "Duet," served as a "home base" for the dancers who were not performing solos. They stood at it in a relaxed but alert manner and occasionally moved it about. According to Rainer:

The activities [in "Sleep"] were eccentric: Taking things out of the bag while examining them and saying, "buzz, buzz, buzz." Crouching in a deep 2nd position plié with arms stretched tautly to the side—each hand grasping a small object—and exploding vocally with "WHAMMM!" Creeping in a squat position to place an object somewhere else in the space (this solo could cover as large an area as the performer wished). Stretching arms between two objects that were too far apart to touch and shifting the gaze from one object to the other (still in a crouched position. The performer never stood erect in this solo). "Sleeping" and sitting. By simply focusing all of the attention on the objects, by never taking notice of anything else going on around one, by clutching the bag or the objects to the body while simulating sleep—by all of this the performer gave an impression of an obsessed, maniacal character. The cool detachment of the dancers who were "not performing" around the barricade contrasted strongly with the idiosyncratic behaviour in both the "Death" and "Sleep" solos.[17]

The distribution of the solos was as follows: "Spencer Holst #1"— Brown and Paxton; "Spencer Holst #2—Davis and Rainer; "Walking"— Davis, Paxton, and Dunn; "Death"—Reid and Dunn; "Sleep"—Reid, Brown, and Rainer.[18]

After "Solo Section," which lasted around twenty or thirty minutes, came intermission, which was followed by thirty to forty minutes of "Play." This section consisted of eleven "games," each with its own sets of rules and structures. Some of them were initiated by a called signal; some signals, when called, had priority over others. One had to respond to called signals, unless one were engaged in one of two "priority" activities—"ball" or "rest." In other events, one could simply choose to initiate them on one's own. Ten of these units could be initiated in any order; the eleventh, "love," was a duet by Rainer and Davis that was performed at the end of "Play." "Ball" was a series of six different movement combinations, designated by the six names of the performers. Each player learned all six, and any one combination could be initiated by calling for a ball (supplied from the choir loft by Alex Hay), calling out the name of a combination and the name of the performers, or by doing it oneself. "Game" was a series of activities for two people with a ball, including passing the ball back and forth and feinting a throw. "Stop" involved running and stopping in a jump that landed in a squat; "jump" was a complicated movement sequence with running, circling, ballet steps, and skips and shuffles that repeated three times; "rest" involved private play (completely choreographed) with the ball while lying on one's back on the floor. Rainer suggested, but did not insist, that these three units in this order could follow "ball." "Pick-up" involved running around the space's perimeter, jumping occasionally, and "picking up" anyone in one's path. "Slow" was a series of seven tableaux, often involving leaning toward or away from the center of the grouping, achieved and dispersed in slow motions; in one of them,

Brown was lifted by two men to sit on their (adjacent) shoulders and, on her signal that she was in position, they stepped apart and she dropped to the floor. In "stance," each dancer struck his or her own fixed stance of relaxed position. "Bounce" was the simple action of standing and bouncing a ball. And "fast" involved passing the ball from hand to hand within a moving huddle of at least four people, with the goal of grabbing the ball and breaking out of the group, only to be chased by the group back into the huddle. When all fifty red balls had been thrown down from the loft, "love"—a slowly unfolding, constantly moving series of erotic poses based on Kama Kala sculpture juxtaposed to a deadpan dialogue about love—began, performed by Rainer and Davis.

After "Play" came "Bach." This section served as a coda. Rainer selected sixty-seven phrases of movement from "Duet," "Solo Section," and "Play," and added most of the traveling movements from "Diagonal." She then made a chance score for each performer, selecting an individual sequence of ten or more actions out of the gamut of movement choices, and adding instructions for speed or slowness, stillnesses, and spatial distances. The dancers stood in a column stage right, in their "stances" from "Play," while the prelude to the second part of Bach's cantata *Ich Habe Genug* played. When the singer began, the dancers performed their scores, traveling across the stage and back in a way that inexorably moved the entire column to stage left; as the music faded and those who had finished assumed their poses from "stance," the lights faded, leaving a few dancers still moving.[19]

Besides the idea for "Diagonal," which originated in Rainer's work with Forti and Ravon, a number of other aspects of *Terrain* had long been present in her work. The various structuring devices were a synthesis of methods from Robert Dunn's class, Ann Halprin's improvisation sessions, working with Forti. The use of the red balls and the games in "Play" simply came from her childhood, when she "played very hard in the streets after school: rollerskating, kick-the-can, hide-and-seek, capture-the-flag, heat, one-foot-off-the-gutter, jumprope, handball," and later, in high school, playing softball regularly. Rainer had begun improvising with Edith Stephen in 1957, and by the spring of 1960, when she was studying technique with Cunningham and improvising with Forti and Nancy Meehan, she was already beginning to explore movement invention in a highly conscious, methodical way. Rainer's notes reveal her thought processes during the course of these sections. Above all she is curious about how one invents movement, maintains control over one's body, and interacts during the dancing with others. During their first meeting, the three set themselves the task of moving about simultaneously but separately to jazz music, a piano solo by Thelonius Monk.

By the end of two hours, I was played-out and somewhat frustrated. My movements felt repetitive — not repetitive through choice, but through a constriction of imagination and technique. I found it hard to get off the ground or to sustain anything but a head-rolling, undulating-torso type of thing. Also it was irritating to work with two people in the room and pretend they weren't there. In fact it was impossible. So I found myself at times following one of them around the room. There was a point where Nancy was moving in a large circle — taking small rhythmic steps with bent knees on half-toe. I started to follow her, aping her movement, then after a while breaking out of it with a lunging spurt of movement, circling around her to return to her side and the hypnotic walk. Repeated this several times and began to get excited, but she broke away finally to work alone....

The next day my neck muscles were so sore I could hardly turn my head. I hadn't realized how little control I exercise over my head — it rolls every which way with no resistance or opposition to what the rest of my body does.

The next week, Meehan brought in recordings of Kabuki and Indian music, and the three began moving to the Kabuki music.

Several things happened. I started to crawl on the floor while holding on to my right ankle with my left hand. Turned, rolled, twisted while retaining this hold. It forced my body into extremes of tautness, and I found myself in several weird positions. Worked with Simone a little bit — sitting upright on floor, rolling from side to side in short, jerky rhythm. Simone related by walking precariously over and around me.

Meehan and Rainer worked on "illogical" dance positions, Meehan offering a turned-in attitude with the left ankle "grasping" the standing right leg.

Experimented with dipping torso forward and trying to make a complete revolution on standing leg while still gripping other leg. Landed on faces. It *can* be worked out, I am sure. Also worked on "turned in" changements....

I've been getting images of and actually finding myself acting out various kinds of fragmented movement. For instance, in the middle of executing a gesture that I feel is overly intimate to my body or too close to what I learn in class, then I "fragment" it, break it up or literally throw it away, or try to do it in an exaggerated manner. Certain mannerisms with my arms, for instance. It is an idea: to try doing this to a classic port de bras. Wobbling of elbows, sudden thrusts of knuckles, pumping shoulders, big arcs with the entire arm, etc. Also find myself in sudden "retreats" from familiar movement: retreat, attack, retreat, attack — until the "stuttering" creates its own dynamic.

In considering Cunningham's use of non sequiturs in body movement, Rainer decided that logic of the dance in any case comes not from the movements themselves but from the presence of the dancer, a realization that would power her own stage presence to a point where she was sometimes criticized for being too present.

Actually, the very effort of the body to move from one thing into a seemingly unconnected something else makes for a relationship between movements. There is no such thing as "disconnection" if the transition is successfully made. And I suspect that this "success" partially depends on the comfort — or appearance of comfort or ease — in the individual dancer, and "sureness of arrival."[20]

Jill Johnston writes that *Terrain* represented "a brilliant culmination" of Rainer's style and method. She notes that Rainer's use of "spontaneous determination" was a refinement of Merce Cunningham's chance methods in which chance and improvisation meet. "The total method is a combination of set material with directives for the free, spontaneous use of that material, limited by rules which further enhance or restrict the freedom of the performer." She lists Rainer's matter-of-fact movement style as a combination of:

> "natural" movements, classical (modern) extensions, hard, fast phrases, soft pose changes, limpid or throwaway relaxations, and the spastic distortions, whimsical or grotesque, which belong to a class of quirky gestures unique to Miss Rainer. The quirks often look like loony-bin material, although the line between what looks insane and what looks child-like is often pretty thin.

Johnston lauds the "Play" section "for its contemporary relevance.... What's more — or less — profound than play? Play is what interests everybody, even those who don't do it." The "love" section of "Play" was pleasurably shocking to Johnston, who found it a refreshing change from "thirteen years of watching dance duets that amount to pretty flirtations or static idealizations and euphemism." Despite the factual nature of this erotic duet — heightened by the flat dialogue of hackneyed romantic phrases — one can still recognize "love" as a dance, and not real lovemaking, Johnston writes. "You know it's a dance because the situation is stylized by subtle deviations from the natural and by the total absence, in the quality of performance, of that emotion which might normally accompany that motion." Finally, Johnston praised Rainer for the way her dancers looked as authentic in the movement as Rainer herself. The concert as a whole, she writes, was perfect in terms of poise and control, "always maintaining that difficult balance on a tightwire over life on the one side and art on the other."[21]

In the spring of 1963, the Washington Gallery of Modern Art, in Washington, D.C., sponsored an exhibition of Pop Art. Titled "The Popular Image," the exhibition ran from 18 April to 2 June. In conjunction with the show of paintings and objects by Jim Dine, George Brecht, Jasper Johns, Roy Lichtenstein, John Wesley, Robert Watts, Tom Wesselmann, Andy Warhol, Claes Oldenburg, Jim Rosenquist, and Robert Rauschenberg, the gallery sponsored a month-long Pop Art Festival, organized by Alice Denney (the assistant director of the Washington Gallery). The festival included scholarly lectures, a lecture-concert by John Cage on the night of the exhibition's opening, two Happenings by Claes Oldenburg, and Concert of Dance #5, by the Judson Dance Theater.[22]

Although the concert was designated "#5" and publicized as "an extension of a concert series at...Judson Memorial Church," it was organized by Billy Klüver with the help and advice of Robert Dunn; the participants in the Washington concert represented a nucleus that would eventually emerge as a splinter group within the Judson group. The flyer, designed by Steve Paxton, followed the Judson tradition of listing dancers and choreographers together in a single list, although the names of the choreographers were indicated by asterisks. The participants listed were Carolyn Brown, Trisha Brown, William Davis, Judith Dunn, Viola Farber, David Gordon, Billy Klüver, Barbara Lloyd, Robert Morris, Steve Paxton, Yvonne Rainer, Albert Reid, Jennifer Tipton; the names of Robert Rauschenberg, Valda Setterfield, and Per Ultvedt are added at the end of the list, as if they were late additions. The names singled out as choreographers are: T. Brown, Davis, Dunn, Gordon, Morris, Paxton, Rainer, Reid, and Rauschenberg. Apparently the plans for the concert were not fixed until after the flyer had been issued, for the printed program omits the names of Farber and Klüver as performers and removes Morris from the roster of choreographers.[23]

An engineer at the Bell Telephone Laboratories in Murray Hill, New Jersey, Billy Klüver was born and educated in Sweden. He moved to the United States and earned a Ph.D. degree in electrical engineering at the University of California at Berkeley. He became friendly with a number of artists, including Jean Tingueley, and he was also a friend of the director of Moderna Museet in Stockholm, Pontus Hulten. Klüver helped Jean Tingueley construct his self-destructing sculpture, *Homage to New York* (1960); the following year, Klüver organized the American contribution by twenty artists to an "Art in Motion" exhibition at Moderna Museet. In 1961, he also performed in Claes Oldenburg's Happening *Store Days I* and began talking with Robert Rauschenberg about constructing a sound sculpture that would come to fruition in 1965 in Rauschenberg's *Oracle*. In 1962, Klüver helped to organize a show by Jasper Johns, Rauschenberg, Alfred Leslie, and Richard Stankiewicz; he also organized an exhibition of Pop Art in Philadelphia. Jill Johnston described him in an article published in 1965, before Klüver organized the Foundation for Experiments in Art and Technology, as a "friend and supporter and avid enthusiast of contemporary forms, as well as an engineer generous with his time and knowledge..., a unique man behind and in front of the scenes." As a collaborator with the artists, Johnston explained, Klüver was interested in consulting and designing to facilitate the translation of the artists' ideas into functional terms. "He is not interested in making a technical 'process,' an invention, like a new kind of musical instrument or any systematic machine, that could be used by artists for composition or execution of work. At the moment, he says, he continues to enjoy contributing a functional unit for one specific purpose."[24]

Concert #5 was performed at America on Wheels, a roller skating rink at Kalorama and Seventeenth Streets in Washington, D.C. on 9 May 1963. According to Steve Paxton, Yvonne Rainer and Judith Dunn went to Washington in order to meet with Alice Denney, and they selected the rink as the site of the performance. He remembers that the rest of the participants arrived at the rink for the first time on the day before the performance.

> It was a hot, muggy, Washington eighth of May, and the skating rink was huge and really hot. We had to climb around up on a moveable scaffolding to do the lighting. The lights hadn't been touched for years, and there was a layer of dust over everything. We were there until about two or three in the morning, doing the lighting, with Alice Denney, who had a pair of roller skates on and had gotten quite drunk, playing the organ with her roller skates and calling out "Remember this one Billy?" We got the lighting done and had a run-through on the afternoon of the concert and realized that our performance was so long that we had to shorten the intermission and, I think, omit one. Some of the dances happened at the same time, but the main reason for that was that we had a vast space to fill. We didn't know how many people were going to come, so we set up islands of seats in various places in the rink. And the performance lasted for four hours and fifteen minutes. I danced in eight pieces including quite a lot of *Terrain*.[25]

Rainer, however, felt that she was not at all involved in the organization of Concert #5. Although Paxton says that he did not know Klüver very well until the time of the concert, Rainer remembers him as a friend of Rauschenberg's and Paxton's, and it was Rainer's impression that Paxton and Rauschenberg went down to Washington to choose the space, and that they, with Klüver, selected the participants in the concert. She remembers that about fifty spectators came to watch. "The place was unbelievably hot; I felt like a fried egg. But we were all ecstatically excited about the place, and doing the work in that place."[26]

Seventeen dances were given during the evening; with six of the dances occurring two at a time, there was a total of fourteen events. Five of the events were actually the five sections of Rainer's *Terrain*. Seven of the dances had been seen on earlier Judson Dance Theater group programs: Judith Dunn's *Index*; David Gordon's *Helen's Dance* and *Mannequin Dance*; Paxton and Rainer's collaboration, *Word Words* (accompanied by Paxton's tape recording of *Music for Word Words*); Paxton's *Proxy*; Trisha Brown's *Lightfall*; and William Davis's *Field*. Five of the dances were new. Robert Dunn remembers planning the order of the events with as much care as he had orchestrated the concerts at Judson, beginning here with the delicate *Trillium*, Brown's solo, in a small spotlight in the exact center of the huge rink, continuing with the contrasts set up between the three sets of simultaneous dances and the fragmented *Terrain* threading its way through the entire evening. The "Bach" section of *Terrain,* with its compendium of movements from the previous sections and the grand yet spare joy of its musical accompaniment, swept through the rink as the concluding dance in the concert. The audience was given a map on the program that told them where each dance would take place.[27]

Trillium had first been performed at the Maidman Playhouse on the American Theater for Poets series, on 24 March 1962. Maxine Munt, in her review of that concert, calls it "the high point of the evening," and notes that it was built on "two movement themes: a sitdown fall and hand stands." Jill Johnston, also writing about the first performance of *Trillium,* praises it for its spontaneity. "The short dance grows, flowers of its own natural accord from its first physical impulse of simply getting up and lying down. It spreads internally, so to speak, and Miss Brown is a radiant performer." Brown herself describes the rules she set up for *Trillium* as follows: "I could stand, sit, or lie, and ended up levitating. In this dance I did not notify myself of my intentions in advance of the performance."[28]

Paxton, who had been learning to improvise with Brown and Forti, and who performed in Brown's *Lightfall* in Concert #4 and later in the evening in Concert #5, thought that *Trillium* was "a very beautiful dance."

> It had a handstand in it and a lot of very beautiful, indulgent movement. Trisha [Brown] told me that a trillium was a flower that she had found in the woods. I'd never seen one; I thought it might be a very large number. She said that she used to pick them in the woods, but by the time she got home they would be wilted and faded. And that's what she thought about movement. It was wild; it was something that lived in the air.
>
> It was odd to see a handstand in a dance at that time. It was odd to see people off their feet doing anything but a very controlled fall.[29]

Brown's movement style was quite different from that of dancers who worked with Cunningham, like Judith Dunn or William Davis. Davis remembers that in *Trillium* Brown was "elastic and floppy. After you watched her for a while, you realized that what might seem quite disturbing or dangerous she had completely under control. I remember that in *Trillium* she fell and touched herself in surprising ways."[30]

The second event in Concert #5 was Judith Dunn's duet for herself and Paxton, *Index,* which took place toward one end of the rink at the perimeter, and, at the same time, Albert Reid's *Bird Solos,* near the center of the space. Reid, who lived with William Davis, had first become involved with the Judson group when he performed in *Terrain.* He had met Rainer in ballet class at the Joffrey studio. Reid was born in Niagara Falls, New York, lived there for ten years, then moved to Canada with his family. As a small child he sporadically took classes in tap dancing, ballet, and gymnastics. But his primary activity was singing. His entire family was musical, and Reid was trained both in piano and singing. When he was eleven, his family moved to Los Angeles, where Reid sang professionally in a boy's choir. At Stanford University, Reid majored in drama, performed in the school productions, and met Davis. Reid's interest in dance was rekindled, and since there was no dance department at Stanford, he studied modern dance with James Truitte at Lester Horton's school in Los Angeles and ballet with Carmelita Maracci. Maracci advised him to go to New York to study ballet with Antony Tudor. After graduating from Stanford and spending a year in the army, stationed in California, Reid moved to New York. He had already seen performances by José Limón's company and Alwin Nikolais a year or two before that, at the American Dance Festival in Connecticut, and soon after settling in New York, he decided to study with Nikolais. Nikolais encouraged Reid to come to the day classes for professional dancers, and Reid supported himself by typing cables at night for American Express. He modestly recalls that "at that time there were so few male dancers that you were always encouraged; even if you weren't good you had opportunities to perform." Reid joined Nikolais's company, and when the first Concert of Dance was held at Judson Church in 1962, he was performing in Spoleto with Nikolais. In 1963 he left Nikolais to work on his own choreography, and he also danced in various other choreographers' works; in 1964 he joined Cunningham's company in time for the world tour. Reid had choreographed *Bird Solos* for a performance at the Henry Street Playhouse. When he performed it again in Concert #5, it was his first participation in the Judson Dance Theater as a choreographer. Looking back on *Bird Solos,* Reid feels that,

> It wasn't a very good piece; it seems like a silly dance. It was literally that: just bird imagery. When I made it I was excited about it, and then it seemed old-fashioned and corny, and I never did it again. Maybe some of the movement in it was interesting, but not the way it was structured.
>
> In fact, I never work with structures; I've never been attracted to games or abstract mathematical formulas. I always have a movement idea, or an interpersonal idea, and the dance emanates from that core reason for the piece. The idea suggests images or movement sequences, and the coherence and logic in the piece comes from working around the core, like building a little pearl around a grain. In that sense I don't think of myself as avant-garde. As a dancer I felt very connected and excited by a lot of the things that went on at Judson, but as a choreographer I felt out of key. I was never attracted to that way of constructing things.[31]

Still, the atmosphere at Judson was one that allowed Reid to experiment with choreography in his own way, giving him a chance to find out in what directions his choreographic inclinations would take him.

After *Index* and *Bird Solos* came *Helen's Dance,* by Gordon, and then the first two sections of *Terrain,* "Diagonal" and "Duet." An intermission followed, and then Gordon's *Random Breakfast.* A duet for Gordon and Setterfield, it was a collage performance of six sections. According to Gordon, the dance was planned as a trio that included Yvonne Rainer, but after one rehearsal with Rainer, Gordon decided he wanted to work with Setterfield only. Gordon describes *Random Breakfast* as a "lavish escapade that included at least a dozen costume changes, innumerable accessories, props, sound cues, and complicated timing. Two of us were to do it in thirty minutes. It was the piece, I remember thinking, that would bring modern dance to an abrupt end." Gordon intended this pastiche as a sardonic comment on "the Judson Church Dance Factory Gold Rush in which choreography ran rampant."

> The policy of the Judson Dance Theater was that no choreographer could be turned away, or rather, there was no policy, because no one would take the responsibility of making qualitative judgments on the work of anyone else. Unlike many of the participants, who were able to perform in each other's work and, in some instances, begging to establish durable associations, I dealt with the situation as a voyeur, which is a tendency of mine....[Judson] and other show business manifestations were the six courses of *Random Breakfast.*[32]

The first section, "The Strip," was a dance for Setterfield. Dressed in a long blue velvet gown that belonged to Waring and had numerous small buttons down the front, long gloves with more buttons, a hat, pearls, and a fur stole, she performed a strip tease to "authentically brassy strip music." Gordon says that,

> She looked like Queen Mary taking her clothes off in public. She walked in a circle forever, taking off one thing at a time, all those buttons to open, the dress, a petticoat, a long-line brassiere, garter belt, stockings, bloomers, limping along in one high-heeled shoe, never breaking the rhythm of the circular walk. She was somehow extraordinarily genteel parading in the circle and dropping her clothing. She discarded all the clothing in a neat pile so that when she was done she could stoop down and gather it all up together in a huge bundle. The dowager empress had become a naked rag lady....
>
> For the first performance...I had not questioned the convention of dancers wearing tights and leotards as a substitute for nudity and Valda ended up in flesh colored tights with an extra pair wrapped around her tits.
>
> Her performance was contained, refined, subdued, and incredibly funny.

When *Random Breakfast* was performed in Concert #7 at Judson Church, Setterfield wore pasties and a mirrored g-string.[33]

The next two sections—"Prefabricated Dance" and "The Seasons"—

were performed simultaneously. In "Prefabricated Dance," Gordon says, he "got rid of enormous hostility by parodying most of the dances I'd seen at the Judson and elsewhere by telling the audience how to make a modern dance. It was totally improvised. I talked about timing, subject matter, content, and how to get the audience in the palm of your hands." Not only did Gordon demonstrate the methods of the avant-garde; he also satirized Louis Horst and the older generation of modern dancers, as well as dance in film and theater. "I conceived of it as a scathing dismissal of current values and methods. The audience thought it was very funny. People I did not attack in a given performance asked why they had been left out." In "The Seasons," Setterfield performed four small dances to Vivaldi's *The Seasons*. Paxton remembers that she wore a bikini under a fur coat at one point and for "Summer" put on a pair of sunglasses and lay down.[34]

In "Lemon Hearts Dance," which took its title from a Taylor Mead film, Gordon did an imitation Spanish dance, wearing a strapless evening gown with the hair on his chest showing above the dress, and a wig, comb and mantilla, and a stole. "I improvised bogus Spanish dialog, songs, and dance steps. In one performance, I ended the section, a berserk Carmen Miranda–Amaya, with the fringe of my stole caught up between all my toes. Uttering dire Spanish curses at the captive shmata, I left the stage as it slithered along the floor after me." In "Big Girls Don't Cry," a satire on the use of various materials and random structures in Happenings, Setterfield spraypainted her own clothing after laying down newspapers and plastic drop cloths. In later performances, dressed as a nun, she "prepared, ran, and leapt upon a pair of child's bedsprings, slowly picked up six plastic washbaskets and knocked them down with a large ball, and shoved a cream pie in her own face after saying 'shit' and 'fuck.' " Finally, in "Garlandiana," Gordon appeared, to the accompaniment of a recording of Judy Garland singing "Somewhere Over the Rainbow." Dressed in a top hat and tails, he smiled and looked shy for four minutes.[35]

Gordon writes of his method of choreographing *Random Breakfast:*

> At the time *Random Breakfast* was made, the subject matter was my prime interest; the newness of the methods through which the subjects were revealed and which formed the structure of the piece was something I took for granted. In retrospect, the somewhat dated aspects of the material enable me to separate and examine those structures more clearly and to evaluate them with a keener eye.
>
> Approximately eighty percent of the material in *Random Breakfast* was improvised around specific subject matter. I sensed at that time that the quality of style of a section could be established without setting specific steps or phrases. I could maintain awareness of the general amount of material I wanted to cover; the order and the details could take care of themselves. Some sections had barely any content other than their style of behavior.[36]

Reviewing the performance of *Random Breakfast* in Concert #7, where it was later performed, Johnston writes:

> Mr. Gordon makes a dance on the spot by explaining to the audience what he might do if he were to make an interesting dance. Each explanation is accompanied by the appropriate illustration: an "exciting" entrance, a thematic movement, a symbolic movement, a religious movement, etc. Very funny parody of some old fashioned ideas and a final statement on any kind of dance making...Gordon and Setterfield are classic wits on the scene. Long live classic wits.[37]

Following *Random Breakfast* in Concert #5 was a simultaneous performance of Paxton and Rainer's *Word Words* and Judith Dunn's duet for herself and Robert Morris, *Speedlimit*. Juxtaposed to the cool nudity of *Word Words,* in which there was no physical contact, *Speedlimit* involved a mixture of reference to tumbling and wrestling with some dance movement. Morris rolled Dunn in on a cart. Both wore white coveralls, and they performed on a gym mat. It was, according to Dunn, a gymnastic struggle. She balanced him on her knees, then they did a double somersault —a forward roll with both bodies curved together. Rainer remembers that there was "some whirling, twisting going down to the floor, and getting up, and some violent-sounding things, where the body would roll over and smack the mat resoundingly." At one point they signaled with small pennants, and at another point, Morris vaulted up against a wall by means of a pole, while Dunn lay still. Finally, they tied each other up with ropes and had to be carted out by helpers.[38]

Speedlimit was performed in New York in Concert #8 and again in Judith Dunn's solo choreography evening, "Motorcycle." Johnston wrote, after Concert #8:

> Miss Dunn began with such basic physical problems as balancing, bracing, pulling— then let these impulses travel naturally into rolls and falls which might then become the new impulses for actions like bumping, rebounding, and quiet grappling. The dance was a horizontal level of tension; the speedlimit is slow, there seemed no reason to hurry beyond one or two accelerations that erupted naturally from the action. The dance takes place in a "round" situation (designed to be seen from any angle), with most of the movement focused on a central gym mat. It includes props—car, pole, flag, ropes— which are secondary to the movement but which bring further dimension to the "environment" and to the field of physically motivated impulses.[39]

Rainer's "Solo Section" from *Terrain* followed these two dances, and then there was an intermission. The audience was requested to remove all chairs from the rink during the intermission, for Robert Rauschenberg's *Pelican*—a dance for two men in rollerskates and on bicycle wheels, and one woman on pointe—followed the intermission.

Rauschenberg had been involved in dance as a costume, decor, and lighting designer since 1953, when he designed costumes for Merce Cunningham's *Septet*. In 1954, he collaborated with Paul Taylor, among other things supplying a dog that cued the beginning and ending of one dance, *Resistance*. The relationships with Cunningham and Taylor continued alongside Rauschenberg's development as a painter, making collages and combine-objects that mixed processes of painting, various methods of transferring images from other sources, and the incorporation of ordinary or extraordinary objects. Born in Port Arthur, Texas, in 1925, Rauschenberg first began to study art after service in the Navy, at Kansas City Art Institute under the G.I. Bill of Rights. He then studied at Academie Julian in Paris; at Black Mountain College and at the Art Students League in New York. Returning often to Black Mountain after moving to New York in 1949, he became friendly with John Cage, Merce Cunningham, David Tudor, Buckminster Fuller, Jack Tworkov, Robert Motherwell, and Franz Kline. He performed in Cage's untitled performance at Black Mountain in the summer of 1952. After working with Cunningham for seven years, Rauschenberg became the company's lighting designer and stage manager in 1961, traveling with the company when it toured (until 1965). Also in 1961, Rauschenberg participated in a performance at the American Embassy in Paris in honor of David Tudor, who was beginning a concert tour of Europe. While Tudor played Cage's *Variations II,* Rauschenberg, equipped with contact microphones, painted a painting. The other performers were Jean Tingueley, Niki de Saint-Phalle, and Jasper Johns. The following year, the same group commissioned a script from Kenneth Koch. *The Construction of Boston,* performed at the Maidman Playhouse in May 1962, was fifteen minutes long, with a cast that included the painter Frank Stella, curator Henry Geldzahler, and the dancers Steve Paxton and Viola Farber. As part of Rauschenberg's contribution, Farber and Paxton inhabited a small furnished apartment on stage and performed a series of everyday activities, beginning when they got out of bed. Rauschenberg also built a rainmaker. The Stewed Prunes, a comedy team, announced various events, and Merce Cunningham directed. Tingueley built a cinderblock wall that finally closed the stage off from the audience, ending the performance.[40]

Rauschenberg had been involved in Judson Dance Theater since its beginnings; he had visited Robert Dunn's classes, and participated in the weekly workshop sessions. He did lighting for concerts and helped in various other ways. He was also involved socially, for he and Paxton lived together. But *Pelican* was Rauschenberg's first venture into choreography on his own.

Rauschenberg gives different accounts of how he decided to make *Pelican*. He claims that Alice Denney had already printed the program and mistakenly listed him as one of the choreographers. "I'd just come along to kill myself on a bunch of rotten ladders five hundred feet up in the air at the roller rink," he says. "I remember Trisha [Brown] helped me name the piece out on Alice [Denney]'s back porch." However, since the flyer Paxton made seems to have been distributed even before the program for Concert #5, as noted above, and it also listed Rauschenberg as the choreographer, and since Rauschenberg rehearsed the dance for three weeks before its performance, his story seems suspect. Perhaps, though, there was earlier publicity distributed by Alice Denney that announced the program. Rauschenberg has also said that:

> The more I was around Merce [Cunningham]'s group and that kind of activity, I realized that painting didn't put me on the spot as much or not in the same way, so at a certain point I had to do theater myself.... I like the liveness of it — that awful feeling of being on the spot, having to assume the responsibility for that moment, for those actions that happen at that particular time.

According to yet another account, Rauschenberg has said that after Alice Denney showed him the skating rink, he decided to use roller skates in a dance and he learned how to skate.[41]

Rauschenberg's method in choreographing *Pelican* was the same as his method in painting or other artmaking: He explored the materials at hand, subjecting them to certain limitations.

> Since I didn't know much about actually making a dance, I used roller skates as a means of freedom from any kind of inhibitions that I would have [as a performer]. That already gives you limitations — puts you in a certain area that you must deal with....
> I auditioned dancers for the piece; and to my surprise, I found that dancers who had skated when they were children, and some of them quite well, couldn't roller skate now because of their dance training. They froze, and it was very awkward. They needed a kind of abandon to actually do it. You see, in their thinking, dancers have a going dialogue between themselves and the floor, and I had put wheels between them and the floor. They couldn't hear the floor any more, and their muscles didn't know where they were.[42]

Rauschenberg has also stated that using roller skates was a "gimmick that would disguise the fact that I couldn't dance." He contrasted his own "lack of danceability" with Carolyn Brown's elegant, dancerly line and precise technique, as she danced in pointe shoes. At first, however, he tried to make a pair of pointe-shoe roller skates by putting ball bearings on the pointes. "It would be her equivalent to skates," Rauschenberg explains.

"But she nearly killed herself on them, and so I thought that wasn't such a good idea and that just dancing on pointe looked just as abstract as rolling around on skates."[43]

The dance was a trio for Rauschenberg, Carolyn Brown, and Per Olof Ultvedt, a Swedish artist who was in New York on a visit. First they rehearsed in Rauschenberg's loft on Broadway, then in a Brooklyn roller-skating rink. The dance lasted for twelve minutes, according to one account, and twenty to thirty minutes according to another account. All three performers wore sweatsuits. To a tape collage Rauschenberg had made from various sources, including march music by Handel and Haydn and sounds from the radio, television, and movies, the two men entered the rink from one end, rolling horizontal to the floor. Each traveled on a set of two bicycle wheels joined by an axle. When they entered, they were hidden by huge winglike constructions made from parachutes. Carolyn Brown moved down the center line of the rink on pointe, while the men rolled down the edges of the rink and, having reached the opposite end, spiraled around, switched paths, and, rolling back to their starting points, swooped around to pick Brown up as she returned along the center line. They partnered her, lifting her and carrying her as they skated in circles and figure eights, until finally they exited, each man kneeling on his axle. Rauschenberg remembers that "It had a flow to it; it had to, because you couldn't stop very well, and everything was moving pretty fast. The main movements were starting and finishing. Those are always the toughest moments in theater: getting on and getting off."[44]

According to Calvin Tomkins:

> [*Pelican*] turned out to be highly romantic in feeling, with the two men in their fantastic parachutes circling and occasionally lifting the ballerina, who wore toe shoes and a sweat suit. There was some anxiety that one of them might drop the incomparable Carolyn Brown, but both Rauschenberg and Ultvedt worked hard at learning to skate, and Carolyn Brown declared afterward that she was never worried. *Pelican*, at any rate, was the hit of the festival.[45]

In Concert #5, *Pelican* was followed by Paxton's *Proxy*; Gordon's *Mannequin Dance* performed simultaneously with Brown's *Lightfall*, for herself and Paxton; another intermission; then Davis's *Field*; and finally, the last two sections of *Terrain* — "Play" and "Bach."[46]

Both the audience and the performers were delighted with the concert. An article in the *Washington Post* on the Pop Art Festival singled out the dance concert as the "most important feature" of the entire festival.

> The program was a long and arduous one, with an extraordinary melange of dance, cal-isthenics, acrobatics, recitals, poetry, imitations, strip teases, rollerskating, and music.

Held in the vast expanses of a roller skating rink, it continued the informal and impromptu air of the Happenings. Chairs were set in groups around the rink so that the audience was surrounded by the performers, who wove in and out of the chairs. [Alan] Solomon pointed out that "the occasion was so stimulating to them (the dancers) that they elaborated and invented as they went along in an unprecedented way. The result was a unique involvement between artist and audience. In this sense it was a major occasion the equal of which I can't recall.

"The performance was a stringent program where you could still feel the classical structure of the ballet with definite sequences, in spite of the improvisation and Happening quality."[47]

Paxton recalls that,

It was a glorious concert. I was high for days and days afterwards. It was not only very different than performing in New York, but it was that we had finally achieved a kind of transformation of theater, because the audience was as active and mobile in making choices about what to see as we were active and mobile in running from place to place to perform, changing our performance style from piece to piece. It made me feel very strongly the differences in the pieces. We had, at one fell swoop, a full panorama of our work in this vast space, almost all at once. And it was very, very amazing. It was also incredibly tiring.

It was very hot in the rink, and it finally started cooling off about midnight. And we finished at 12:15 or so and got to Alice Denney's house, where we were staying, at 1:30 to 2:00. I remember that it was cool at that point, and that there was a full moon, and the mockingbirds were mewing and calling because of the brightness. It was a blue sky at night. And I remember lying there in a state of fatigue and ecstasy with this incredible moon filtering through a tree and brightness all around. I felt that in this performance, Concert #5, the work and the thinking and the organization concept had all come together to make something that was new and full and rich. And I was really pleased to have been there.[48]

Both *Terrain* and Concert #5 were watersheds in a number of ways. *Terrain* was a choreographic achievement for Rainer and a revelation for her dancers and spectators about the nature of dance movement and the identity of a dance. Concert #5 was an expansion in terms of the use of space, new audiences, moving outside of New York, the strengthening ties with the artworld. Although the dancers did not feel identified in terms of their work with the Pop Art exhibition in Washington, Rauschenberg was a pivotal figure involved with both aspects of the event. And certainly connections could be drawn between the factual realism of much of the work at Judson and the new, figurative paintings of the Pop artists. The use of sports images, of flags, of popular genres and Hollywood myths, radio music, and even of the ballerina image served as raw source material for the Judson choreographers, just as highways, beer cans, Coca-Cola bottles, and pictures of Marilyn Monroe served the Pop artists. The found gesture — whether from everyday life or "commercial" dance — was used in dance in much the same way that the found object—either junk or the imagery of commercial art or ordinary industrial products—was used in fine art. Impersonal methods of creating a dance—through chance or distancing techniques—had their parallels in the silkscreens, projected enlargements, and factory-made objects by Pop artists. Pop Art was a reaction to Abstract Expressionism just as post-modern dance repudiated both the personal expressionism and the abstract gestures of an older generation of modern dancers. In fact, Pop Art "arrived" in New York in 1962, the year of the first Judson concert. But, as Lucy Lippard points out, there are many different views on which artists constitute the Pop Art movements; Lippard herself recognizes only five: Andy Warhol, Roy Lichtenstein, Tom Wesselmann, James Rosenquist and Claes Oldenburg. And compared with the hard-edged, representational styles of these artists, the diversity of the Judson work cannot be strictly defined.[49]

But these two concerts were a turning point in the Judson Dance Theatre in other ways. For Rainer, organizing her own ambitious projects became more demanding on her time and resources than working on the collaborative ventures of the workshop. For those, like Lucinda Childs and Deborah Hay, and certainly others, who were not invited to participate in Concert #5, a feeling of exclusion and resentment arose. There began to be undercurrents in the larger group of a division between an "in" group and an "out" group.[50] The seeds of dissension that would eventually disperse the Judson group had been sown.

5

Dance in the Sanctuary
and in the Theater

During the month of May 1963, a number of Fluxus people and other artists put on a Yam Festival (spelling May backwards), which was sponsored by the Smolin Gallery. Dance and music performances, Happenings, Events, and private performances done following instructions occurred at various locations around the city. A calendar listed events and instructions; the Smolin Gallery served as information center. A number of Judson Dance Theater workshop participants performed in the Yam Festival. "The Billy Linich Show," happening throughout the month, included appearances by members of Waring's company. Also throughout the month, Al Hansen's *Silver City at Ground Zero* "evolved" at Canal Street and Broadway. Robert Ashley, a member of the Once Group, contributed a six-day sculpture, *Chair,* which was a set of instructions for destroying a chair one day at a time, then resting on the seventh day. On 11 May began "an endless and continuous program of performance beginning about noon on Saturday through evening and Sunday." This Yam Day program, held at the Hardware Poet's Playhouse on West 54th Street, included works by George Brecht, Robert Breer, Earle Brown, John Cage, Philip Corner, Malcolm Goldstein, Red Grooms and Rudy Burckhardt, Al Hansen, Dick Higgins, Spencer Holst, Ray Johnson, Jill Johnston, Brooklyn Joe Jones, Alison Knowles, George Maciunas, Jackson MacLow, Robert Morris, Yvonne Rainer, James Tenney, James Waring, Christian Wolff, and La Monte Young. On 19 May, during an afternoon at George Segal's farm in North Brunswick, New Jersey, Allan Kaprow did a Happening, Wolf Vostell presented a Decoll/age, La Monte Young played music, Dick Higgins made *All Kinds of Trouble,* and Yvonne Rainer and Trisha Brown improvised on the roof of Segal's chicken coop. The first of May was Clock Day, 7 May Box Day, 13 May Moon Day, 14 May Balloon Day, 15 May Necktie Day, 16 May Newspaper Day, 17 May Water Day, 18 May Food Day, 21 May Key Day, 27 May Problem Day, 29 May Poetry Day.

On 16, 17, and 18 May, Ben Patterson gave tours. On 27 May, Michael Kirby presented performances of *The First and Second Wilderness (A Civil War Game)*. The thirty-first of May saw the conclusion of a three-year piece by George Brecht and Al Hansen, *Blues for Marcel Duchamp,* as well as a panel "concussion."[1]

On 10 June, James Waring organized The Pocket Follies, a benefit for the Foundation for the Contemporary Performance Arts — a foundation whose board included John Cage and Jasper Johns, and which raised money through sales of art works to help finance performances by Merce Cunningham and the Judson Dance Theater. The Follies included collaborations by Fred Herko and Michael Malcé (*Cleanliness Event, with Poo-Poo Cushion Music*) and by Jill Johnston and Robert Morris (*New Poses Plastiques*). There were dances and performances by George Brecht, Trisha Brown, David Gordon with Valda Setterfield, Ray Johnson, Allen Marlowe, John Herbert McDowell, Aileen Passloff, Yvonne Rainer, Robert Rauschenberg. There were also several plays: Ruth Krauss's *A Beautiful Day,* directed by Remy Charlip; and N. F. Simpson's *Oh; A Compendium of Everyone's Remarks, Act II,* directed by Waring. The Pocket Follies Academic Festival A Capella Group sang a "Serio-Comic Choral Overture," a "Grand Nostalgic Vocal Entr'Acte," and the evening ended with a "Spectacular Musical Finale."[2]

From 23 through 25 June, the Judson Dance Theater workshop put on three more group concerts. With five group programs and one solo choreography concert to its credit, the workshop was forging an identity. It was known from the beginning that the group included fine dancers, but by now a number of gifted choreographers had begun to emerge in the context of the group activities. Even more importantly, the workshop had become a nexus of divergent artistic concerns, a "clearing," as Robert Dunn had called his class, where the choreographer felt free to experiment or even to work traditionally but independently; where a grass-roots audience in the artists' communities of Greenwich Village and the East Village knew they could come, for free admission or a small contribution, to see dances that would often provoke the senses and the intellect; where artists in various fields could participate as equals in making dances; where all that was despised in modern dance and ballet could be commented on or temporarily corrected; where all that was admired in traditional theatrical dancing could be utilized. Cunningham's technique and choreography had created what often looked like an alienated, fragmented style. Waring's witty, elegantly wrought ballets at times seemed campy. The older modern dance seemed artificially dramatic and preternaturally stylized. The Judson choreographers wanted their work to be both serious and enjoyable, to make art without acquiring the aloof godlike persona of The Artist. They wanted to restore to their works the down-to-earth humanity they felt was sometimes erased in the dances of the masters they emulated. "You had to be a *person* at Judson," Judith Dunn says, "with enough energy to throw yourself around, to do your own work and help others as well. A different kind of effort was required in performance [than was required by Cunningham]: You had to find the essence of what you were doing or supposed to be doing. It was demanding in a completely different way."[3]

Because since the days of Robert Dunn's classes the emphasis had been on the choreographic process rather than on the perfection of a particular technique—even though the dances sometimes demanded technical rigor or called attention to a choice or repudiation of technique, the dances at Judson often seemed more accessible, metaphorically more free and matter-of-fact, than those of the older modern dance. Some of the pragmatism of the new dance was circumstantial: If one had no money for special lighting instruments, elaborate costumes, a well-appointed theater, or a skilled staff, one made do with what one had. The Judson Church was available; simple lighting was inexpensive; participants in the workshops had various skills that could be exploited in stage managing, costume design, musical direction, graphic design. But also, the same aesthetic that could value the nontechnical movements of an untrained dancer could value the simplicity of clear, plain lighting and of leotards or street clothing. And the social principles that led the workshop to insist on collective procedures and nonevaluative criticism led the dancers to reject the typical hierarchy of the modern dance company and the traditional mystique that prevailed in the relations between artist and audience in the dance world. The earnest curiosity that fueled the experiments in choreography and in performance, the willingness to borrow freely from other art forms while extending the definitions of dance as a form, the rejection of personal choice through the use of chance techniques and photographic scores, all seemed to lead to an unaffected, unvarnished style. The critics— especially Jill Johnston, who tried to open her writing style in parallel ways —rhetorically associated these aspects of the Judson work to the political and social ambiance: the freedom and youth valorized during the Kennedy era.

Reviewing Concerts #6, #7, and #8, Johnston raises the issue of legitimacy and notes that:

> The basic virtue of these concerts continues to be the open door policy. No holds barred.
>   From the beginning this has meant the entry of "situations" into a scene which contained a legitimate "dance" foundation. Legitimacy is an odd notion. I'm using the term to describe, so far as it's possible, that motion by people which might be any nonfunctional exaggeration of natural action and which is traditionally conceived to be the result of some "training" in a professional dance studio where the exaggeration and/or

distortion of natural action is roped off into structural, rhythmic (metric) divisions.

The Judson dancers have thrown the idea of legitimacy into lovely confusion. For one thing, the dancing itself is often so physical in such a natural way that it bears little resemblance to any conventional "attitudes" of dance. Secondly, the choreographer may be a painter, a sculptor, or a composer as well as a dancer, and that means the emphasis often settles on a theater "situation" ("happening"), "event," rather than on legitimate dancing as defined above. Thirdly, there is an attitude of pure non-dance which is neither physical nor theatrical but a state of being. The notion of legitimacy becomes absurd. Dancing is what you think it is. Possibly the whole world of movement is dancing. So the question is: What is dancing, and if you know what dancing is, what is non-dancing?[4]

The three concerts were given in the sanctuary, as *Terrain* had been. According to Robert Rauschenberg, the limitations of the physical space in the gymnasium had begun to place tiresome constraints on the choreography.

We graduated up to the church [sanctuary] when we got really tired of every piece having certain things in common. Everything appeared on a basketball court. After a while, that visual limitation began to bug everybody. You always had to figure out what you were going to do with the baskets. And the radiators were impossible, too.

With the baskets, you could take the lights off them, use them to put the lights on, let them be seen, try to hide them, throw something over them. All those things you could do only once, though. And it didn't always work at one time.[5]

Although only two concerts had been given in the gymnasium, the weekly workshops met there, and the space had become quite familiar to the group. Carolee Schneemann, however, thought that the dancers were not visually aware enough of their performance environment. They seemed to her to be aware of space only kinesthetically.

Their eyes reached into space without touching it. They were alone. The distance between "art" and life. Space was anchored in their bodies, space was where they felt their spines. They didn't realize a radiator behind them equaled their mass, asserted verticals against their legs.

I want a dance where a body moves as part of its environment; where the dancer says Yes to environment incorporating or says No transforming it...where the choice is visual as a dancer is Visual Element moving in actual real specific dimensions. I want a dance where dancers can fall, can crash into a wall; aim movement beyond their line of spine INTO space, into materials, into each other—projective, connective! A dance where dancers can fart, can start and stop, are aware of the impulse, the necessity by which they move and its implicit diminution or contrary flow. A dance where dancers can leave the performance...and return...or not return.[6]

Concerts #6, #7, and #8 were again structured by Robert Dunn, who is listed on the program as program advisor. The other technical credits are: lighting design, William Linich, assisted by Michael Katz; musical direction, Malcolm Goldstein; costume consultant, Ruth Emerson; publicity,

Lucinda Childs and Alex Hay. Judith Dunn was stage manager for all three programs, assisted by a different person each night: Elaine Summers, for Concert #6; Alex Hay, for Concert #7; and Yvonne Rainer, for Concert #8.[7] Alex Hay designed the flyer in the style of the breakfast paintings he was working on at the time: a vertical sheet of white paper with a large photographic image of a fried egg, around whose perimeter the information on the concerts is printed.[8]

Once again, the dances were arranged in unexpected alternations of large- and small-scale numbers, pieces with and without musical accompaniment, with and without sets and special costumes, various choreographic techniques. There were nine dances in Concert #6, eight in Concert #7, and three in Concert #8.[9]

Concert #6 opened with Elaine Summers's *Dance for Carola,* a solo without music that was structured as "one thing." This was the beginning of Summers's choreographic involvement with "kinetic awareness," a discipline she has evolved and synthesized from various approaches to anatomical and kinesiological study and therapy. Summers's kinetic awareness method relates the physical condition of the body to the person's emotional and psychological states. In trying to change the individual body/personality, Summers takes on the role of "a guide on a voyage of self-discovery," in which the subject learns to free tensions and discover his or her total movement potential.[10] One of Summers's teachers who contributed to her development of this work was Carola Speads, and *Dance for Carola* was dedicated to her. Summers was making discoveries about her choreographic process through the Judson group, and about certain movement preferences in teaching her own classes, but learning how to reach "the core of one's inner and outer movement" she credited to her teachers Speads and Charlotte Selva.

I spent a lot of time by myself doing that work, and one summer I felt, "If I'm really honest about it, all I want to do is lie on the floor. I really don't want to move." So for two-and-a-half months, during the three-hour period I spent dancing every day, I didn't get up off the floor. And in that time, I began to rediscover my own energy.

I thought, "I'm living according to an energy pattern, a body imagery, that isn't mine. Maybe I don't have any energy. If that's true, then I'm just going to have to face it."

Then, from that came a feeling that I had a tremendous amount of energy that was really mine, but also an understanding that I don't like to move fast, necessarily, which is what I was always doing.

I started to walk more slowly down the street, and I couldn't seem to go slowly enough. I felt that every time you change the direction of your eyes or the lift of your head, you see something completely differently. So if you took one step and you looked into everything that could be happening, every possibility of what you could perceive in that one step, or who would go by you, you could take an infinite amount of time for one step. That's what I was doing on the streets of New York. And out of that I made *Dance for Carola.*[11]

A similar thirst for the experience of total perception, of infinitely expanding consciousness, led others in the Judson group and in the Village artists' community to learn physical and spiritual disciplines like Tai Chi Chuan and Zen meditation, or to experiment with consciousness-expanding drugs.

In *Dance for Carola,* Summers's single action was to move from standing to crouching and then back to standing again, all in even, slow motion.

> It took eight to ten minutes. Now that same activity would probably take me forty-five minutes.
>
> The support I received from everyone in the group felt wonderful. I had been doing this work for ten years, and this was the first dance that came out of it. I was scared to do it. But everyone liked it very much. The luxury to be able to commit yourself to something, for whatever length of time it took to explore that thing was very valuable.[12]

Ironically, in terms of Summers's motivation to find the inner and outer cores of her own movement impulses, Johnston commented that *Dance for Carola* "is a single, slow lyric line of motion which misses itself only because the performance is not completely consonant with the intention."[13]

The second dance was a group work by Fred Herko, with the music, which was also the set, by Joe Jones, a Fluxus member, and construction by George Herms. The dancers were Lucinda Childs, Ruth Emerson, Deborah Hay, Fred Herko, Arlene Rothlein, and Polly Stearns. The title of the dance was *Binghamton Birdie.* This was also the nickname of one of the "A-men" from the San Remo coffeeshop who visited Linich at Warhol's Factory. The performers twice danced in the lobby space, visible because the curtains that ordinarily hung from the choir loft during the dance concerts had been opened.[14] Then the curtains closed and Joe Jones's musical set lowered and played itself.

> A big, chandelier-like construction of self-playing drums rose from the lowered position in which it had been playing (agitatedly but quietly) in almost total darkness. A spotlight focused abruptly on a white curtain. An imperious whirring sound arose and through the curtain Fred Herko flashed in, looking beatific.
>
> He wore black tights, a yellow-and-blue jersey with "JUDSON" emblazoned across the front, and, on one foot, a black shoe and his means of locomotion—a roller skate. His other foot was bare.
>
> Continuing to look beatific, he skated around the floor for a time, moving his arms and the unencumbered foot through various balletic positions. Before vanishing behind the white curtain, he did a bit of toe-dancing—roller skate and bare foot notwithstanding.[15]

The structure of Herko's dance was a list of five sections. The strategy was a defamiliarization of ballet techniques and line by changing the standard costume, especially the shoes. Wrote Johnston:

> The five sections of Mr. Herko's *Binghamton Birdie* cohere with that strange logic of parts that have no business being together, but which go together anyway because anything in life can go with anything else if you know what you're doing. The only moment that missed for me was the over-extended display of Brooklyn Joe Jones' marvelous mechanical musical construction (suspended from the balcony). Mr. Herko danced around after that on one roller skate, but I don't think he did it soon enough. The pure choreography of the second and last section, six dancers moving before and behind the pillars supporting the balcony, is lovely. So is the first event: Herko squat-walking in a black cape with a black umbrella for canopy, making a few sweet notes on a flute.[16]

Third on the program was a duet choreographed and danced by Joseph Schlichter and Sally Stackhouse, two dancers with José Limón's company. Schlichter joined the Judson workshop through Trisha Brown, whom he married that summer. He had studied dance in college at Cornell University, served in the Navy for a three-year enlistment, then resumed his dance studies with Martha Graham, Antony Tudor, and Limón.[17] Before joining the Judson workshop, Schlichter had shown two dances in group concerts. His *Ekstasis,* performed in May 1961 at the Master Institute, was on a program produced by Contemporary Dance Productions. Ernestine Stodelle wrote that this solo was about the "religious transports of a medieval monk," reminding her of the cathedral sculptures of Gislebertus.[18] His *Stones of Time,* shown at the YM-YWHA by Contemporary Dance, Inc. in May 1962, was, according to Louis Horst, a "novel and sometimes humorous pre-pre-primitive trio from the era of the troglodytes before the year 1;...'way back with the Neanderthal man."[19] The duet *Fauna* was Stackhouse's only involvement with the Judson Dance Theater.

Fauna was "a taut, sometimes violent, pas de deux," according to Hughes.[20] The photographs of the dance show the two performers in leotards painted with splotches like camouflage or animal markings. In one image Stackhouse perches on Schlichter's back; in another she sits on his thighs as he balances on hands and feet, close to the floor, stomach facing the ceiling. He holds her legs as she moves, then seems to throw her away from him. She jumps up at him, and in a final image he stands over her as she lies on the floor.[21]

According to Schlichter, he and Stackhouse made *Fauna* in response to some of the discussions in Dunn's class about what material could be allowed in a dance.

> Robert Dunn was the most freeing choreography teacher I had ever studied with—and I had studied with a lot of teachers. I mean, a teacher who still called himself a teacher. If you worked with Simone Forti, or Trisha [Brown], that was freeing but you didn't

think of them as teachers in a conventional way. We had this argument in Dunn's class about "What could you do with dance? Was that allowed?" Could I really put my hand on her breast? There were rules. Yvonne [Rainer] and I got into an argument: "What if you want to put your hand up her crotch?" And I said, "Yes!"

So Sally [Stackhouse] and I did a dance specifically about that. Not putting my hand up her crotch, but putting my hand on her crotch as if it were just another part of the body. Put your face in her armpit. Put your foot on her face.

Another interest that informed the dance was the physical experience of two bodies colliding.

We got into the question of how two bodies collide in the air. And that led to something we called "breast bangs." How could we throw ourselves in the air, hit, come down, and go on with the movement? So the dance was about two creatures that did that. It was a love duet about creatures that would hurl themselves in the air, collide and then go on. The movement was very set, except for the bangs. You had to know exactly what you were doing, but you didn't have to do it exactly that way the next time; that was what kept it alive. So there were lots of open spaces within set phrases.

The other thing about that dance was that it was a love duet and we were really into each other's bodies, in ways that you did not expect. But not in ways that had a sexual focus, but simply that every part of the body was used — in lifting, for the most part.

We were also beginning to talk about faces, to experiment with faces. "Did your face express anything?" Yvonne doesn't express a lot facially, for instance. We had all these wonderful arguments about that. "Is that what dance is about? Do you have to move to be a dancer!"[22]

Johnston, who saw this series of three concerts as a refreshing return to the "unburnished physical nature" of dancing typical of the early modern dance of the 1930s — albeit often departing radically from the technical dance basis of the "woolen" period of Graham, Humphrey, Weidman, and Holm — saw *Fauna* as a violent action in the traditional manner.

Fauna is physical in the older sense of throwing yourself around with dramatic contact and violent exertion, always maintaining learned attitudes of dance, in this case attitudes derived more from Limón than from anybody else, but with overtones of Nijinsky and undertones of an Apache dance.[23]

Intermission followed *Fauna,* then fourth on the program was Ruth Emerson's *Cerebris and 2,* another dance built on a spatial grid. The dancers were Lucinda Childs, Deborah Hay, Arlene Rothlein, Ruth Emerson, and Yvonne Rainer. The music was by Malcolm Goldstein.[24] Childs, Hay, and Rothlein danced a trio in designated spaces. Taking cues from each other, they had to think constantly, because they were also given a chart with different movement possibilities, and they threw dice to determine other phrases they performed. Their part of the dance was

Cerebris; Rainer and Emerson danced a duet (hence, *and 2*). Movement possibilities for the duet included tongue to nose, yawn, slap ass, scratch, fluff hair, laugh, talk, cough.[25] Emerson explains:

> I tried to work on cuing off one another, having your own movement and then also having things that were cued from what other people did. I remember Yvonne [Rainer]'s surprising me by asking whether it was okay to make faces, as part of her material, which was obviously of interest to her and something I wouldn't have thought of. I said, "Sure." Sometimes you have an idea and something else turns out to happen. Something interesting happens, although it has nothing to do with what you had in mind.
>
> Here nothing very interesting happened, and the thing I had in mind didn't happen either. Essentially, it was a study. Nowadays you might say it doesn't belong on a concert. I think there were too many instructions, so that nothing much would be visible or understandable to an audience.
>
> The dancers were very nice about working on it, to their credit. Nobody said, "Oh Ruth, come on...."[26]

The fifth dance was John Herbert McDowell's *Auguries*. This time McDowell did write his own musical score. He had originally made the dance while studying movement therapy with Alec Rubin at Master Institute; it was made as a study of hand movements from the exercises Rubin had given. According to McDowell:

> A few years later, Yvonne Rainer told me, "You know, you did five things in that piece that are impossible. They can't be done."
>
> I was very flattered and pleased. I didn't know any better. The dance came totally out of Alec [Rubin]'s class, going by feeling and experiencing. And thinking of funny things to do with hands.
>
> I leapt up in the air and collapsed in the middle of the air. I fell to the floor in a heap. I ran into a pillar as hard as I could. I should have hurt myself, but I didn't. I whirled around several times, so many times I couldn't walk. Then I walked. I sort of fell, and got up, and walked across the stage and got up onto a platform.
>
> Then I did all this stuff with my hands. And finally, I was wearing a sweatshirt with pockets, and I put my hands in the pockets so they disappeared for the first time. Then my hands became very active, very wild. The last thing that happened was that I pulled my hands out and looked at them in total horror.[27]

The sixth dance on the program was Schlichter's *Association(Improvisations)*. The performers were Trisha Brown, Ruth Emerson, Deborah Hay, and Elizabeth Keen.[28] Schlichter had given the dancers a specific structure within which they invented movements. The structure was a process of association, in which one person initiated a movement and that activity sparked a chain of reactions, from copying the movement, to varying it, to bouncing from it to a new action by free association. Schlichter explains:

In "association," you do something like this: you suck your straw, I suck my straw, she sucks her straw. And you might get variations. You get a continuous wave of action. As soon as you as the originator have done what you thought of as the action, you were free. You could initiate a new action, or I could change your suck-the-straw action into something else. It was a wonderful interplay; it was about "How does something roll on in a circle that is ever-changing?"

It was a kind of follow-the-leader structure, but not that literal, and since there were only four, the leader was always changing, and there was no way to tell who was the originator and who was the follower. It's a matter of playing with that mirror. When you get so good at it, it's a symbiotic evolvement.[29]

Following *Association* came a second intermission, then Lucinda Childs's *Three Piece.* This was a solo that extended the movements in the first section of Childs's *Pastime,* which was performed in Concert #4. The music was by Malcolm Goldstein. Childs recalls:

I felt that *Pastime* had been gimmicky. I wanted to just work on exploring something more limited to the first section of *Pastime.* It was a rather traditional piece. I was working with movement, but limiting myself to a very tight area of movement.[30]

Goldstein's *Sanctuary Piece,* for three instruments (piano, treble instrument, and bass instrument), accompanied *Three Piece.* James Tenney played the piano, Goldstein the treble instrument (violin), and Philip Corner the bass instrument (trombone). The three musicians stationed themselves in different places around the sanctuary. The written score for the music provides melodic figures for each player, but also includes unscored silences and the spontaneous choices of repeating and arranging tones taken from the given figures.[31]

According to Childs,

Malcolm Goldstein did the music because he and Arlene Rothlein and I were very close. I was spending a lot of time with Arlene, going back and forth between Waring and Judson rehearsals. I was also dancing with Merle Marsicano and Beverly Schmidt. It was a very busy time. I liked Malcolm and wanted him to do something [with me]. And I didn't want to dance in silence—that was too spooky.

His music was abstract, non-melodic. It had nothing to do with the dance. I didn't relate to it musically at all in my counting structure. That collaboration was in the Cunningham tradition of musical accompaniment that had nothing to do with the actual dancing.[32]

About *Three Piece,* Johnston simply writes, "*Three Piece* is a short, neat, clean, concise dance, well done, in the Cunningham style."[33]

The eighth dance on the program was McDowell's mammoth *Eight Pas de Deux, Pas de Trois, and Finale.* Subtitled "a small token for James Waring's Hallelujah Gardens" (Waring's *At the Hallelujah Gardens,* a dance with Events embedded in it, had been given its premiere earlier that year), McDowell's dance featured seventeen performers and a tape collage with music — all waltzes — by more than forty composers. The set was by Remy Charlip. The performers were Eddie Barton, Trisha Brown, Ruth Emerson, Laura de Freitas, Mark Gabor, Tony Holder, Susan Kaufman, Elizabeth Keen, Deborah Lee, Suzanne Levine, Clare Lorenzi, McDowell, Rudy Perez, Yvonne Rainer, Fred Vassi, Arthur Williams, and Shirley Winston.[34]

Like *Auguries, Eight Pas de Deux* had been made at the Master Institute. For the Judson performance, McDowell recalls,

I asked Remy [Charlip] to make the set. We went to a junk shop and got all these terrible trophy things, about three of them, and piled them on a wooden pillar. The music started — Johann Strauss — and a spotlight came on this pillar with all these terribly shlunky silver things piled up. I had seen the Moiseyev, where they throw a man. So I got the tallest bearers I could find, came out in a fancy costume, with my legs spread, and was thrown, right into the set, and demolished it. It was very spectacular.

The overture had gone on for a long time. And while the music was playing, the audience was looking at this fool thing, for a long time. Maybe two minutes. Then the Strauss came on. The whole thing was waltzes.

I danced the first pas de deux with Trish [Brown]. And then, after I danced with her, she had to surreptitiously go around and pick up all these things I had dropped all over the stage. My next partner and I had to hide the fact that she was picking up the set.

Afterwards, Paul Taylor said to me, "John, that was very dangerous to dance with all this stuff on the stage."

In the pas de deux with Yvonne [Rainer], she came in with a mask over her face, giggling. She kept patting me on the back very hard. And finally, I collapsed and ran offstage and came back on with blood running all over me.

The pas de trois was right after I'd been wounded by Yvonne. I went off, and the two girls came on to do the pas de trois. But I wasn't there. So they had to do a pas de trois as if the third person were there. But they looked horrified and discomposed. It was very funny.

The pas de deux with Ruth Emerson was the last one. I knew I'd be pretty tired by then. Ruth was very big. So I leapt up, put my legs around her, and she waltzed with me for forty-five seconds, and I got my breath back.

Finally six of the girls lifted me over their heads and carried me and four other girls threw roses.

Then everything started to go wrong, and all these new people started coming out on stage. Four men came out of the corners of the stage and did a thing which in some cases was incredibly competent and in some cases totally incompetent.

Eddie Barton came out in a g-string, practically naked, and did three back flips. Then all the dancers were on the stage. The follow spot started going crazy, all over the audience. Then the tape started going crazy, too. From the Neilsen Fourth Symphony to an English recording of "I Feel Pretty." And the thing started to go to pieces, totally. And then the curtain started to open and close arbitrarily. The lights came on for a moment to reveal a huge pyramid of people, precariously balanced. The lights went out and came on again, and the stage was littered with dead people. The curtain closed for the last time, and then Trish Brown came crawling out through the curtain and pulled it back, and that was the end of the piece.[35]

Johnston writes of this extravaganza:

> McDowell...presented his silly spectacle of himself in hundreds of ridiculous rendez-vous (actually *Eight Pas de Deux, Pas de Trois, and Finale*) with a lot of crazy ladies. This may be a one-shot dance, but the injection of big doses of well-considered ham can be a soothing hypodermic in serious times.[36]

Again, rather than ending with the lavish finale of *Eight Pas de Deux, Pas de Trois, and Finale,* Dunn chose an austere conclusion in *Arizona,* by Robert Morris, a solo in four sections that was a paradigm for the "minimalist" strand of dance that was one of many to develop out of Judson Dance Theater.

Morris was born in Kansas City, Missouri, in 1931 and grew up there, attending the University of Kansas City, where he studied engineering, and then Kansas City Art Institute and the California School of Fine Arts. He served in the Army for two years, then attended Reed College from 1953 to 1955. Morris moved back to San Francisco with his wife, Simone Forti, in 1955. He painted Abstract Expressionist paintings, and both of them worked with Ann Halprin and the musicians, painters, and actors in her circle. When the Morrises moved to New York, in 1960, Robert Morris had given up painting, and in fact, no longer thought of himself as an artist. He began making objects, such as a tapering grey plywood tunnel and the *Box with the Sound of Its Own Making,* that were results of a refined strategy of calculation and decision making.[37] He rejected the notion of the art-work as a highly crafted, "beautiful" object that displays the artist's skills and emotional state. As Jill Johnston wrote of his practice:

> Clearly, Morris is *not* an artist in the tradition of making things "work" by an intuitive co-ordination of materials. His sculpture is never the result of those continuous deci-sions whereby an artist accepts and discards each gesture in a conflict and resolution of forces. For Morris, the personal gesture is the assertion of an impenetrable facade.[38]

The concreteness and functional appearance of Morris's sculptures, his attention to the measurement, perception, and involvement of the human body in his objects and their sense of human scale, and his inclu-sion and revelation of the process of making the objects in the objects themselves seem to have led naturally to the use of live performance, spe-cifically dance. The manipulation of objects and materials in live perform-ance allowed Morris to give his works duration and temporality. His insis-tence on the neutral presence—both in the objects and in performance—and his tasklike attitude toward making art fit well with the investigations of the Judson group in regard to the mechanics of performance. Unlike the painters whose activities on the canvas extended logically into Happenings

—manipulations of materials, colors, and textures that often involved fantastic imagery—Morris's manipulations primarily concerned the human body and its matter-of-fact relations to itself, other bodies, articulations of time and space.

Morris's first performance, in fact, involved no visible human presence. In 1960, he presented a performance at the Living Theater in which his *Column,* a grey rectangular column measuring eight feet by two feet by two feet, stood vertically for three-and-one-half minutes, then fell—Morris pulled it with a string—and stood horizontally for three-and-one-half minutes. According to Johnston, "Morris said he wanted a change from the vertical to the horizontal with a rest in each position. His own role as a performer was simply that of facilitating the fall of the column."[39] Morris had been assigned seven minutes for the length of his performance, and his initial decision was to bifurcate that duration drastically.

Morris performed in Forti's *See-Saw* in 1960 and in her evening of dance constructions in 1961.[40] Morris writes, about the ideas underlying dance he shared with Forti:

> My involvement in theater has been with the body in motion. However changed or reduced the motion might have been or however elaborate the means used might have been, the focus was this movement. In retrospect this seems a constant value which was preserved. From the beginning I wanted to avoid the pulled-up, turned-out, anti-gravitational qualities that not only gave a body definition and role as "dancer" but qualify and delimit the movement available to it. The challenge was to find alternative movement.
>
> I was not the first to attempt such alternatives. Simone [Forti] Whitman, together with others, had already explored the possibilities inherent in a situation of "rules" or game-like structures which required the performer to respond to cues which might, for example, indicate changes in height or spatial position. A fair degree of complexity of these rules and cues effectively blocked the dancer's performing "set" and reduced him to frantically attempting to respond to cues—reduced him from performance to action.... [In Forti's 1961 concert] focused clearly for the first time were two distinct means by which new actions could be implemented: rules or tasks and devices (she termed them "constructions") or objects.[41]

For Morris, objects were the preferred means to solve problems and thus create a structure for the dance. The manipulation of an object generated movement without becoming more important than the performer or performance.[42]

In *Arizona,* Morris's movement was nearly as reductive as it had been in the *Column* event. The performance was somewhat more elaborate in terms of the objects and structure. In section one, Morris contrasted the nearly imperceptible, slow turn of his torso from front to left during the course of five minutes, while his voice on tape described the animatedly laborious process of sorting cows. In section two, Morris carefully aimed and threw a javelin; in part three, he swung a small light as the stage lights dimmed; in part four, he adjusted a T-form.

> The objects I used held no inherent interest for me but were means for dealing with specific problems. For example the establishment of an inverse ratio between movement, space, and duration was implemented by the use of a "T"-like form which I could adjust and move away from, adjust again and move away from, and so on until the sequence of movements according to the ratio had been completed. Or again, the establishment of a focus shifting between the egocentric and the exocentric could be accomplished by swinging overhead in a fully lighted room a small light at the end of a cord. The lights in the room fade as the cord is slowly let out until finally in total darkness only the moving point of light is visible as it revolves in the large space above the heads of the audience.[43]

Morris points out that from the time of this dance (but obviously present in the *Column* event also) the coexistence of static and mobile elements has been an essential part of his work. Time, while a necessary aspect of the performance, was "less a focus than a context"; similarly, Morris used space "at most as a way of anchoring the work, riveting it to a maximum frontality." The motivation for using slow motion in *Arizona* also involved a ratio between time and space: Morris had noticed that in the rollerskating rink at Concert #5 the vast space seemed to absorb and dissipate the individual dancer's movements. "It was apparent that only the smallest movements kept their weight or mass in such a large, nonrectangular space."[44]

Concert #6 had begun and ended with solo, reductive, slow-motion dances. Concert #7, comprising eight dances, began and ended with structured improvisations. In the first dance, Joseph Schlichter's *Faces of the Coin,* eight dancers carried out instructions they found on cards placed on the seats of chairs. Instructions were also given to audience members by the dancers. The dancers were Trisha Brown, Ruth Emerson, Mark Gabor, Deborah Hay, Elizabeth Keen, Yvonne Rainer, Arlene Rothlein, and Elaine Summers. Schlichter remembers:

> There were chairs placed around the space, and on each chair was a pile of cards, and you were to go on stage and take a pile. There were some overlaps. One of them might say, "Climb a wall for thirty seconds." And you did whatever that meant to you. You could have a screaming fit the way Yvonne Rainer might, or whatever. Each chair was designated by a number, and one instruction might say, "Go to chair #4." If you were in the audience, and you didn't know which chair was number four, you just had to do it. Everything was done according to a time schedule. There was no music, but there were parts where you were told to sing something. I was interested in what different people interpret something as.[45]

Johnston wrote enthusiastically about the "formlessness" of *Faces of the Coin*:

> Here the chaos was a result of eight performers making spontaneous interpretations from instructions they found on cards when they first arrived at a chair. The isolation, interference, or collaboration that ensued had no precedent in a rehearsal, so the performers were as surprised as the audience and the action was like bouncing molecules.[46]

Second on the program was another dance structured by poses, Rudy Perez's *Take Your Alligator with You,* danced by Perez and Elaine Summers.[47] This was the first dance choreographed by Perez, who had danced in the Judson concerts since Concert #1, in which he performed in Summers's *The Daily Wake.* Perez had grown up in New York City, studying art in school, and beginning dance classes relatively late, at age twenty-one. Perez studied dance first at the New Dance Group and then at the Martha Graham studio.[48]

Take Your Alligator with You was a combination of short nontechnical movement phrases, spoken lines, and stillnesses. Perez wore a suit and hat and carried an umbrella, and Summers wore a dress and high-heeled shoes. They posed in attitudes halfway between a bourgeois couple and a vaudeville team, their bodies stiff and mannered. Finally, he lifted her as if she were a suitcase and carried her as she lay horizontally.[49]

Third in Concert #7 was Deborah Hay's *All Day Dance,* which Johnston called "one of the most exciting dances on this series." It was performed by Lucinda Childs, Ruth Emerson, Fred Herko, Tony Holder, Arlene Rothlein, and Joseph Schlichter, to music by John Herbert McDowell, played by Edward V. Boagni, Malcolm Goldstein, Kenneth Sarch, and McDowell. *All Day Dance* extended some of Hay's concerns with the scoring of sounds and movements in *City Dance.* According to McDonagh, each dancer followed separate cues in the sound score, which dictated both the movements and their durations. Then each one repeated a single phrase until exhausted. Tony Holder remembers that some activities depended on what the other dancers were doing, and that one rule allowed for interruptions of other people's activities. "I remember Joe [Schlichter] holding Cindy [Childs] by the neck and lifting her off the ground. Freddy Herko was hanging onto a pillar and Ruth [Emerson] was dragging his foot, twisting his leg. The dance was very fragmented." Hay remembers that Schlichter "was very rough and everybody else had to watch out for him so they wouldn't get hurt."[50]

For Johnston, *All Day Dance* was an exemplar of the new, fundamental physicality of this dance that fell somewhere between theatrical dancing and free play.

> The pure vitality of thrusting jumps (the kind you might see in a child careening down a sand dune), of crashing falls or baseball slides, and of hard swift rolls on the floor combine easily and probably after no thought of combination, with a different kind of vitality more dance-like, in the flat arm flings, long jet-stride walks, vibrations, triplets with port du bras, wide zingy turns, and high fast leg extensions. The six dancers, in shirts and faded dungarees, make all this activity cling and separate in a clear open space in a continuum of dynamic tension and release.[51]

Intermission followed *All Day Dance,* then Elaine Summers's *Dance for Lots of People,* for fifteen performers, to music by John Herbert McDowell. The performers were Leroy Bowser, Pearl Bowser, Lucinda Childs, June Ekman, Ruth Emerson, Mark Gabor, Tony Holder, Harold Johnson, Deborah Lee, Rudy Perez, Katherine Pira, Arlene Rothlein, Carol Summers, Elaine Summers, and John Worden. Choreographed intuitively, rather than by Summers's preferred method of chance, the dance looked like a silent communal ritual, or a cathartic scene from a German Expressionist drama. In fact, Summers says it was inspired by the Japanese film *Ugetsu.*[52]

The group entered slowly and noiselessly, taking gliding steps and moving as a single clump, starting at the upstage right corner of the sanctuary space. Three people in succession were lifted up out of the cluster, as it began to move imperceptibly to the left. Next everyone in the group extended some body part; backlit dramatically, this clump with outstretched hands and feet had the visual impact of one of Mary Wigman's mass dances. Each person lifted his or her face slowly toward the ceiling, then lowered it and snapped it to the right, then back to center. As a group, the dancers jumped small jumps, then rushed out into the space and fell, rose in slow motion, then descended back to the floor in slow motion. While the group fell and rose and fell, finally lying motionless for a full minute, soloists came out of the mass to dart and gesture among the scattered bodies. When the cluster reassembled with a sudden rush toward center, it began to vibrate quickly, moving further, to the upstage left corner, where the dancers formed a box configuration in which, with machinelike regularity, they filed from the back line to the front line. Finally, the box became a line of dancers holding hands to snake back across the stage and off.[53]

Summers remembers that,

> I had seen it in the beginning as huge masses with lines spinning out from the mass. Then I realized I wanted lots and lots of people. And in making the dance, I learned that when you have masses of people, the movements get very large. I had to keep making the steps tinier and tinier. When we did the jumps, they had to be tiny little jumps, because with everyone jumping, it looked enormous in terms of weight.[54]

Fifth on the program was Elizabeth Keen's *Bird Poem,* another solo done to the jazz of Don Friedman. Keen simply describes *Bird Poem* as "images of flight." She was not interested, she explains, as some of the other Judson dancers were, in "taking five movements and putting them in a certain order." She choreographed intuitively and improvisationally, working from images of sensation. She recalls:

> I felt that even if you employed chance techniques, the selections that you made very much reflected what you were and what you chose. When I make a dance, I try to destroy the order anyway; I try to do what's unpredictable. I felt that as a method it didn't lead me to something that was beyond myself. I just said, "There I am; I just came at it a different way."
>
> You never get away from yourself. You just can't You'd better use yourself, because that's what you've got. You can cloak it in whatever method is popular at the time, which you'll either have a superficial or a deep connection with.

Keen remembers that she was very drawn to improvisation, and used avant-garde jazz as accompaniment partly because of that fascination, but that after she studied composition with Bessie Schönberg, while working on her master's degree at Sarah Lawrence, she rejected it as something to show on stage. "I felt that you can get things from actually choreographing something that you cannot get from improvisation. I improvise when I'm going to make things up. But extraordinary things can happen in improvisation that I don't think you can get choreographically."[55]

The sixth dance in the concert was Carolee Schneemann's *Chromelodeon (4th Concretion),* performed by Lucinda Childs, Ruth Emerson, Deborah Hay, Carol Summers, and John Worden. The music was a sound collage by Schneemann and James Tenney that included barrel organ music, J. S. Bach, and electronic sounds created by Tenney. Working from images of silent films, children's games, toys, ballet dancers, and chickens, Schneemann used lights, painted costumes, food, words, and physical interactions to create "a wild and lyrical assemblage of rags, hemp, costume, paint, movement, and objects."[56] The women dressed and undressed themselves, were pulled and carried, dressed and undressed by the men. Worden began the piece by coming down from the balcony to set up the decor — a rack of costumes. Childs wrote words with her body and a long yellow ribbon; two men turned the tall Emerson over and over as she lay on the floor; people spoke in Japanese; Worden turned the women like spinning tops and then covered them with a blanket, where the men struggled with them. Emerson and Childs climbed into the church balcony and played Bach's *Em Fugue* on the church organ. Worden carried food in on an apron made out of an American flag, then ate. Carol Summers, disguised as a "Wolfman," pursued Deborah Hay, who shrieked as the lights flickered in a slow-motion, dream-like impression. The lights played a palette of bright colors: gold, white, magenta, yellow, green, blue. Childs and Emerson put on tutus made of curtains and performed ballet steps as Worden called out the names of the steps in a flat, Midwestern accent: "Reel levy. Tan do. Pass de ducks." Finally, all five imitated chickens as the lights dimmed.[57]

Schneemann had originally planned, as a finale, a rooster solo for Rainer, inspired by *Three Seascapes*. An early score, written in March 1963, names "John [Worden], Alex [Hay], Cindy [Childs], Debby [Hay], Ruth [Emerson], and Yvonne [Rainer]" as performers. In a letter to Rainer, Schneemann explained "Why you-for-rooster-madness":

> Any movement appears to be the quality of its physical source—intention is only what is done, how it is possible at all. (A small compact body will not cut space with propulsion of a long, thin limbed body.)...
>
> Axis can be described; I can't describe the variation of axis from one body to another....it *is* felt.
>
> The body is a unit. (I would like the arms to fly out of the sockets, the head to levitate a few feet above the shoulders...to the left...to the right and Spin around!)
>
> The face: plastic concentration of expressive details—psychological focus. (Have the body grin, wink, stare, subdue a question.)
>
> Glass fragments for a construction. The green glass: bottle shoulder, curved edge, three raised letters COI. Can't place it where the rectangular brown fragment is placed, each moving to its particular function, not interchangeable. Where I need an arched strip of wood, I do not put a vertical strip of wood.
>
> Rooster. Rooster music has greater dramatic variation than chicken music. Figure of independent movement. Continually in quest. Standing self-absorbed....something about the floor...the look of it...not grass, not water, not a hand. Following slow motion of eye passage—crack between boards—walking into minute space may be the sense....that the body could be where the eye is, actually!... Walking quickens. The floor patterns are set by where you need to be. Head moves to free itself from eye peel; quick succession of staccato head assertions and the arms begin to grow rhythms *against* this head, (eyefull). Squalk could be breath release on tension between head-arm movement. And quickening. Independence of head from arms and neck provoke the feet, the knees...they are lifting...jumping...fingers fly apart. (A bird can fly...a rooster flies a little more than a man can.) A way of becoming another source of energy; its necessity takes on our own aroma, hue. Strangeness of exceeding, incorporating banality of chicken feet image (in soup, in chicken shit, in pebble, grass, a wood railing edge by them). Flapping wings, flapping arms. Indulge it: flapping, squalking, flying, screeching, scratching. No more space. All time drawn into rooster (figure of independent movement, eh?). This ends the piece.
>
> Why you to do it. What I mentioned about the goose on stage, in fright during concert, and your turn to help it, that you assumed its gestures, and its intent. Range of energy you control is what I see for this part, and No One else has a comparable range.[58]

Rainer, however, refused the part. She was in the midst of preparations for *Terrain,* and she wanted to work on her own choreography. She felt that even with Schneemann's instructions, the improvisatory nature of *Chromelodeon* required more thought and participation from her than she could commit. Schneeman replaced the rooster solo with a chicken cluster for five dancers. "It took [five] dancers to do the part Yvonne [Rainer] wouldn't do," she claims.[59] Schneemann's conception of choreography was unconventional in part because of this flexibility, stemming from an image rather than a kinetic assignment of steps.

Schneemann refers to the movements in the work as "object equivalences" of three kinds: the spins, leaps, pushes, runs, and whirls that correspond to a child's spinning top; the focused, slicing energy of the chase; and the resolution in the chicken cluster. The title came from the words "nickelodeon" (barrel organ) and "*chromo*: combination of forms, colored vision; *chromatic*: having notes not included in diatonic scale, admitting notes marked with accidentals."[60]

Johnston discusses *Chromelodeon* in her review of Concerts #6, #7 and #8 as an example of the "extreme range of interest" displayed in the programs.

> *Chromelodeon...* is essentially a messy, brainless "happening" with lots of clothes, paper, rags, burlap, and paint. The five performers get dressed up, move things from one place to another, get under piles of stuff, manipulate each other into odd positions. The gassy werewolf duet, the monkey-man on a mound with a megaphone, the jungle of paper, color, sounds (which could be more complete in a small environment) all made the kind of scene where nothing is coherent or formulated, where the activity is without premeditation or afterthought, like some form of life prior to the development of the forebrain — plankton or paleolithic.[61]

If McDowell's *Eight Pas de Deux, Pas de Trois, and Finale* had satirized ballet by taking its conventional dramatic structures and stuffing them with unexpected movements and a mixture of trained and untrained dancers, Schneemann aimed a blast at ballet by putting its technical movements in an unexpected environment.

An intermission followed *Chromelodeon,* then David Gordon's *Random Breakfast* and Trisha Brown's *Trillium,* both of which had been performed in Concert #5, in Washington (see Chapter 4). Again, Dunn's Zen-like taste for asymmetry led him to close the concert with the lavish *Random Breakfast* as the penultimate number, surprising the senses with the delicate clarity of the final dance, *Trillium.*

Concert #8 consisted of three long dances, with an intermission between each one. The program began and ended with two large-scale pieces — Arlene Rothlein's *Another Letter to the Sun (for Charles Ives)* was first and Philip Corner's *Flares* last — and in the middle was Judith Dunn's duet, *Speedlimit.*[62]

Rothlein's *Another Letter to the Sun (for Charles Ives)* was performed by Lucinda Childs, Philip Corner, June Ekman, Ruth Emerson, Deborah Hay, Fred Herko, Elizabeth Keen, Deborah Lee, Norma Marder, John Herbert McDowell, Elizabeth Munro, Rudy Perez, Diana Reil, Arlene Rothlein, Beverly Schmidt, Carol Summers, and Elaine Summers. The music was by Charles Ives and Domenico Scarlatti, and it was performed by Norma Marder (voice) and James Tenney (piano). Elizabeth Munro painted the backdrop.[63]

According to Rainer, *Another Letter to the Sun* was a series of tableaux quoting epic paintings by the French painters David and Delacroix. Waring, who though it "very impressive," also assumed it was based on paintings. According to McDowell,

> It was based on statues. There were two groups of people and — she showed us pictures of sculpture by these two people whose names I can't think of — and one group was fairly static, taking at will poses as they decided to interpret them from these pictures of sculpture, and the other group had a sort of general movement that went in terms of the other sculptor, and then at the end everybody sat down on the floor and a piano came out and Norma Marder sang an art song.[64]

Johnston writes, "Miss Rothlein's tribute to Charles Ives contains an interesting sculptural section in which one group of dancers moves in a slow classical tableau after the painter David and the other group moves with slow baroque expansion after the painter Delacroix."[65]

Like the choreographers who turned to sports movements, games, films, and photographs to shape their dances, Rothlein turned to a non-dance source for her movements. But the nature of that source — a static art form, from another era — lent the dance a quality of slow and constant motion.

Judith Dunn's *Speedlimit* was the balancing duet for herself and Robert Morris that had first been performed at the Washington concert (see Chapter 4). The dynamic changed from the slowly moving vertical groupings of *Another Letter to the Sun* to the pinpointed tensions and balances, much of it taking place on the floor, of *Speedlimit.*

The last piece in Concert #8 was Corner's *Flares,* a dance that involved slide projections and the simultaneous translation into musical and movement terms of a written score. The performers were Corner, Malcolm Goldstein, Dick Higgins, Norma Marder, Elizabeth Munro, Max Neuhaus, Arlene Rothlein, Beverly Schmidt, James Tenney, and Vincent Wright.[66]

Corner gave each performer an individual "design sheet," which scored activities in terms of time and either space or pitch. All of the activities were structured as bursts, with silence and darkness intervening. The silences averaged nineteen seconds, but could be as short as eleven seconds and as long as thirty-one seconds. In interpreting their individual scores, the performers—"players," as Corner called them—had a number of ways to respond to the shapes and colors. For instance, Corner wrote in his instructions, "for musicians, the shape may come off as the actual sound, or it may be a possibly very different sound resulting from an action in the specified shape." The performers were not divided into musicians and dancers; any "player" could realize his or her score or parts of it either visually—in movement—or sonically. Also, slides of these score-drawings were projected on the wall and these projections were moved around, according to the same loose rules for interpretation. The rules for the "game" directed its movement in space as well as time, and specified the ways in which groups cohered and dispersed as players became attracted to each other's activities.[67]

Beverly Schmidt remembers that,

> *Flares* was at the end of a very long program. It was very hot, and people began walking out through it at the end. The audience got restless, and in order to get out they had to walk through it.
>
> People expressed themselves more then. There were often squabbles in the audience, and if people didn't like something, they'd express it. Or if they got bored, they'd express that. The audiences were lively and interesting, that was part of the whole thing.
>
> I remember watching two people walking through the dance and thinking, "You've got your nerve!"[68]

In general, Corner's musical interests diverged from those of Cage and other new American composers in that he was less interested in rhythmic structures and the measurement of time than in "the direct presence of sound."

> That meant color, dynamics, and pitch to the extent that it was wobbling, full of sensual, emotional implications. The only thing defined was how a tone moves.
>
> Learning calligraphy loosened up my sense that you could get a beautiful harmony between a rather precise method of conception and something free.[69]

Corner thought of his Judson performances as musical compositions, not as dances. "I extended what it is to be a musician, but I never did a piece that wasn't music. I did pieces that might have been something else also."[70] In *Flares,* as in all of the works on the Judson programs, the participants are called "performers" in the printed program, leaving the responsibility of defining the art form up to the audience.

According to Johnston,

Philip Corner's *Flares* was the last event on the entire series. Everybody was hot and tired, so the interminable alternation of activity and blackouts became unbearable. That was too bad, because there were many beautiful moments—of dancing, lights, costumes, painting, singing, and instrumentation. The short span of each scattered assemblage really did flare up and die off like scenes lit by lightning in partially unknown places. But the blackout intervals were at least eleven seconds long, and since there were about 35 of them, the pleasurable sensation of not knowing exactly what you've just seen turned into an intense desire to be sure of something, just once.[71]

The Judson group had not only changed the methods by which dances were made and the content of the dances; their practice of putting on concerts during the summer—traditionally a quiet time in New York for the arts, and especially for dance performance—and of presenting their concerts free of charge to a community audience were two factors that affected the social institution of dance viewing. In a Sunday article in the *New York Times* in August 1963, Allen Hughes suggested that the dance world had changed its habits partly because "the proposition that summertime automatically relieves city-bound people of esthetic sensibility has been proven false." Other reasons for the expansion of dance in all seasons, he thought, were that people had begun to realize that dancing is theater, and that as theater it "may be a more reliable source of literate entertainment" than Broadway theater. And, he announced, "the tenet that stage dancing is enjoyable only to connoisseurs, initiates, 'eggheads,' or something worse continues to lose place in the American credo."

Last year, only the avant-garde Judson Dance Theater had the courage to put on mid-summer events (two), and they constituted the only serious dance offerings we had until the Rebekah Harkness Foundation Dance Festival was presented at the Delacorte Theater as a post-Labor Day postscript to the Shakespeare Festival.

Compare that with what we have had and are having now. The Judson people put on three consecutive performances at their home base on Washington Square and then moved to the Gramercy Arts Theater to do four more in two weeks.

The Harkness Festival added three single Monday-evening events in full summer to its scheduled post-Labor Day week-long series. The Heights Opera Association, which began by giving operas on the Mall in Central Park, included two dance programs on its schedule. . . .

In June, dance got rather prominent play in the New York Philharmonic's Prominade Concerts in Philharmonic Hall. Now, dance is having a three-event summer series of its own in Lincoln Center's "August Fanfare."[72]

Concerts #9 through #12 were given at the Gramercy Arts Theater on 30 July, 1, 6, and 8 August—two Tuesday and two Thursday evenings. The concerts were produced by Herbert Semmel, who either donated the theater or "angeled" the concerts by providing financial backing.[73] The Judson Poets' Theater was using the church for their summer production of two plays by Paul Goodman, and Elaine Summers had been asked to present a concert at the Gramercy Arts Theater, so she organized the series there.[74] The credits for all four concerts were the same. William Linich and Johnny Dodd did the lights; Malcolm Goldstein and John Herbert McDowell were responsible for the music; Al Hansen did the sets and served as stage manager; Alex Hay and Lucinda Childs did the publicity; and Ruth Emerson, William Linich, and Yvonne Rainer served as the program committee.[75] Twenty-five pieces, some of which were primarily musical, were shown on the four evenings. The participation of Al Hansen, who was involved in Happenings, as stage manager and set designer, as well as the creator of one of the pieces in Concert #12, broadened the Judson network further. So did the participation of some of the previous generation of avant-garde choreographers — James Waring, Aileen Passloff, and Beverly Schmidt — who had taught or influenced members of the Judson Dance Theater but had not performed at the church. According to Rainer, Waring did not consider the church a space where "real" concerts could be performed, but thought of it as an informal workshop situation.[76] It was not until later in August 1963, after the Judson group had given twelve cooperative concerts and one individual concert, both at the church and in other locations, that Waring decided to perform at the church.

The first concert at the Gramercy Arts Theater comprised six pieces. The first, *Acapulco,* was made by Judith Dunn and performed by Lucinda Childs, Judith Dunn, Alex Hay, and Deborah Hay. Dunn juxtaposed a variety of unrelated activities. It was the only dance she choreographed that did not depend on conventional dance technique. She had planned the entire work in advance and held one rehearsal to teach the performers their parts.[77] For Johnston, *Acapulco* was a paradigm for the incorporation of "real" situations into a dance.

> A woman irons a dress in a natural manner, but the dress she irons is on her body, and she does it while leaning on a diagonal tilt. Two women sit down together and play cards the way they might on the floor of anybody's living room. A girl in a nightgown [Lucinda Childs] rises in slow motion on the chair where she had been seated, immobilized, for some time, and turns her torso, arms in second position, until she falls off balance into the arms of a man who has been standing for quite a while waiting for her to fall. This particular piece is more in the nature of an event than a dance. Yet the emphasis rests on movement.[78]

As Childs sat on her chair downstage right, Dunn came toward her very slowly from upstage left, holding a comb, and, still in slow motion, combed Childs's hair. Childs said "Ouch," also in slow motion.[79]

The second piece was McDowell's *First Act Finale,* another theatrical extravaganza. It was performed by Joanna Vischer, Eddie Barton, Jose

Evans, Michael Malcé, David Schiller, and Arthur Williams. The music, by Johann Strauss, Jr., was "Genug, damit, genug," from *Fledermaus* — a second act finale, as the program noted.[80]

Eddie Barton remembers that in *First Act Finale,*

> Joanna Vischer was sitting, dressed in a white dress, with flowers, and there were different things going on around her. I didn't do very much. I leaned against a wall, mostly, and watched David Schiller. He'd go upstage, and then come downstairs, and look, and look at Joanna, who'd get up to sing, or be about to sing and then sit down again. I didn't mind not doing much; I was getting used to being on stage.[81]

According to McDowell,

> It ended up with Joanna Vischer getting stabbed in the belly with real fake blood spurting all over the stage. It was marvelous and we worked for a long time to get that effect. Spurted all over. She had a pouch. And Arthur Williams tore up a book and let a bird fly.... It was a theater piece.[82]

The third dance on the program was Sally Gross's *Back Country,* a solo done to a recording by jazz pianist and singer Mose Allison of "Back Country Blues." Gross was lowered onto the stage sitting in a tire and wearing a blue chiffon dress, then performed a dance that was an abstraction of familiar movements and that ended with her on the floor with her legs up on the wall of the stage, spinning around on the floor and coming up stomach first.

Gross remembers:

> I had this image of myself descending from the ceiling in a tire. Why couldn't I fly like they do in Hollywood, like Peter Pan? So I talked to Al Hansen about it, and he said, "There's no reason why it can't be done." He got me a big truck tire, because you can't fit in a car tire.
>
> Then I really got a concept about weight and what it is to lift somebody, and once they get them up, how to lower them without letting them fall. I remember Al saying it was one of the hardest things he could ever have imagined, that if he'd had any idea it was going to be like that he never would have done it.
>
> He got me up there on a pulley. That was wonderful. They lowered me down, the tire hit the ground (it wasn't supposed to), and I kind of flipped out of it. Then the tire went back up and I got to do the dance.[83]

After *Back Country* came intermission, then Ruth Emerson's *Cerebris,* an abbreviated version of her *Cerebris and 2,* performed in Concert #6. Here it was danced by Lucinda Childs and Deborah Hay, using Goldstein's music from the original.[84]

Philip Corner's *Big Trombone,* fifth on the program, was a piece of music. Corner played the trombone over a collage of other sounds.[85] The piece was done several times, besides at the Gramercy, once as a musical accompaniment for a dance by Phyllis Lamhut. Corner speaks about *Big Trombone* having come out of his involvement with physical movement, through Judson, and also out of his interest in jazz music.

> I was just playing the trombone in a vigorous, physical way, organically related to the music itself. There were no gratuitous theatrics. I thought new music, in terms of a harmonic and rhythmic language, lacked a dimension jazz had—that is, a certain rawness. I wanted to create in my own terms something that had an unimpeded, uninhibited rush of physical energy.[86]

Big Trombone lasted five or six minutes of full-bodied sound. "It's exhausting to play," Corner remarks. In a reversal of the practice of musical scoring, Corner began to use the tape of his own performance of *Big Trombone* as its score, transmitting the piece to other performers more like a choreographer might have dancers learn their roles by watching a film or videotape than like a composer usually communicates his or her musical composition. "One has to listen to my tape, absorb the general aspect of what's going on, and then recreate it." Later, Corner added some written instructions to supplement listening to the tape, such as "Big sounds, full sounds," "Move the trombone around in space," and "You really play your head off."[87]

The sixth piece on the program was Lucinda Childs's *Minus Auditorium Equipment and Furnishings,* performed by June Ekman, Ruth Emerson, Sally Gross, Alex Hay, and Deborah Hay. The dance was a structured improvisation given form by the rule that the dancers had to navigate their ways around the stage without making contact with the actual surface of the stage. They had to use chairs and benches, or each other. "The one surface you could not use was what everyone was accustomed to using in a theater," explains Childs. "It was more of an obstacle course [than a dance]. It had the quality of a Happening." Alex Hay provided the sound by accomplishing a separate task: He sawed through a large cardboard box with a hand saw. Standing inside the box, he was at first invisible. After he sawed through it, along a spiral path, the box fell away; when he got to the bottom of the box, the dance ended.[88]

The first dance in Concert #10, Elaine Summers's *Country Houses,* was also a direct exploration of theatrical space and conventions. It was a piece about entrances and exits. The performers were Eddie Barton, Lucinda Childs, June Ekman, Ruth Emerson, Sally Gross, Deborah Hay, Al Kurchin, and Kathy Pira. The sound was provided by Robert Dunn.[89]

Summers recalls:

> The theater had a low, overhanging proscenium arch, and it was a long drop to the

stage. Some people came in from the audience, some came up from a trap door, some came in from the side of the balcony down a ladder. I asked Robert Dunn if he would do the music and he said yes.[90]

Dunn arranged dialogues for the dancers by taking lines from plays by Oscar Wilde. The title of the dance derives from one of the spoken lines. Dunn chose Wilde because he found the lines:

suitable as the kind of verbal material I was looking for, a formal text in English, which yet restrained itself to "personal" matter, and was not immediately identifiable as to author or by content. Of course, I had to avoid the famous paradoxes, and today would probably look for such material in the dialogue of the novels of Anthony Trollope.[91]

Summers remembers that Dunn insisted on rehearsing the dancers so that they would say the lines in a specific, flat style.

The dancers did the lines exquisitely, although it took a great deal of work for Robert [Dunn] to get the exact tone he wanted.

First there were the entrances. Then there was a section with everyone lying in a circle and talking about going to the club and the evening's entertainment. Then there was a section where they're rushing about and as they pass each other, they make assignations and comment on each other. Then there was a dance where one woman was held in the air by two men. She was not to touch the ground, and they constantly changed positions. She had lines like "Love changes one," and "I am changed," all quotes about love. Then there were the exits.[92]

James Waring thought that *Country Houses* was one of Summers's best dances, and remembered that in it "Everyone wore white...and it had people climbing over the proscenium, and Bob Dunn got words from Oscar Wilde." Adds McDowell, "And there were ladders, and there was a lot that happened up in the air. Ruth Emerson saying something about German grammar while hanging from the ceiling."[93]

Second on the program for Concert #10 was Eddie Barton's *Pop #1,* a solo. Barton was born in Missouri but grew up in Columbus, Ohio. As a child he had no dance training—except for imitating dancers he saw in movies on his own—but he was active in gymnastics, and involved with the local swimming and diving team, initially because he had asthma "and couldn't do anything else." McDowell had asked him to do some gymnastics in *Eight Pas de Deux, Pas de Trois, and Finale.* After that performance, Alec Rubin held a party, and there Barton met James Waring, who invited him to come to his classes at the studio on St. Mark's Place. Barton went to a few of the workshop sessions, but felt shy about not having much to contribute. *Pop #1* and *Pop #2* (in Concert #11) were the two dances he choreographed in Judson Dance Theater programs. He danced in the works of various other choreographers, and especially in those of Passloff and Waring.[94]

Barton describes *Pop #1*:

> I walked out on stage with a small mat rolled up, wearing a tan leotard with a string around my waist, carrying a balloon. I came in, rolled the mat down, took the balloon out, showed it, blew it up, tied it, set it down on the mat, walked away from the mat on the diagonal. I knelt down, stood up to check the wind, then knelt down again and did a back three-quarter. That's like a back flip, but instead of landing on your feet, you land on your body. I landed on the mat, bursting the balloon.[95]

After Pop #1 came Rudy Perez's *Take Your Alligator With You,* the duet that had been performed in Concert #7. This time it was danced by Perez and Elizabeth Keen. John Herbert McDowell's *Auguries,* from Concert #6, followed, then intermission.[96]

The fifth event on the program was *Blue Suede,* a piece of collage music by James Tenney. *Blue Suede* had been performed already in "A Program for Sounds and Bodies" in December 1962. There it was listed as one of three tape pieces by Tenney; the other two were *Improvisation for Medea* and *Noise Study.*[97]

Two dances by Elizabeth Keen followed: *Blinkers* (the title was later changed to *Blinders*), originating from a feeling of blindness, and *Thumbs* (later called *Reins*), a dance about control.[98]

The concert closed with Beverly Schmidt's *The Seasons,* a solo excerpt from Roberts Blossom's "filmstage" work, *Blossoms.* A mixed-media performance, the dance used music by Philip Corner, Malcolm Goldstein, and Henry Purcell, and a film by Mario Jorrin.[99] *The Seasons* had first been performed, as *Duet for One Person,* as part of *Blossoms* on 27 May 1963, at the Square East Theater on West Fourth Street, where it ran on Monday nights; during the rest of the week Second City appeared there. In the mixed-media form he called "filmstage," Blossom wanted to separate the eye and the ear, rather than synthesizing their sensations as most theater does. His strategy was to combine film, slide projections, live action, dramatic acting, singing, and music. *Blossoms* was a series of vignettes performed by Taylor Mead, Schmidt (who by then had married Blossom), and Blossom himself. Blossom directed Schmidt's improvisation, which was accompanied by films of Schmidt dancing in the studio. Someone from the Judson group saw that performance and asked Schmidt to repeat it in the upcoming series of concerts. Schmidt changed the dance by studying the film of herself, memorizing her own movements, and then choreographing a dance in four sections that was more tightly structured and coordinated with the film than the dance in *Blossoms.* Walter

Gutman, who also saw *Blossoms,* gave Schmidt a grant to produce her concert at the YMHA in 1964.[100]

Schmidt already knew several members of the Judson group and had attended a workshop session. A member of Alwin Nikolais's company from the early 1950s, she presented concerts of her own work and taught at Henry Street Settlement House until she left Nikolais in 1962. That year (1962–1963), she taught at Sarah Lawrence College, replacing Bessie Schönberg, who was on sabbatical leave. Schmidt had a studio at 2 Pitt Street, in the same building in which Philip Corner lived, next door to the Henry Street Playhouse. Schmidt's studio was the one large, open space in the building, which was otherwise divided into apartments; Corner kept his piano there, and friends of both Schmidt's and Corner's gave performances there. Schmidt met Malcolm Goldstein and Arlene Rothlein through Corner. She had already met Yvonne Rainer, when Rainer was married to the painter Al Held and Schmidt was married to Hank Jensen, a sculptor. Jensen worked closely with Hans Hoffman, and Rainer had been working as a model at Hoffman's school on Eighth Street before she began to dance. Schmidt remembers seeing Rainer at art world parties. Schmidt recalls:

> After I left the Nikolais company, Yvonne [Rainer] asked me, "Why don't you come to the workshop?" After Robert Dunn had finished teaching, she continued it in her loft on St. Mark's Place and Second Avenue. So I did go, once. What they did was very much like what we had done in class at Henry Street, in the improvisation class in which we brought things in, and did structured improvisations.
>
> But it was very time-consuming at the workshop, because everything was very long. These were not pieces; this was a lab. Some of it I thought was interesting and some wasn't. I really wasn't that interested in improvisation any more, except in the context of a piece.[101]

When Schmidt remade her dance for the Gramercy Arts Theater, she found that it seemed to express four different moods, so she named it *The Seasons.* In the first section, Schmidt wore a costume that suggested a circus performer—black tights and tunic, a bolero and a plumed derby hat—and she carried a hoop. She thought of this section as late spring. Her movements were sharp and energetic, centering around the hoop; circling it, twirling it on her wrists, tracing figure-eights. Corner played the trombone. For the next season, early fall, Schmidt wore a long blue gown and her movements were more subdued. Her spine and arms undulated, she posed in profile, she turned slowly, then quickly, she mimicked the film, in opposition. Then she quoted steps from the dance she would do in the fourth section. In the third section, Indian summer, Schmidt wore a red flowered muumuu, entered with Goldstein, and both held a frozen position. A slide of red flowers was projected on the screen. Schmidt slowly lowered herself to the floor while Goldstein began to play the violin. She rolled over, got up to run back and forth on a diagonal, then danced with her own projected image and swished her hair fourteen times. Finally, in the winter section, she wore an ice-blue nightgown and performed a "formal dance in neat walking patterns" to Purcell's *Rondo,* on tape, as the film returned to black and white.[102]

Schmidt recalls that,

> I was dancing in synchronization with myself, but in spatial opposition. I was facing myself on the screen, doing the same movements, but in opposition.
>
> The movements did not refer to any dramatic reality; there was no story, no event in time. There was a lot of lyrical gesture. There was a back screen and then a smaller screen in front that interrupted the image. I stood in front of that screen for a while and then lay down for a while. The timing was not metrical, except in the dancey section at the end. Most of it was timed according to the way the film happened, rather than on any metrical beats.
>
> I didn't do anything flashy that would detract from the total picture. You can't be too spectacular, or the dance will fly out of the total picture.[103]

Johnston, who did not review this series of concerts as a group, singled out Schmidt's performance, in an article on Merle Marsicano, Aileen Passloff, and Schmidt titled "Romantic Dancers," as a "high-class romantic experience."

> I have no sharp opinion of what made this event so beautiful for a lot of people. For myself, I think Miss Schmidt is the kind of performer who can do anything and be beautiful because she has a true center and the emanation from that center is always a palpable reality. Exactly what a center is I have no idea. It's like trying to talk about angels, and there are many things people know that are impossible to talk about. Anyway, Miss Schmidt performed several dances with simple, unassuming lyric movement, accompanied by an offstage violin, and before a movie of her own enlarged image projected on the back wall and on a smaller downstage panel. The interplay of images — the soft, majestic volume of the figure on the screen with the diminutive flesh and blood on the stage — made a shifting mirror of the kind of dimension that reached far beyond, in the past and future, the moments of reckoning on that small stage. Near the end I had the uncanny feeling of an ancient presence when her head loomed huge in an instant of immobilized totemistic grandeur. Another timeless breath lay suspended when she appeared in a long red flowered dress against the panel and the movie stopped on a lush scene of red flowers — abstract enough to be the garden of the world. And the Corelli duet, as she broke the tension of duality to dance the same solo that she was dancing on the screen, came to me like a heroic emphasis. Miss Schmidt's lyricism has a pure, straightforward quality which includes the wit of an obliquely directed humor and the courage to be nothing more than what anybody really is. The image is so substantial, so factually grounded, that the romantic tones never seem out of touch with the grey wonder of an ordinary day.[104]

The first dance in Concert #11 was Susan Kaufman's *Animals*, per-
formed by Joan Baker, Eddie Barton, Joe Evans, Irv Hochberg, Michael
Malcé, John Herbert McDowell, Arthur Williams, Al Hansen, and Ray
Johnson. The music, by Joseph Byrd, was performed by Philip Corner,
Harry Diakoff, Malcolm Goldstein, Annette Mendel, Dorothy Moskowitz,
and Max Neuhaus.[105] Barton remembers that Kaufman got boxes from F.
A. O. Schwartz and built them into shapes and that the dancers performed
in them.[106]

Second on the program was *Woton's Wake,* a thirty-minute black and
white film by Brian de Palma, starring Christine Callahan and William
Finley. The soundtrack, mixing "dramatic" movie music with found
sounds and satirically pseudointellectual German pronouncements, was by
John Herbert McDowell. In retrospect, *Woton's Wake,* one of de Palma's
earliest films, looks like a period piece. A goofy trance figure who looks
like a Hasidic version of Tiny Tim — an alchemist named Woton Wretchi-
chevsky — malevolently prowls Manhattan, often in pursuit of a young
blond woman. The film is full of quotations; the central character climbs
to the top of an ersatz Empire State Building before his tragic end cum
stock footage and a bombardment of paper airplanes. The film anticipates
de Palma's later work, in that it is full of parodic but loving quotations of
film classics — not only from Ingmar Bergman and Maya Deren, but also
The Bride of Frankenstein and *King Kong.*[107]

Intermission followed *Woton's Wake,* then third on the program was
Eddie Barton's *Pop #2.* This was a variation on *Pop #1,* a play on the
expectation that the same spectators would return to each concert and
would appreciate the subtleties of repetition and variation over the course
of two evenings. "It was exactly the same thing [as *Pop #1*] up to the back
three-quarter. In the back three-quarter, instead of landing on the mat, I
landed beside the mat, and then flipped over on the mat, bursting the
balloon."[108]

A tape collage of electronic music, by Malcolm Goldstein, was fourth
in the concert, and fifth and last was Aileen Passloff's *Salute to the New
York World's Fair,* in which Toby Armour, Joan Baker, Aileen Passloff,
and Joanna Vischer played turn-of-the-century prostitutes who never
received customers. Armour, who was pregnant at the time, played the
madam and wearing spectacles, counted the house and wound up a Victro-
la. The others did specialty dances. One did a Japanese "number," they all
jumped rope, and Passloff did a "little gym dance."

> It was a funny, sweet, little dance that one of the dancers in the piece had learned in
> gym, and she showed it to me. It was "You put your little foot, you put your little foot,
> you put your little foot right out." It was one of those dances. It had no seductions.

The dance had a lot to do with who was in it. It also had to do with the place where I was doing it, the Pocket Theater on Third Avenue and Thirteenth Street. Back of the backdrop was a wonderful old staircase, and underneath the staircase was where the lighting technician ran the lights from. And I thought, "This is a very beautiful set."

We did an official gun drill, with parasols — people of all different sizes, wearing all different costumes. We were a real conglomerate.[109]

Concert #12 opened with a piece by James Waring that had no human presence, *Imperceptible Elongation No. 1.* Waring describes it:

It was five seconds long, literally. It was a Happening, quite beautiful. Everything happened together. There was this big white screen on the stage, and five or six jars of colored confetti. And suddenly, hands burst through the paper and grabbed the jars of confetti and emptied them. And at the same time big white puff balls were thrown from the balcony and it was over. It was probably the only Happening I've ever done. It should have had music.[110]

Second on this program was Malcolm Goldstein's *Ludlow Blues,* a mixture of live musical performance with prerecorded electronic sounds. Philip Corner played the trombone, Vincent Wright played alto saxophone, and Rhona Ginn played flute. According to Goldstein,

I was working with the spatial sense of the instruments. The melodic sense was masses of instruments, and a contrast with distinct instrumentation. There was an improvisation section at the end of that.

I don't know why it was on this program. It was just a piece I had written. It was named *Ludlow Blues* after the town in Colorado where striking miners were machine gunned by the army reserves. But it wasn't meant to represent that.[111]

Following *Ludlow Blues* was Elizabeth Keen's *Sea Tangle,* which had been performed in Concert #2 (see Chapter 3). Fourth on this program was Al Hansen's *Parisol 4 Marisol,* performed by the members of the New York Audio-Visual Association, with music by Brooklyn Joe Jones.[112] *Parisol 4 Marisol* was a Happening that had originally taken place on 24 and 25 May at the 3rd Rail Gallery, at 49 East Broadway, on a program of "Electrifying Events: Happenings," which also included Art Brenner's *Dragonblood* and Wolf Vostell's *New York Décollage.* A floorplan for *Parisol 4 Marisol* shows a loft space with twenty-three tables, a fireplace containing two figures, three mirrors, two films, four mimes, a second fireplace with a speaker plus Elna Rapp or two mimes, and doors leading out to a garden, a store room, and two bathrooms. Notes on the floorplan give the duration as twenty-four minutes and list as participants Mark Saffron (film), Joe Greenstein, Lanny Powers, Paul [no last name given], Chuck Connor, Zena Weiss, Carol Ehrlick, Arnlene Rubawsky, Yvonne Rainer, Freddie Herko, Elna Rapp, Rachel Drexler.[113] The program for Concert

#12 does not list the names of the performers in the New York Audio-Visual Association.

Photographs of the performance at the Gramercy Arts Theatre show a stage littered with buckets, newspapers, cardboard cartons, and ladders and other vertical structures festooned with fabric and toilet paper. A bare-foot man in a long paper tunic, wearing a paper-bag mask, grasps a long stick as though it were a spear; another person does a shoulder stand and seem to be "bicycling" his or her legs. In another photograph, Philip Corner stands under a wooden frame lined with toilet paper rolls; behind him sits Malcolm Goldstein. The caption reads: "Malcolm Goldstein fiddles while Philip Corner rests after an incredible trombone ride." The performance ended with a performer hitting Hansen in the face with a pie in a way that left the audience uncertain whether the action was scored or spontaneous. Hansen describes the incident:

> I am in a clinch with a girl; we are kissing each other, each is tearing the shirt off the other (The shirts are prepared with little razor blade nicks along the back so that something can be gotten hold of to tear.) During our kissing and tearing down strips, another performer taps me on the shoulder. I ignore him and continue to kiss the girl. He looks at the audience and taps me on the shoulder again, and I ignore him again and continue to kiss the girl. The third time he taps me, I count to three and turn to look at him as if to say, "What could be more important than kissing the girl?" Whereupon I get a pie in the face.[114]

After *Parisol 4 Marisol* came intermission, then Aileen Passloff's *Boa Constrictor.* Johnston, who preferred Passloff's solos and duets to her group pieces, admired the "slight, slurping feminine cannibalism of *Boa Constrictor.*" According to Passloff,

> *Boa Constrictor* was a dance about the fact that I love eating. It was about sucking and getting caught up in appetite. I was covered in about fifty feather boas. There was no real food. I ate bones and grapes — what ever was around, in my mind. I practically ate myself. It was ugly, and comic, and melodramatic. It used gestures no one used, except in ballet pantomime. Or Jimmy Waring. It was meant to be a kind of madness.
>
> I hardly did any real moves. I was covered with all the feather boas, and every time I moved, everything shook.[115]

The sixth dance on this program was Arlene Rothlein's *Morning Raga with Yellow Chair,* another dance that stayed in one spot. It was a solo for Rothlein, who remained on the chair, to recorded Indian ragas played by Ustad Ali Akbar Kahn on sarod and Pandit Chatur Lal on tabla.[116] Goldstein remembers that:

> She took a chair from our house that had already been painted yellow — she didn't make a prop — and she just sat on the chair and did various kinds of motions, always on the

chair. Only at one point did she get really far from the chair, where she kept only her fingertips and her toes on the chair and extended very far from it. Otherwise, it was a matter of reaching past the chair, or leaning on the chair. It was all very lyrical and soft.[117]

Passloff remembers *Morning Raga* as "full of passion," and Summers recalls that:

It was just a chair, and Arlene. She did everything to such extremes of movement; everything was on the chair, but beyond it. You knew she had absolutely no concern for how she looked, but total concern for going into the extremity of whatever movement it was. She did everything you could do with a chair. Her movement was extremely sinuous and indirect, continuous, flowing. It wasn't lyrical in the sense of being pretty, because she was a very strong and intense woman.[118]

The final dance in Concert #12 was a collaboration between Deborah Hay and Fred Herko, *Elephant Footprints in the Cheesecake-Walk: For Shirley*. The music was by Edward V. Boagni, "with insights into Schubert, Rednar, Steiner and Bach." Each partner contributed movements—Hay's included a tap dance in tribute to her mother, Shirley—and Herko came up with the title.[119] According to McDowell:

It started with Freddie on a swing with the curtain closed, so that suddenly the whole curtain went PUCCCHHHHH and blew out at the audience, he swang in the swing against the curtain and knocked the curtain way out into the audience. And then there was a long dance, a very romantic pas de deux, and it finally ended up with the hammock, yeah; there was this love scene where they kept climbing up into a hammock.[120]

Waring thought the dance "really rather awful."[121]

In many ways the dances in Concerts #6, #7, and #8 at the church explored the qualities of the performance space and the features of dance with equal emphasis. Jill Johnston remarked on the overall sense of raw physicality in the dances, and if some of them exploited the concentrated nature of slow motion activity, many of them used energetic, even violent movement, structured in a variety of ways, from chance to improvisation to copying poses. The expansive space with its balconies and pillars invited exploitation: a number of choreographers used large groups; several set their dances moving into or under the balcony formed by the choir loft; Morris decided to pit time (slow motion) against space (the absorption of movement by a large area).

The works performed at the Gramercy Arts Theater, in Concerts #9 through #12, on the other hand, were constrained by the size of the stage. The choreographers were not afraid to let their dances spill past the proscenium. But many of them choreographed dances that stayed in one place or a limited amount of space, and several of them refer to their own works or the works of others on the series as Happenings or theater pieces. It is as if in their fascination with the theater space as a theater they forsook dancing.

The group may have expanded its audience by moving temporarily to the Gramercy Arts Theater. Artists, musicians, dancers, and theater people had been cognizant of the Judson Dance Theater ever since it began. With the Gramercy concerts, the Judson network grew to include the independent film world. Not only did Brian de Palma show *Woton's Wake* and Beverly Schmidt use film and slide projections in her work, but also, on Monday nights that summer the Filmmakers' Showcase sponsored screenings at the Gramercy Arts Theater. On 29 July, the night before Concert #9, one could see an evening of eight-millimeter films that included work by the Kuchar brothers, Red Grooms, SNCC, Linda Talbot, and Ed Emshwiller. On 5 August, the night before Concert #11, Jack Smith's films, including *Flaming Creatures,* were shown.[122]

In many ways the Gramercy concerts represented a crisis of the identity that had been consolidated by Concerts #6, #7, and #8. For the first time since the cooperative workshops began, Robert Dunn neither advised nor arranged, although his connection to the group continued.[123] Although Yvonne Rainer served on the program committee, neither she nor Steve Paxton — two of the most active organizers of the workshop — choreographed or danced in the series. Several members of the workshop were away for the summer, and although Jill Johnston may have seen Concerts #10 and #12, she declined, for the first time, to review the group concerts; she wrote only about the works of Schmidt and Passloff, neither of which came out of the workshop. Also for the first time since the workshop began (except for the Washington concert), dances from previous concerts were repeated. On each program a musical piece that was distinctly a musical piece, and not a marriage of music and dance, was played. After thirteen concerts and a year of weekly activity, the Judson Dance Theater had produced nearly ninety dances. It had expanded the audiences for dance and enlivened the calcifying dance scene by amplifying the definitions of dance to embrace art, film, music, and movement of every sort.

6

From Great Collective to Bus Stop

On 25 and 26 August, James Waring gave a concert with his dance company at Judson Church. Nearly all of the dancers in Waring's company were members of the weekly workshop that called itself Judson Dance Theater. Of the performers in this concert, Lucinda Childs, Deborah Hay, Fred Herko, Yvonne Rainer, and Arlene Rothlein were in the workshop; only Gary Gross and Waring himself were not. Besides these dancers, other members of the Judson Dance Theater workshop contributed to Waring's program. John Herbert McDowell composed the music for *Poet's Vaudeville*, here given its premiere—a work dedicated to Harry Langdon, with words by Diane di Prima. McDowell also played the piano for *Phrases*, originally choreographed in 1956, to music by Satie. Norma Marder, who had sung in several Judson Dance Theater performances, sang in *Poet's Vaudeville*. And William Linich designed the lighting for the concert. In fact, the printed program indicated that the concert was presented by Judson Dance Theater. It was the first time since the workshop began that a concert of work by a person not in the workshop was identified with Judson Dance Theater.[1]

Perhaps it was around this time that Al Carmines asked Steve Paxton and Judith Dunn to form a more permanent group that would be the Judson Dance Theater and to direct it, in a manner more like the Poets' Theater than the somewhat anarchic, loose organization of the workshop. According to Paxton, "We said we'd think about it. We were unable, as far as I can see, to ever pull it together." According to Judith Dunn, the two brought the idea before the group, which vetoed it, preferring to remain an uninstitutionalized, cooperative entity. In certain ways, however, even within the cooperative, there were differing statuses in regard to authority and power. Judith Dunn remembers that she often felt like a "house mother," partly because she was older than the others, and partly because she was a member of the prestigious Merce Cunningham company. Rainer had already given a concert of her own choreography. And Rainer and Paxton were seen as "movers and shakers" by some of the other members of the group. As with the Robert Dunn choreography class, the dynamic inevitably changed over time. As early as Concert #5, divisions began to appear within the group. According to Rainer, when Rauschenberg's involvement with the group increased to include choreography, "—through no error in his behaviour but simply due to his stature in the art world—the balance was tipped, and those of us who appeared with him became the tail of his comet. Or so I felt."[2] By the second year of the Judson workshop, a consolidation had long since taken place, new participants had joined, and nonmembers of the workshop gave individual concerts under the aegis of Judson Dance Theater. The identity of the group, or at least of its name, moved during a short period of time, as Judith Dunn puts it, from "the Great Collective Period to the Solo Period to the Bus Stop period."[3]

During the second year, solo choreography concerts were given by three members of the workshop—Paxton, Judith Dunn, and Summers. Paxton's concert, although not given at the church, was publicized as a Judson Dance Theater production. Besides these three independent concerts, both Waring and Katherine Litz, another member of the generation preceding the Judson group, gave individual concerts at the church. But also, the various members of the workshop gave concerts elsewhere—often identifying themselves as part of Judson Dance Theater, a situation that gave rise to divisiveness in the workshop itself. With the four "commercial" concerts by the Surplus Dance Theater, in February and March 1964, a distinct nucleus had emerged. More work was shown outside of the four group concerts given by the workshop at the church then in them. And, with Concerts #14, #15 and #16, at the end of April 1964, the workshop had almost entirely dissipated. More solo concerts were given after Concert #16—by Herko, Waring, Passloff, Judith Dunn, and Schneemann in 1964; by 1965, a new group of dancers and choreographers had appeared on dance programs at the church, although members of the original workshop continued to present old and new choreography there. But once the workshops had ended, the "Bus Stop Period" had begun. That is, concerts were no longer collaboratively produced, but planned by individuals or smaller groups who requested the use of the space directly from the church office.[4]

When in September 1963 the workshop sessions resumed, the exploration of space, materials, technique, and performing presence continued in various ways. On 6 October, at 1:30 PM, Steve Paxton's *Afternoon (a forest concert)* was given at 101 Appletree Row in Berkeley Heights, New Jersey. Although not given at the church, the concert was presented by Judson Dance Theater and, like the other Judson concerts, provided admission free of charge. The advertisement for the concert in the *Village Voice* offered bus transportation for up to fifty spectators. Paxton designed his flyer for the concert.[5]

Paxton wanted to create a dance outdoors for several reasons. One was that, as with his other experiments, it was another thing he hadn't yet done; the Judson group had used unconventional spaces, but they had not yet moved outside. The use of the church itself was considered highly untheatrical in the dance world. Doris Hering had complained that James Waring's concert in August, although rewarding, would look better on a "proper stage." According to Paxton,

> The Living Theater was far out, but the proscenium stage was our basic training. We moved away from that conventional place. We were going in another direction. We had moved into 3-D, to performances in the round and horseshoe formations. That still kept us from using the back of the theater. You still have to move forward in that case. I wanted to go further afield.[6]

Another motivation for working out-of-doors was that Paxton was interested in transplanting that fixed expression of concentration, which had long concerned him, out of the studio and into a space that dissipated focus.

> I had become interested in that phenomenon that happened in dance classes, that glazed, interior-focused look that people have, and I wanted to use that focus as material. It made them look not like thinking people to me. I guess I was perceiving the difference between forebrain, being-stage activity and something deeper, more physical, and more into the lower part of the brain. I wanted to use that as material. So I trained them in the studio, and we got into that state, doing technical work. And then I took them into the forest, and we did it there. They still had that glazed look, which was what I was interested in. To me it's a very animal look, they're concentrating on their muscles and their senses, and I [tried] to use that concentration as a theatrical element.[7]

The site that Paxton chose for the performance was the forest near Billy Klüver's house. This choice was due to both practical and aesthetic considerations.

> It was a convenient place to work even if it was an hour from the city, convenient in the sense that once you got there you could go to the bathroom or get a drink of water or stay overnight if it was late. Rauschenberg had a jeep which I borrowed to run in and out of town, which was difficult otherwise.
>
> When I first saw the forest, there was a lovely green light over everything. That's why I picked that particular place. By the time I did the performance, however, which was about three or four weeks after I had decided to do it, I had [all the choreography] made, but it had turned fall, and that lovely green light was gone. The leaves had all turned yellow. And it was much more ordinary-looking light.[8]

Paxton had rehearsed five dancers—Lucinda Childs, Tony Holder, Barbara Dilley, Yvonne Rainer, and Paxton himself—in Rauschenberg's studio. He brought them to New Jersey for only one or two rehearsals, just before the performance, so that they would not get used to dancing out-doors and lose their studio appearance.[9] The dance itself, Holder recalls, included:

> Cunninghamesque things, twisting things, and a lot of consciousness of other people. Steve [Paxton] was very didactic about how to do things, not what I would call flexible. And Steve was very conscious, as we rehearsed, of the size of the clearings we would be performing in.[10]

Rainer remembers,

> We rehearsed it for quite a while, and it was very difficult movement. It was leggy and formal: relevés, ronds de jambe. It taxed me to my utmost.
> We rehearsed it out there on Sunday, a week before the performance. And that was when I discovered that the movement was supposed to be done in the dirt.
> There were various events—dancing in the dirt, then something took place on a platform.[11]

Paxton chose five trees to serve as markers for the five "stations" where the dancing took place. Olga Adorno, Klüver's wife then, acted as guide. The trees and the six performers (the five dancers plus Dilley's son, Benjamin Lloyd, who was listed on the program) wore camouflage and day-glo polka dot garments. The dancers wore natural colored turtleneck shirts with polka dot windbreakers over them. The trees had more elaborate costumes. Paxton explains:

> A number of trees had fake bark—an outer bark made of cloth and painted over that could be taken off. Underneath were the polka dots. One tree, up to about forty feet where its branches started, was covered with white cloth with orange polka dots. The trees were so successfully camouflaged that I lost tree #5 several times.
> I had five ideas for different kinds of polka dot creations. One tree—it was a small clump of trees, actually—had rainbow sections that went up it and that covered various branches that went out maybe twelve feet. Then there was the forty-foot extravaganza. Only the three other polka dot variations occurred under fake bark.
> Work happened near the trees or around them, often without revealing the fact that they were polka dot underneath. And people would walk into a section that there would be dance happening. On their way from one station to the next they might pass a dancer, or sometimes they got there and the dancers came with the audience, making excursions occur.[12]

Jill Johnston, who had not written about Concerts #9 through #12, resumed the chronicling of Judson Dance Theater with a review of *Afternoon*.

> In New Jersey last month, the leaves were beginning to turn pretty colors, and Steve Paxton brought a group of dancers into the woods surrounding Billy Klüver's house in Berkeley Heights for an *Afternoon (A Forest Concert)*. The spectators were led by a

guide (her cap said "follow me") from one leafy grove to another where the troupe of five...danced and did some natural things like disappearing. I wasn't keen about the dancing because the ground made balancing difficult and the forest was more exciting than human technique. But I liked the unexpected entrances, the nonchalant disappearances, and not knowing or caring too much where to look when something was going on in more distant places. The scene I thought best suited to the environment was a sweet transaction between mother, son, sky, and trees when we were led to a clearing where Barbara [Dilley] Lloyd sat with her baby, Benjamin, who played with a leaf, hugged his mother, glanced imperturbably at the spectators, and took a big view of the sky. A little later he had the presence of mind to crawl under a space made by the dancers, who were placing their limbs over and under each other on a wooden plank.[13]

Although Paxton considered *Afternoon* "an okay little piece" and a "side trip" from his ongoing concerns with the walking and photographic poses that had begun in *Proxy*,[14] in many ways the themes of *Afternoon* are present throughout his career. The confusion of categories between inside and outside, human and nonhuman organisms, culture and nature in a number of Paxton's dances is an embodiment of the process of stripping and leveling that, according to Victor Turner, creates a social situation of raw "communitas." Turner's term refers to the "potentially free and experimental region of culture" that stands in opposition to institutional, generally rigid structure. In communitas, spontaneity, equality, and social cohesion are valued and lived; situations of instruction often arise, such as those of ritual transformation of status.[15]

Soon after the Judson workshops resumed, Charles Ross, a young sculptor who had worked with Ann Halprin in San Francisco, came to a few sessions and proposed a collaboration. Rainer wrote a letter to the Foundation for Contemporary Performance Arts to request a $200 grant for materials and construction; the letter was signed by Rainer, Robert Dunn, and Alex Hay, as the "program committee for the next Concert of Dance." According to this letter, the collaboration would take place between three artists — Ross, Alex Hay, and Al Hansen — and at least six choreographers. It also explained that "an elaborate environment, constructed mostly of metal, is to be the focal point of the [evening-long] piece." The letter, written in September, projected a November date for the concert. Apparently, in the intervening months the nature of the collaboration changed in a number of ways: The flyer, although designed by Alex Hay, announced that the collaboration was with the Judson dancers and Charles Ross; the program notes indicate that Robert Dunn dropped off the program committee. The other program credits are: lighting, Alex Hay and Carol Summers; sound, Lanny Powers; stage manager, David Lee, assisted by Janet Castle; "galumpf squad," Al Hansen (captain), assisted by Mac Benford, Arthur Cohen, Michael Pass; chair sculpture, Charles Ross, assisted by Felix Aeppli. The group received a grant from the

Foundation for Contemporary Performance Arts and gave the money to Ross to pay for the construction of a huge trapezoid made of metal pipes and a platform on which Ross and Aeppli piled numerous chairs of all kinds. Other materials included tires and bedsprings. The collaboration took place at Judson Church on 19 and 20 November 1963.[16]

A number of newcomers to the group appeared in this concert, which also had changed from the original plan in that the evening consisted of twelve different dances, interlaced with periods of "free play." The names of all the performers appeared, in alphabetical order and without regard to any difference in status between choreographer and dancer, on the first page of the program: Felix Aeppli, Joan Baker, Carla Blank, Lucinda Childs, Philip Corner, Judith Dunn, June Ekman, Ruth Emerson, Lulu Farnsworth, Marty Greenbaum, Sally Gross, Al Hansen, Alex Hay, Deborah Hay, Tony Holder, Jerry Howard, Susan Kaufman, David Lee, Deborah Lee, Elizabeth Munro, Rudy Perez, John Quinn, Yvonne Rainer, Charles Ross, Arlene Rothlein, Carolee Schneemann, Larry Segal, Elaine Summers, James Tenney, and John Worden.[17]

This self-admittedly ambitious concert took place during an active season in New York's avant-garde. The November issue of *The Floating Bear* carried reviews of the opening of Robert Morris's show at the Green Gallery and the Judson Poets' Theater production of Gertrude Stein's *What Happened*, both in October. It announced, besides the upcoming Concert of Dance on 19 and 20 November, a proposed modern dance repertory company for the work of new choreographers, organized by James Waring and sponsored by the American Theater for Poets; a new distribution center for books and little magazines, called Mandrake; LeRoi Jones's new anthology of avant-garde American writing, *The Moderns*; a new poetry magazine, *Blue Beat,* with work by Ed Sanders, Tuli Kupferberg, Norman Solomon, and Gerard Malanga; *An Anthology,* edited by La Monte Young [and Jackson MacLow], with work by George Brecht, Claus Bremer, Earle Brown, Joseph Byrd, John Cage, David Degener, Walter DeMaria, Henry Flynt, Yoko Ono, Dick Higgins, Toshi Ichiyanagi, Terry Jennings, Ray Johnson, Ding Dong, Jackson MacLow, Richard Maxfield, Robert Morris, Simone Forti Morris, Nam June Paik, Terry Riley, Dieter Rot, James Waring, Emmett Williams, Christian Wolff, and La Monte Young. It also announced two new productions by the Paper Bag Players; a double bill by the Judson Poets' Theater; a drama workshop at Judson Church; an auction of paintings by New York artists at Judson Gallery for the retrial costs of poet Ray Bremser; a Kurt Schwitters exhibition at Galeria Chalette on Madison Avenue ("You'll want to go twice, at least," was the comment by Waring appended to this announcement); poetry readings at Hardware Poet's Playhouse. It announced "Fred Herko's kind of ballet class," given on Saturday mornings at Waring's studio. And it announced several literary, arts, and poetry magazines, including *Stable*, designed by Andy Warhol, edited by Gerard Malanga, and published by Eleanor Ward of Stable Gallery.[18]

Concert #13 was a joyous, expansive, energetic performance. The use of the space within the sanctuary expanded even further than it had in the past, spreading to the altar, the balcony choir loft, and every square foot of the sanctuary space. According to Johnston, all the principles of natural movement, concentration, and cooperation seen so far in Judson Dance Theater's work were brought to a climax in this concert. Although composed of discrete dances, all the activity seemed to coalesce into one seamless whole.

> The collaboration at Judson Memorial Church on November 19 and 20 between Charles Ross, sculptor, and the Judson Dancers brought all the previous concerts into dynamic focus. Although there were dances by program, the evening was like a single unit because the dances occasionally overlapped, or one dance followed another without pause, and, more important, because Ross's sculptural environment was a constant factor tying everything together by both the limitations it imposed and the possibilities it suggested.
> His basic objects were a big iron trapezoid, a long seesaw, and a platform of wood planks set about eight feet above the floor. The balancing, climbing, sliding, swinging, hanging, jumping, and falling activities made possible by these constructions set the dominant tone of natural physical movement that the Judson dancers have projected on a smaller scale from the beginning. Also, a broad, uncontrolled physicality seemed the natural result of performing in such a huge area, the audience seated in a wide circle around the outside edges.[19]

The playful spirit with which the choreographers responded to Ross's sculptures during their rehearsals and workshop sessions crystallized in dances that chiefly resembled games of various sorts. The first dance listed on the program was *Qui à* [sic] *mangé le baboon?*, by Charles Ross. Ross and Susan Kaufman played with a large balloon, beginning the concert with intimations of children's toys. During *Qui à mangé le baboon?*, according to Johnston's account, ten minutes of free play began.

> Ross blew up a huge black balloon behind the scenes, then tapped it out into view, where he and a young lady and the audience played with it a while, continuing as the dancers slowly mobilized into many activities involving the constructions as well as a bed spring, a noisy piece of sheet metal, chairs, tables, ropes, and tires. I liked these periods best when the wilder action evolved from a quiet beginning, especially since the balloon set the atmosphere to begin with of soft suspense.[20]

The second dance was Ruth Emerson's *Sense,* a gymnastic exploitation of the large trapezoid. Wearing a leotard that she had made herself, with her legs bare, Emerson looked more like a sports gymnast than a dancer. She walked around the edges of the structure, then leaped up to grasp a horizontal pipe on top, swung up into a handstand on the pole, and moved along the entire sculpture. Emerson remembers that,

> People thought that structure was a bit heavy and scary. For a while there was [in the gym] this big sort of not quite trapezoid of pipes, like a tetrahedron. People would try turning it over and climbing it. I remember a bunch of women trying to deal with it one day and getting quite scared. If you dropped it, it would clang to the floor. Everyone was afraid it would hit them or squash them. I got quite impatient, because as a kid I had a jungle gym and swung around a lot and climbed trees a lot. I thought, "Why is everybody so pussyfooting about it?" That trapezoid was the thing I ended up on the most. There was a big seesaw and a bed; I don't remember spending so much time on them.
>
> I finally made the piece called *Sense*, expressing my impatience, saying "It's really possible to do this. It's not hard, it's easy, it's fun." That word said all those things to me. All I did was to traverse it without touching the ground, a little bit like a gymnastic routine. I did it in a very straightforward way. Maybe it looked harder than it was; it was never particularly difficult. I made that solo very quickly and after a lot of fiddling.[21]

Rainer remembers that *Sense* was "extraordinary: This enormous person swinging. I think she went around the entire perimeter of the structure, hand over hand, just swinging. It was very beautiful." Johnston called *Sense* "a lovely sculptural solo...moving with slow equipoise around all the bars, making two sudden breathless springs on to the top bars, wrapping her long legs around them and sliding in smooth hoists."[22]

Elaine Summers recalls that at one point (perhaps in the free play section, or during a session in the gym) she arrived at the top of the sculpture and spontaneously turned to Emerson, also at the top, to ask if she was afraid of heights. Summers remarks,

> I don't know why I asked her that question. And she said, "I'm terrified!" We started to come down, and when I got very close to the bottom, I realized that I was afraid to let go, even though intellectually I knew I was only a foot away. I realized that when you're working you're not always aware of your psychological feelings about space.[23]

The next dance was Carolee Schneemann's *Lateral Splay*, repeated two or three times during the course of the evening.[24] The performers were Judith Dunn, June Ekman, Sally Gross, Alex Hay, Deborah Hay, Tony Holder, Jerry Howard, Deborah Lee, John Quinn, Larry Segal, Elaine Summers, and John Worden. *Lateral Splay* was a running dance that set up specific, minimal goals for the performers: to run as fast as possible, for as long as possible, in random directions, until a collision with an object or another runner occurred. Schneemann used sensory awareness exercises in her rehearsals with her dancers. These exercises included telling the runners to imagine that they were particles bombarding space; blindfolding them and having them crawl around among one another, to get used to physical contact; having them walk blindfolded through the space individually to familiarize themselves with its geography. She asked them to walk very quickly, changing directions while remaining aware of each other's movements. She also used an exercise she calls "Grab and Falls," in which one person pulls another person to the ground, while the one pulled surrenders impulses to resist; this drill has continued in Schneemann's "Kinetic Theater" work since then. Schneemann says about the rehearsal process for *Lateral Splay*, "Exercises of collision and impact were practiced over and over again until we actually felt secure and free crashing into one another."[25]

There were four distinct styles of running that Schneemann made available to the runners: a backwards, upright run: a forward, upright run; a low crawling position with knees bent and arms swinging; a run interrupted by turns and falls. Within the context of the concert, she thought of this dance as an event integrated into the totally designed environment, as "an explosive and linear refrain, a propulsive jet of movement cutting through the sequences of other works and the materials of the environment. It involves a maximum expenditure of directed energy." Besides running on the floor of the room, the dancers used the balcony, "over the heads of the audience, where steel sheets had been laid, making tremendous thundering noises as the runners passed over them."

> In order to stop a run, the rule was to collide with an obstacle. The obstacles were the walls of the church, the audience, the steel girders, the mountain of chairs, and the other runners. When collision occurred, the runner had to meet the obstacle at full speed, merge with it, and fall down. Rests lasted until the impulse to run again. Because the runs were exhausting, the sequences could last for only three minutes. . . . I was convinced that proper concentration — an instantaneous yielding on impact, rather than resistance — could prevent us from injury.[26]

Johnston called *Lateral Splay* "the wildest dance on the program," noting that it was one of the few that did not utilize the constructions.

> The dancers tore across the space with all the speed they could manage, tumbling heels over head when they collided or when they felt like it into gasping inert heaps. The pace of alternating explosion and silence was like extreme energy running down quickly into collapse. The alternation was not a predictable bore, however, because each performer was going at his own pace, and sometimes it seemed a contagious current would sweep them into a common propulsion or a common collapse. Alex Hay, a non-dancer with a tight, wiry body, pitched forward with such speed — his body laterally off center, as I believe they were instructed to run some of the time — that he looked like a bat out of

hell with one wing scorched and the other left behind. Larry Segal, another non-dancer, was a masterpiece of frenetic inspiration. Spinning and running at the same time, he might have been careening helplessly off the whirl of a centripetal force. Once he grabbed a vertical bar of the trapezoid and flew around it in big fantastic arcs.

Johnston considered Segal "equally amazing" during the free play interludes,

gathering the legs of a few spectators together with the frenzied pleasure of doing something silly or nothing special, turning somersaults around an upper bar of the trapezoid, and other spectacular monkey business, playing a witty game of shoes-on-hands with Yvonne Rainer on top of the platform, or making like Christ at the bottom of the church's big wooden cross with some ecstatic jerks and gyrations.[27]

Morris had noted the usefulness of objects in directing one's focus in performance. The sculpture by Ross seems to have engendered an unusually free and imaginative response from all its users, even those who didn't particularly like it. Here in full force was the spontaneity and abandon to movement of all kinds that so many of the Judson choreographers had been moving toward.

Alex Hay was one of those who was dissatisfied with the Ross project. He felt that the collaboration was not, in fact, a truly cooperative venture.

[Ross] presented us with these lumps of stuff that we could hardly use. He was doing sculptures, but that didn't have too much of a relationship to really getting together with people and describing their needs. Collaboration means each party has input into it, so you arrive at a solution that's adequate for both parties, but this was not the case [with Ross]. He just made these two great big things which then we had to employ in our concert because we were doing a "collaborative" concert. So *Prairie* was my attempt to use this thing.

It was really the first piece I did—in *Rafladan* I didn't know what I was doing—and I got involved in thinking about the problem and the solution. The whole basis of the dance was "How could you really use this structure?" It was about ten feet tall at the tallest point. It was a strange shape; there were no parallel sides in it, and it had four corners and four sides. It was made out of 2-inch or 2½-inch steel, joined together at the corners.

I got three pillows and tied them to myself with ropes, so they wouldn't fall while I was on top of the structure, and I just moved around on top of the structure with these pillows, trying to keep them under me. I made a tape, which just said "Are you comfortable?" "That's not very comfortable." There were about five or six comments and questions. And I would talk, in the same vein, on top of the tape, answering the questions and making statements about how I felt on the structure.

It lasted five minutes, and I wore everyday clothing.[28]

Photographs of *Prairie* show Hay not only on top of the structure, but also wrapped around the vertical bars of the construction, sometimes upside down. For the most part he encountered the pipes on his stomach, with the pillows providing the padding in front. The resulting combination of incongruous and awkward positions, nonchalance, and off-hand comments created a very deadpan humor.

Emerson remembers *Prairie* as "super, absolutely super."

> It was so funny and charming. I had done this whole pro, Olga Corbut act on the structure. Then [Hay] strapped himself with a belt and a pillow somewhere quite high up. There he was with this damn pillow! And a tape came out of the balcony, saying "Are you comfortable?" It was outrageous. He looked horribly uncomfortable. He was really funny, and here I was always so self-conscious about wanting to look nice, wanting people to like the way I looked. He looked awful. I was rather amazed that somebody could treat themselves like that.[29]

After *Prairie* came Carla Blank's *Turnover*, a dance deriving from the simple task of having all the women turn the huge trapezoid over. Because the structure was so tall, some of the women, who had been at the bottom when the dance began, ended up hanging from the top of the sculpture.[30]

Blank had just graduated from Sarah Lawrence College, where she had studied with Bessie Schönberg, Judith Dunn, Beverly Schmidt, and Ruth Lloyd, who taught music analysis. During Blank's years at Sarah Lawrence, the visiting faculty included Donald McKayle, David Wood, Katherine Litz, and Henry Danton, from whom she first learned ballet. Blank had been dancing and choreographing, studying modern dance and various kinds of folk dance since childhood. Growing up in Pittsburgh, Pennsylvania, her first dance teachers were two friends of her mother's who had trained with Martha Graham. "It was like Stanislavsky method," Blank recalls. "There had to be justification for the movement; when I choreographed a dance I had to say what I was thinking." She went to a progressive private school and, beginning in third grade, she wrote and choreographed plays and performed in them. She went square-dancing regularly with her family and learned Balkan, Irish, Israeli, and traditional English folk dances. At first Blank went to college at Carnegie Mellon, then she transferred to Sarah Lawrence when she realized that she wanted to dance professionally. In her senior year at Sarah Lawrence, she joined Merle Marsicano's company, where she worked for three years. Moving to New York after graduation, she studied ballet at the Joffrey school and modern dance with James Waring and Judith Dunn. She remembers going to a concert at Judson Church in July 1963 (it may have been one of the concerts at the end of June), and then in the fall, when the workshops resumed, she began to attend.[31]

The next dance in the concert was a collaboration between Yvonne Rainer and Charles Ross, called *Room Service*. This is the only dance on the program that is billed separately as a collaboration between Ross and a choreographer. Ross's role was to rearrange the stage equipment with two helpers; Rainer's role was to set up a game of follow-the-leader with three teams of three, one of which Rainer led. Ross's team also included Aeppli and Emerson. Of those playing Rainer's game, there was an all-woman team (Rainer, Sally Gross, Carla Blank); an all-man team (Alex Hay, Tony Holder, Al Hansen); and an integrated team (Lucinda Childs, Marty Greenbaum, and Lulu Farnsworth). The leaders were the names listed first, the middle players the middle names, and the tails of the team the final names. On each team, the players stayed close together, climbing on and around the various objects. The platform, which had not yet been piled with chairs, served in a number of ways; people jumped off it or, when it was set on end, stuck their hands through the slats to gesture. One photograph shows the three women climbing over the platform in its vertical position. Another group of photographs shows the three men lying on the floor, their arms outstretched and their hands moving; the women's team approaches and crawls over them.[32] Rainer remembers,

> The men's team would do these hair-raising things. And at one performance Ross and Aeppli tied up my team so we couldn't move.
>
> It was kind of dangerous. People would jump off that platform onto a piece of sheet metal on a spring. There were a couple of mattresses, and then a bedspring, and sheets of metal. They'd jump onto this thing, and it would catapult them off. I think someone got cut in one of the performances.

Rainer had invited Marty Greenbaum to be in her piece, and he had brought along his girlfriend, Lulu Farnsworth, who was also incorporated into the dance.

> Marty Greenbaum was a Judson character. When I first met him he was taking magazines and painting them and burning them. He was a kind of Abstract Expressionist, junk painter. He presented himself as a complete eccentric; he'd go around with dice and little whistles. He give you some dice and say "Let's play," and you'd make up the game as you went along. He loved hanging out at Judson. He was in Peter Schumann's *Totentanz* and he was quite good. So I asked him to be in this. Lulu Farnsworth was his girlfriend, and I never saw her before or after that.[33]

Steve Paxton, who was on tour with Cunningham at the time of the concert, remembers seeing several of the dances in rehearsal. *Room Service* seemed to him outstanding.

> I loved *Room Service*. I don't remember some of the other works. It was like watching ants climbing, at times with all different kinds of ants, hunting around, doing different kinds of activities. One team changed the environments. It was quite lively—a lot of running and sliding and playing and the fun of watching the first person able to do something naturally and then everybody else struggling to achieve it.[34]

Paxton's way of looking at *Room Service*—with the leader of each team "able to do something naturally" and the followers "struggling to achieve it"—encapsulates the problem and the challenge of choreography that many of the Judson group were grappling with. How can one crystallize extemporaneous movement without dessicating it? How does one learn another person's movement, so natural to that person, without changing it? How does one repeat in dance? The history of modern dance is full of choreographers whose technique, based on movement natural to the maker, lost its originality and expressive power in translation to other bodies. *Room Service* showed, with the simplicity of a child's game that does not usually frame movement as the center of aesthetic attention, that these choreographic questions are true even of unstylized, "natural" movements.

Paxton thought about his colleagues' work with the Ross sculptures while he was on tour, and two weeks before the concert, he wrote a note to Rainer from Colorado Springs, suggesting means for using the trapezoid in "more approachable" ways. Apparently he had seen a rehearsal with the constructions in the upstairs sanctuary.

> The pieces look much better in the room upstairs, and I liked a lot of the construction ideas I saw being tried.
>   But the cockeyed trapezoid remains a problem, and I wondered if it would be more approachable if auxiliary pieces and props were made: bridges and ladders, or things to hang from a cross-piece which would be easy to stand on, easier than a loop in a rope, which might support movement more freely.
>   Also a hook affixed to a halter fastened to the body would provide a means of resting one's arms etc. which tire when hanging from that thing, one of the most obvious possibilities.

He includes in the note a sketch of a dancer suspended from a pole with such a hook and halter, looking rather like a monkey's tail curling up from the base of the dancer's spine.[35]

For Rainer, who had been exhausted after *Terrain*, Concert #13—and *Room Service*, in particular—signaled a turning point in her work. After presenting *Room Service* at Judson Church and repeating it, with Robert Morris replacing Charles Ross as the leader of the team that moved props, at the 24 April concert in Philadelphia (see p. 194), Rainer became intrigued with the stylistic constraints placed on the dancer's movements and performance demeanor by carrying objects. In Philadelphia the performance took place on a proscenium stage, and Rainer reports that

> At this performance it spilled off the stage into the aisles, into the seats—displacing audience—and out the exits. I was excited by a particular piece of business: 2 of us carrying a mattress up an aisle, out the rear exit, around and in again thru a side exit.

> Something ludicrous and satisfying about lugging that bulky object around, removing it
> from scene and re-introducing it. No stylization needed. It seemed to be so self-con-
> tained an act as to require no artistic tampering or justification.[36]

Out of her thoughts about this experience and a later incident of furniture
moving during Concert #14 (see p. 197), Rainer began to plan her *Parts of
Some Sextets*, "a dance for ten people and twelve mattresses" completed in
1965.[37] In narrowing the gap between "real life" and art, Rainer's dance,
like many of the works in Concert #13, shared a modernist preoccupation
with demystifying art that informed the paintings and sculptures of Robert
Rauschenberg, Jasper Johns, Robert Morris, and Andy Warhol and other
visual artists who were the Judson Dance Theater's exact contemporaries,
even members of the workshop or of its audience.[38]

Even the intermission of Concert #13 was a performance, as in Concert #1 (see Chapter 2). Philip Corner's *Intermission* was a functional artwork: Ross's sculpture had to be deconstructed and reassembled for the
second half of the program, and Corner made the amplification of that
activity—both physically and aurally—his piece. Corner explains:

> *Intermission* came out of my own involvement with the people who were doing Happen-
> ings—Life is Art, and all that. That was a life I had outside of Judson, with people like
> Alison Knowles, Dick Higgins, George Maciunas, George Brecht, and Yoko Ono.
>
>   I organized the dismantling and reassembling of the structure; it was done very pur-
> posefully and artistically. What it looked like was not what it would look like if people
> were just doing it functionally. That was my first experimentation with electronics and
> it probably could have been done better, but I rigged up contact microphones, and it
> was played in the lobby. Most people didn't even pay any attention to it, which was all
> right with me.
>
>   It seemed that was quite appropriate—doing the job in an elegant way. The actions
> were not elaborated, but focused. If you do something, you do it. You're always aware
> of the rhythmic thing. Whatever opportunity there is to make a sound, you use. If you
> can roll something across the floor, you do. It's not supposed to be something that's
> gratuitously arty. All the inherent artistic qualities are clarified.[39]

What was important to Corner— and what he stresses in his score for
the piece, "Beforehand or Afterward"—is the revelation of the mechanics
of the performance, dispelling illusion and valuing work, just as *Room
Service* did in its way. "Complete the construction; put it into play," Corner instructs. The piece is a way of continuing the dance in the interval of
the performance that is usually reserved for "real life"—the intermission.
The resulting score is a way of not only bringing life into art, but art into
life, as well. Corner concludes his score by saying that "it applies also, if
you wish it, to preparing your meals."[40]

Corner enjoyed the collaboration, although he did not see it as "a
great breakthrough," but rather as one more collaboration in what was, for

him, an ongoing series of collaborations. "We had so many collaborations with so many people. I thought it was a very nice thing that he made, the whole idea was very beautiful. People did things that they couldn't have done otherwise, having that sculpture. People worked basically within the sense of their own style, and adapted it to the sculpture."[41]

The first dance after *Intermission* was Deborah Hay's *Would They or Wouldn't They?*, performed by Alex Hay, David Lee, Yvonne Rainer, and Deborah Hay to music by Al Hansen. The women danced near the trapezoidal structure, while the men, on a mat inside the sculpture, pressed their heads together to create enough tension to rise from lying to standing. When the women called out, the men picked them up, carried them, and put them down. The men hung from a rope attached to the trapezoid and stood on their heads in two corners of the structure. Finally, the men held the women up, so that they could grasp the top bar of the sculpture to hang from it; then the men also grasped the bar, facing in the opposite direction from the women.[42] Deborah Hay recalls,

The collaboration—working with a sculptor on a piece—seemed unreal to me, in a way. So the only way I could relate to it was in the most mundane way. If there were a pole, you could hang from it, you could lean against it, et cetera. So in *Would They or Wouldn't They?*, there were resting places. We did things together and separately. Women had parts; men had mostly supportive roles. It didn't have emotional intentions. It was formal; it was [a way of] using the structure. Although in retrospect, [I see that] I might have been working out certain things. Alex [Hay] was a shitty husband. It was an opportunity to call him over, have him pick me up and carry me! I could have been working things out subconsciously.[43]

According to Alex Hay,

People were materials. That's what Judson was all about—materials. Critics shouldn't get involved in interpreting what the emotional relationships [in the dances] were.

We were responsible to go and pick them up when they called us. That was what we were in the piece for. We weren't there to have some sort of relationship with them; we were there to do these things, particularly to carry them around.

He does think, however, that "a couple of times it may have gotten a little cute, in the way they called us."

All these concerts were pretty low-key, so you started playing around with the pieces. You would start doing things that were not really straightforward. You'd start getting cute or something. It had nothing to do with the piece; it had to do with the relaxed atmosphere. That's the reason no one was uptight, no one felt pressured. You never had any feeling that you might fail, when you could redeem yourself on the next night, or in another concert, or in another workshop. There was no pressure. And there was nothing precious about it.[44]

Rainer claims that she suggested the title of Deborah Hay's dance. "It was my response to the ambiguities in the piece. I thought these configurations really meant something. So I suggested in the title some action that was or wasn't being consummated." Rainer remembers, at one point in the dance, being carried "like a baby sloth. The men were on all fours, and the women were holding on them and hanging underneath. It probably was a sexually loaded collection of images."[45] Expressive meaning was present in the dances even when the explicit goal of the choreographer was simply to manipulate the formal terms of the composition.

Another session of free play followed *Would They or Wouldn't They?*, and then a solo by Arlene Rothlein. Unlike Hay, Rothlein was interested in investing her dances with emotional content. According to Rainer, Rothlein was an "ecstatic" performer. Rothlein's dance in Concert #13 was a solo of hand and facial gestures dedicated to Isadora Duncan. Johnston called *Enceinte for Isadora Duncan* "a strange, introverted solo." Rothlein, dressed in black, sat on a table in front of the church altar, in a seated fourth position — with her right leg bent in and her left leg bent behind her. She stretched out her right hand and stared at it, holding her left hand limp. She leaned to the right and held splayed hands to her head, in a gesture of agony; her mouth opened wide to complete the image of a scream. The dance ended when Rothlein stood up and simply walked out of the sanctuary. Rainer recalls that "Arlene did not know that 'enceinte' means pregnant. She was shocked when I told her. She thought it meant ritual, or full, or something mystical. Pregnant *with* [the spirit of] Isadora Duncan."[46]

The next dance was Rainer's *Shorter End of a Small Piece.* It included elements that Rainer later put into *Dialogues,* first performed in February 1964. Rainer and Childs swung around violently on the ropes attached to the trapezoid. "You'd just fall out, and you'd know exactly where to grasp so that you wouldn't hit anything. You'd catch your weight at the last minute before hitting the ground," Rainer explains. Three men continually rushed through on the diagonal. Deborah Hay entered, dressed in a black dress and high-heeled shoes. According to Rainer:

> I knew it was not a complete work. It was a small piece, and the shorter end of a small piece. So the title just indicated its minuscule nature, and that there was more of it, or would be soon.
>
> That was another reason this place was so great. You could try out an idea. Or that's the way I felt. Everything I did didn't have to be resolved. Sometimes by trying an idea out in the workshop, I'd see how it wasn't resolved. And sometimes I wouldn't really get a notion of it, and I'd do it anyway, in the performance.[47]

Like *Intermission* and *Enceinte for Isadora Duncan,* Joan Baker's dance, which followed *Shorter End of a Small Piece,* imbued its movements with a mystical feeling. In fact, the name of the dance was *Ritual*. It was a series of repetitions of a single action: Someone would separate from the group, which stood inside the trapezoid, climb to the top, and drop to the floor. The performers wore yarmulkes, and Philip Corner remembers that they bounced rhythmically, like Orthodox Jews at prayer. According to Baker:

> *Ritual* was an authentic mystical-type number. Every once in a while, a sacrifice was chosen, who came through the gang and climbed up the whole thing, got to the top and fell. It was repetitious. It was a ritual.
>
> Then the group would do mutterings and incantations until another figure came out, climbed up, fell down, and disappeared.
>
> Originally there were to be no special costumes. But then my sense of humor and my theatrical bent got the better of me and I tie-dyed yarmulkes. That became a real bone of contention. Ruth Emerson and several other people were horrified that I should put such a decoration on such an essentially clear form of ritual repetition.[48]

The performers propelled themselves through space again in Schneemann's *Lateral Splay*, and finally, the last dance on the program, Lucinda Childs' *Egg Deal*, was performed. Compared to the wild, fervent activity of the free-play sections, *Lateral Splay,* and *Room Service,* the manipulation of ropes and boxes in *Egg Deal* was quiet and spare. A tiny chair was tied to the rope attached to the trapezoid, and Childs stood on the chair, leaning out from the structure. People walked, lay down at intervals on the floor, and tossed the boxes, which were the cartons that large quantities of eggs are delivered in. Childs recalls,

> This was the first small group piece in which I actually choreographed movements. There were different things that you could do with the boxes. You could move a box in such a way that there's a box between you and some other person, continuing that on the structure. You could kick the box in a certain way. One box was suspended on a rope, and we had a routine in which you swing this way, and the box comes that way, and you try to kick it—something hard to do because it depends on the suspension of the box and your motion connecting. When you succeeded, you could drop that activity. You could stack the boxes. Ross' sculpture was a very beautiful environment to work in.[49]

As Robert Morris stated about his own work, the solving of a task or the handling of an object can focus the performer's concentration. Working with the objects that made up Ross's environment made the Judson Dance Theater relaxed and alert as performers and inventive as choreographers. The sculptures unified the concert by providing a physical link among the dances, and also by giving the dancers something extemporaneous to do in the interludes between dances, so that there was a natural connective. The sculptures also made for a very diverse concert, in terms of the responses of the choreographers, who used the structures to play games, create tasks, structure rituals, practice athletics, or simply handle them as materials.

On 6 and 7 December, Judith Dunn gave an evening of old and new works. Both the evening and the first dance on the program were called *Motorcycle*. The program varied from the first night to the next. On both nights, *Acapulco* followed *Motorcycle*. On Friday, 6 December, *Speedlimit* came third, then *Witness II* and *Witness I*, accompanied by Robert Dunn's *Doubles for 4*. On Saturday, 7 December, the third item was *Index I* and *Witness I*, with *Doubles for 4*; the fourth item comprised *Index II*, *Witness III*, and *Doubles for 4*. On both nights, the fifth dance was *Airwave* and the sixth dance was *Astronomy Hill*. Robert Rauschenberg, who designed the lighting, was given billing on the first page of the program. Alex Hay assisted Rauschenberg; Tony Holder was the stage assistant; Steve Paxton designed the flyer and the costume for *Witness II*; Robert Dunn served as musical director. The flyer was printed on the inside of a plain white envelope.[50]

Judith Dunn says that the streets of Greenwich Village inspired the dance *Motorcycle*. She felt that the rawness of the street life could be translated into dance in a nonliteral way.

> It was motorcycle time in the Village. There was all this energy from the motorcycles. Those were rough and tough times, with people wearing strange clothes. Merce Cunningham's dances were so refined. I wanted to make a dance that had a different kind of energy. But the dance didn't look anything like a motorcycle.[51]

Steve Paxton remembers that Dunn "had gotten very excited by Larry Poons' motorcycle, and she wanted him to bring it into the church as part of the performance, but I don't think he agreed to do that. But I don't think the dance had anything in particular to do with the word, more just the image."[52] In the same year, Kenneth Anger had returned from Europe and, inspired by motorcycle gangs he saw in Brooklyn, made the film *Scorpio Rising*, a montage film with a sound track of pop songs. Anger correlates the motorcycle cult with James Dean, Jesus Christ, Marlon Brando, and Hitler—mythic figures in popular culture. According to Anger, "I see the bike boys as the last romantics of this particular culture. They're the last equivalents of the riders of the range, the cowboys."[53]

Jill Johnston wrote, in her review of Dunn's evening,

> Motorcycles are more exciting than rockets and jet planes. Fast living and leather jackets. Not that other things aren't faster and more dangerous, but motorcycles are local color. The glory of it is a street romance.
>
> Judith Dunn got off to a good start by calling her concerts "Motorcycle" (at Judson Church on December 6 and 7). The letters of the word appeared in the lobby, strung across on various dangling objects, and in the performing area, spelled out on a con-

struction lying against the sanctuary altar. Otherwise there was no sign of a motorcycle, real or simulated, in the concert itself. Motorcycle was to the concert as scooter is to a church service. The connection is perfectly clear. (Frank O'Hara has a poem about sardines and oranges; how *Sardines* is the title of a painting that has no sardines in it, and "Oranges" is the title of one of his poems and he never mentions orange.)

Anyway, the power of the word is such that I had the feeling of motorcycle, regardless of what I was looking at.[54]

The dance *Motorcycle* was a solo for Judith Dunn, accompanied by Arlene Rothlein singing and John Worden playing trumpet. Dunn wore leg warmers and a leotard that had been cut off at the midriff to make a halter top. Among other actions, she struck a yoga pose, "the lion," squatting on the floor with eyes and mouth open wide and tongue stuck out. After holding "the lion" pose for twenty seconds, she fell over to do a dance that remained close to the floor, and at one point she rested her head on her arms, crossed on her knees. "It was some kind of liberation dance," Dunn reflects. On the first night, Lucinda Childs, Ruth Emerson, Deborah Hay, and Yvonne Rainer provided a movement "backup" for the dance; on the second night, only Emerson and Rainer did this. According to Rainer, "You felt like a football player. You had to do exact unison: hold hands stiffly and sing 'da da da dum' while stepping out on the same foot on the same beat."[55]

Johnston, who saw the concert both nights, preferred the second version.

> [Dunn's] first solo, *Motorcycle*, is a strong dance with many beautiful, evocative gestures in it. There [is] a series of delicate falls near the end. She crouches with her head down on arms folded across the knees, then falls by a slight impulse onto one hand so that her body opens sideways into a cradled suspension. The first night the solo was accompanied by four women who occasionally dashed into the space and fell into a huddle. The lack of connection between the group and Miss Dunn didn't make any spatial sense to me. But the second night she eliminated the dashing group and kept two women, who entered and stayed, for the most part in static positions reflecting the mood of the dance, and then crawled off with Miss Dunn at the end. The balance of changing distances between single figures somehow activated the space as the previous arrangement had not.[56]

Acapulco, which had been performed at the Gramercy Arts Theater in Concert #9 in July (see Chapter 5), was repeated this time with Rainer taking Dunn's role. Johnston explains in her review that the dance derived its structure from a child's game. She calls it "a beautiful visual event, abstracted from the simple actions of a hand game (scissors, rocks, and paper), of ironing a dress, playing cards, and brushing the hair."

> The central section, a long slow-motion walk of Deborah Hay and a "sit" of Lucinda Childs, the former approaching the latter (dropping a scarf on the way) finally to brush

her hair, is an exquisite picture, especially as it is lit by Robert Rauschenberg into gold lights and shadows, reminding me of a George de la Tour or some chiaroscuro painter like that. The tension of the scene snaps perfectly as Yvonne Rainer is wheeled in on a cart and dumped off, at which moment Miss Hay stops the hair brushing, runs over to sit down and play cards with Miss Rainer, and Miss Childs quickly turns to stand on her chair. She immediately reverts to slow, rising and twisting until she falls off balance into Alex Hay's arms.[57]

Index was the duet for Judith Dunn and Steve Paxton that had been performed first in Concert #4 (see Chapter 3). Performed on Saturday night on this program, it was divided into two parts—*Index I* and *Index II*—and interrupted by *Witness I* and intermission. Johnston describes it as,

A dynamic engagement, full of lyric encounters, big travels, virtuosic speed and coordinations, and those gestures I have mentioned [matter-of-fact or allusively expressive, but always like biomorphs in a generally abstract context], which complicate the pure dancing with currents of psychic energy. Like the wild precise allegro of feet and legs that stops abruptly as Mr. Paxton throttles his partner with a hand at the neck. Or the wonderful sequence of awkward balances followed each time by a lunge of one at the other to make both collapse hard and like in some sprawling communion.[58]

Doubles for 4 accompanied both *Indexes,* and on Friday night it accompanied both *Witnesses.* Robert Dunn describes his 1959 composition:

Four dancers who were "out" entered with a cardtable and four folding chairs, set [them] up, and sat down to [the table], each dealing out for himself shuffled cards bearing instructions for performing simple clapping patterns which played against each other in a more complex way. At the end of the assigned number of "deals," they put away the cards, folded up the table and chairs, and left the space, while the dance continued as before.[59]

Witness was one long phrase that traveled in four directions, danced in three different versions in the course of the two evenings: a solo, a duet, and a trio. Judith Dunn describes the structure of the dance as a mandala. When she performed the phrase as a solo in *Witness II*, she wore a special costume that Paxton designed—a leotard and tights in different shades of brown, missing one leg and with the other leg painted blue. Twigs stuck out of the tights, and a special shoe made it seem that grass was growing up between Dunn's toes. On Friday night, the duet version, *Witness I*, was danced by Dunn with John Worden, after *Witness II*. On Saturday night, Paxton and Worden danced *Witness I* after *Index I*. The trio version, *Witness III*, was danced by Childs, Emerson, and Deborah Hay, overlapping with the end of *Index II*. *Witness* functioned as a fluid link between the sections, making a segue both nights into *Airwave*.[60]

Childs, Emerson, Deborah Hay, Rainer, Rothlein, and Worden danced in *Airwave*, a dance that for the choreographer was about "people working together." The dancers formed huddles and gave signals to each other initiating various dance actions. But the dance was not improvised; Dunn says that it was completely set, although Johnston describes it as "a tight collage of phrases, the order of which was determined by signals and discussion hurdles." Rainer remembers that "rather than someone calling out something, we'd have to get into a huddle and agree, and then we'd do it." Later it seemed to Dunn that she might better have satisfied her intentions in *Airwave* by allowing the dancers to improvise. But at the time, "I thought improvisation was crazy; I was all for chance and perfection," she states.[61]

Astronomy Hill, the final solo, juxtaposed a spoken sound track against movement phrases. According to Dunn, the movements were sometimes humorous and included a Sophie Tucker imitation. The text was composed of letters Dunn had written home when, at nine years old, she had been sent to a boarding school that she hated. Johnston considered the juxtaposition of sound and movement in *Astronomy Hill* overly literal.

> Both the content and the delivery verged on illustrating the movement, or vice versa. I think if the order of the content (something about a letter home to mother from a girl at camp) was jumbled up and put on tape by a voice with a strong bland delivery (keeping "dramatic" inflections at least to a minimum) that the corny might have had a chance to become absurd. A corny illustration of the corny always turns out to be corny.[62]

Besides composing *Doubles for 4*, Robert Dunn provided a subliminal musical accompaniment to the entire concert by turning a small radio on and off, at a low volume, according to a predetermined time structure. Dunn writes,

> The radio was tuned to a Spanish-speaking station and was adjusted to stay out of the foreground awareness of the audience, but [to] provide a subliminal alerting to the small sounds in other parts of the building (there was always basketball going on in the gymnasium below) and from the streets around the church (passing fire-engines, a common event at the concerts, were the great sound-hit of the evening) and drawing all this into the experience of the dance.[63]

"Motorcycle" was an important concert not only because of the technical proficiency of Dunn and her dancers, and not only because it marked a point in Dunn's choreographic career independent of her career as a Cunningham dancer. The way the concert was unified, both through Robert Dunn's musical events that expanded sound perception and through Judith Dunn's weaving together of the dances; the way the personnel, the choice of dances, and even the content of the dances changed, all marked an artfulness in production of an entire evening and an attempt to experiment with a form that superficially seemed like a conventional concert of repertory works.

Johnston considered Dunn "not terribly original but lucid and solidly inventive" as a choreographer. But Johnston noted:

> I think people were happy to see the strong professional dancing of this concert. The last program (by the Judson dancers) was a sprawling jamboree by comparison. Changes keep things lively. Miss Dunn herself is a dancer of considerable poise and skill. She's a modern dancer of the '60s, I mean that she possesses an extensive technique which is related to the classical dancing of the ballet without looking like ballet, for the kinesthetic continuity of her dancing is that of a modern dancer and the range of movement is never inhibited by formulas. I have an idea that many modern dancers of the '60s were in a state of panic about technique. They rushed to the ballet studios to get stronger because the demands of the dance world were becoming more complex. The reign of several important vocabularies (Graham, Holm, etc.) was coming to an end and was no longer enough to meet the new demands. But since the demands were not clear, these modern dancers got stranded between the old ideas and their new strength. The confusion is still going on, but Miss Dunn is quite hip to the past and the present. She's been involved in the directions modern dance has rightly been taking away from the impasse of literature, logic, and the legalities of one academy or another.[64]

The concert also marked a shift in the Judson dynamics. The members of the workshop had always performed in other theaters and under other auspices even during the time of the cooperative concerts. But after Concert #13, there were only three more cooperative concerts planned from the workshop—Concerts #14, #15, and #16, given at the end of April 1964. In between Concerts #13 and the final series of three were two solo concerts at the church—Dunn's and Summers's—and several events that ultimately constituted divisive spinoffs from the workshop itself.

In January 1964, seven members of the Judson Dance Theater put on a concert at the State University of New York at New Paltz. The seven were Lucinda Childs, Alex Hay, Deborah Hay, Tony Holder, Steve Paxton, Yvonne Rainer, and Robert Rauschenberg. Holder was the only one whose choreography was not shown but, in the Judson tradition, he got equal billing with the six dancer-choreographers. Some of the dances had been shown before on Judson programs—Childs's *Minus Auditorium Equipment and Furnishings*; Deborah Hay's *All Day Dance*, here performed as a duet and called *All Day Dance with Two*; her *Would They or Wouldn't They?*, here retitled *They Will*. Six new dances were also given: Rauschenberg's *Shotput*; Childs's *Cancellation Sample*; Rainer's *At My Body's House*; Paxton's *Flat*; Rainer's *Thoughts on Improvisation (for the painter James Byars)*; and Alex Hay's *Colorado Plateau*. The concert was titled "Concert for New Paltz (Performed by Seven of Judson Dance Theater)," and the program note emphasized the links between the visual art-world and the concerns of the Judson choreographers:

> In the curious way in which the art world changes, painters have made inroads into theatrical performances. Artists find that there are no unacceptable sources for material. The repertoire of Judson Dance Theater reflects the latest of this recent tendency to allow freer play. Dancers, mixed with painters on the stage, point out how there is another quality to bodies than just the arrived at differences dancers have discovered in themselves—there is the whole look of the body, which knows a lot on its own, and, whether "trained" or not, relays much of its history with action.[65]

In February and March, the same people plus Albert Reid and Robert Morris gave two different programs on a four-week series at Stage 73, 321 East 73rd Street, calling themselves Surplus Dance Theater. Paxton organized the series, which ran on Monday nights, explaining to the press that the only relationship between Judson Dance Theater and Surplus Dance Theater was some overlapping of personnel. Allen Hughes wrote admiringly of this group's and Judson Dance Theater's ability to adapt itself to any space, in a Sunday article entitled "At Home Anywhere":

> The subject of this column last week was the lack of theaters in New York that are both suitable and available for dancing and dance-watching. Most dance people, be they of balletic or modern persuasions, acknowledge this deficiency and feel themselves limited by it.
> There is one hardy band, however, that seems serenely unperturbed by the matter. This is the group of dancers, painters, actors, musicians, writers, and goodness knows what else that calls itself the Judson Dance Theater....
> These are the avant-garde of the dance world, and if they are unified in any way, it is only by the belief that dancing must be done, that anyone can do it, that almost anything anyone does qualifies as dancing, that it can be done anywhere, and that conventions of artistic thought and practice exist only to be smashed.

After naming the various locales in which members of the Judson Dance Theater workshop had performed over the previous two years, Hughes ventured to explain how they succeeded, offering two reasons:

> 1) They tailor their dances to fit the limitations of the performing area.
> 2) They can, if necessary, maintain a sublime disregard for the comfort of their audiences. (They have been helped in this by the fact that many of their performances have been given free of charge.)
> Much of what they do enrages practitioners and devotees of conventional ballet and modern dance. They often do nonsensical, outrageous, and boring things, and many of the things do not amount to much, even, I would guess, by their own inscrutable esthetic measurements. Sometimes they seem to carry on like children at play who want to be watched by adults, and who do not understand that the adult attention span for such play is apt to be limited.
> Nevertheless, they have been watched by more and more people....

> Now, they seem to be fanning out in a number of directions simultaneously, giving
> further proof to the fact that wherever they land they can dance something somehow.[66]

As with the Concert for New Paltz, some of the dances on the Surplus
programs had been performed in Judson Dance Theater concerts. Some
had been performed first at New Paltz. But several were new. The first
program, "sur +," included *21.3* by Robert Morris, *All Day Dance with
Two* by Deborah Hay, *Flat* by Steve Paxton, *Colorado Plateau* by Alex
Hay, *Dialogues* by Yvonne Rainer, *Acapulco* by Judith Dunn, and *Shotput*
by Robert Rauschenberg. The second program, "Exchange," given on 2
and 9 March, included *They Will* by Deborah Hay, *Pastime* by Lucinda
Childs, *Prairie* by Alex Hay, *Three Seascapes* by Yvonne Rainer, *A Brief
Glossary of Personal Movements or The Modern Dance: A Solo: 1. Sav-
ings and Loan* by Albert Reid, *At My Body's House* by Rainer, and *Site* by
Robert Morris.[67]

During Surplus Dance Theater's uptown run, Elaine Summers presented her mixed-media evening, *Fantastic Gardens,* at Judson Church, on
17, 18, and 19 February. *Fantastic Gardens* mixed film projections, friezes
with live performers, dancing, music, singing, speaking, and audience participation, all taking place throughout the space in the sanctuary.

Summers decided to use the whole space because, she says, she wanted
to structure the performance to be reality, in the sense that everything
would be going on around the audience and each spectator would only be
able to observe part of the totality.

> In working with film, I realized that out of the same materials you could make different
> edits. And in thinking about choreography—whether you improvise or whether you use
> set structures—, I realize that you never really see the same dance twice. *Fantastic Gar-
> dens* was made with the rather bitter acknowledgement that you can't see in the back of
> your head. You were not meant to see everything. You were meant to deal with that
> question: "Where shall I look?" If you came back another night, you would see a whole
> different thing.[68]

By using film projections as well as live performance, Summers felt
she could express in another way the issue of looking at the same phenomenon in different ways. In one section, a film of Sally Stackhouse was projected onto a screen in the balcony while Stackhouse danced in front of it.
The movement of filmed dancer and live dancer was not always identical;
sometimes the film showed a closeup of a movement or a different part of
the dance. In "Film of Joan and Al," near the end of the program, a
sixteen-millimeter black and white film, shot by Summers, showed Al
Hansen and Joan Baker building a house out of materials they found in an
empty lot. Ka Kwong Hui, a friend of Summers's, shot the same scene in

color, in super-eight millimeter film, and the smaller, color image was projected in the corners of the black and white image.[69]

Summers later wrote this description of *Fantastic Gardens*:

> *Fantastic Gardens* was the first full-evening intermedia concert in New York City combining film, dance, music, and sculpture. The concert was presented in three parts with two intermissions. The first section consisted of a film collage of dances, using chance methods inspired by John Cage. In the second section, "All Around the Hall," members of the audience were seated around the edge of the Judson Memorial Church in the form of a pyramid. Film images were splashed over the ceiling, floor, walls, and audience, who were given small hand mirrors with which to pick up additional images. As the projected images, partially aided by mirrors placed near the projector lens, splashed very slowly over the audience, dancers began to dance inside of large sculptural pieces which were placed within and outside the perimeters of the audience. The audience was then invited to participate in the dance by using their mirrors to light the dancers. In the third section, "Other People's Gardens," one of the sculptures, a large metallic "tree" built of junk, became the instrument played by composer Malcolm Goldstein. Several films were shown successively. One of these, a film of Sally Stackhouse dancing, was projected onto a split screen before which Stackhouse performed a choreographed "shadow dance."[70]

The printed program, made of small sheets of colored paper stapled together, like the petals of a variegated flower, lists thirteen sections in *Fantastic Gardens*: "Overture," film by Carol Summers, "Statues," film by Elaine Summers, "Projection Piece," and "The Sun King" made up the first section, in which the audience was seated facing the altar. A note on the program explained to the audience that mirrors would be distributed during the first intermission, and that "when the 1st intermission is over, the audience is requested to walk around the sculptures and reseat themselves wherever they can. Upon sitting, please let your mirrors catch the light so that they will then reflect on and around the dancers. Kindly return mirrors during the 2nd intermission." The audience was also warned to take its belongings during both intermissions, when the seating would be changed. The second section consisted of "Sculpture, Dancers, & People," "Film All Around the Hall" (*Illumination; Ice Freezes Red; Im Mim in Ages' "Communism Is More Palatial Than a Gold Mine"; Preditor's* [sic] *Dream,* and *Twenty by Twos Twenty-five*)," "Creatures." The third section consisted of "Other People's Gardens," "Film of Joan and Al," "Playing the Tree," and "Wind Dance." The program explained that Summers had choreographed the dances and given the dancers movement scores, which they used as frameworks within which to improvise. The dancers were Eddie Barton, Carla Blank, June Ekman, Ruth Emerson, Sally Gross, Al Hansen, Fred Herko, Christine Meyers, Roger Morris, Bill Myers, Sandra Neels, Rudy Perez, Arlene Rothlein, Larry Segal, Sally Stackhouse, and John Worden.

The music was by John Herbert McDowell (for "Other People's Gardens") and Malcolm Goldstein. The sculptures were made by Al Hansen, Ira Matteson, Bill Myers, Robert Ranieri, and Carol Summers. Photography was credited to Elaine Summers, Stan Vanderbeek, Carol Summers, Eugene Friedman, Ka Kwong Hui, and Billy Linich. The projectionists were Dorothy Hoppe, John Hoppe, and Maurice Elanc; the technical crew was Bill Myers, James Wilson, and Al Hansen. Johanna Vanderbeek did the costumes, and Carol Summers did the lighting. Andrew Peck was the lighting assistant.[71]

According to Jonas Mekas, who reviewed *Fantastic Gardens* in his "Movie Journal" in the *Village Voice,* the evening was not the first such experiment — he gave as recent precedents the work of Roberts Blossom, Stan Vanderbeek, and Robert Whitman — , but it was "by far the most successful and most ambitious attempt to use the many possible combinations of film and live action to create an aesthetic experience."

> Specifically, one could see here a huge ballet-happening, often involving the entire audience and using the entire presence of the church itself, its walls, its columns, balconies, ceiling. Mirrors were distributed which the audience used to catch the beams of light crisscrossing the church. When one looked at the audience, it seemed to be dancing too, going through a variety of fluttering, floating movements, hands moving in the air as if they were chasing and following the light beams, in a strange ritual of light.

Mekas describes the technical set-up for the various projection schemes.

> There were screens at both ends of the auditorium and three or four projectors, with the images being projected at various times, singly or in chorus, on the screens, on the walls of the church, the ceiling, and the columns, and on and around the dancers and the audience. Superimpositions were created right there by throwing two and three images one upon the other, or around each other; and there was a man working a hand-held projector like an image-gun or a light-brush, swinging it the way he felt like, in images of color and black-and-white, changing their size and background.
>
> Fantastic effects were produced by using a split screen, a screen made of several dangling strips of white material which moved and separated, and there were human figures appearing through the partings, moving into and out of the screen, submerging, disappearing into it, participating in it, so that at times one didn't know or knew only vaguely what was the photograph and what was the real live presence. Actions of images overlapped or repeated or extended actions of dancers and people — the same figures, often, appearing on the screen as in the dance arena or around the balcony. Etc.[72]

The "Overture" was a composition by Malcolm Goldstein, sung by Carolyn Chrisman, Robert Rainieri, Norma Marder, Al Carmines, Lou Rogers, and John Patton. Goldstein played piano and percussion. He created a notation for the singers that was a sketchier notation than the score for the same piece he wrote in 1976. Duration, loudness, and range of pitch were indicated. Goldstein improvised on the piano, using gestures similar to the 1976 score and perhaps, as indicated in the later score, playing both the keyboard and the inside of the piano. "Overture" was performed a second time, during "Wind Dance," with the vocalists behind the audience, using the same score but articulating wind sounds.[73]

After the film by Carol Summers came a section, called "Statues," of dancers posing in white leotards and tights. Then came the film collage, by Elaine Summers, which included a recurring image of Fred Herko wearing an overcoat and watering a garbage can — until finally he lifts the cover to find flowers sprouting. The next section was "Projection Piece," a variation of Emerson's *Narrative,* from Concert #1, in which the "characters" wore costumes and spoke in nonsequiturs, written by James Wilson.[74] According to Summers,

> "Projection Piece" came from the fact that I wanted to structure a work that would be like a magnet for your projections. I noticed that whenever you do anything, most people in the audience try to make a story out of it, whether it has a story or not. I did this piece to magnetize them. I wanted to keep it as evocative as possible, and as abstract as possible at the same time. It started on the altar, with the women on the altar and the men at the bottom. The women lay down over the shoulders of the men. The clothing was meant as a trap; I have been interested for a long time in the incongruity of costumes, and again, the tremendous projection [they evoke]. As soon as you put a piece of clothing on, it carries a social past, your personal past, and then the body that it is going onto [has meaning, too]. So all the men wore tails and bare feet and white gloves. The women all wore black gowns, except Sally Gross, who wore an 18th century silk dress, as the only figure in white.
>
> One of them jumped diagonally, saying "Let go of my tongue, mother, I'll say it myself." All sorts of phrases like that.[75]

According to Johnston's review, spectators objected to not being able to see everything, but as far as she was concerned,

> You could have been hanging from the rafters to enjoy everything [that followed "Statues."] A bird's eye view might have been quite interesting, especially after the first intermission when the seating arrangement changed and the audience formed a kind of flower, the majority remained in a deep outside circle while a group sat in a nuclear mass in the center....
>
> ["Projection Piece"] consisted of words and movement by the women in sexy black dresses and the men in "dress" black pants and jackets. Here the space was a big arena for the independent actions of the dancers and the accidental juxtapositions of movement and spoken lines. Since it was impossible to see and hear each line and action, it seemed unnecessary. Anyway, not straining to get it all, one could bask in the total atmosphere, which was off-beat and romantic, like an elegant garden party going somewhat haywire. The end of it was quite beautiful. Collapsing over each other as though

spent from an orgy of sentiment, the voices of the singers cascaded over the bodies in long, full-throated intonations to resolve the fantasy where it lay sleeping.[76]

The singing Johnston refers to was Goldstein's "Illuminations from Fantastic Gardens," with text by Arthur Rimbaud—"After the Deluge," from *Illuminations.* The notation for this music had originally come about when Arlene Rothlein had asked Goldstein for something to sing while dancing. Goldstein created a graphic treatment of the words that indicated, through the size, spacing, thickness of lines, and appearance (angular, rounded, smooth, fragmented) of the letters, what the loudness, rhythmic articulation, intensity, and timbre of the singing should be. The singers were spaced throughout the church and, according to Goldstein's directions, each one acted as a soloist "each with their own specific manner of realizing the notation and each moving at their own pacing," with the exception of the line that reads "Then in the violet and budding forest, Eucharis told me it was Spring."[77]

Next came "The Sun King," a section Summers refers to as "the Louis XIV arrangement," and then a section in which the dancers moved around the sculptures, and the "Film All Around the Hall," which she thought of as "the grand ball." "The eye," Jill Johnston noted, "was challenged to catch it on the run, to stay with it or leave it at the risk of missing it or something else. I liked the element of missing things in the concert."[78]

After the second intermission came "Other People's Gardens," a series of satires of other choreographers. Carla Blank, who danced with Merle Marsicano at the time, imitated Marsicano; Tony Holder played Paul Taylor; John Worden and Ruth Emerson did a satire on Judith Dunn's choreography. The other spoofs were on Hanya Holm, Yvonne Rainer, Alwin Nikolais, Aileen Passloff, and Martha Graham. Malcolm Goldstein's "Playing the Tree" was a section in which he used one of the sculptures as a percussion instrument. And finally, all the dancers, the singers, and Goldstein on piano created the "Wind Dance."[79]

Like Rainer in her *Terrain,* Paxton in *Afternoon,* and Judith Dunn in "Motorcyle," Summers was forging a direction for future work in *Fantastic Gardens*, which was a synthesis of her concerns in Robert Dunn's class, in the Judson workshop, and with the other arts. Her collaborators on *Fantastic Gardens* reflected the expanding network in the world of independent film, continuing from the Gramercy concerts. And, as with the other solo concerts, Summers's ambition in *Fantastic Gardens* showed that for the original members of the workshop, the cooperative concerts, in which short works by individual members were best suited to the demands of the group as a whole, could no longer suffice.

On 27 February, the same members of the Judson Dance Theater who had formed the Surplus Dance Theater (Childs, Dunn, Hay, Hay, Holder,

Morris, Paxton, Rainer, and Rauschenberg) appeared in the Once Festival in Ann Arbor, Michigan. The festival had been organized by the Once Group, an organization of avant-garde composers and performers based in Ann Arbor; it included, besides the evening of dance (which comprised two concerts), six music concerts with compositions by Donald Scavarda, George Cacioppo, Robert Ashley, Gordon Mumma, George Brecht, Terry Jennings, Udo Kasemets, Mary Traltas, Barney Childs, Bruce Wise, Kazuo Fukushima, Roman Haubenstock-Ramati, Michael Adamis, Henri Pousseur, John Cage, Robert Sheff, Morton Feldman, Anton Webern, Joseph Byrd, George Crevoshay, Roger Reynolds, Lejaren Hiller, Pauline Oliveros, Herbert Brun, Benjamin Johnston, Charles Hamm, Salvatore Martirano, Christian Wolff, Philip Krumm, Bob James, Robert Pozar, and Eric Dolphy. Besides the Once Group, the performers included the Brandeis University Chamber Chorus, the University of Illinois Contemporary Chamber Players, and the Bob James Trio with Eric Dolphy. The Judson group was billed "From the Judson Dance Theater" in the program, but the advance flyer had announced the appearance of "The Cream of the Crop — from the Judson Dance Theater" and named William Davis, Judith Dunn, Alex Hay, Deborah Hay, Barbara Lloyd, Robert Morris, Sandra Neels, Steve Paxton, Yvonne Rainer, and Albert Reid. However, ultimately William Davis, who planned to show *Sulfurs* (with Barbara Lloyd and Sandra Neels), and Albert Reid, who planned to show a new solo and a duet, did not appear with the group. The final program was as follows: Morris's *Arizona*, Rainer's *Dialogues*, Deborah Hay's *They Will*, Paxton's *Flat*, Childs's *Cancellation Sample*, Rainer's *Some Thoughts on Improvisation*, and Judith Dunn's *Acapulco* with Robert Dunn's *Doubles for 4*, all on the seven o'clock program; Paxton's *Proxy*, Deborah Hay's *All Day Dance for 2*, Morris's *21.3*, Rainer's *At My Body's House*, Judith Dunn's *Speedlimit*, Alex Hay's *Prairie*, Rauschenberg's *Shotput*, and Alex Hay's *Colorado Plateau*, all on the ten o'clock program.[80]

Apparently it was the Once Group that added "Cream of the Crop" to the title "From the Judson Dance Theater," which the dancers had submitted. But this label, added to the fact that the group earned nine hundred dollars to appear at the Once Festival, created a great deal of friction within the workshop. Those who had not been asked to appear resented the others' use of the Judson Dance Theater name. They hadn't minded the lack of pay when no one was being paid and no admissions charged, but now the situation had changed.[81]

When Jill Johnston produced another group concert, this time sponsored by the Institute of Contemporary Art in Philadelphia and held at the Annenberg auditorium at the University of Pennsylvania on 24 April 1964, the words Judson Dance Theater were nowhere to be seen. The program and flyer simply stated that the performance was by the April 24th Concert

Group. Once again, Rainer's *At My Body's House*, Alex Hay's *Colorado Plateau*, Rainer's and Ross's *Room Service*, Reid's *A Brief Glossary of Personal Movements of the Modern Dance: A Solo: 1. Savings and Loan*, and Morris's *Site*, from previous Judson, New Paltz, or Surplus programs were shown. Premieres at the Philadelphia concert were *Natural History* by Judith Dunn, *Silver Pieces* by David Gordon, *Carnation* by Lucinda Childs, *Untitled Duet* by Carla Blank and Sally Gross, and *We Three* by Deborah Hay.[82]

Katherine Litz gave a concert at Judson Church in March, and from March through April James Waring organized seven Monday night concerts, "Events and Entertainments," presenting "dances, diversions, and what nots" by artists in and out of the Judson workshop, at the Pocket Theater. The end of April also saw the last three numbered concerts by the Judson Dance Theater workshop.[83]

Like Concert #13, in which all the dances were spawned by working with a commonly agreed-upon environment, in Concert #14, given on Monday, 27 April 1964, a unifying factor of method had been chosen: improvisation. Concert #15, on 28 April, was a program of six dances, and Concert #16, on 29 April, was a program of nine dances. Robert Morris designed the flyer for the series, a blue rectangle with a footprint that moved, smudging the print, across the paper. The three programs, designed by Andrew Sherwood, were different color pastel sheets with tracings of feet and hands. There was no program committee listed on the programs. Philip Corner and Max Neuhaus are credited for sound; Janet Castle for lighting; Phoebe Neville as assistant. For Concert #14, June Ekman was stage manager and James Tenney operated the tape; for Concert #15, Deborah Hay was stage manager and Malcolm Goldstein operated the tape; for Concert #16, Yvonne Rainer was stage manager and James Tenney operated the tape.[84]

The first half of Concert #14, according to the program notes, consisted of thirty minutes, within which seven improvisations "choreographed" by individuals would take place at any time. During intermission, the seating was changed—the audience was warned to take their hats and coats with them—and after the intermission, the second half of the concert consisted of a twenty-five minute improvisation choreographed by Deborah Hay.

The seven improvisations in the first half of the concert were *Pearls Down Pat* by Carla Blank and Sally Gross, *Improvisation* by Lucinda Childs, *The Other Side* by Judith Dunn, *Dredge* by Alex Hay and Robert Rauschenberg, *Rialto* by Steve Paxton, *Thoughts on Improvisation (for the painter James Byars)* by Yvonne Rainer, and *Execution is Simply Not* by Elaine Summers. The participants in Deborah Hay's untitled improvisation were: Carolyn Brown, Lucinda Childs, William Davis, Judith Dunn, David Gordon, Alex Hay, Deborah Hay, Tony Holder, Barbara Lloyd, Steve Paxton, Yvonne Rainer, Robert Rauschenberg, Albert Reid, Carolee Schneemann, Joanna Vischer, and Marilyn Wood.[85]

Pearls Down Pat may have been the same improvisation that Blank and Gross had performed in Philadelphia the previous week as *Untitled Duet*. Gross remembers it as a dance with certain rules about making physical contact, performed at the same time that a recording of Bach's *Goldberg Variations* played—although the dancing did not work with or against the music. Gross remembers,

> If there was contact, then we had to keep the contact for a number of seconds before we could break away, or maybe a certain body part making contact meant you couldn't turn around or you couldn't bend down. There were certain rules, certain limits, but we didn't write them down, so I don't remember exactly what they were.
>
> We worked together well and had the confidence that we wouldn't get hurt. We felt fairly free to fall and recover, although it wasn't like *32.16 Feet per Second Squared*, which had a lot of backward falls and spiral recoveries, after which you would halt and start again. In that dance we thought that we would never bump into each other, and we never did.
>
> With Carla my feeling was that we could do more body contact and we wouldn't get hurt. We weren't afraid. That fall we had begun a lot of weight-lifting and body-lifting stuff. She would lie on my back and I would carry her. That was part of the dance. But it didn't come out of anything specific; we left ourselves open to take chances. There were a lot of off-center balances. And a lot of it was about leaning into that weight.[86]

Blank recalls that the rules, whatever they were, restricted the movement choices so that although the two performed the dance several times, it changed very little.[87]

The essential characteristic of improvisation is its elusiveness. If all dance is evanescent, disappearing the moment it has been performed, improvisation emphasizes that evanescence to the point that the identity of the dance is attenuated, leaving few traces in written scores, or even muscle memory. For this reason, very few of the participants in Concert #14 remember what it is, exactly, they did. Neither Childs, nor Dunn, nor Alex Hay, nor Rauschenberg remembers the work in the concert. Paxton does remember *Rialto*:

> I took two pictures of the audience. I left the stage for long periods of time. I used cardboard boxes as a costume, getting inside them and tipping them. I laid a big stack of boxes on top of myself, reaching for one more edge and putting it up on top. One of them had a rope in it, which was not revealed to the audience. And I put it in so that by pulling down on that rope I could compress all of them and make a unit; I could tip without the boxes falling over.
>
> The name comes from Venice: the bridge, and also the name of theaters. An

awareness of performance was involved, because I took pictures of the audience instead of the audience taking in a picture.[88]

Rainer's *Thoughts on Improvisation* (also called *Some Thoughts on Improvisation*) was a solo with a spool of white thread. Rainer was dressed in a black dress and high-heeled shoes. The dancing was accompanied by a taped reading of a text on improvisation Rainer had written after dancing at the Green Gallery in an event by James Lee Byars, to whom *Some Thoughts...* was dedicated. The essay forces the audience not only to watch the movements in the improvisation closely, but also challenges the viewer in two ways: by presenting a description of the process, it presents conflicting information—i.e., the act of listening to the spoken information might distract the viewer from the dancing; and secondly, by suggesting the kinds of choice and element that structure an improvisation, it leads the spectator to make correlations between the dance currently viewed and the stimuli informing every moment. Rainer began:

> Well see, it's like this see. I get into place and I size up the situation. That doesn't take much doing. You just size up the situation, and you let your blood flow and then there is an obvious opening: There is an aisle completely surrounding the platform of boxes, an aisle between the platform and the people standing against the wall. So I walk....
> So I keep on sizing up the situation, see. And I keep on walking. And I made decisions: He has left the room, I will run; she is standing stockstill, I will bring my head close to hers; that man is moving his arms around, I will do as he does; the wall looms close, I will walk until I bump into it; my black dress is white from the wall, I will brush it off; they are finished, I will rest in this position for a long time; the man is using the magnifying glass, I will look at him from the other side; he and she are standing together, I will stand with them; the woman removes her cellophane bag from the reach of my steam-rolling foot, I WILL NOT MAKE AN ISSUE OF IT.

Rainer describes the physical impulses, the feeling of physical connection to the performing space—"They are the pulse and tongue of the body in the place." She lists three aspects of choice-making in improvisation: impulses, antiimpulses, ideas. The action, she notes, can come from choosing not to follow an impulse. It is, finally, the performer's instinct—the "sense of fitness," the confrontation with anxiety, the control over concentration, and, in improvising with one other person or in a group, the treatment of social dynamics—that fuels the performance. "At the moment of moving into an action, one must behave and feel as though no other choice exists even while running the risk of acting out a thoroughly private illusion." Yet even the lack of conviction, if manifested, can be exploited in the performance. "Like saying 'Look at my dirty underwear. I forgot to change it today, but you see, it too exists.' An improvisational equivalent of dirty underwear might be the letting go of one's concentration and just *being* there looking at the people who are looking at you." Finally, Rainer concluded,

> My own every action and decision brings to bear an element of control and certainly influence, thus returning to my hand a limited power to push the thing where I want it to go at that moment. If I seem to be concerned with the idea of a power conflict, I am not (though the possibility exists). As frequently happens, two people in an improvisation are as much pushed by *it* as by each other. When it goes forward it moves with an inexorable thrust and exerts a very particular kind of tension: spare, unadorned, highly dramatic, loaded with expectancy—a field for action. What more could one ask for.[89]

The engaging of the audience in a dialectic of experience and analysis is another thread that continues through Rainer's choreography as well as her filmmaking. In *Some Thoughts on Improvisation*, the audience is not simply given a dance whose structure is improvisatory; it is induced to participate in the decisions made during the improvisation, and challenged to think about the process of improvisatory performance in general.

At first, according to Elaine Summers, the improvisations were planned as sequential pieces. But then the group changed their minds and decided to improvise the order of the dances as well. Alex Hay remembers that the one limit in planning when one's dance would come in the first half of the program was that sounds could not conflict. Summers recalls that she performed her *Execution is Simply Not* simultaneously with Paxton's and Rainer's solos. Summers's improvisation was a walking dance, performed in two different costumes—a street dress and sandals, and, for the second half of her dance, an antique, turn-of-the-century black lace dress.

> I became interested during the performance in the difference between the dress I was wearing and Yvonne [Rainer]'s dress, and I decided right during the concert to make a dialogue with her, a kinetic discussion, about this dichotomy. I took the dance movements—it was all walking, of course—and suited them to this nineteenth century feeling. I juxtaposed that to Yvonne's straightforward movement pattern. We weren't supposed to be doing the dances together, but there was a time problem and they said to me, "You must go out and do your dance now," which was a surprise. The juxtaposition had a controversial feeling; I enjoyed being in a situation in which the sparks were flying.[90]

At some point during the concert, probably during the long improvisation in the second half of the concert, Philip Corner and Max Neuhaus performed Corner's *Rope Pull Sounds,* a tug of war with a rope loaded with bells, slats, chains, cans, and balloons. During *Thoughts on Improvisation*, Rainer asked Morris to help her move furniture, a continuation of the lugging of the mattress during the 24 April concert in Philadelphia that had excited Rainer. She writes, "We moved all the furniture in the lounge into the sanctuary (which was the playing area), including the filthy dusty carpet. Thoroughly irritated everybody by interfering with their activities, broke a leg off the couch, spilled ashes and sand inadvertently all over my black dress. The situation was definitely not satisfying." The disparity between her reaction to the Philadelphia "moving" and this experience led Rainer to consider her use of materials, giving rise to her use of mattresses in *Parts of Some Sextets,* the following year. "Was the difficulty in the nature of the materials? Could it be that a living room couch is not as 'plastic' as a mattress? Hard materials versus soft — or more flexible — materials? (An absurd area of speculation? — like comparing the virtues of plastic or wood toilet seats?)" Returning to the subject of the improvisation in Concert #14, Rainer continues, "Having completed the job I found myself with no ideas. In exasperation Bob [Morris] left, and in desperation I fell back on some of my more eccentric improvisatory techniques. (At that time I had not yet made the decision to abandon the loony bin and the NY subways as sources of inspiration.)"[91] The program does not list Morris as one of the participants in the group improvisation, but Paxton also remembers the furniture-moving by Rainer and Morris, and he suggests that Morris's name may simply have been omitted by accident.[92]

Jill Johnston, looking back at the demise of Judson Dance Theater, in a *Village Voice* column published in 1965, wrote about Concert #14:

> Ironically, one of the concerts on this last series in [April] was a great improvisation, with minimal restrictions on freedom, and the most impressive collection of vanguard dancers and artists (including most of the Cunningham company) couldn't get this tacitly accepted Open Sesame (free play) of the Judson Dance Theater off the ground. Everybody was very polite except for Yvonne Rainer, who doesn't care to be assimilated in the mass, and the response to her nerve should have been pandemonium if anybody had faced the assertion squarely. I wasn't looking for a climax but for a "situation" that would develop of electric necessity out of a collective atmosphere of private sideshows. In isolation, a number of performers were interesting enough, if that was all you wanted. The conditions for the different types of improvisations at the church have varied considerably. The conditions for success usually boiled down to a viable contract between guide lines (ground rules) supplied by the choreographer and the performers who were alert and imaginative enough to be existing under any circumstances. This last group improvisation (arranged by Deborah Hay) demonstrated the temptation to loosen guide lines under the cover of previous successes where the situations were more circumscribed. (At the other extreme, greater restrictions have illustrated that the same or even better effects can be achieved when the choreographer is in complete control; at such a point the method becomes inconsequential.)

Johnston contrasts the improvisation in Concert #14 to the collaborative work in Concert #13.

> Occasionally, certain external factors have supplied the motive force. The mess of objects and structures in the collaborative concert with sculptor Charles Ross was an

effective trapping for extended moments of the two free-play sections. For Rainer's [and Ross's] *Room Service* it was even more effective, because the leadership psychology of improvisation was made explicit in the follow-the-leader form of the piece, and the materials provided a setting for the three leaders, who would have to be dull as doldrums not to take advantage of such an environment.[93]

Concert #15 opened with a trio, William Davis's *Sulfurs,* to new music, continued with a solo without music, Tony Holder's *Plus,* and a trio without music, Carla Blank's *Potlatch.* Three more dances followed the intermission: Judith Dunn's *Natural History,* a trio to Romantic piano music; Al Kurchin's solo *Garlands for Gladys*; and David Gordon's duet for himself and Valda Setterfield, *Fragments.*[94]

Sulfurs was choreographed by William Davis and performed by Davis, Barbara [Dilley] Lloyd, and Sandra Neels, to Christian Wolff's string quartet *Summer,* which was played by Ira Lieberman, Malcolm Goldstein, Mimi Hartshorn, and Lucy Reisman. Davis thought of the trio as an idyllic nature dance, with social commentary of his *Crayon* or *Field,* and without *Field's* ironies. He writes, "Here the music was a kind of natural landscape (what Christian Wolff called it) for the dance to happen in: open, spacious, rather dry and astringent. (Open in the sense that it has no modular rhythm.) It generates an atmosphere, clear and light, but with a kind of tension."[95]

The costumes were hand-knitted legwarmers, sleeves, and tights, striped in bands of different widths in cream, yellow, and yellow-orange, over leotards and tights that were in shades of ivory and pale yellow. The title of the dance refers to sulphur butterflies. Davis notes that he also wanted to suggest volatility or combustibility, the sun, and the color pale yellow. He describes the movements:

> There was no animal mimicry, but a lot of the space patterns and couplings derived from images of animal activity, like the wheeling flocking of birds, or the tumbling together of the flight patterns of two butterflies. I remember some of the groupings of twos and threes as being quite rapid and intricate, and also some of the movement as being a little dangerous, particularly several eccentric jumps, and some swiftly dovetailed duets and trios. Barbara [(Dilley) Lloyd] sprained her ankle landing on relevé from a long, low leap in which I had her arms and her head splayed and arched backward so that it was hard for her to see where the ground was. She had a wonderful abandon in her dancing (a little like Lynn Seymour) that I went a bit far in taking advantage of.
>
> There were a lot of spinning turns, especially in a solo for Sandra [Neels], and I also remember doing a strange sequence of lifts and carrys with Sandra, but can't recall any detail of it.[96]

Davis remembers thinking that in certain ways his choreography may have resembled Cunningham's, but that Carolyn Brown, Cunningham's lead dancer, told him she saw more of Balanchine's influence than Cunningham's in the dance.[97]

Although Tony Holder had performed in more than ten dances at the Judson Dance Theater programs, and had attended the workshop since it began, *Plus* was his first choreography at Judson. Like Deborah Hay, he was one of the youngest members when the workshop began. He had arrived in New York in September 1962, specifically to study at Cunningham's studio as a scholarship student. He took over Paxton's job of cleaning the studio after Paxton joined the company. Holder had grown up in Indiana, where he began to study dancing in high school as an aspiring athlete, at the suggestion of his stepmother, who said the classes would help. By the time he won a swimming scholarship to the University of Nebraska, he decided that the sports would take too much time away from his dancing, and he went to another college. After a year in college, he decided to study dancing full-time. His stepmother, who had been friendly with John Cage and Merce Cunningham both in Seattle and in New York, wrote to Cunningham to tell him how Holder danced. Cunningham, Holder remembers, was full of advice and suggestions for his friend's son.

> He was very solicitous: "Don't get malnutrition, eat your breakfast." "Do you know how to get places on the subway?" He said to go to all the dance concerts that I could, so I started going, but I got bored with them. The ballet looked good to me. When the Judson workshops started in October and I'd been in New York a month, Merce [Cunningham] said, "Why don't you go? There are people there from class." I said I didn't know anything. He said it didn't matter. It wasn't easy to meet people. So I went.[98]

Like the others in the workshop, Holder was immediately incorporated into the dances the group produced, and in Concert #3 and #4 he performed in Rainer's *We Shall Run* and Paxton's *English*, and after those concerts in numerous other dances. He became very friendly with Alex and Deborah Hay, and later, with Lucinda Childs, Steve Paxton, and Robert Rauschenberg. During the summer of 1964, he worked for Rauschenberg, taking care of his loft and printing silkscreens for him while he was in Europe. He remembers that,

> Before they left, I went to help Rauschenberg at his studio. It blew my mind to watch him work. I would arrive at ten in the morning, and he would already be drinking vodka and orange juice. And then he'd start painting, and the dog would walk across the painting, and he would erase three of the footsteps and not the others. Then he left [for Europe] and paid me to print all the silkscreens on paper and then destroy the screens.

Holder and Alex Hay had found weighted vests that basketball players use to practice jumping, and Holder decided to use one of the vests in a dance he had made, a series of short phrases arranged by chance. He performed the dance once with a vest on and once without it, and the two-part piece constituted *Plus*.

> Rauschenberg made me a costume that looked like a bacon, lettuce, and tomato sandwich. It was green and red and white. I thought the vest looked like bread; it was a white canvas vest. I rehearsed the dance with the vest on, and it was very arduous. I got to the point where I could do all the movements and not fall down. I took the vest off. I was going to lay it on the floor in performance so no one would notice. But I was so exhausted by dancing in it that I dropped it, and there was a smash. And then I did the dance again, and it was totally different.[99]

Carla Blank's *Potlatch* was performed by Blank, Deborah Lee, and Sandra Neels. Blank only remembers one movement from that dance: a slow-motion walk that she thinks of as "a kind of bicycle walk, a tight-rope line walk, too. The arms were circling, palms facing the floor, and it caused a mesmeric feeling when you performed it. There was a relevé to deep plié going on at the same time." The title was based on the dance's structure, which had to do with an exchange of movements between the dancers.[100]

Judith Dunn's *Natural History*, following intermission, was danced by Dunn, Lucinda Childs, and Tony Holder. The music, by Robert Schumann, was played by Robert Dunn on the piano.[101]

The next dance was Al Kurchin's *Garlands for Gladys*, to a tape he had put together. Kurchin, not a trained dancer, had performed in Summers's *Country Houses* in Concert #10. Don McDonagh describes *Garlands for Gladys*:

> A series of chairs [was] set in an arc. Kurchin sauntered out and came to a foot-hopping halt to stare at them. This was repeated a few times until the last entrance, when wearing a naturalistic mask, he assaulted one of the more "feminine" and delicate looking chairs.[102]

The final dance on the program was Gordon's *Fragments,* the same dance that in Philadelphia the previous week had been called *Silver Pieces*. Gordon explains the work's genesis:

> Someone said I should do an evening of my own work and they could arrange it. So I went about making separate pieces. Then that whole deal fell through. But Jill Johnston asked if I could go to Philadelphia.
>
> I took the bits and pieces I had been working on, glued them together, and called it *Fragments*. I needed something to serve as the glue. So I had a television set and two chairs. We sat on the stage, watched TV, and every now and then we got up to do things.
>
> In Philadelphia, I took the TV out of the student lounge. It was on a five-foot scaffold and it was enormous.

> At Judson, I took our own TV, sprayed it silver, sprayed gray leotards and tights sil-
> ver, had us wear children's plastic wigs sprayed silver, and performed the dance under
> the name *Silver Pieces.*
> It included things like Grape Jokes, like the Empire Grape Building.
> It was a bunch of parts of pieces all stuck together. The lights were out at the begin-
> ning. We turned on the TV. Then the lights came up. We were watching it. The first
> thing you saw was the TV screen. We weren't allowed to adjust it. And only one time
> was there tracking on the screen.[103]

Jill Johnston later described the dance in a discussion of the use of
objects in the new dance, especially the factual projection of objects.

> On a program in [April] 1964, David Gordon and Valda Setterfield presented a tele-
> vision dance, *Silver Pieces.* The television set was turned to various stations at whim,
> while the two dancers performed ten sequences of action of an indeterminate order. As
> a mass media product the fact of the TV set loomed large in its ironic presentation
> before a captive audience. The association of images—the movement of the dancers and
> the picture on the screen—was intentionally haphazard (life in the living room has the
> same quality) and produced some interesting, often hilarious, results. In one perfor-
> mance a commercial advertising a cure for headaches was accompanied by a sequence
> of repetitive head-clutching and belly-aching gestures.[104]

Again, the juxtaposition of expressive accompaniment—here, both the
sound and the image of the television broadcast—to abstract movement
sequences created a fortuitous set of meanings in the dance.
    In another article, Johnston called *Fragments/Silver Pieces:*

> Gordon's and Setterfield's television Pop dance...in the best tradition of these two art-
> nouveau comedians, whose airs and ironies might be as appropriate at the tired end of a
> movement as they can be at the beginning, when everything goes and too much serious
> endeavor is offset by anyone who can plagiarize and satirize at the same time with styl-
> ish independence. Gordon and Setterfield have been the unwitting commentators on the
> scene they helped to create.[105]

Concert #16, held on 29 April, comprised nine dances. The first was
Villanelle, a group dance by Fred Herko, danced to *Nuits d'été* by Hector
Berlioz. The performers were Herko, Carla Blank, Abigail Ewert, Deborah
Lee, and Sandra Neels. A villanelle is a pastoral poem consisting of five
groups of three lines and a quatrain, with the first and third lines of the
first tercet alternating as a refrain in the succeeding stanzas and appearing
as the final two lines of the quatrain. Perhaps Herko used the formal structure of this poetic form as a basis for his choreographic structure in the
dance. It was one of the sections in the full-length evening *The Palace of
the Dragon Prince,* which Herko gave at the church, although not as a Judson Dance Theater production, on 1 and 2 May. Carla Blank recalls,

It was technically beyond most of us, I think. It really called for toe dancers. [Herko] had a vision that was very nineteenth century, a kind of Theater of Marvels. This dance was much more in the ballet tradition than his previous dances, many of which had been pure experiments. This was really based in a sense of the history of dance.

[Herko] always reminded me of Nureyev in his own movement. There was something about the use of the head and arms and back. It was influenced by James Waring, but it was even more balletic, I think.

I remember a lot of jumps and stretched feet. Everything was very extended, high-energy, stretching everything out as much as possible. A lot of the piece was done as unison work, but I think Deborah Lee was the soloist. She had a very perfect body, very correct in terms of ballet lines. There were a lot of movements in line formations, four in a line, and I remember him running wildly through it. He didn't do much in the dance, as I recall.[106]

The second dance in Concert #16 was Albert Reid's *A Brief Glossary of Personal Movements*, which Reid had performed with the longer title *A Brief Glossary of Personal Movements or The Modern Dance: A Solo: 1. Savings and Loan* on the Surplus "Exchange" program and in Philadelphia on 24 April. Reid made the dance a list of various kinds of movement that he felt had come from working in other choreographer's techniques and from trying to discover what his own movements were. He remembers that he was thinking a great deal at the time about the cult of personality in modern dance.

My theory of modern dance was that you had certain strong, central figures like Merce [Cunningham] or Paul Taylor, who had their own way of doing something and everybody formed around them and tried to emulate them as best they could. With Graham, you have to do all that floor business and your knees have to be a certain way, or you will have problems with that technique. I studied with Graham for about two weeks and immediately had problems. You had to be a certain physical type to fit in with a particular choreographer's way of doing things. Even with Merce, whose technique was more classically derived and accessible to anyone whose body worked well, has personal ways of doing gestures and things with his back, and a dramatic aura that eluded everyone else when they performed his movement.

I thought of modern dance as being personalities and idiosyncracies, with everyone but the leaders trying to fall into those idiosyncracies. Whereas ballet is a tradition that no one person is big enough to overwhelm.

So in *A Brief Glossary of Personal Movements*, I was just dealing with that: my own ways, my own particular dance, things I liked to do. I intended to do a longer piece, and that's why I subtitled it *1. Savings and Loan. Savings* was what I hadn't found in myself or used in myself yet, or what other people hadn't used of me, I felt, and *Loan* was what I borrowed from other choreographers I had worked with. I wasn't doing parodies of other people, though, as Merce had in *Antic Meet.*

I can't think of a movement that I did in it. But I remember whistling, which was very hard. I was in the middle of the piece, and I was breathless and dry, and it seemed not to work. The dance was eccentric, and it was a list of idiosyncracies.[107]

The third dance was Lucinda Childs's *Carnation*, a solo that was completely based on the manipulation of objects. Like Rainer, Childs was considering the differences between heavy, rigid objects, and the ways in which the body accommodates to moving or lifting them, and softer, more flexible, more "plastic objects. The materials Childs used were a blue plastic bag, a sheet, two socks, sponges, plastic curlers, and a colander. Jill Johnston, who devoted an entire column to Childs's *Carnation* and Morris's *Site*, both in Concert #16 and both involving the factual manipulation of objects with efficiency and, at the same time, evocative power, describes *Carnation* succinctly:

> [Childs] sits at a small table with a visage of contained intensity, contemplating a plan of action with foam-rubber curlers and sponges, as momentous as a call to battle. She puts the curlers between the sponges, places a salad colander on her head, pulls out each curler with a neat swift pull, and places them around her head on the prongs of the colander. That done, she sticks the sponges in her mouth, removes the curlers, the colander, gets up and dumps them with unceremonious relief into a blue plastic bag, into which she injects her foot. The next section involves a head stand, a sheet, and two socks (attached to the sheet) with some difficult maneuvering. Finally, she caps this perfect and meticulous nonsense with a meaningless assault on the blue plastic bag. After careful placement of the bag, she runs toward it, jumps on it, stands immobilized, glares in frenetic silence until her face starts to cry, and, at the final moment of wrinkled distortion, returns to deadpan normal and prepares for another attack on the bag.[108]

Childs explains that she was working with the rather surrealistic image of all those objects being contained in her body and being spit out. She thought of the first section as a process of making "sandwiches," with the sponges as bread and the curlers as frankfurters. Once the sponges, curlers, and colander had gone into the plastic bag, which already had a sheet on it, Childs did a handstand that made everything inside the bag fly out. Childs describes the maneuvers of the second section:

> I was doing a handstand against a flat which was just to the left of the table. At the end of the handstand, the sheet was partially covering my body, because it was attached to a sock on my right foot. At the other corner of the sheet there was another purple sock, which my foot was not in yet. Then I lowered myself from the handstand to a headstand so that I could free my left hand in order to put on the sock, which was hard because it was upsidedown. When I got the purple sock on and pulled it into place, I went back into a handstand and opened my legs in such a way that the sheet dropped and completely covered me.
> In the next section, I held the ends of the sheet with my hands. The two other ends were attached to my feet below. I did movements with the sheet covering my whole body, then folded it in half and in quarters and eights and sixteenths, until finally the whole sheet was wrapped up into a tiny ball. Then I took the socks off and disentangled myself.

Childs remembers the handstand section as particularly arduous to perform.

> It's pretty hard to put on a sock while you're standing on your head. I was very nervous before the performance, because it's almost not humanly possible to keep your balance. The trick was to lower my leg enough so that I could actually feel my foot with my hand. Just to get my foot to my hand was hard. It was always such a relief when the sock was finally on. The other problem was to do the handstand in such a way that I didn't throw the whole bag over the flat, because then the sheet would go over the flat too. There were these hazards, and I felt that I had to be like a paratrooper; I had to pull the right string at the right minute, or I'd be strangled by the parachute. It had that feeling of precision to it. It was very scary.

She describes the final section as a repetitive walk on the diagonal, from the downstage to the upstage corner, where she stood on the bag.

> At one point, the bag made me cry, supposedly. I grimaced, crying, as if the bag did something to me. I jumped off it, then I repeated the diagonal again, doing exactly what I had been doing, only this time it didn't work. Then I tried walking calmly to the bag, then leaving it indifferently, then jumping back on it suddenly to see if that would produce a result, but it didn't work. Then I ran past it and did a backward somersault onto it. There was still no result. Then I did that three times, and that was the end of the piece. [109]

Like the beer cans and Coca-Cola bottles that loomed large in the paintings of Pop artists, the objects Childs used in *Carnation* are indices of an industrialized society. But they are the signs of a particular role in industrial America: the housewife. It is as if in *Carnation* the laundry, the hot dog lunches, the beauty aids, and the garbage apparatus attack the housewife in a nightmare embodiment of the metaphor "enslaved by objects."

The fourth dance in Concert #16 was Deborah Hay's *Three Here*, danced by Hay, Judith Dunn, and Tony Holder, to John Cage's *Williams Mix #5*. [110]

After intermission came Sally Gross's *Conjunctions*, a dance for a large group of people, to a taped reading of a text that primarily consisted of the words "but," "and" and "or." The dance was two minutes long. Each conjunction was assigned a single, acrobatic movement; the movements were a headstand, a cartwheel, and a somersault. When the performers heard the words on the tape, they performed the corresponding movements. According to Gross:

> It was an enormous group of people, maybe twenty or thirty, whoever was there and was willing to do it could do it. I just told them earlier what they would have to do. You just started in the space, and you just kept doing the movements. I was concerned with

being able to work in a space and being able to move and not worry that somebody behind you is going to be stupid enough to get stepped on. You're not supposed to turn around and look; you're supposed to take your own responsibility for your movement.[111]

The sixth dance on the program was *Site* by Robert Morris, which had already been performed on the "Exchange" program of Surplus Dance Theater and in Philadelphia on 24 April. In Philadelphia, it had been performed by Morris and Olga Adorno Klüver. On the Surplus program and in Concert #16, Morris performed the dance with Carolee Schneemann. As with his *21.3*, also performed on a Surplus program, in which Morris mouthed a prerecorded reading of the introduction to *Studies in Iconology* by Erwin Panofsky while standing at a lectern, *Site* also invoked art history with a quotation. This time the quotation was a visual one—Schneemann was revealed in the pose of the woman in Manet's *Olympia*. And, as in *21.3*, *Box with the Sound of Its Own Making*, and some of Morris's other performance and sculptural works, juxtaposed to the artistic "product" were the signs and traces of a workman's process. In her review, "The Object," Johnston describes *Site* at the Judson:

Dressed in white, wearing work gloves and a skin-tight, flesh-colored mask, Morris stands before a white box containing a tape recorder which makes the constant rumbling sound of a pneumatic drill (previously recorded from his studio window). To his right is a stack of three large rectangular plywood boards, painted white. He removes one and stands it up vertically a few yards away. He removes the second and takes it off-stage. After a few moments he returns, grasps a corner of the third, and pulls it away swiftly to reveal a reclining odalisque, backed with white pillows, her skin covered with faint white make-up so that she looks somewhat dewy and transparent. She is also a facsimile of Manet's *Olympia*. Morris makes the famous Manet painting his "found" object as a live entity on the stage. She remains transfixed while he manipulates the plywood board, making a moving sculpture of body and object, with the additional visual effect of shifting relationships between Morris, the odalisque, the small white box, and the stationary vertical board.[112]

Paxton remembers Morris's manipulation of the plywood board as "an amazing dance, bending it and balancing it and twirling it and letting go of it."[113] As Johnston points out, the workmanlike activity of Morris as a performer and the sound of the drill, juxtaposed to the "ideal poetic image of the transfixed lady," creates a revealing opposition between the work of the artist and the cultural meaning of the work, an opposition that is nevertheless a connection.[114] By surrounding the cultural icon with work gestures, Morris demystifies the fetishized art object in *Site*.

The seventh dance on the program was Deborah Lee's *Dance in a Black Dress*, a solo performed to music by James Waring. The music was played by Philip Corner (on trombone) and Malcolm Goldstein (on violin).[115]

The next dance was Sally Gross's *In Their Own Time*, with music by Philip Corner. The dance was an improvisation for six performers. Gross gave each performer a two-hour span of time, without specifying morning or evening, then traced an imaginary clock face on the floor. The task of the dancers was to abstract movement they ordinarily did during the span of time they were assigned. They could leave their time span by leaving the space assigned to it, either by sitting in a chair in the center of the circle, or by moving on the circumference of the circle. Gross explains:

> You didn't actually do whatever it was you did during that time of day, but you used that movement as vocabulary. In other words, you didn't sleep, but you might choose to "sleep" standing up. It wouldn't be interpreted as sleep.
>
> Each person knew which wedges of the circle corresponded to which times. And you could choose to leave your time and go to another space. But you couldn't move into a new space until someone vacated it. So, often there would be two people on the circumference.
>
> If you didn't want to move at all, you had the option to go sit in the chair. If someone was already in the chair, the next person had to sit in that person's lap. Sometimes there would be a pileup on the chair.
>
> It was just a very simple structure on which to base a dance.
>
> I called it *In Their Own Time* because each person stayed in the wedge that represented their own time span, but also because everyone did movements according to their own sense of timing. So time had multiple meanings.[116]

Philip Corner's music was generated by a set of tiny scrolls with calligraphic notations that served as a score for playing the inside of a piano. It was called *from keyboard dances*. It was one of Corner's first pieces of music that was physical in a rhythmic sense. Although the hammering inside the piano created a set of regular pulses, the dancers did not match their movements to the music.[117]

In May 1964, Merce Cunningham, with his dance company, began a world tour that lasted for six months and ended by changing the composition of the company as well as creating a rift between Cunningham and Cage, on the one hand, and their collaborator Robert Rauschenberg, on the other. The tour stripped the Judson Dance Theater of a number of its participants: Alex Hay went with the company to assist Rauschenberg, and Cunningham's dancers included William Davis, Barbara Dilley, Deborah Hay, Sandra Neels, Steve Paxton, and Albert Reid. After *Fantastic Gardens*, Ruth Emerson had married and moved to California. Before the Cunningham company left, Fred Herko presented, on 1 and 2 May, at the church but not under the auspices of Judson Dance Theater, his *The Palace of the Dragon Prince*, a story ballet to music by Berlioz and St.

Saens, performed by Carla Blank, Herko, Robert Holloway, Deborah Lee, Elsene Sorrentino, Sandra Neels, Phoebe Neville, Abigail Ewert, and Terry Foreman. On 19 and 20 May, James Waring and Dance Company performed at the church; the performers included Arlene Rothlein, Lucinda Childs, Deborah Hay, Fred Herko, Deborah Lee, Yvonne Rainer, as well as Gary Gross, Toby Armour, Vincent Warren, Diana Cernovich, and Waring himself. The composers for one of the dances included Philip Corner, John Herbert McDowell, and Malcolm Goldstein. On 31 May and 1 June, Aileen Passloff and Company gave a concert at the church. Passloff's dancers included, of the Judson group, Childs, Rainer, Blank, Rothlein; Philip Corner did the music for her *Bench Dance*.

In the summer of 1964, Robert Dunn once again offered a choreography course, which he taught at Judith Dunn's studio on East Broadway, in Chinatown. Dunn writes that in the time intervening between his classes from 1960 through 1962 and the summer workshop of 1964, James Waring was teaching composition; Dunn went to one or two class sessions and heard Waring reading aloud from *Philosophy and Psychology in the Abhidharma*, a book about the Buddhist theory of mind, perception, and action by Herbert V. Guenther. According to Dunn, it was Waring who suggested that Dunn give another class, because Waring "felt things were sagging a bit again." Dunn writes about the new class:

> Among the new people in the class were Meredith Monk, Lucinda Childs, Phoebe Neville, Sally Gross, and Robert Morris, dragged along by Yvonne Rainer. Early versions of Meredith's *Break* and Lucinda's *Street Dance* were shown in the class. In spite of the continuing richness of personnel and events in the class, I believe I had become more concerned with the problems of my own existence and had less imagination left over for others at that time. At *no* time did I have the idea of dealing out the dispensations of the new revelation which had occured at Judson Church and its far-flung environs. (I was always looking for *more*.)
>
> At any rate, I had somewhat less of a sense of excitement and accomplishment about this class. However, I find the experience of the first performance of *Street Dance* quite unforgettable. Lucinda [Childs] and another dancer (who?) turned on a tape and began some simple activities leading them to the freight elevator, in which they disappeared downward out of sight. The tape kept us company in our bereavement and after a while said, "Go to the window...go to the window." We did, and looked up and down rather grungy East Broadway, until someone, myself or another, suddenly sang out on sighting Lucinda standing still in the recessed doorway of a storefront far over to our left. After actions coordinated between the tape and the small figures some four or five floors below (stopwatches were involved), the dancers crossed the street again to our side, going out of sight, the tape continued, and after a while they re-arrived on the elevator and went over to turn off the tape, to wild applause. This dance remains one of the most mysteriously beautiful events I have seen, perhaps because of the distance and glass-separated soundlessness in which we experienced Lucinda's miniaturized physical

presence, in the same moment with immediacy of her somewhat flattened but sensuous voice on the tape in the room with us.[118]

By that fall, when Judith Dunn presented her *Last Point*, a collaboration with Gene Friedman and Robert Dunn (19-21 October); when Fred Herko jumped out a window on Cornelia Street and died, and a ceremony was held for him at the church (5 November); when Carolee Schneeman presented her Kinetic Theater orgiastic *Meat Joy* (16 through 18 November); and when the members of the Cunningham company returned from the world tour, and Yvonne Rainer and Robert Morris returned from their four-month European tour, all in November — Judson Dance Theater had clearly ended as a workshop and as a cooperative venture. Each member of the workshop has a slightly different sense of when the end came, but the reasons given are quite similar: the group had served its purpose, and it was time to go on to other things; individuals were emerging from the group whose needs were no longer satisfied by the collective concerts; an influx of new younger participants made the content of the workshop sessions redundant for the original group; the somewhat utopian community that had developed over several years was rent by the conflicts over the out-of-town concerts and, ultimately, over the identity of the group.

Philip Corner remembers:

I spent that summer going to Mississippi — that was a big summer for civil rights action — and when I came back, Judson Dance Theater was finished. It was so obviously finished that it was a surprise to me that there were still more concerts and dances going on at Judson Church. Some people, like Meredith Monk, had just come to the city; she used the structure that had been set up. But the Judson Dance Theater, the exploration and the group of people and the working together — that was over. It was clear. That thing was completely dead when I came back; It was like returning to a different place.

I think people used it to pioneer their styles, their work. Then people began to get companies together. There began to be conflicts about out-of-town gigs, and who should be invited. People began to get a sense of whose work they liked and whose work they didn't like. There was less of a cooperative thing, and that was a disappointment to me. I saw that as a community — art as a substitute for religion as a cohesive principle for organizing a community. For me it was the promise of something, the idea of cooperating and everybody working together. That promise was maybe less precious to some than to others, or it became less so.

And there were negative things, too. There were, in fact, problems in the differences of the quality of people's work. What could have held everybody together was a sense of personal exploration, a certain newness, and that could be stretched very far if everybody were committed to exploration, or even to a rejection of something already established. When people start coming in doing familiar stuff — not pioneering, not exploring, not even against established dance — then you start multiplying the possibilities of misunderstanding the lack of sympathy between people. It had to end. And aside from that, people were developing their own careers; they had less time for it and less need for it.[119]

According to Robert Rauschenberg:

In the beginning the whole thing was as democratic as you could ever imagine. That's what I consider the miracle of the whole thing. And then gradually the emphasis shifted from the group activity of making pieces and sharing ideas to a more traditional academic idea—"I'm getting ready for a concert." It just happened naturally, as everybody got a little better or their directions were defined. Gradually that work attitude was replaced by the feeling that Judson Church was one of the most interesting and most available spaces to do performances in. And even people who'd never been involved in Judson Dance Theater, like Katie Litz and Jimmy Waring, started coming in and scheduling concerts. And just at that time, it seemed to me, came the end of what one would call the Judson group.[120]

Elaine Summers thinks that it was partly the very freedom from rules that the group cherished that led to its eventual demise. Her sense was that long before she put on *Fantastic Gardens*—perhaps in October 1963—the Judson Dance Theater had begun to dissipate.

Judson was a complex, bubbling, boiling, hot place, full of people really working on their ideas, and getting their ideas out, and being involved in the opportunity to "do their own thing," with a commitment not to get in each other's way. There was a great generosity on everyone's part, a commitment to making it possible by cooperating in the shit work and taking responsibility for change. No one objected to any chore that might come their way. And on top of that, there was a real interest in what each one was doing, what we were all dealing with in terms of dance.

There were no rules about who could join, and that finally closed down the Judson Dance Theater. People came in and were disappointed. Their image of what happened at Judson was that you came in, did your dance, and then you got to perform it. You joined a group and it was all very social. They thought we were hostile because we wanted to work, not socialize. Then they would go away, and there would be another group, who had no idea of what we were doing, who would get up and talk for twenty minutes during the criticism period, but who weren't trained in perception and had no commitment to each other's work.

Finally, everybody had to leave Judson, because we couldn't work there. Too many people came in whose work was antithetical to ours, who wanted to bring in outside people to lecture on dance as choreography, who wanted to take over and get some organization into the group. They couldn't believe that the chairmanship rotated. I think they thought there was some secret organization that they couldn't see, and that they didn't want any part of. The original group withdrew, just went away quietly and left it to them.

We could have said, "Our group is closed, and if you want to start your own group, go on another night." But I think most of us felt the idealism of the group would have been lost if we had closed the group. We had had an open but heavily structured relationship, which was very efficient; if you didn't follow the structure, you couldn't get any work done.

Yvonne [Rainer] hung on for a long time. And I hung on for a long time. And finally I realized that there was nothing we could do. We'd lost it. The only alternative would have been to set up something new and different. To do it again. But there was also the growth that each person had gone through as a result of this experience, and a lot of us were strong enough to go off on our own.[121]

Judith Dunn writes:

The exchanges, interchanges, assimilations—the experiences that have taken place at Judson reach beyond the previously established traditions of concertizing and theater-making. There is a certain reality here—persons, performers, that is—are called dancers when they "dance." Their works are called dances because they so name them, because they exist, and because they exist they are performed. Word spreads, audiences come from the community and "uptown." It was really that simple, right from the start. . . .

A question I have not been able to resolve for myself is what effect the large influx of new persons to the workshop with the resulting changes I have described [changes in organization, including elected committees to administrate group concerts], was. Certainly communication was more cumbersome, and intimacy and spontaneity were reduced. At the same time, the interests of the early members shifted to individual concerns. This was reflected in the solo concerts which took place and will continue to do so over the coming year [1965].

From the start the Judson Dance Theater has been an open situation with a wide range of activity and flexibility. I tend to remain optimistic as to future developments.[122]

Allen Hughes, the *New York Times*'s dance critic, who had always been sympathetic to Judson Dance Theater, saw it very simply "They had become known. The were on the center, and they realized they had to shift, to get off-center. It had to go somewhere."[123]

Jill Johnston, who had pronounced Judson Dance Theater the wave of the future, had devoted most of her columns during 1963 and 1964 to covering it, and had begun to produce concerts of work by its members, announced in January of 1965 that it had been over for a year. She writes:

Looking back, I think the Judson Dance Theater, the first vanguard movement in dance since the early '30s, lost its initial momentum by the end of 1963. The first concert of the Judson series was in July of '62. Within a two-year span, the idea was well-established. The consolidation of talent in the early Judson concerts was a fortuitous and spontaneous affair. Nobody set out to "make" a movement. The dancers and non-dancers who had been studying composition with Robert Dunn at Merce Cunningham's studio decided they needed a place to perform, and they found the church. Such a consolidation, vital as it may be, contains the seeds of its death in the increasing independence of its members.

Yvonne Rainer was the most adventurous and prolific choreographer of the group. After she gave her first evening-long work, *Terrain*, in April of '63, she found the milieu of the weekly workshops from which the programs emerged to be increasingly superfluous to her own needs. Judith Dunn, another pivotal member of the group, gave her first solo presentation a few months later. The focus of the workshops blurred with an influx of late-comers and a division of the original core through outside performing opportunities....

The church was a great launching pad for new ideas and vital collaborations. No doubt most of the choreographers now feel that the need for the "democratic" ensemble has expired. The last three concerts presented as the Judson Dance Theater (May [actually, April], '64) indicated the end of an inclusive milieu and the beginning of a more political structure based on achievements to date....

Judson was never a stable institution, thankfully, and Herko was not the only choreographer who found the concerts a casual convience in his peregrinations around town. If some of the others were less casual about their involvement, it has become clear, nevertheless, that the entire arrangement was a momentary expediency and that the modern dance at its best remains an individual affair and not an institutional business. The milieu created by the Judson collaborations was tight enough to afford a stimulating exchange of influence, and loose enough not to constrict personal ambitions.

Johnston concludes that, after the aesthetic revolution of the previous two years, the direction of new choreographers must be consolidation; her view of change in art and in history is a cyclical one.

Dunn's intention and essentially laissez-faire approach remained the same [in his summer, 1964 course], but the fearless talents who attended his first course, several of whom attended the second, had already shot their insurgent wad, and the next historical step is development and variation. The quick emancipation of dance from its old anchorage in literature and dependence upon musical forms and idealized movement derived from the professional studios (all prefigured by Cunningham in the '50s) makes another major insurrection unthinkable right now. There is no collective dissatisfaction in any case. And as the excitement which drew a number of individuals into the generalized orbit of a movement has diminished, the problem of the survival of fresh methods in new or authentic modes now most clearly devolves upon those individuals who can maintain whatever measure of dissatisfaction is necessary to withstand the pressure from the tradition of this new thing.

The collective enterprise is far from finished, as is clear from future plans, but the character of the enterprise, as I have indicated, has become more exclusive. Without muddling over nature's course, I might suggest it would be a pity if new or outside talent were intimidated in the search for a milieu to support more adventure. The dance world is so minute in the scheme of things that a barricade around the only vanguard movement in the country seems undesirable without anybody saying so. More to the point, no doubt, is the need for better communications to publicize activities and attract the talent that ends up in the ballet studios learning about musical comedy auditions, or at Juilliard to be indoctrinated by the old regime, or at any other dreary homes for the aged....

So, *salut* '64, and more rooms with a view in '65![124]

In many respects Johnston was right. The original Judson group both consolidated their gains and dispersed geographically and artistically. Johnston herself organized three concerts outside of New York — in Buffalo, Boston, and Richmond — in 1965. A group consisting of Paxton,

Rauschenberg, Hay, Hay, Childs, and Brown performed in another Once Group festival that September. In 1965 there were a number of one-choreographer or two-choreographer concerts at Judson Church, beginning with a program by Susan Kaufman and Toby Armour in January. In March, when Yvonne Rainer and Robert Morris gave a concert of new works, the church was nearly ousted from the American Baptist Convention because Rainer and Morris appeared nude in Morris's *Waterman Switch*. In May 1965, Steve Paxton and Alan Solomon organized the First New York Theater Rally, a month-long festival of dance, Happenings, and a guest appearance by the Once Group, which took place in a television studio at Eighty-first Street and Broadway, at Judson Church, and at Al Roon's Health Club. By 1966, there were several programs of "Judson Revivals." In April 1966, Childs, Hay, Hay, Rainer, Paxton, and Rauschenberg appeared at the NOW Festival in Washington, D.C. Rainer premiered her first version of *The Mind is a Muscle* in Washington and in New York at the Judson later that month. In the spring, Childs, Hay, Hay, Paxton, Rainer, and Rauschenberg began to work on the series "Nine Evenings: Theater and Engineering," a collaboration between artists and engineers, produced by Billy Klüver and the Foundation for Experiments in Art and Technology. In 1965 and 1966, Beverly Schmidt organized dance concerts and film showings at the Bridge Theater in the East Village.[125] The arts were expanding beyond their own borders and beyond any single place or any single group. And the expansion of dance as an art, so much of which had taken place at the Judson Dance Theater workshops and concerts, proliferated.

Notes

Introduction

1. See Selma Jeanne Cohen, "Avant-Garde Choreography," *Criticism* 3 (Winter 1961): 16–35, reprinted in three parts in *Dance Magazine* 36 (June 1962): 22–24, 57; (July 1962): 29–31, 58; (August 1962): 45, 54–56, for a discussion of the older avant-garde.

Chapter 1

1. Robert Ellis Dunn, unpublished notes, 30 March 1980, p. 1.

2. John Cage, "[The New School]," in Richard Kostelanetz, ed., *John Cage* (London: Penguin Books, 1974), p. 119; Ellsworth J. Snyder, "Chronological Table of John Cage's Life," in *John Cage,* pp. 39–40.

3. Cage, "[The New School]," p. 119.

4. Al Hansen and Dick Higgins, "[On Cage's Classes]," in *John Cage,* pp. 123–24.

5. Ibid., p. 121.

6. Ibid., pp. 121–22.

7. Interview with Remy Charlip, Bennington, Vermont, 8 July 1980.

8. Ibid; "Choreographics,"*Dance Observer* 27 (June-July 1960): 95.

9. Dunn, notes, 30 March 1980, p. 1.

10. Anita Feldman, "Robert Dunn: His Background and His Developing Teachings," unpublished paper, Fall 1979, pp. 3–4; Dunn, Vita, 1980, p. 1.

11. Dunn, notes, 30 March 1980, p. 2.

12. Interview with Robert Dunn, New York City, 25 March 1980.

13. See Louis Horst, *Pre-Classic Dance Forms* (New York: The Dance Observer, 1937; reprint ed. Dance Horizons, 1972); Louis Horst and Carroll Russell, *Modern Dance Forms* (San Francisco: Impulse Publications, 1961); and Doris Humphrey, *The Art of Making Dances* (New York: Rinehart, 1959; reprint ed. Grove Press, 1962).

14. Interview with Robert Dunn, New York City, 16 May 1980.

15. Interview with Dunn, 25 March 1980.

16. Dunn, notes, 30 March 1980, p. 2.

17. Ibid.

18. Interview with Dunn, 16 May 1980.

19. Ibid.

20. Dunn, notes, 30 March 1980, p. 4.

21. Yvonne Rainer, *Work 1961–73* (Halifax, Nova Scotia: The Press of the Nova Scotia College of Art and Design; New York: New York University Press, 1974), p. 5.

22. Feldman, "Robert Dunn," p. 7.

23. Don McDonagh, *The Rise & Fall & Rise of Modern Dance* (New York: New American Library, 1971), p. 79.

24. Interview with Yvonne Rainer, New York City, 24 June 1980.

25. Horst and Russell, *Modern Dance Forms,* pp. 73–75.

26. Ibid., pp. 44–45.

27. Ibid., p. 26.

28. Ibid., p. 39.

29. McDonagh, *The Rise & Fall,* p. 79. "Mickey mousing" is a term used in film and dance to mean mimicking the rhythms and emotional shading of musical accompaniment.

30. Quoted by McDonagh, *The Rise & Fall,* p. 77. This statement is published in Cage, *Silence* (Middletown, Connecticut: Wesleyan University Press, 1961), p. 62, and was originally published in Cage, "Forerunners of Modern Music," *The Tiger's Eye,* March 1949.

31. Dunn, notes, 30 March 1980, pp. 2–3.

32. Martin Heidegger, "The Origin of The Work of Art," *Poetry, Language, Thought,* trans. Albert Hofstadter (New York: Harper and Row, 1975), p. 46.

33. Ibid., p. 54.

34. Interview with Dunn, 16 May 1980.

35. Ibid.

36. Merce Cunningham, *Changes: Notes on Choreography,* ed. Frances Starr (New York: Something Else Press, 1968), pp. 43–44.

37. Interview with Dunn, 16 May 1980.

38. Rainer, *Work,* p. 5.

39. Interview with Marni Mahaffay, New York City, 19 June 1980.

40. Ibid.

41. Ibid.

42. Ibid. Rainer told me (on 20 June 1980) that she thinks the dance Mahaffay described and demonstrated to me might be *Stove Pack Opus,* a collaboration between Rainer, Forti, and Ruth Allphon.

43. Interview with Mahaffay, 19 June 1980.

44.   Sally Banes, *Terpsichore in Sneakers: Post-Modern Dance* (Boston: Houghton Mifflin, 1980), p. 58.

45.   Steve Paxton with Liza Béar, "Like the Famous Tree," *Avalanche* 11 (Summer 1975): 27.

46.   Interview with Steve Paxton, Washington, D.C., 30 June 1975.

47.   Ibid.

48.   Banes, *Terpsichore in Sneakers,* p. 22.

49.   Ibid., pp. 23-24.

50.   Simone Forti, *Handbook in Motion* (Halifax, Nova Scotia: The Press of the Nova Scotia College of Art and Design; New York: New York University Press, 1974), p. 34.

51.   Banes, *Terpsichore in Sneakers,* pp. 24-25.

52.   Ibid., p. 25.

53.   Meg Cottam, Videotaped interview with Simone Forti by Bennington College Judson Project, New York City, 8 February 1980. All of the Bennington College Judson Project interviews cited here were videotaped in New York City and will be abbreviated BCJP hereafter.

54.   Interview with Charlip, 8 July 1980.

55.   Forti, *Handbook,* pp. 36-46.

56.   Dunn, notes, 30 March 1980, p. 8.

57.   Rainer, *Work,* pp. 4-5; Yvonne Rainer's note to me, 29 July 1980.

58.   Rainer, "Account of My Career," unpublished manuscript, [1966], p. 1.

59.   Rainer, *Work,* p. 4; Rainer, unpublished notes, 23 May 1980.

60.   Rainer, *Work,* pp. 312-13; Rainer, unpublished notes, 23 May 1980.

61.   Rainer, "Account," p. 1.

62.   Rainer, Untitled score, 1960 or 1961.

63.   Ibid.

64..   Rainer, Score with dots, body parts, actions, and rates of speed.

65.   Interview with Rainer, 24 June 1980.

66.   Ibid.

67.   Rainer, Notebook [1962].

68.   Rainer, *Work,* pp. 281-82.

69.   Ibid.

70.   Rainer, Notebook.

71.   Ibid.

72.   Rollo H. Myers, *Erik Satie* (New York: Dover, 1968), p. 69.

73.   Interview with Rainer, 24 June 1980.

74. Rainer, *Work,* p. 7. Rainer also says that Ruth Emerson began to come to the Dunn class in spring 1961, but Emerson in my interview with her on 11 June 1980 in New York City says she only took the course once (or for one year).

75. Interview with Dunn, 25 March 1980.

76. Judith Dunn, "My Work and Judson's," *Ballet Review,* vol. 1, 6 (1967): 24. She also confirmed this view in my interview with her, Burlington, Vermont, 8 July 1980.

77. Jack Anderson, "Judith Dunn and the Endless Quest," *Dance Magazine* 41 (November 1967): 50; Judith Dunn, "My Work and Judson's," p. 22.

78. Judith Dunn, "My Work and Judson's," p. 24.

79. Anderson, "Judith Dunn," p. 50.

80. James Waring, John Herbert McDowell, Judith Dunn, Arlene Croce, and Don McDonagh, "Judson: A Discussion," *Ballet Review,* vol. 1, 6 (1967): 34.

81. Rainer, Score with floorplan for Ruth, Marnie, Steve, and Paul, 1961.

82. Rainer, *Work,* p. 7.

83. Ruth Allphon, Simone Forti, and Yvonne Rainer, Score, *Stove Pack Opus,* 1961.

84. Conversation with Yvonne Rainer, 28 July 1980. Forti's "dance reports" are published in *An Anthology,* ed. La Monte Young (New York: Something Else Press, 1963; reprint ed. Cologne: Heiner Friedrich, 1970), unpaged.

85. H. Sohm, *Happening and Fluxus* (Cologne: Kölnischer Kunstverein, 1970), unpaged.

86. Forti, *Handbook,* pp. 56–67.

87. Rainer, *Work,* pp. 6–7.

88. Advertisement, *Village Voice,* 27 July 1961, p. 11.

89. Rainer, Score, *The Bells,* 1961.

90. M.S. [Michael Smith], "James Waring, etc.," *Village Voice,* 3 August 1961, p. 10.

91. Dunn, notes, 30 March 1980, p. 8. Rauschenberg, the painter and collagist, was at the time Cunningham's designer for lighting, costumes, and decor. Johnston was the dance critic for the *Village Voice* (since 1960). Remy Charlip was a dancer in Cunningham's company, a designer and illustrator, and he worked with the Paper Bag Players, a children's theater group. David Vaughan, a good friend of James Waring's, was a performer and the administrator of the Cunningham company. Robert Morris was making wood and mixed-media sculptures. Ray Johnson was a collagist and mail artist. Peter Schumann, soon to found the Bread and Puppet Theater, had recently arrived from Germany; his *Totentanz,* with the Alchemy Players, was given at Judson Memorial Church in May 1962.

92. Rainer, *Work,* p. 7; and Score for *Satie for Two.*

93. Rainer, Score, *Satie for Two,* 1962.

94. Anne Livet, ed., *Contemporary Dance* (New York: Abbeville Press, 1978), p. 44.

95. Forti, *Handbook,* pp. 31–32.

96. Ibid., p. 68.

97. Livet, *Contemporary Dance,* pp. 44–45.

98. Ibid., p. 45.

99. Paxton with Béar, "Like the Famous Tree," p. 30.

100. Interview with Trisha Brown, Alex Hay, and Robert Rauschenberg, New York, 17 February 1980, BCJP.

101. Interview with Elaine Summers, New York, 15 March 1980.

102. Ibid.

103. Score with drawing by Kyle Summers for Ruth Emerson, 1961 or 1962.

104. Ibid.

105. Interview with Elaine Summers, New York, 16 April 1980.

106. Ibid. According to Rainer, in *Work,* p. 7, Paxton used his index finger; according to Paxton, in Paxton with Béar, "Like the Famous Tree," p. 28, he used a piece of glass.

107. Interview with Summers, 26 April 1980.

108. Sally Banes and Amanda Degener, Interview with Ruth Emerson, New York, 10 June 1980, BCJP; Ruth Emerson, Vita [1963?].

109. Banes and Degener, Interview with Emerson, 10 June 1980.

110. Ibid.

111. Emerson, Vita.

112. Banes and Degener, Interview with Emerson, 10 June 1980.

113. Ibid.

114. Emerson, Chance score, 1961 or 1962.

115. Emerson, Score, chance dance with windows, 1961 or 1962.

116. Emerson, Score with improvisation with chance cues, 1961 or 1962.

117. Ibid.

118. Interview with John Herbert McDowell, New York, 17 May 1980.

119. Waring, McDowell, Dunn, et al., "Judson: A Discussion," p. 31.

120. Ibid.

121. Banes, *Terpsichore in Sneakers,* pp. 98–99.

122. Ibid., p. 99.

123. Interview with David Gordon and Valda Setterfield, New York, 6 April 1975.

124. Sally R. Sommer, "Valda Setterfield: The Performer," *Soho Weekly News,* 12 April 1979, p. 25.

125. Interview with Gordon and Setterfield, 6 April 1975.

126. Ibid.

127. Ibid.

128. Ibid.

129. Ibid.

130. Interview with Rainer, 24 June 1980.

131. Dunn, notes, 30 March 1980, pp. 3–4.

132. Announcement and prospectus, American Theater for Poets, Inc. [1962?]. The board of directors is listed as: Alan Marlowe, Diane di Prima, James Waring, Fred Herko, LeRoi Jones, and Nicola Cernovich.

133. Ibid.

134. Program, Poets Festival, Maidman Playhouse, 5 March 1962.

135. Lillian Moore, "Rainer-Herko Dance Recital," *New York Herald Tribune,* 6 March 1962, p. 12.

136. M.M. [Marcia Marks], "Dance Works by Yvonne Rainer and Fred Herko," *Dance Magazine* 36 (April 1962): 54, 57.

137. Lelia K. Telberg, "Yvonne Rainer and Fred Herko," *Dance Observer* 29 (May 1962): 72.

138. Interview with Jill Johnston, New York City, 13 June 1980.

139. Johnston, "Fresh Winds," *Village Voice,* 15 March 1962, p. 13.

140. Maxine Munt, "For Dancers Only...," *Show Business,* 7 April 1962, p. 6. I have changed the punctuation.

141. H. Sohm, *Happening and Fluxus,* unpaged; Johnston, "Boiler Room," *Village Voice,* 29 March 1962, p. 14.

142. Johnston, "Boiler Room."

143. Johnston, "Fresh Winds."

Chapter 2

1. Waring, McDowell, Dunn, et al., "Judson: A Discussion," p. 32.

2. Interview with Paxton, Bennington, Vermont, 11 April 1980.

3. Rainer, *Work,* pp. 8–9; Interview with Paxton, 11 April 1980.

4. Paxton, in my 1980 interview with him, thinks that he, Rainer, Emerson, and Robert Dunn went to the audition; Rainer, in *Work,* p. 9, only mentions that she, Paxton, and Emerson went there to dance; Emerson remembers that she, Rainer, and Paxton went (Banes and Degener, Interview with Emerson, 10 June 1980); and Elaine Summers (in my interview with her, 15 March 1980) thinks that it was Rainer, Paxton, and Robert and Judith Dunn who went. In a note to me, 29 July 1980, Rainer stated that Judith Dunn was there and Robert Dunn was not.

5. Rainer, *Work,* p. 9; Banes and Degener, Interview with Emerson, 10 June 1980; Paxton doesn't remember what he performed (Interview with Paxton, 11 April 1980).

6. Interview with Paxton, 11 April 1980.

7. Banes and Degener, Interview with Emerson, 10 June 1980.

8. New York Community Trust, Plaque on the front of Judson Memorial Church, 1966; Stanley Kauffmann, "Music by Al Carmines," *New York Times,* 3 July 1966, sec. 2, p. 1; "Judson Jubilee: Restoring a Well-Used Place," flyer about Judson Memorial Church, December 1976.

9. Kauffmann, "Music by Al Carmines"; "Judson Jubilee" flyer.

10. "Judson Jubilee" flyer; Judson Archives.

11. Judson Archives.

12. Ibid.

13. Kaufmann, "Music by Al Carmines."

14. Kaufmann, "Music by Al Carmines"; Jack Anderson, "The Other Theater at Judson," *Ballet Review,* vol. 1, 6 (1967): 74; Wendy Perron, Interview with Al Carmines, New York City, 1 July 1980, BCJP. Kaprow, however, did not make Happenings before 1959 (see Michael Kirby, *Happenings* [New York: Dutton 1965], pp. 46–47). Perhaps Carmines saw an Environment by Kaprow. Or perhaps he refers to *Ray Gun Spex* in 1960.

15. Program, Judson Poets' Theater, 18 November 1961. A play by William Packard, *In the First Place,* had been performed in the organ loft of the church on 23 through 26 March 1961 by a group called the Judson Gallery Players, directed by Robert Nichols. The program and announcement for this production are in the Judson Archives.

16. Sohm, *Happening and Fluxus,* unpaged; Judson files. I have changed the punctuation in the quotation.

17. Ibid.

18. Judson Archives; Kauffmann, "Music by Al Carmines."

19. Perron, Interview with Carmines, 1 July 1980. But, in fact, the first concert did take place upstairs in the church sanctuary, according to numerous accounts.

20. Interview with Robert Dunn, 16 May 1980.

21. Interview with Robert Dunn, 25 March 1980.

22. Interview with Paxton, 11 April 1980.

23. Interview with Paxton, 30 June 1975.

24. Rainer, *Work,* p. 8.

25. Interview with Summers, 15 March 1980.

26. Press release, A Concert of Dance, June 1962. Maclane should be spelled MacLane.

27. "Dance at Judson," *Village Voice,* 28 June 1962, p. 17.

28. Interview with Summers, 15 March 1980.

29. Program, A Concert of Dance, Judson Memorial Church, 6 July 1962. Freeman should be spelled Friedman.

30. I know this from photographs of later concerts, numerous verbal descriptions of the concert, and my own viewing of the space.

31. Perron, Interview with Carmines, 1 July 1980.

32. Program, 6 July 1962.

33. According to Steve Paxton (Interview, 11 April 1980), and McDowell (Waring, McDowell, Dunn, et al., "Judson: A Discussion," p. 37).

34. Waring, McDowell, Dunn, et al., "Judson: A Discussion," p. 37; Michael Rowe and Amanda Degener, Interview with John Herbert McDowell, New York City, 19 February 1980, BCJP.

35. Interview with Summers, 26 April 1980.

36. Rowe and Degener, Interview with John Herbert McDowell, 19 February 1980.

37. Allen Hughes, "Dance Program Seen at Church," *New York Times,* 7 July 1962, p. 9.

38. Ruth Emerson, Score, *Narrative.*

39. Interview with Emerson, New York City, 11 June 1980.

40. Ruth Emerson, Score, *Timepiece.*

41. Banes and Degener, Interview with Emerson, 10 June 1980.

42. Interview with Paxton, 11 April 1980.

43. Ibid.

44. Jill Johnston, "Democracy," *Village Voice,* 23 August 1962, p. 9; Johnston, "The New American Modern Dance," in Richard Kostelanetz, ed., *The New American Arts* (New York: Collier Books, 1967), p. 191.

45. Hughes, "Dance Program Seen at Church."

46. Interview with Remy Charlip, Bennington, Vermont, 8 July 1980.

47. Interview with Paxton, 11 April 1980.

48. Interview with Allen Hughes, New York City, 8 April 1980.

49. Perron, Interview with Carmines, 1 July 1980.

50. Andy Warhol and Pat Hackett, *POPism: The Warhol 60s* (New York and London: Harcourt Brace Jovanovich, 1980), p. 55.

51. Interview with Edward Bhartonn, New York City, 23 June 1980.

52. Warhol and Hackett, *POPism,* pp. 55–57.

53. Paxton with Béar, "Like the Famous Tree," p. 26.

54. Interview with Paxton, 11 April 1980.

55. Ibid.

56. Interview with John Herbert McDowell, New York City, 17 May 1980; Rowe and Degener, Interview with McDowell, 19 February 1980.

57. Johnston, "Democracy."

58. Diane di Prima, "A Concert of Dance — Judson Memorial Church, Friday, July 6, 1962," *The Floating Bear* 21 (August 1962): 11; reprinted in *The Floating Bear: A Newsletter. Numbers 1–37, 1961–1969,* eds. Diane di Prima and LeRoi Jones, Introduction and Notes adapted from interview with Diane di Prima (La Jolla, California:

Laurence McGilvery, 1973): 239. Hereafter, references to *The Floating Bear* will be to the reprint edition.

59. Interview with McDowell, 17 May 1980.

60. Geoffrey Hindley, ed., *The Larousse Encyclopedia of Music* (Secaucus, New Jersey: Chartwell Books, 1971), pp. 222–23.

61. Elaine Summers, Score for Ruth Emerson, *Instant Chance.*

62. Ibid.

63 Elaine Summers, Scores and notes, *Instant Chance.*

64. *Instant Chance* was reconstructed by Elaine Summers on 29 June 1980 at Judson Memorial Church. It was videotaped in black and white by Tony Carruthers for the Bennington College Judson Project, and in color by Davidson Gigliotti.

65. Interview with Summers, 15 March 1980.

66. Hughes, "Dance Program Seen at Church." Hughes says there were six performers in *Instant Chance* but the program lists seven. Perhaps one of the performers did not finally dance in it.

67. David Gordon, "It's About Time," *The Drama Review* 19 (T-65, March 1975): 44; Christina Svane, Interview with David Gordon, New York City, 28 February 1980, BCJP.

68. Program, 6 July 1962.

69. Banes, *Terpsichore in Sneakers,* p. 114; Interview with Deborah Hay, New York City, 2 August 1980, BCJP.

70. Interview with D. Hay, 2 August 1980.

71. Interview with Rainer, 20 July 1980.

72. Interview with Gretchen MacLane, New York City, 19 June 1980.

73. Interview with Paxton, 11 April 1980.

74. Interview with MacLane, 19 June 1980.

75. Program, 6 July 1962.

76. Rainer, *Work,* p. 287.

77. Program, 6 July 1962; Interview with Brown, Hay, and Rauschenberg, 17 February 1980.

78. Rainer, *Work,* pp. 287–88.

79. Johnston, "Boiler Room." I have changed the punctuation.

80. Munt, "For Dancers Only...," 7 April 1962.

81. Interview with William Davis, New York City, 3 March 1980.

82. Conversation with Rainer, New York City, 4 July 1980.

83. Program, 6 July 1962.

84. Elaine Summers, Score, Ruth Emerson's part in *The Daily Wake.*

85. Interview with Summers, 5 April 1980.

86. Program, 6 July 1962.

87. Gordon, "It's About Time," p. 44.

88. I saw *Mannequin Dance* as part of Gordon's *The Matter plus and minus* in December 1979.

89. Svane, Interview with Gordon, 28 February 1980.

90. Gordon, "It's About Time," p. 44.

91. Di Prima, "A Concert of Dance." I have changed the punctuation.

92. Johnston, "Democracy."

93. See for instance, the essays in Virgina Stewart and Merle Armitage, eds., *The Modern Dance* (New York, 1935; reprint ed. New York: Dance Horizons, 1970).

94. Di Prima and Jones, *The Floating Bear,* p. xii. I have changed the punctuation.

95. Ibid., p. xiv.

96. Herko, "[Theater Reviews]," *The Floating Bear,* p. 118.

97. Herko, "Paul Taylor — A History," *The Floating Bear,* p. 192.

98. "Notices," *The Floating Bear,* p. 192.

99. Note 31, *The Floating Bear,* p. 568.

100. Edwin Denby, "Letter to the Editors," *The Floating Bear,* p. 216.

101. Koenig [LeRoi Jones], "Note," *The Floating Bear,* p. 56.

102. Michael McClure, "!The Feast!, for Ornette Coleman," *The Floating Bear,* pp. 143–55.

103. Alan Marlowe, "Review," *The Floating Bear,* p. 180; Gilbert Sorrentino, "Rollins' Return," Ibid.

104. LeRoi Jones, "New York Loft and Coffee Shop Jazz," *Down Beat* (1963); reprinted in LeRoi Jones, *Black Music* (New York: William Morrow, 1967), pp. 92-98.

105. LeRoi Jones, *Blues People* (New York: William Morrow, 1963), pp. 225-26.

106. Interview with Charlip, 6 July 1980.

107. Warhol and Hackett, *POPism,* p. 55; di Prima and Jones, *The Floating Bear,* p. xvi.

108. Di Prima, "A Concert of Dance." I have changed the punctuation.

109. Interview with Paxton, 11 April 1980.

110. Banes, *Terpsichore in Sneakers,* p. 59; Paxton with Béar, "Like The Famous Tree," p. 26; Interview with Paxton, 11 April 1980.

111. Interviews with Paxton, 30 June 1975 and 11 April 1980.

112. Paxton with Béar, "Like The Famous Tree," p. 29.

113. Interview with R. Dunn, 15 May 1980.

114. Interview with Paxton, 11 April 1980.

115. Interview with Paxton, 30 June 1975.

116. Interview with Paxton, 11 April 1980.

117. Banes and Degener, Interview with Emerson, 10 June 1980; Program, 6 July 1962; Interview with Brown, Hay and Rauschenberg, 17 February 1980.

118. Emerson, Score, *Shoulder r.*

119. Banes and Degener, Interview with Emerson, 10 June 1980.

120. Hans Richter, *Dada: Art and Anti-Art* (New York: Harry N. Abrams, 1964), p. 69.

121. Tristan Tzara, "Manifesto on feeble love and bitter love," in *The Dada Painters and Poets: An Anthology,* ed. Robert Motherwell (New York: George Wittenborn, 1951), p. 92.

122. Richter, *Dada: Art and Anti-Art,* pp. 51, 57–59.

123. Raoul Hausmann, "Dada ist mehr als Dada," *De Stijl* 4 (March 1921): 42; translated and quoted in Richard Sheppard, "Dada and Mysticism: Influences and Affinities," in *Dada Spectrum: The Dialectics of Revolt,* eds. Stephen Foster and Rudolf Kuenzli (Madison, Wisconsin: Coda Press; Iowa City, Iowa: University of Iowa, 1979), p. 99.

124. William Davis, Unpublished notes, 24 March 1980; Interview with Rainer, 20 July 1980; Interview with Davis, 3 March 1980.

125. Davis, notes, 24 March 1980.

126. Ibid.

127. Ibid.

128. Walter Sorell, "Phyllis Lamhut, Albert Reid, William Davis, and Yvonne Rainer," *Dance Observer* (March 1963):

129. Interview with Paxton, 11 April 1980.

130. Interview with Rainer, 24 June 1980.

131. Rainer, *Work,* pp. 288–89.

132. Interview with Rainer, 24 June 1980; the first photograph of Rainer was taken at KQED-TV in San Francisco in August 1962 and was published in Yvonne Rainer with Liza Béar and Willoughby Sharp, "Yvonne Rainer: The Performer as a Persona," *Avalanche* 5 (Summer 1972): 46; the second photograph taken at KQED-TV, was published in Rainer, *Work,* p. 289. The descriptions of these movements came from my interview with Rainer, 24 June 1980.

133. Rainer, Notebook.

134. Interview with Davis, 3 March 1980.

135. Interview with Lucinda Childs, New York City, 16 April 1980.

136. Sorell, "Phyllis Lamhut, Albert Reid..."

137. Munt, "For Dancers Only," *Show Business,* 23 February 1963.

138. Johnston, "Democracy." I have changed the punctuation.

139. Di Prima, "A Concert of Dance." I have changed the orthography.

140. Interview with Brown, Hay, and Rauschenberg, 13 February 1980; interview with Alex Hay, New York City, 23 March 1980.

141. Interview with Paxton, 11 April 1980.

142. Hughes, "Dance Program Seen at Church."

143. Interview with Hughes, 8 April 1980.

144. Di Prima, "A Concert of Dance." I have changed the orthography.

145. Johnston, "Democracy."

146. Rainer, *Work,* p. 8.

Chapter 3

1. "African Leader Sees U.S. Ballet," *New York Times,* 23 May 1962, p. 39.

2. Doris Hering, "Dance," in *The American Peoples Encyclopedia Year Book 1963,* ed. Dorothy Carew (New York: Grolier, Inc., 1963), p. 210.

3. Ruth Emerson, Notes, July 1962, on back of flyer announcing class.

4. Interview with Robert Dunn, New York City, 25 March 1980.

5. The dance is discussed by Cunningham in Merce Cunningham, *Changes: Notes on Choreography,* ed. Frances Starr (New York: Something Else Press, 1968), pp. [22]-[41].

6. Interview with Emerson, 11 June 1980; Interview with Rainer, 24 June 1980; Interview with Lucinda Childs, New York City, 16 April 1980.

7. Interview with Summers, 15 March 1980; Waring, McDowell, Dunn, et al., "Judson: A Discussion," p. 38. The date given in "Judson: A Dance Chronology," *Ballet Review,* vol. 1, 6 (1967), p. 54, is August 1962. Jill Johnston says in her review "Central Park; At Woodstock," *Village Voice,* 20 September 1962, p. 9, that the date was 1 September.

8. Program, A Concert of Dance [#2], no date, Turnau Opera House, Woodstock, New York. I have corrected the punctuation.

9. Ibid.

10. Anna Kisselgoff, "Variety Is the Norm for Elizabeth Keen," *New York Times,* 31 December 1976, p. C11; Program, Elizabeth Keen and Margaret Beals, 27 April 1963, Judson Hall, New York City; Press release, Paul Taylor Company, November 1961.

11. Natalie Jaffe, "Contemporary Dance," *New York Times,* 26 April 1963, p. 25.

12. McDonagh, *The Rise and Fall,* pp. 241-42.

13. Ibid., p. 240.

14. Interview with Sally Gross, New York City, 20 March 1980.

15. Ibid.

16. Ibid.

17. Ibid.

18. Ibid.

19. Interview with Jill Johnston, New York City, 13 June 1980.

20. Johnston, "Central Park; At Woodstock."

21. Walter Gutman, "[Jill Johnston]," *Culture Hero,* Special issue on Jill Johnston, [1970?], p. 18. I have changed the punctuation.

22. Interview with Summers, 26 April 1980.

23. Rowe and Degener, Interview with McDowell, 19 February 1980.

24. Ibid; Waring, McDowell, Dunn, et al., "Judson: A Discussion," p. 39.

25. Interview with Summers, 15 March 1980.

26. Interview with Gross, 20 March 1980.

27. Program, A Concert of Dance [#2].

28. Judith Dunn, "My Work and Judson's," p. 24. I have changed the punctuation.

29. Rainer, *Work,* p. 8.

30. Interview with Rainer, 24 June 1980; Banes and Rowe, Interview with Philip Corner, New York City, 25 February 1980, BCJP.

31. Di Prima and Jones, *The Floating Bear,* p. 240.

32. Interview with Rainer, 24 June 1980.

33. Rainer, Chance lecture written on colored construction paper, 1961 or 1962.

34. Robert Morris, unpublished notes on the workshop at Waring's studio, written 30 October 1962.

35. Ibid.

36. Interview with Rainer, 24 April 1980. Rainer does not remember exactly why the group moved from her studio to the Judson Church, nor do others I have interviewed. Various interviewees remember various nights of the week for the workshop meeting, but most agreed on Tuesday.

37. Waring, McDowell, Dunn, et al., "Judson: A Discussion," p. 37. I have changed the punctuation.

38. Interview with Brown, Hay, and Rauschenberg, 13 February 1980.

39. Ibid.

40. Interview with Childs, 16 April 1980.

41. Interview with Summers, 15 March 1980. If Summers is right about Christmas Eve and New Year's Eve falling on the workshop night in 1963, then Tuesday is the night the group met.

42. Ibid.

43. Banes and Degener, Interview with Emerson, 10 June 1980.

44. Interview with Summers, 15 March 1980.

45. Judith Dunn, "My Work and Judson's," p. 26. In the fourth sentence I have substituted "decisions" for the original "discussions" which I think is a typographical error. Also, I have changed the punctuation.

46. Interview with Summers, 15 March 1980.

47. Interview with Paxton, 11 April 1980.

48. Program, A Concert of Dance #3, Judson Memorial Church, New York City, 29 January 1963.

49. Ibid.

50. Interview with Paxton, 11 April 1980; Interview with Childs, 16 April 1980; Flyer, A Concert of Dance #3 and #4, Judson Memorial Church, New York City, 29 and 30 January 1963.

51. Interview with Childs, 16 April 1980; Rainer, note to me, 29 July 1980.

52. Press Release, Concerts #3 and #4 [January 1963].

53. Program, Concert #3.

54. Interview with Rainer, 20 July 1980.

55. Interview with Childs, 16 April 1980. Rainer, in my interview with her 20 July 1980, says that Linich had been "hanging around" with the Waring group, in which Linda Sidon also danced. Linich had worked the lighting in May 1962 for Carolee Schneemann's environment at the Living Theater. (Carolee Schneeman, *More Than Meat Joy* (New Paltz, New York: 1979), p. 22.)

56. Warhol and Hackett, *POPism,* p. 61.

57. Ibid., pp. 64–65.

58. Interview with Paxton, 11 April 1980, and my examination of the space in the gymnasium.

59. Interview with Paxton, 11 April 1980.

60. Banes and Rowe, Interview with Corner, 25 February 1980.

61. Schneemann, *More Than Meat Joy,* p. 23.

62. Program, Concert #3.

63. Program, A Concert of Dance #4, Judson Memorial Church, New York City, 30 January 1963.

64. Johnston, "Judson Concerts #3, #4," *Village Voice,* 28 February 1963, p. 9.

65. Munt, "For Dancers Only, "*Show Business,* 9 February 1963, p. 11.

66. Johnston, "Judson Concerts #3, #4."

67. Rainer, *Work,* pp. 290–92; My viewing of the reconstruction of *We Shall Run,* directed by Rainer, at Bennington College, Bennington, Vermont, 18 April 1980.

68. Rainer, *Work,* p. 290. The program for Concert #3 omits Ruth Emerson. But Rainer lists these twelve names; and Allen Hughes, in "Dancers Explore Wild New Ideas," *Times Western Edition,* page and date unknown, says there were twelve dancers. So does Johnston in "Judson Concerts #3, #4," p. 9.

69. Rainer, "Rreeppeettiittiioonn iinn mmyy Wwoorrkk," Unpublished essay, May 1965, p. 1.

70. Interview with Childs, 16 April 1980.

71.　Interview with Tony Holder, New York City, 4 March 1980.

72.　Hughes, "Dancers Explore Wild New Ideas."

73.　Johnston, "Judson Concerts #3, #4," p. 9.

74.　Banes and Degener, Interview with Emerson, 10 June 1980.

75.　Interview with Emerson, 11 June 1980.

76.　Jaffe, "Contemporary Dance."

77.　Paxton with Béar, "Like the Famous Tree," p. 26.

78.　Rainer, *Work,* p. 293.

79.　Interview with Rainer, 20 July 1980.

80.　Waring, McDowell, Dunn, et al., "Judson: A Discussion," p. 41.

81.　Interview with Rainer, 20 July 1980.

82.　Program, Concert #3.

83.　Hughes "Dancers Explore Wild New Ideas."

84.　Johnston, "Judson Concerts #3, #4."

85.　Ibid.

86.　Munt, "For Dancers Only," 9 February 1963.

87.　Program, Concert #3.

88.　Interview with Emerson, 11 June 1980.

89.　Tom Borek, "The Connecticut College American Dance Festival 1948–1972," *Dance Perspectives* 50 (Summer 1972): 56.

90.　Munt, "For Dancers Only," 9 February 1963; Interview with Rainer, 20 July 1980; Johnston, "Judson Concerts #3, #4," p. 19.

91.　Rainer, *Work,* p. 286.

92.　Rainer, "Rreeppeettiittiioonn," p. 1.

93.　Marks, "Dance Works by Rainer and Herko," p. 57.

94.　Johnston, "Fresh Winds."

95.　Telberg, "Yvonne Rainer and Fred Herko."

96.　Interview with R. Dunn, 25 March 1980. Waring had choreographed his *Dances Before the Wall* in 1957.

97.　Johnston, "Judson Concerts #3, #4," p. 19.

98.　Johnston, "Judson 1964: End of an Era," *Ballet Review,* vol. 1, 6 (1967): 9.

99.　Munt, "For Dancers Only," 9 February 1963. I have changed the punctuation.

100.　Program, Concert #3.

101.　Davis, notes, 24 March 1980.

102.　Ibid.

103. Johnston, "Judson Concerts #3, #4."

104. Interview with Davis, 3 March 1980.

105. Davis, notes, 24 March 1980.

106. Dan Cameron and Michael Rowe, Interview with Carolee Schneemann, New York City, 27 February 1980, BCJP; Schneemann, *More Than Meat Joy,* p. 23.

107. Cameron and Rowe, Interview with Schneemann; Schneemann, *More Than Meat Joy,* pp. 25–32.

108. Schneemann, *More Than Meat Joy,* p. 18.

109. Ibid., p. 15.

110. Ibid., p. 10.

111. Ibid., p. 9.

112. Ibid., pp. 9–11.

113. Ibid., pp. 32–33.

114. Ibid., pp. 33–35.

115. Ibid., p. 33.

116. Johnston, "Judson Concerts #3, #4," p. 19.

117. Hughes, "Dancers Explore Wild New Ideas."

118. Paxton with Béar, "Like the Famous Tree," p. 26.

119. Interview with Paxton, 11 April 1980. The program for Concert #3 says that *Music for Word Words* was the accompaniment for *Word Words;* however, both Paxton (Paxton with Béar, "Like the Famous Tree," p. 26) and Rainer (Interview, 20 July 1980), say that *Word Words* was performed in silence on Concert #3.

120. Munt, "For Dancers Only," 9 February 1963.

121. Program, Concert #4.

122. Paxton with Béar, "Like the Famous Tree," p. 26.

123. Interview with Holder, 4 March 1980.

124. Interview with Childs, 16 April 1980.

125. Interview with Rainer, 20 July 1980.

126. Interview with Childs, 16 April 1980.

127. Program, *Exchange,* Surplus Dance Theater, Stage 73, New York City, 2 and 9 March 1964.

128. Interview with Childs, 16 April 1980; Childs, "Lucinda Childs: A Portfolio," *Artforum* 11 (February 1973): 50.

129. Interview with Childs, 16 April 1980.

130. Childs says she sat on a table (Interview with Childs, 16 April 1980). But photographs show her on the floor and Yvonne Rainer (Note to me, 29 July 1980) distinctly remembers her on the floor. Childs may be remembering the table from subsequent performances.

131. Interview with Childs, 16 April 1980.

132. Ibid.

133. Interview with Corner, 25 February 1980.

134. Interview with Paxton, 11 April 1980.

135. Interview with Childs, 16 April 1980.

136. Louis Horst, "The Contemporary Dance, Inc., Kaufmann Concert Hall, April 25, 1963," *Dance Observer* 30 (June–July 1963): 88–89.

137. Jaffe, "Contemporary Dance." In the original article the lines are jumbled; I have corrected them here.

138. Johnston, "Judson Concerts #3, #4," p. 19.

139. Banes, *Terpsichore in Sneakers,* p. 133; Interview with Childs, 16 April 1980.

140. Program, Concert #4; Banes, *Terpsichore in Sneakers,* p. 78. See Banes, p. 78, for a description of "violent contact" improvisation.

141. Interview with Brown, Hay, and Rauschenberg, 13 February 1980; demonstration by Gretchen MacLane in my interview with her, 19 June 1980.

142. Interview with Paxton, 11 April 1980.

143. Munt, "For Dancers Only," 9 February 1963.

144. Johnston, "Judson Concerts #3, #4," p. 19.

145. Program, Concert #4.

146. Interview with Rainer, 20 July 1980.

147. Ibid.

148. Interview with Paxton, 11 April 1980.

149. Johnston, "Judson Concerts #3, #4," p. 19.

150. Program, Concert #4.

151. Johnston, "Judson Concerts #3, #4," p. 19.

152. Interview with Emerson, 11 June 1980.

153. Program, Concert #4.

154. Al Giese, Photographs of Concerts #3 and #4, Judson Memorial Church Archives.

155. Program, Concert #4.

156. Ibid.

157. Interview with Malcolm Goldstein, New York City, 9 March 1980.

158. Interview with Paxton, 11 April 1980; Interview with Childs, 16 April 1980.

159. Munt, "For Dancers Only," 9 February 1963.

160. Johnston, "Judson Concerts #3, #4," p. 19.

161. "Arlene Rothlein, Dancer, Is Dead; Won Obie in 1968 as Best Actress," *New York Times,* 22 November 1976, p. B 12.

162. Munt, "For Dancers Only," 9 February 1963.

163. Jaffe, "Contemporary Dance."

164. Program, Concert #4.

165. Interview with Judith Dunn, Burlington, Vermont, 8 July 1980.

166. Interview with Paxton, 11 April 1980.

167. R. Dunn, unpublished notes, 4 April 1980, p. 1.

168. Johnston, "Judson Concerts #3, #4," p. 19.

169. Program, Concert #4.

170. Interview with Rainer, 20 July 1980.

171. Interview with Beverly Schmidt Blossom, New York City, 6 April 1980.

172. Johnston, "Judson Concert #3, #4," p. 19.

173. Munt, "For Dancers Only," 9 February 1963.

174. Ibid.

175. Johnston, "Judson Concerts #3, #4," p. 19.

Chapter 4

1. Advertisement, *Village Voice,* 25 April 1963, p. 8; Interview with Rainer, 20 July 1980.

2. Program, "A Program for Sounds and Bodies," 2 Pitt Street, New York City, 1 December 1962.

3. Rainer, *Work,* pp. 18–20, 32–33; Interview with Rainer, 20 July 1980; Spencer Holst and Beate Wheeler, *Thirteen Essays/Sixty Drawings* (New York: By the author and artist, 1960), pp. 32–36, 92–96. The two Holst essays are reprinted in *Work,* pp. 18–20, with descriptions of the "Solo Section." Full descriptions of the movements in the solos are given in *Work,* pp. 32–33. The essay on his great-grandfather that Holst refers to in "On the Truth" is published in *Thirteen Essays/Sixty Drawings,* pp. 22–26.

4. Rainer, *Work,* p. 34. Rainer demonstrated the "walk with wail" and other movements to me in my interview with her, 20 July 1980. In the program for *Terrain,* these solos are simply called "Walking" and "Death."

5. Scott MacDonald, "Interview with Hollis Frampton: The Early Years," *October* 12 (1980): 107. I have changed the punctuation. Rainer told me, in my interview with her, 20 July 1980, that she performed *Three Satie Spoons* at Pitt Street. But it is not listed on this program.

6. Ibid., pp. 106–7.

7. "Duet Section," which on the program for *Terrain* was simply called "Duet," is thoroughly described in Rainer, *Work,* pp. 16 and 30–31.

8. Sorell, "Phyllis Lamhut, Albert Reid, William Davis, and Yvonne Rainer." I have changed the punctuation.

9. Munt, "For Dancers Only," 23 February 1963.

10. Interview with Rainer, 20 July 1980.

11. Interview with Paxton, 11 April 1980.

12. Interview with Albert Reid, New York City, 16 May 1980.

13. Interview with Paxton, 11 April 1980.

14. Interview with Rainer, 20 July 1980.

15. Rainer, *Work,* pp. 14–15, 28–29. Again, the movements in "Diagonal" are thoroughly described.

16. Doris Humphrey, *The Art of Making Dances,* ed. Barbara Pollack (New York: Grove Press, 1962), p. 75. Humphrey devotes seven pages to a discussion of the diagonal line of the stage space; Interview with Rainer, 20 July 1980.

17. Rainer, *Work,* p. 21. I have changed the punctuation.

18. Ibid., p. 18.

19. "Play" and "Bach" are thoroughly documented in Rainer, *Work,* pp. 22–27, 35–43.

20. Rainer, *Work,* p. 1; Interview with Rainer, 20 July 1980; Rainer, unpublished notes, 23–30 May 1960; In my interview with Paxton, 11 April 1980, he recalled that he often criticized Rainer for too strong a stage presence.

21. Johnston, "Yvonne Rainer: I," *Village Voice,* 23 May 1963, p. 17; Johnston, "Yvonne Rainer: II," *Village Voice,* 6 June 1963, pp. 11 and 18.

22. Washington Gallery of Modern Art, *The Popular Image,* Washington, D.C., 18 April–2 June 1963, exhibition catalog, text by Alan Solomon, phonograph record of statement by artists; Leslie Judd Ahlander, "At Washington Gallery: Pop Art Festival Hailed," *Washington Post,* 26 May 1963, p. G 10; "Judson Dancers at Washington Roller Rink," *Village Voice,* 2 May 1963, p. 14.

23. "Judson Dancers at Washington Roller Rink"; Flyer, A Concert of Dance #5, America on Wheels Skating Rink, Washington, D.C., 9 May 1963; Program, A Concert of Dance #5, America on Wheels Skating Rink, Washington, D.C., 9 May 1963.

24. Johnston, "Billy Klüver," *Village Voice,* 12 August 1965, p. 7.

25. Interview with Paxton, 11 April 1980.

26. Interview with Rainer, 20 July 1980.

27. Program, Concert #5; Interview with Robert Dunn, 16 May 1980.

28. Munt, "For Dancers Only," 7 April 1962; Johnston, "Boiler Room"; Banes, *Terpsichore in Sneakers,* p. 78.

29. Interview with Paxton, 11 April 1980.

30. Interview with Davis, 3 March 1980.

31. Interview with Reid, 16 May 1980.

32. Gordon, "It's About Time," pp. 45–46.

33. Ibid., p. 46; Svane, Interview with Gordon, 28 February 1980.

34. Svane, Interview with Gordon, 28 February 1980; Gordon, "It's About Time," p. 46; Interview with Paxton, 11 April 1980.

35. Svane, Interview with Gordon, 28 February 1980; Gordon, "It's About Time," p. 46.

36.   Gordon, "It's About Time," p. 46.

37.   Johnston, "From Lovely Confusion to Naked Breakfast," *Village Voice,* 18 July 1963, p. 12.

38.   Interview with Judith Dunn, 8 July 1980; Interview with Paxton, 11 April 1980; Interview with Rainer, 20 July 1980.

39.   Johnston, "Judson Speedlimits," *Village Voice,* 25 July 1963, p. 10.

40.   National Collection of Fine Arts, Smithsonian Institution, *Robert Rauschenberg,* Washington, D.C., 30 October 1976–2 January 1977, exhibition catalog, pp. 25–39; Calvin Tomkins, *Off the Wall* (Garden City, New York: Doubleday, 1980), pp. 192–97.

41.   Interview with Brown, Hay, and Rauschenberg, 17 February 1980; Flyer, Concert #5; Program, Concert #6; Richard Kostelanetz, *The Theater of Mixed Means* (New York: The Dial Press, 1968), pp. 80–81.

42.   Kostelanetz, *The Theater of Mixed Means,* p. 82.

43.   Interview with Brown, Hay, and Rauschenberg, 17 February 1980.

44.   Floor plan and description of *Pelican* in Swedish, from unidentified source, given to me by David Vaughan, Spring 1980; National Collection of Fine Arts, *Robert Rauschenberg,* p. 184; Interview with Brown, Hay, and Rauschenberg, 17 February 1980.

45.   Tomkins, *Off the Wall,* p. 227. I changed the spelling of Ultvelt in the quotation to Ultvedt, as it appears in the program for the concert and in several other sources.

46.   Program, Concert #5.

47.   Ahlander, "At Washington Gallery: Pop Art Festival Hailed."

48.   Interview with Paxton, 11 April 1980.

49.   See Lucy Lippard, "New York Pop," in Lucy Lippard, ed., *Pop Art* (New York and Toronto: Oxford University Press, 1966), pp. 69–138.

50.   Interview with Rainer, 20 July 1980; Interview with Childs, 16 April 1980.

Chapter 5

1.   Yam Festival Calendar, New York City, May 1963; Michael Kirby, "The First and Second Wilderness," *Tulane Drama Review* 10 (T-30, Winter 1965), p. 94. Trisha Brown joined Yvonne Rainer, whose name appears alone on the publicity, in the improvisation on a chicken coop roof, according to photographs of the event by Peter Moore and my various interviews with Trisha Brown, 1973–1980.

2.   Allen Hughes, "Judson Dance Theater seeks New Paths," *New York Times,* 26 June 1963, p. 34; "Judson: A Dance Chronology," *Ballet Review,* vol. 1, 6 (1967): 56.

3.   Interview with Judith Dunn, 8 July 1980.

4.   Johnston, "From Lovely Confusion to Naked Breakfast," p. 12.

5.   Interview with Brown, Hay and Rauschenberg, 17 February 1980.

6.   Schneemann, *More Than Meat Joy,* p. 18.

7. Programs, A Concert of Dance #6, #7, and #8, Judson Memorial Church, New York City, 23, 24, and 25 June. There is a small joke in the program credits that would only be apparent to someone who read all three programs. For Concert #6 it seems that Michael Katz was William Linich's "helper." On Concert #7, Linich was "aided by" Katz. And on the third night, Concert #8, Linich was "supported by" Katz.

8. Interview with Paxton, 11 April 1980; Flyer, Concerts #6, 7 [and 8], Judson Dance Theater, New York City, June 23, [24], 25, 1963. The flyer announces only two concerts—#6 and #7—but gives the dates erroneously as 23 and 25 June.

9. Programs, Concerts #6-8.

10. Ellen Webb, "Teaching from the Inside Out," *Soho Weekly News,* 2 August 1979, p. 51.

11. Interview with Summers, 15 March 1980.

12. Ibid.

13. Johnston, "Judson Speedlimits," p. 10.

14. Program, Concert #6; Warhol and Hackett, *POPism,* p. 61; Photographs of Concert #6 by Al Giese, Judson Church Archives.

15. Hughes, "Judson Dance Theater Seeks New Paths."

16. Johnston, "Judson Speedlimits." I have corrected the order of the lines in the articles, some of which were printed out of proper sequence.

17. Interview with Joseph Schlichter, New York City, 25 August 1980.

18. Ernestine Stodelle, "Contemporary Dance Productions," *Dance Observer* 28 (August–September 1961): 103.

19. Horst, "Contemporary Dance, Inc.," *Dance Observer* 29 (August–September 1962): 106.

20. Hughes, "Judson Dance Theater Seeks New Paths."

21. Giese, Photographs, Concert #6.

22. Interview with Schlichter, 25 August 1980.

23. Johnston, "Judson Speedlimits."

24. Program, Concert #6.

25. Emerson, Score, *Cerebris and 2.*

26. Interview with Emerson, 11 June 1980.

27. Program, Concert #6; Interview with McDowell, 17 May 1980.

28. Program, Concert #6.

29. Interview with Schlichter, 25 August 1980.

30. Program, Concert #6; Interview with Childs, 16 April 1980.

31. Letter from Malcolm Goldstein, 21 March 1980; Goldstein, *Sanctuary Piece,* 1963.

32. Interview with Childs, 16 April 1980.

33. Johnston, "Judson Speedlimits." I corrected a typographical error in the text.

34. Program, Concert #6.

35. Interview with McDowell, 17 May 1980.

36. Johnston, "Judson Speedlimits."

37. Michael Compton and David Sylvester, *Robert Morris* (London: The Tate Gallery, 1971), p. 7; Johnston, "Robert Morris," unpublished article, [1965?].

38. Johnston, "Robert Morris," p. 1.

39. Johnston, "The New American Modern Dance," p. 190.

40. Program, "five dance constructions + some other things," New York City, 26 and 27 May 1961.

41. Robert Morris, "Notes on Dance," *Tulane Drama Review* 10 (T-30, Winter 1965), p. 179.

42. Ibid., pp. 179–80.

43. Johnston, "Robert Morris," pp. 9–10; Morris, "Notes on Dance," pp. 180–83. The text "A Method for Sorting Cows," is reprinted in its entirety in Compton and Sylvester, *Robert Morris,* p. 8.

44. Ibid., pp. 183–84.

45. Program, Concert #7, Interview with Schlichter, 25 August 1980.

46. Johnston, "From Lovely Confusion to Naked Breakfast."

47. Program, Concert #7.

48. McDonagh, *The Rise & Fall,* pp. 231–32.

49. Ibid., pp. 232–33.

50. Johnston, "Judson Speedlimits"; Program, Concert #7; Interview with Deborah Hay, New York City, 2 August 1980; McDonagh, *The Rise & Fall,* p. 127; Interview with Holder, 3 April 1980.

51. Johnston, "Judson Speedlimits."

52. Program, Concert #7; Interview with Summers, 15 March 1980.

53. Elaine Summers, Score, *Dance for Lots of People,* 1980. Summers reconstructed this dance for videotaping purposes on 28 July 1980. I performed in the reconstruction and also studied the tapes made of this reconstruction for the Bennington College Judson Project by Joan Blair and Tony Carruthers.

54. Interview with Summers, 5 April 1980.

55. Program, Concert #7; Interview with Elizabeth Keen, New York City, 19 August 1980.

56. Program, Concert #7; Johnston, "The New American Modern Dance," p. 189.

57. Schneemann, *More Than Meat Joy,* pp. 36–46. The performance is fully documented here with written descriptions and photographs.

58. Ibid., p. 37; Schneeman, "(Brown Overalls...or Costume Event...or Welcome Home Baloney)," unpublished score, March 1963; Schneeman, Letter to Yvonne Rainer, 19 March 1963. I have changed the punctuation.

59. Interview with Rainer, 20 July 1980; Cameron and Rowe, Interview with Schneeman, 27 February 1980. Schneemann says "six dancers" but I assume she means five, as her book documents.

60. Schneeman, *More Than Meat Joy,* p. 37.

61. Johnston, "From Lovely Confusion to Naked Breakfast."

62. Program, Concert #8.

63. Ibid.

64. Interview with Rainer, 20 July 1980; Waring, McDowell, Dunn, et al., "Judson: A Discussion," p. 44.

65. Johnston, "Judson Speedlimits."

66. Banes and Rowe, Interview with Corner, 25 February 1980; Program, Concert #8.

67. Philip Corner, Score, *Flares,* 1963.

68. Interview with Beverly Schmidt Blossom, New York City, 6 April 1980.

69. Banes and Rowe, Interview with Corner, 25 February 1980.

70. Ibid.

71. Johnston, "Judson Speedlimits."

72. Hughes, "All This Dancing," *New York Times,* 11 August 1963, sec. 2, p. 2.

73. Programs, A Concert of Dance, #9–#12, Gramercy Arts Theater, New York City, 30 July, 1, 6, and 8 August 1963; Interview with Emerson, 11 June 1980; Interview with Blossom, 6 April 1980.

74. Interview with Summers, 5 April 1980; Ad, *Village Voice,* 1 August 1963, p. 12.

75. Programs, Concerts #9–12.

76. Interview with Rainer, 20 July 1980.

77. Interview with Judith Dunn, 8 July 1980.

78. Johnston, "The New American Modern Dance," in *The New American Arts,* ed. Richard Kostelanetz (New York: Collier Books, 1967), p. 184.

79. Interview with Blossom, 6 April 1980.

80. Program, Concert #9.

81. Interview with Edward Bhartonn, New York City, 25 June 1980.

82. Waring, McDowell, Dunn, et al., "Judson: A Discussion," p. 44.

83. Program, Concert #9; Interview with Gross, 20 March 1980.

84. Program, Concert #9; Interview with Emerson, 11 June 1980.

85. Program, Concert #9; Corner, unpublished note, Judson Church Archives.

86. Banes and Rowe, Interview with Corner, 25 February 1980.

87. Ibid.

88. Program, Concert #9; Interview with Childs, 16 April 1980.

89. Interview with Sumers, 5 April 1980; Program, Concert #10.

90. Interview with Summers, 5 April 1980.

91. Robert Dunn, notes, 4 April 1980, p. 1.

92. Interview with Summers, 5 April 1980.

93. Waring, McDowell, Dunn, et al., "Judson: A Discussion," pp. 44–45. I have changed the punctuation.

94. Interview with Bhartonn, 25 June 1980.

95. Ibid.

96. Program, Concert #10.

97. Ibid.; Program, "A Program for Sounds and Bodies," 2 Pitt Street, New York, New York, 1 December 1962.

98. Program, Concert #10; Interview with Keen, 19 August 1980.

99. Program, Concert #10.

100. Interview with Blossom, 6 April 1980; Ad, *Village Voice,* 6 June 1963, p. 12; Saul Gottlieb, "Theater: Blossoms," *Village Voice,* 6 June 1963, p. 12.

101. Interview with Blossom, 6 April 1980.

102. Ibid; Beverly Schmidt, Score and cue sheet, *The Seasons,* 1963–1964.

103. Interview with Blossom, 6 April 1980.

104. Johnston, "Romantic Dancers," *Village Voice,* 22 August 1963, p. 14. I have corrected spelling errors in the article. Also, there are discrepancies between Johnston's article and Beverly Schmidt Blossom's descriptions of the dance. Blossom says that she and Goldstein entered the stage space together, but Johnston says the violinist is offstage. Johnston writes Corelli instead of Purcell.

105. Program, Concert #11. I have changed Dorthy to Dorothy.

106. Interview with Bhartonn, 25 June 1980.

107. Program, Concert #11; My viewing of *Woton's Wake,* 17 August 1980.

108. Program, Concert #11; Interview with Bhartonn, 25 June 1980.

109. Program, Concert #11; Interview, Aileen Passloff, New York City, 25 July 1980, BCJP. Passloff says she did the performance in the Pocket Theater, but I think she means the Gramercy Arts Theater, where the performance took place, I believe for the first time, in Concert #11, and where the stage was also quite small.

110. Waring, McDowell, Dunn, et al., "Judson: A Discussion," p. 45.

111. Program, Concert #12; Interview with Goldstein, 21 March 1980.

112. Program, Concert #12.

113. Flyer, Happenings, 24 and 25 May 1963, reprinted in Sohm, *Happening and Fluxus,* unpaged; Al Hansen, Floorplan with Notes on *Parisol 4 Marisol,* reprinted in Sohm, *Happening and Fluxus,* unpaged; I have corrected the spelling of Rainer's name but have copied the others with possible misspellings as they appear in Hansen's notes.

114. Al Hansen, *A Primer of Happenings and Time/Space Art* (New York: Something Else Press, 1965), pp. 16, 18 and 25. The photographs reproduced in the book are by Peter Moore. I have changed the punctuation in the quotation.

115. Program, Concert #12; Johnston, "Romantic Dancers"; Interview with Passloff, 25 July 1980.

116. Program, Concert #12; Yvonne Rainer demonstrated Rothlein's pose on the chair during my interview with her on 20 July 1980; Bhartonn also demonstrated a similar pose during my interview with him on 25 June 1980.

117. Interview with Goldstein, 21 March 1980.

118. Interview with Passloff, 25 July 1980; Interview with Summers, 26 April 1980.

119. Program, Concert #12; Interview with Deborah Hay, 2 August 1980.

120. Waring, McDowell, Dunn, et al., "Judson: A Discussion," p. 45. I have changed the punctuation.

121. Ibid.

122. Ad, *Village Voice,* 25 July 1963, p. 13; Ad, *Village Voice,* 1 August 1963, p. 13.

123. Robert Dunn arranged the dialogue for Summers's *Country Houses* but also continued his friendship with some of his former students and in that way sometimes served unofficially as an adviser. (Interview with Emerson, 11 June 1980.)

Chapter 6

1. Program, James Waring and Dance Company, Judson Memorial Church, New York City, 25 and 26 August 1963.

2. Interview with Paxton, 11 April 1980; Interview with Judith Dunn, 8 July 1980; Interview with Emerson, 11 June 1980; Rainer, *Work,* p. 9.

3. Interview with Judith Dunn, 8 July 1980.

4. Ibid.; Interview with Paxton, 11 April 1980; Interview with Summers, 15 March 1980.

5. Flyer, *Afternoon (a forest concert),* 101 Appletree Row, Berkeley Heights, New Jersey, 6 October 1963; Advertisement, *Village Voice,* 3 October 1963; Interview with Paxton, 11 April 1980.

6. Interview with Paxton, 11 April 1980; Doris Hering, "James Waring and Dance Company, Judson Memorial Church, August 25, 1963," *Dance Magazine* 37 (October 1963): 60. (This review by Hering was the first review in *Dance Magazine* of a concert at Judson Church, and it was not about a concert by the Judson Dance Theater.)
   Although the Judson Dance Theater as a group had not performed outdoors, Yvonne Rainer and Trisha Brown had performed their improvisation on the roof of George Segal's chicken coop, and certainly several Happenings and Events had taken place out of doors.

7. Interview with Paxton, 11 April 1980; Paxton with Béar, "Like the Famous Tree," p. 28.

8. Interview with Paxton, 11 April 1980.

9. Ibid.

10. Interview with Holder, 4 March 1980.

11. Interview with Rainer, 20 July 1980.

12. Interview with Paxton, 11 April 1980.

13. Johnston, "Fall Colors," *Village Voice,* 31 October 1963, p. 7. Johnston says that the concert took place "last month," but in fact it had taken place earlier in October. I have changed the punctuation.

14. Paxton with Béar, "Like the Famous Tree," p. 28.

15. Victor Turner, "Passages, Margins, and Poverty," in *Dramas, Fields, and Metaphors: Symbolic Action in Human Society* (Ithaca and London: Cornell University Press, 1974), passim; Banes, *Terpsichore in Sneakers,* p. 62.

16. Robert Dunn, Alex Hay, and Yvonne Rainer, Letter to the Foundation for Contemporary Performance Arts, 7 September 1963; Flyer, A Concert of Dance #13, Judson Memorial Church, New York City, 19 and 20 November 1963; Program, Concert of Dance #13, Judson Memorial Church, 19 and 20 November 1963; Interview with Rainer, 20 July 1980.

17. Program, Concert #13.

18. Di Prima and Jones, *The Floating Bear,* pp. 316–28.

19. Johnston, "Judson Collaboration," *Village Voice,* 28 November 1963, p. 18.

20. Ibid.

21. The description of *Sense* comes from my viewing of Peter Moore's photographs of Concert #13, in the Judson Archives. The quotation is from my interview with Emerson, 11 June 1980.

22. Interview with Rainer, 20 July 1980; Johnston, "Judson Collaboration."

23. Interview with Summers, 15 March 1980.

24. Schneemann, in *More Than Meat Joy,* p. 47, says that *Lateral Splay* was performed three times; Program #13 says that it was performed twice—once after Emerson's *Sense* and once after Baker's *Ritual.*

25. Schneemann, *More Than Meat Joy,* pp. 47 and 49. I have changed Schneemann's spelling of Siegal to Segal, as written in the program.

26. Ibid., pp. 47–48. I have changed the punctuation.

27. Johnston, "Judson Collaboration." Again, I have changed the spelling, this time of Siegel, to Segal. I do not know which spelling is correct.

28. Interview with Alex Hay, 23 March 1980; Interview with Brown, Hay and Rauschenberg, 17 February 1980.

29. Interview with Emerson, 11 June 1980.

30. My viewing of Peter Moore's photographs; Interview with Carla Blank, via telephone from Oakland, California, 29 May 1980.

31. Interview with Carla Blank, 29 May 1980.

32. Program, Concert #13; Peter Moore, photographs; Interview with Rainer, 20 July 1980; Rainer, *Work,* p. 294.

33. Interview with Rainer, 20 July 1980.

34. Interview with Paxton, 11 April 1980.

35. Steve Paxton, Letter to Yvonne Rainer, Colorado Springs, Colorado, 2 November 1963.

36. Rainer, "Some retrospective notes on a dance for 10 people and 12 mattresses called *Parts of Some Sextets*, performed at the Wadsworth Atheneum, Hartford, Connecticut, and Judson Memorial Church, New York, in March, 1965," *Tulane Drama Review* 10 (T-30, Winter 1965): 168, reprinted in Rainer, *Work,* p. 45.

37. See Rainer, "Some retrospective notes...," pp. 168–78 (in *Work,* pp. 45–51) and *Work,* pp. 52–61 for an account of *Parts of Some Sextets.*

38. See Sally Banes and Noël Carroll, "Working and Dancing: A Response to Monroe Beardsley's 'What Is Going On in a Dance?' " in *Dance Research Journal,* vol. 15, 1 (Fall 1982): 37–41, for a discussion of *Room Service,* task dance, and expressiveness in post-modern dance.

39. Banes and Rowe, Interview with Corner, 25 February 1980.

40. Corner, "Beforehand or Afterward," *Big Deal* 3 (1975): 14–18.

41. Banes and Rowe, Interview with Corner, 25 February 1980.

42. Program, Concert #13; Peter Moore, Photographs; Interview with Alex Hay, 23 March 1980. Don McDonagh describes the dance, but adds an interpretation, in *The Complete Guide to Modern Dance* (Garden City, New York: Doubleday and Company, 1976, p. 386.

43. Interview with Deborah Hay, 2 August 1980.

44. Interview with Alex Hay, 23 March 1980.

45. Interview with Rainer, 20 July 1980. I asked Deborah Hay, in my interview with her on 2 August 1980, whether Rainer had, in fact, made up the title, and Hay was not sure.

46. Johnston, "Judson Collaboration"; Peter Moore, photographs; Interview with Rainer, 20 July 1980.

47. Interview with Rainer, 20 July 1980.

48. Program, Concert #13; Peter Moore, photographs; Banes and Rowe, Interview with Corner, 25 February 1980; Interview with Joan Baker Prochnick, New York City, 5 March 1980.

49. Interview with Childs, 16 April 1980.

50. Program, "Motorcycle," Judson Memorial Church, 6 and 7 December 1963; Flyer, "Motorcycle," Judson Memorial Church, 6 and 7 December 1963.

51. Interview with Judith Dunn, 8 July 1980.

52. Interview with Paxton, 11 April 1980.

53. George Sadoul, *Dictionary of Films,* trans. and ed. Peter Morris (Berkeley and Los Angeles: University of California Press, 1972), s.v. "Scorpio Rising."

54. Johnston, " 'Motorcycle,' " *Village Voice,* 19 December 1963, p. 11. I have changed the punctuation.

55. Program, "Motorcycle"; Interview with Judith Dunn, 8 July 1980; Interview with Rainer, 20 July 1980.

56. Johnston, " 'Motorcycle,' " pp. 11–12. I have changed the punctuation.

57. Ibid., p. 11. I have changed the punctuation.

58. Program, "Motorcycle"; Johnston, " 'Motorcycle,' " p. 12. I have changed the punctuation.

59. Robert Dunn, Notes, 4 April 1980, p. 2.

60. Interview with Paxton, 11 April 1980; Interview with Judith Dunn, 8 July 1980; Program, "Motorcycle."

61. Program, "Motorcycle"; Interview with Judith Dunn, 8 July 1980; Johnston, " 'Motorcycle,' " p. 12; Interview with Rainer, 20 July 1980.

62. Johnston, " 'Motorcycle,' " p. 11.

63. Robert Dunn, Notes, 4 April 1980, p. 2.

64. Johnston, " 'Motorcycle,' " p. 11. I have changed the punctuation.

65. Program, Concert for New Paltz, State University of New York at New Paltz, New Paltz, New York, 30 January 1964. Don McDonagh, in *The Complete Guide to Modern Dance,* p. 389, says that the title of *Would They or Wouldn't They?* was changed in 1964 to *They Will,* but also says that it was performed with or choreographed with Fred Herko.

66. Hughes, "At Home Anywhere," *New York Times,* 9 February 1964, sec. 2, p. 18. I have changed the punctuation.

67. Hughes, "Dance: An Avant-Garde Series Begins" *New York Times,* 11 February 1964, p. 45; Johnston, "Pain, Pleasure, Process," *Village Voice,* 27 February 1964, pp. 9 and 15; Flyer, Surplus Dance Theater, Stage 73, New York City, 10 and 17 February and 2 and 9 March 1964; Program, "Exchange," Surplus Dance Theater, Stage 73, New York City, 2 and 9 March 1964. Johnston's "Pain, Pleasure, Process" describes the first program, "sur + ," quite thoroughly.

68. Interview with Summers, 15 March 1980.

69. Ibid.

70. Hans Breder and Stephen C. Foster, eds., *Intermedia* (Iowa City, Iowa: Corroboree: Gallery of New Concepts, School of Art and Art History, University of Iowa, [1979]), p. 149.

71. Program, *Fantastic Gardens,* Judson Memorial Church, 17–19 February 1964. I have changed the spelling of Sandra Neels's name (from Nols) and Larry Segal's name (from Siegel).

72. Jonas Mekas, "Movie Journal," *Village Voice,* 27 February 1964, p. 12. Lines in the article were scrambled, and I have corrected their order here. I have also changed "flattering" to "fluttering."

73. Letter from Malcolm Goldstein, 21 March 1980; Program, *Fantastic Gardens;* Goldstein, Score, *Overture to Fantastic Gardens,* revised and extended 1976.

74. Program, *Fantastic Gardens*; Interview with Summers, 5 April 1980; Johnston, "Summers' Gardens," *Village Voice,* 12 March 1964, p. 9; my viewing of part of Elaine Summers' film for *Fantastic Gardens* on 26 April 1980.

75. Interview with Summers, 5 April 1980.

76. Johnston, "Summers' Gardens."

77.   Goldstein, Score, *Illuminations from Fantastic Gardens,* 1964, reprinted in Richard Kostelanetz, ed., *Text-Sound Texts* (New York: William Morrow, 1980), pp. 84–91.

78.   Interview with Summers, 5 April 1980; Johnston, "Summers' Gardens."

79.   Interview with Summers, 5 April 1980; Johnston, in "Summers' Gardens," also says that Merce Cunningham was the subject of one of the parodies.

80.   Flyer, The Once Festival, VFW Ballroom, Ann Arbor, Michigan, 25 February–1 March 1964; Program, The Once Festival, VFW Ballroom, Ann Arbor, Michigan, 25 February–1 March 1964. Deborah Hay's title is a variant of *All Day Dance with Two,* given at New Paltz.

81.   Gordon Mumma, Letter to "Robert, Judith, etc." [i.e., Judson Dance Theater], 31 October 1963. In this letter from Mumma for the Once Group to the Judson Dance Theater, now in Yvonne Rainer's files, Mumma asks for a title for the concert, the number of participants, and the names of the individuals who would be coming. He mentions a maximum fee of $900.00 for six or seven performers, and a proportionate or better than proportionate amount for fewer performers. On the back of this letter, in Judith Dunn's handwriting, is written "Title—From the Judson Dance Theater," under which is written a list of dances, some with question marks following and times and personnel required for the dances. Different alternatives are sketched out in terms of solo performances and the necessary cast for group dances. In the end, nine performers went to the festival. Tony Holder, in my interview with him 4 March 1980, told me about the anger of the rest of the group, as have other interview subjects.

82.   Program, April 24th Concert Group, Annenberg Auditorium, University of Pennsylvania, 24 April 1964. Albert Reid's title is listed as *A Brief Glossary of Personal Movements of the Modern Dance*...rather than *A Brief Glossary of Personal Movements or the Modern Dance*..., as it was listed on the "Exchange" program of Surplus Dance Theater. It is probably a typographical error here. Also, Childs's *Carnation* is not marked as a premier in the program, but I have no evidence that it was performed anywhere before this.

83.   Judson Archives.

84.   Flyer and programs, Concerts of Dance #14, #15 and #16, Judson Memorial Church, 27, 28, and 29 April 1964. A note in the Judson Archive corrects the program for Concert #15, which had stated that June Ekman was the stage manager and James Tenney the tape operator.

85.   Program, Concert #14. I have corrected the spelling of several names. Also, the title of Rainer's dance was sometimes given as *Some Thoughts on Improvisation (for the painter James Byars).* I have written this version of the title as it appears on the program for Concert #14.

86.   Interview with Gross, 20 March 1980.

87.   Interview with Blank, 29 May 1980.

88.   Interview with Paxton, 11 April 1980.

89.   Rainer, *Work,* pp. 298–301. I have changed the punctuation. The entire text is given in Rainer's book.

90.   Interview with Summers, 15 March 1980; Interview with Alex Hay, 23 March 1980.

91. Corner, Score, *Rope Pull Sounds,* 1964/1975; Rainer, "Some retrospective notes...," pp. 168–69.

92. Interview with Paxton, 11 April 1980.

93. Johnston, "Judson 1964: End of an Era: I," *Village Voice,* January 1965, p. 12; reprinted in *Ballet Review,* vol. 1, 6 (1967): 8–9. Johnston writes that Concert #14 took place in May, but she is mistaken.

94. Program, Concert #15.

95. Davis, Notes, 24 March 1980. In his notes, Davis spells the title "*Sulphurs,*" but in the program it is spelled "*Sulfurs,*" as it is on the flyer for the Once Festival, where it was not, in fact, performed. That flyer also lists the musical accompaniment as composed by Mauricio Kagel.

96. Ibid. Lynn Seymour is a Canadian ballet dancer.

97. Interview with Davis, 3 March 1980.

98. Interview with Holder, 4 March 1980.

99. Ibid.

100. Interview with Blank, 29 May 1980; Program, Concert #15.

101. Program, Concert #15.

102. Ibid.; McDonagh, *The Rise & Fall,* pp. 277–78.

103. Svane, Interview with Gordon, 28 February 1980. Contrary to both Gordon's memory of the two performances and Jill Johnston's account of the April series—in which she again says, erroneously, that the concerts were in May and also states that *Silver Pieces* [sic] was performed on the same program with Childs's *Carnation*—in "The New American Modern Dance," in *The New American Arts,* Richard Kostelanetz, ed. (New York: Horizon, 1965; reprint ed. New York and London: Collier Books; Collier-Macmillan, 1967), pp. 185–86, the dance is called *Silver Pieces* in the program for the April 24th Group Concert and *Fragments* in the program for Concert #15. Also, the Philadelphia program implies that Gordon and Setterfield cochoreographed the dance, while the Judson program lists Gordon as the choreographer.

104. Johnston, "The New American Modern Dance," pp. 185–86. I have changed the punctuation.

105. Johnston, "Judson 1964: End of an Era," p. 8.

106. Program, Concert #16; Interview with Blank, 29 May 1980.

107. Interview with Reid, 16 May 1980. See Footnote 82 in regard to the title.

108. Interview with Childs, 16 April 1980; Johnston, "The Object," *Village Voice,* 21 May 1964, p. 12. I have changed the punctuation.

109. Interview with Childs, 16 April 1980.

110. Program, Concert #16.

111. The program does not list the names of the performers in *Conjunctions.* The quotation and description come from my interview with Gross, 20 March 1980.

112. Johnston, "Pain, Pleasure, Process"; Johnston, "The Object." In "Pain, Pleasure, Process," Johnston thoroughly documents the "sur +" program of Surplus Dance Theater.

113. Interview with Paxton, 11 April 1980.

114. Johnston, "The Object."

115. Program, Concert #16.

116. Interview with Gross, 20 March 1980.

117. Banes and Rowe, Interview with Corner, 25 February 1980.

118. Interview with Davis, 3 March 1980; Interview with Emerson, 11 June 1980; Program, *The Palace of the Dragon Prince,* Judson Memorial Church, 1 and 2 May 1964; Judson Archives; Robert Dunn, Notes, 30 March 1980, pp. 6–7. Childs' *Street Dance* is documented in Lucinda Childs, "Lucinda Childs: A Portfolio," *Artforum* 11 (February 1973): 52, and reprinted in Banes, *Terpsichore in Sneakers,* pp. 146–47.

119. Judson Archives; Interview with Rainer, 20 July 1980; Johnston, "Judson 1964: End of an Era: I"; Banes and Rowe, Interview with Corner, 25 February 1980.

120. Interview with Brown, Hay, and Rauschenberg, 17 February 1980.

121. Interview with Summers, 15 March 1980.

122. Judith Dunn, "My Work and Judson's," pp. 25–26. I have changed the punctuation.

123. Interview with Hughes, 8 April 1980.

124. Johnston, "Judson 1964: End of an Era: I and II."

125. Judson Archives; Johnston, "Judson 1964: End of an Era," expanded version in *Ballet Review,* vol. 1, 6 (1967): 12–14; Interview with Blossom, 6 April 1980; Yvonne Rainer, files.

Illustrations

1. Robert Huot and Robert Morris, *War*, Concert of Dance #4, Judson Memorial Church gymnasium

2. Trisha Brown and Steve Paxton in Brown's *Lightfall*, Concert of Dance #4, Judson Memorial Church gymnasium

3. Judith Dunn and Albert Reid in foreground, Yvonne Rainer, William Davis, Trisha Brown (only leg visible), and Steve Paxton in background, in Rainer's *Terrain,* Judson Memorial Church sanctuary

4. *Room Service* by Yvonne Rainer and Charles Ross, Concert of Dance #13, Judson Memorial Church sanctuary

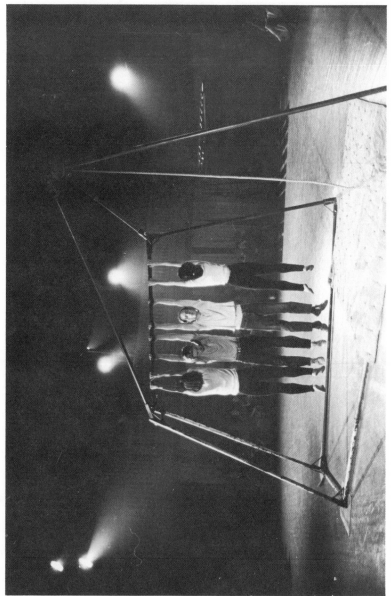

5. (L to R) Yvonne Rainer, Alex Hay, David Lee, and Deborah Hay in Deborah Hay's *Would They or Wouldn't They?*, Concert of Dance #13, Judson Memorial Church sanctuary

Photo © 1963 by Peter Moore. 351 W. 30th St., NYC 10001

6. "Motorcycle"; Judith Dunn in her *Witness II* and (l to r) Tony Holder, Alex Hay, John Worden, and Steve Paxton in Robert Dunn's *Doubles for 4*, Judson Memorial Church sanctuary

7. *Fantastic Gardens* by Elaine Summers, Judson Memorial Church sanctuary

Photo © 1964 by Peter Moore. 351 W. 30th St., NYC 10001

8. Steve Paxton in his *Rialto*, shown here at the Pocket Theater in "Events and Entertainments," 16 March 1964, and later performed at Concert #14, Judson Memorial Church

9. Philip Corner, *From Keyboard Dances,* Concert of Dance #16,
Judson Memorial Church sanctuary

Photo © 1964 by Peter Moore. 351 W. 30th St., NYC 10001

Bibliography

Books, Articles, and Catalogs

Ahlander, Judd. "At Washington Gallery: Pop Art Festival Hailed." *Washington Post*, 26 May 1963, sec. G. p. 10.

Anderson, Jack. "Judith Dunn and the Endless Quest." *Dance Magazine* 41 (November 1967): 48–51, 66–67.

Ballet Review, Vol. 1, no. 6 (1967). Judson Issue.

Banes, Sally. *Terpsichore in Sneakers: Post-Modern Dance*. Boston: Houghton Mifflin, 1980.

Banes, Sally, and Carroll, Noël. "Working and Dancing: A Response to Monroe Beardsley's 'What Is Going On in a Dance?'" *Dance Research Journal*, Vol. 15, no. 1 (Fall 1982): 37–41.

Breder, Hans, and Foster, Stephen C., eds. *Intermedia*. Iowa City, Iowa: Corroboree: Gallery of New Concepts, University of Iowa [1979].

Cage, John. *Silence*. Middletown, Connecticut: Wesleyan University Press, 1961.

"Choreographics." *Dance Observer* 27 (June-July 1960): 93–95.

Cohen, Selma Jeanne. "Avant-Garde Choreography." *Criticism* 3 (Winter 1961): 16–35. Reprinted in *Dance Magazine* 36 (June 1962): 22–24, 57; (July 1962): 29–31, 58; (August 1962): 45, 54–56.

Corcoran Gallery of Art and Detroit Institute of Arts. *Robert Morris*. Washington, D.C., and Detroit. Exhibition catalog. Text by Annette Michelson. 24 November–28 December 1969; 8 January–8 February 1970.

Corner, Philip. "Beforehand or Afterward." *Big Deal* 3 (1975): 14–18.

Cunningham, Merce. *Changes: Notes on Choreography*. Edited by Frances Starr. New York: Something Else Press, 1968.

di Prima, Diane, and Jones, LeRoi, eds. *The Floating Bear: A Newsletter*. Numbers 1–37, 1961–1969. La Jolla, California: Laurence McGilvery, 1973.

Dunn, Judith. "My Work and Judson's." *Ballet Review*, Vol. 1, no. 6 (1967): 22–26.

Fatt, Amelia. "Designers for the Dance: Robert Rauschenberg." *Dance Magazine* 41 (April 1967): 57–58.

Feldman, Anita. "Robert Dunn: His Background and His Developing Teachings." New York, 1979. Typewritten.

Forti, Simone. *Handbook in Motion*. Halifax, Nova Scotia: The Press of the Nova Scotia College of Art and Design; New York: New York University Press, 1974.

Foster, Stephen, and Keenzler, Rudolf, eds. *Dada Spectrum: The Dialectics of Revolt*. Madison, Wisconsin: Coda Press; Iowa City, Iowa: University of Iowa, 1979.

Griffiths, Paul. *A Concise History of Avant-Garde Music from Debussy to Boulez*. New York and Toronto: Oxford University Press, 1978.

Hansen, Al. *A Primer of Happenings and Time/Space Art*. New York: Something Else Press, 1966.

Heidegger, Martin. *Poetry, Language, Thought.* Translated by Albert Hofstadter. New York: Harper and Row, 1975.

Hering, Doris. "Aileen Passloff and Dance Company, Judson Memorial Church, June 1, 1964." *Dance Magazine* 38 (July 1964): 65.

————. "James Waring and Dance Company, Judson Church, May 20, 1964." *Dance Magazine* 38 (July 1964: 29, 64.

————. "James Waring and Dance Company, Judson Memorial Church, August 25, 1963." *Dance Magazine* 37 (October 1963): 28, 60.

"Herko Memorial." *Village Voice,* 5 November 1964, p. 11.

Higgins, Dick. *Postface.* New York: Something Else Press, 1964.

Horst, Louis. *Pre-Classic Dance Forms.* New York: The Dance Observer, 1937; reprint ed., New York: Dance Horizons, 1972.

Horst, Louis, and Russell, Carroll. *Modern Dance Forms.* San Francisco: Impulse Publications, 1961.

Hughes, Allen. "An Avant-Garde Series Begins." *New York Times,* 11 February 1964, p. 45.

————. "At Home Anywhere." *New York Times,* 9 February 1964, sec. 2, p. 18.

————. "Dance: *Last Point* Given at Judson." *New York Times,* 20 October 1964, p. 42.

————. "Dance Program Seen at Church." *New York Times,* 7 July 1962, p. 9.

————. "Dance Programs Have Premier." *New York Times,* 17 March 1964, p. 30.

————. "Dance: The Avant-Garde." *New York Times,* 21 May 1964, p. 41.

————. "Dancers Explore Wild New Ideas." *Times Western Edition,* date and page unknown.

————. "Judson Dance Theater Seeks New Paths." *New York Times,* 26 June 1963, sec. 2, p. 34.

————. "Whither Avant-Garde Dance?" *New York Times,* 7 June 1964, sec. 2, p. 12.

Humphrey, Doris. *The Art of Making Dances.* New York: Rinehart, 1959; reprint ed., New York: Grove Press, 1962.

Jackson, George. "Naked in Its Native Beauty." *Dance Magazine* 38 (April 1964): 32–37.

Johnston, Jill. "The Artist in a Coca-Cola World." *Village Voice,* 31 January 1963, pp. 7, 24.

————. "Billy Kluver." *Village Voice,* 12 August 1965, p. 7.

————. "Boiler Room." *Village Voice,* 29 March 1962, p. 14.

————. "Central Park/At Woodstock." *Village Voice,* 20 September 1962, p. 9.

————. "*December* Romance." *Village Voice,* 13 August 1964, p. 9.

————. "Democracy." *Village Voice,* 23 August 1962, p. 9.

————. "Fall Colors." *Village Voice,* 31 October 1963, p. 7.

————. "Fresh Winds." *Village Voice,* 15 March 1962, p. 13.

————. "From Lovely Confusion to Naked Breakfast." *Village Voice,* 18 July 1963, p. 12.

————. "The Gentle Tilt." *Village Voice,* 26 March 1964, p. 5.

————. "Judith Dunn." *Village Voice,* 5 November 1964, pp. 11, 17.

————. "Judson Collaboration." *Village Voice,* 28 November 1963, p. 18.

————. "Judson Concerts #3, #4." *Village Voice,* 28 February 1963, pp. 9, 19.

————. "Judson '64: I." *Village Voice,* 21 January 1965, p. 12. Reprinted in *Ballet Review,* Vol. 1, no. 6 (1967): 7–10.

————. "Judson '64:II." *Village Voice,* 28 January 1965, p. 11. reprinted in *Ballet Review,* Vol. 1, no. 6 (1967): 10–12.

————. "Judson Speedlimits." *Village Voice,* 25 July 1963, p. 10.

————. *Marmalade Me.* New York: E.P. Dutton, 1971.

————. "Miss Marsicano." *Village Voice,* 21 June 1962, p. 10.

————. "Meat Joy." *Village Voice,* 26 November 1964, p. 13.

————. "Motorcycle." *Village Voice,* 19 December 1963, pp. 11–12.

————. "The Object." *Village Voice,* 21 May 1964, p. 12.

————. "Pain, Pleasure, Process." *Village Voice,* 27 February 1964, pp. 9, 15.

———. "Romantic Dancers." *Village Voice*, 22 August 1963, p. 14.

———. "Summers Gardens." *Village Voice*, 12 March 1964, p. 9.

———. "Yvonne Rainer: I." *Village Voice*, 23 May 1963, p. 17.

———. "Yvonne Rainer: II." *Village Voice*, 6 June 1963, pp. 11, 18.

Jones, LeRoi. *Blues People*. New York: William Morrow, 1963.

Kauffmann, Stanley. "Music by Al Carmines." *New York Times*, 3 July 1966, sec. 2, p. 1.

Kirby, Michael. *The Art of Time*. New York: E.P. Dutton, 1969.

———. *Happenings*. New York: E.P. Dutton, 1965.

Klosty, James, ed. *Merce Cunningham*. New York: E.P. Dutton, 1975.

Kostelanetz, Richard. *The Theater of Mixed Means*. New York: The Dial Press, 1968.

———, ed. *John Cage*. London: Penguin Books, 1974.

———. *The New American Arts*. New York: Horizon, 1965; reprint ed., New York and London: Collier Books; Collier-Macmillan, 1967.

———. *Text-Sound Texts*. New York: William Morrow, 1980.

Lippard, Lucy, ed. *Pop Art*. New York and Toronto: Oxford University Press, 1966.

Livet, Anne, ed. *Contemporary Dance*. New York: Abbeville Press, 1978.

M.M. [Marcia Marks]. "Dance Works by Yvonne Rainer and Fred Herko, Maidman Playhouse, March 5, 1962." *Dance Magazine* 36 (April 1962): 54, 57.

———. "Phyllis Lamhut, Yvonne Rainer, William Davis, Albert Reid, Judson Hall, February 15, 1963." *Dance Magazine* 37 (April 1963): 20-21.

Maskey, Jacqueline. "Judson Dance Theater, Judson Memorial Church, October 17-19, 1964." *Dance Magazine* 38 (December 1964): 20-21.

McDonagh, Don. *The Complete Guide to Modern Dance*. Garden City, New York: Doubleday, 1976.

———. *The Rise & Fall & Rise of Modern Dance*. New York: New American Library, 1971.

Mekas, Jonas. "Movie Journal." *Village Voice*, 27 February 1964, p. 12.

Moore, Lillian. "Rainer-Herko Dance Recital." *New York Herald Tribune*, 6 March 1962, p. 12.

Motherwell, Robert, ed. *The Dada Painters and Poets*. New York: George Wittenborn, 1951.

Myers, Rollo H. *Erik Satie*. New York: Dover, 1968.

Munt, Maxine. "For Dancers Only..." *Show Business*, 7 April 1962, p. 6.

———. "For Dancers Only." *Show Business*, 9 February 1963, p. 11.

———. "For Dancers Only." *Show Business*, 23 February 1963, p. 7.

National Collection of Fine Arts, Smithsonian Institution. *Robert Rauschenberg*. Washington, D.C. Exhibition catalog. 30 October 1976-2 January 1977.

Paxton, Steve, with Béar, Liza. "Like the Famous Tree..." *Avalanche* 11 (Summer 1975): 26-30.

Rainer, Yvonne. *Work 1961-73*. Halifax, Nova Scotia: The Press of the Nova Scotia College of Art and Design; New York: New York University Press, 1974.

Richter, Hans. *Dada: Art and Anti-Art*. New York: Harry N. Abrams, 1964.

Schneemann, Carolee. *More Than Meat Joy*. New Paltz, New York: Documentext, 1979.

Smith, Howard. "Strange Excitement." *Village Voice*, 24 May 1962, p. 7.

M.S. [Michael Smith]. "James Waring, etc." *Village Voice*, 3 August 1961, p. 10.

Smith, Michael. "Theater: Meat Joy." *Village Voice*, 26 November 1964, pp. 17, 21.

Sohm, H. *Happening & Fluxus*. Cologne: Koelnischer Kunstverein, 1970.

Sommer, Sally R. "Valda Setterfield: The Performer." *Soho Weekly News*, 12 April 1979, pp. 25-26.

Sorell, Walter. "The Dance: Phyllis Lamhut, Albert Reid, William Davis, and Yvonne Rainer." *Dance Observer* 30 (March 1963): 41.

The Tate Gallery. *Robert Morris*. London. Exhibition catalog. Text by Michael Compton and David Sylvester, 28 April-6 June 1971.

Telberg, Lelia K. "Yvonne Rainer and Fred Herko." *Dance Observer* 29 (May 1962): 72–73.

Tomkins, Calvin. *The Bride and the Bachelors.* New York: Viking Press, 1965.

———. *Off the Wall: The Art World of Our Time.* Garden City, New York: Doubleday, 1980.

Tulane Drama Review 10 (T-30, Winter 1965). New Theater issue.

Warhol, Andy, and Hackett, Pat. *POPism: The Warhol '60s.* New York and London: Harcourt Brace Jovanovich, 1980.

Waring, James; McDowell, John Herbert; Dunn, Judith; Croce, Arlene; and McDonagh, Don. "Judson: A Discussion." *Ballet Review*, Vol. 1, no. 6 (1967): 30–53.

Washington Gallery of Modern Art. *The Popular Image.* Washington, D.C. Exhibition catalog. Text by Alan Solomon. Phonograph record of statements by artists edited by Billy Klüver. 18 April–2 June 1963.

Young, La Monte., ed. *An Anthology.* New York: Something Else Press, 1963; Second edition Cologne: Heiner Friedrich, 1970.

Interviews

Bhartonn, Edward. [Eddy Barton.] New York, New York. Interview, 23 June 1980.

Blank, Carla. Oakland, California, and New York, New York. Telephone interview, 29 May 1980.

Blossom, Beverly Schmidt. New York, New York. Interview, 6 April 1980.

Brown, Trisha; Hay, Alex; and Rauschenberg, Robert. New York, New York. Videotape Interview, 17 February 1980. Bennington College Judson Project.

Carmines, Al. New York, New York. Videotape Interview by Wendy Perron, 1 July 1980. BCJP.

Charlip, Remy. Bennington, Vermont. Interview, 8 July 1980.

Childs, Lucinda. New York, New York. Interview, 16 April 1980.

Corner, Philip. New York, New York. Videotape Interview by Sally Banes and Michael Rowe, 25 February 1980. BCJP.

Davis, William. New York, New York. Interview, 3 March 1980.

Dunn, Judith. Burlington, Vermont. Interview, 8 July 1980.

Dunn, Robert. New York, New York. Interview, 25 March 1980.

———. New York, New York. Interview, 4 April 1980.

———. New York, New York. Interview, 15 April 1980.

———. New York, New York. Interview, 16 May 1980.

Ekman, June. New York, New York. Interview, 15 April 1980.

Emerson, Ruth. New York, New York. Interview, 11 June 1980.

———. New York, New York. Videotape Interview by Sally Banes and Amanda Degener, 10 June 1980. BCJP.

Forti, Simone. New York, New York. Videotape Interview by Meg Cottam, 8 February 1980. BCJP.

Friedman, Gene. New York, New York. Interview, 25 March 1980.

Goldstein, Malcolm. New York, New York. Interview, 9 March 1980.

Gordon, David. New York, New York. Videotape Interview by Christina Svane, 28 February 1980. BCJP.

Gordon, David, and Setterfield, Valda. New York, New York. Interview, 6 April 1975.

Gross, Sally. New York, New York. Interview, 20 March 1980.

Hay, Alex. New York, New York. Interview, 23 March 1980.

Hay, Deborah. New York, New York. Videotape Interview, 2 August 1980. BCJP.

Holder, Tony. New York, New York. Interview, 4 March 1980.

Hughes, Allen. New York, New York. Interview, 8 April 1980.

Johnston, Jill. New York, New York. Interview, 13 June 1980.

Keen, Elizabeth. New York, New York. Interview, 19 August 1980.

McDowell, John Herbert. New York, New York. Interview, 17 May 1980.

―――. New York, New York. Videotape Interview by Michael Rowe and Amanda Degener, 19 February 1980. BCJP.

MacLane, Gretchen. New York, New York. Interview, 19 June 1980.

MacLow, Jackson. New York, New York. Videotape Interview by Michael Rowe, 29 January 1980. BCJP.

Mahaffay, Marni. New York, New York. Interview, 19 June 1980.

Passloff, Aileen. New York, New York. Videotape Interview, 25 July 1980. BCJP.

Paxton, Steve. Washington, D.C. Interview, 30 June 1975.

―――. Bennington, Vermont. Interview, 11 April 1980.

Prochnik, Joan Baker. New York, New York. Interview, 5 March 1980.

Rainer, Yvonne. New York, New York. Interview, 24 June 1980.

―――. New York, New York. Interview, 20 July 1980.

Reid, Albert. New York, New York. Interview, 16 May 1980.

Schlichter, Joseph. New York, New York. Interview, 25 August 1980.

Schneemann, Carolee. New York, New York. Videotape Interview by Dan Cameron and Michael Rowe, 27 February 1980. BCJP.

Summers, Elaine. New York, New York. Interview, 15 March 1980.

―――. New York, New York. Interview, 5 April 1980.

―――. New York, New York. Interview, 26 April 1980.

Miscellaneous Unpublished Materials

American Theater for Poets, Inc. Announcement and prospectus. 1962?

Corner, Philip. Scores.

Davis, William. Notes. 24 March 1980.

Dunn, Robert Ellis. Notes. 30 March–4 April 1980.

―――. Vita. 1980.

Emerson, Ruth. Scores and Notes.

―――. Vita. 1963?

Goldstein, Malcolm. Scores.

Mahaffay, Marni. Scores and Notes.

Rainer, Yvonne. Notebooks and Scores.

―――. Notes. 23–30 May 1960.

Summers, Elaine. Notes and Scores.

Wynne, Peter. "Judson Dance: An Annotated Bibliography of the Judson Dance Theater and of Five Major Choreographers—Trisha Brown, Lucinda Childs, Deborah Hay, Steve Paxton, and Yvonne Rainer." Englewood, New Jersey, May 1978.

Archives

Archives, Judson Memorial Church, New York, New York.

Philip Corner. Files.

Dance Research Collection of the Library and Museum of the Performing Arts (New York Public Library at Lincoln Center).

Trisha Brown. Files.

David Gordon. Files.

Peter Moore. Photographic Files.

Yvonne Rainer. Files.

Elaine Summers. Files.

Index